A2-Level Psychology

The Revision Guide

Contents

Section 13 — Psychology of Sport and Exercise

Section 14 — Child Psychology

Section 15 — Psychology of Education

Section 16 — Research Methods

Section 17 — Issues and Debates

Do Well in Your Exam

Published by Coordination Group Publications Ltd.

Editors:
Katie Braid, Polly Cotterill, Katherine Craig, Rob MacDonald, Kate Redmond

Contributors:
Radha Bellur, Lauren Burns, Richard Carciofo, Elisa M Gray, Nigel Holt, Christine Johnson, Tracy Jones, Kate Robson, Denise Say, Stuart Wilson

Proofreaders:
Charley Darbishire, Angela Jones, Raffaella Parris

With thanks to Laura Phillips for copyright research.

ISBN: 978 1 84762 275 4

With thanks to Science Photo Library for permission to use the image on page 111.
Groovy website: www.cgpbooks.co.uk
Jolly bits of clipart from CorelDRAW®
Printed by Elanders Ltd, Newcastle upon Tyne.

Based on the classic CGP style created by Richard Parsons.

This book covers:

AQA A
OCR
Edexcel

There are notes on the pages to tell you which bits you need for your syllabus.

Introduction to A2 Psychology

These pages are for everyone. *They're here to give you a quick intro to A2 Psychology — recapping some stuff that you did at AS and giving a brief overview of what exciting topics A2 has got in store for you. Ooh, the excitement...*

The **Different Exam Boards** Cover Slightly **Different Topics**

A2 Psychology is made up of two units — **Unit 3** and **Unit 4**. Their content varies between exam boards.

AQA A

- **Unit 3** contains eight topics — **Biological Rhythms and Sleep**, **Perception**, **Gender**, **Relationships**, **Aggression**, **Eating Behaviour**, **Intelligence and Learning**, and **Cognition and Development**. The good news is you only have to answer questions on **three** of these topics and you get to choose which ones you do.
- **Unit 4** covers **Psychopathology** (where you'll have to choose **one** disorder to study out of **three**) and **Psychology in Action** (where you'll study one application of psychology from a choice of three). There's also a visit to the old favourite, **Research Methods**.

Edexcel

- **Unit 3** contains four topics — **Criminological Psychology**, **Child Psychology**, **Health Psychology** and **Sport Psychology**. You have to answer questions on **two** of these — you get to choose which ones.
- **Unit 4** covers **Clinical Psychology** and **Issues and Debates**. There's some choice in the Clinical section, but you have to learn all of Issues and Debates.

OCR

- **Unit 3** contains four topics — **Forensic Psychology**, **Health and Clinical Psychology**, **Psychology of Education** and **Psychology of Sport and Exercise**. You only need to study **two** of these topics and you get to choose which ones you do.
- **Unit 4** brings together loads of things — **Research Methods**, **Approaches**, **Perspectives** and **Issues and Debates**.

You learnt about the different **approaches** that are used to study psychology during AS level. You'll need these again for A2, so here's a quick recap:

The **Cognitive Approach** Focuses on **Internal Processes**

1) Cognitive psychologists focus on **internal processes** to understand behaviour — for example, how we perceive or remember things.
2) They compare the human mind to an advanced **computer** system, so they use **computer models** to try to understand human cognition (thinking).
3) Using concepts from information processing, cognitive psychologists describe the brain as a **processor** — it receives **input**, **processes** it, and produces an **output**. Obviously it's ridiculously more complicated, but the general idea is the same.
4) Cognitive psychology studies are often laboratory-based and **artificial**, so they can lack **validity** in the **real world** (**ecological validity**).

If brains are like computers, Sarah's crashed the day she packed for her holiday.

Developmental Psychology is About How Humans **Develop**... Obviously...

If you're doing **AQA** or **OCR** you covered **developmental psychology** at AS level. **Edexcel** people didn't, but do need to know about it this time around. In fact, this book's got a whole section on it just for you lot (see Section 14).

Developmental psychology is a bit of a jumble of ideas from different approaches. It deals with how people **develop** and **change** over their lifetime. It also involves looking at how children are **qualitatively different** to adults in their understanding, abilities and feelings.

Chloe had just seen that solid food was next on her timetable and she couldn't wait.

Researchers like **Piaget** and **Samuel and Bryant** looked at children's **cognitive** development. They studied the way children approach problems depending on their age and the stage of development they've reached.

They found that the brain appears to have a **timetable** of **what** we can do and **when** we can do it — e.g. children don't start speaking or progress with potty training until they reach a certain stage of development.

Introduction to A2 Psychology

The **Biological Approach** Explains Behaviour as a Product of **Nature**

You've all come across the **biological approach** before (if you do **OCR** you'll know it as the **physiological** approach). There are three **key assumptions**:

Human behaviour can be explained by looking at internal, biological stuff, like hormones and the nervous system.

Experimental research that uses **animals** can be generalised to **human behaviour**.

Abnormal behaviour can be removed using **biological treatments** — e.g. medication for mental illnesses such as schizophrenia.

So, as far as this approach is concerned, it's what's inside that counts...

1) Researchers look at **genetics**, **hormones**, the **brain**, and the **nervous system** to explain behaviour.
2) It's very scientific — research is mostly carried out in **laboratory experiments**.
3) Common research techniques include **animal studies**, **brain scans** and **correlational studies**.

Individual Differences is About **Differences** Between... erm... **Individuals**

You've all met **individual differences** before as well. It's another one that's made up of bits from loads of approaches. The main thing that researchers want to find out is **how** and **why** we're all **different** from each other. You might think it's pretty obvious that we're all different, but psychologists have got to find something to fill the day.

1) Other areas of psychology tend to assume that people are broadly the **same** — e.g. developmental psychologists assume that we all go through the same basic stages of development.
2) However, this usually isn't the case. Not everyone hits the stages of development at the same **age**, and we all differ to some extent in our **psychological characteristics** — for example, our levels of motivation, aggression and intelligence, etc.
3) So, the individual differences approach looks at what **causes** these differences.

For example, Brian and his friend Flippy differ from each other in a few ways.

Social Psychologists Look at How We **Interact** with Each Other

Last one, hurrah. You've all met social psychology before during AS.

1) This approach is all about how we **influence** each other's thoughts, feelings and behaviour — either as **individuals** or as **groups**.
2) Major areas of research include **conformity** and **obedience**.

> Probably the most famous experiment in social psychology is **Milgram's Behavioural Study of Obedience** (1963). In the experiment he tested people's obedience by asking participants to give someone electric shocks if they made mistakes in a learning task. Most of his participants carried on giving the shocks, even when they thought they were causing harm. He concluded that most people will follow orders even if it means doing something they don't think is right. Pretty scary stuff.

3) Other areas of research include **persuasion**, **attitudes** and **relationships**.
4) Common research methods include **correlational studies**, **observational studies** and **experimental methods**. If you don't remember what these are don't fret — there's a whole section on research methods starting on page 214.

Two pages down — two hundred and forty nine to go...

But don't freak out, there's good news — some pages aren't for all exam boards. In fact, you'll come across whole sections that you can skip merrily past — just check the top of each page to see whether it's for you or not. So it's really more like 2 down, a lot less than 249 to go. You've covered loads of pages in the time it's taken to read these three lines. Good work.

Biological Rhythms

You only need these pages if you're doing the AQA exam. *George Gershwin. Gloria Estefan. 90s dance maestros Snap. They all had rhythm, and so do you. Only you don't have to write a song about it... unless you really want to.*

Biological Rhythm Cycles **Vary** in **Length**

Biological rhythms can be classified according to how long their cycle lasts.

1) **Circadian rhythms** — have cycles that generally occur **once every 24 hours**. For example, we will usually go through the **sleep-waking cycle** once every day.

2) **Infradian rhythms** — have cycles that occur **less than once every day**. For example, the menstrual cycle. **Sabbagh and Barnard (1984)** found that when women live together their menstrual cycles may **synchronise**. It isn't clear why, but it may be linked to **pheromones** (chemicals that can affect the behaviour or physiology of others).

Stan and Paul had more than enough rhythm for everyone.

3) **Ultradian rhythms** — have cycles that occur **more than once every 24 hours**. For example, the sleep cycle has several repeating stages of light and deep sleep (see p.6). Research using **EEGs** (electroencephalograms) to monitor brain activity during sleep has shown that a **regular** sleep pattern is really important. Disrupting these cycles can have very **serious consequences** — see the next page.

Biological Rhythms are **Regulated** by **Internal and External Influences**

The timing of biological rhythms is determined by factors both **inside** and **outside** our bodies.

Endogenous pacemakers

1) Some aspects of our biological rhythms are set by **genetically determined** biological structures and mechanisms **within the body**.
2) The **suprachiasmatic nucleus** (SCN), part of the **hypothalamus**, seems to act as an **internal clock** to keep the body on an approximate 24-hour sleep-waking cycle.
3) It is sensitive to light and regulates the **pineal gland**, which secretes **melatonin** — a hormone which seems to induce sleep. When there is **less** light, more melatonin is produced. When there is **more** light, secretion is reduced and waking occurs.
4) **Menaker et al (1978)** lesioned this structure in hamsters — their sleep-waking cycle was **disrupted**.

Exogenous zeitgebers

1) These are influences outside of the body that act like a **prompt**, which may trigger a **biological rhythm**.
2) **Light** is the most important zeitgeber. **Siffre (1975)** spent six months in a cave. He had **no clocks** and **no natural light** as zeitgebers. His sleep-waking cycle **extended** from a 24-hour to a 25-30 hour cycle. It therefore seems that natural light is needed to fine-tune our normal 24-hour cycle.

Endogenous and Exogenous Factors **Interact**

Endogenous and exogenous factors **interact** to regulate the timing of our biological rhythms.

1) In some cases, endogenous factors may **completely determine** a cycle. **Pengelly and Fisher (1957)** found that squirrels will hibernate even when kept in laboratory conditions very different from their natural environment.
2) However, many animals can **react more flexibly**, especially humans who are able to adapt to their surroundings. We can make ourselves stay awake and **change the environment** to suit our needs, e.g. by using artificial light.
3) **Cultural factors** are also important. For example, Eskimos often live in permanent daylight or permanent night-time but can maintain **regular daily sleep cycles** — so the cycle can't just be determined by levels of light acting on the pineal gland.
4) **Individual differences** can also affect the rhythms. **Aschoff and Wever (1976)** found that in a group of people isolated from daylight, some maintained their **regular** sleep-waking cycles. Other members of the group displayed their own very **extreme** idiosyncracies, e.g. 29 hours awake followed by 21 hours asleep. This also shows that factors must interact to control or influence biological rhythms.

Biological Rhythms

Disrupting Biological Rhythms can have **Negative Consequences**

1) In the natural environment, zeitgebers normally **change slowly**, e.g. light levels during the year change gradually.
2) However, in modern society, zeitgebers can change quickly. This can have **negative effects** on our ability to function — slowing **reaction times**, impairing **problem-solving skills**, and limiting our **ability to concentrate**.

Jet lag

1) Jet planes allow fast travel to **different time zones.** Leaving the UK at 9am means that you'd get to New York at about 4pm UK time. New York is 5 hours behind the UK, so the local time would be about 11am.
2) Consequently you'll feel sleepy at an **earlier (local) time.** If you then went to sleep you would wake-up earlier and be **out of sync** with local timing. It appears easiest to **adapt** by forcing yourself to stay awake.
3) It can take **about a week** to fully synchronise to a new time zone. **Wegman et al (1986)** found that travelling east to west (**phase delay**) seems easier to adapt to than travelling west to east (**phase advance**).
4) **Schwartz et al (1995)** found that baseball teams from the east coast of the USA got **better results** travelling to play in the west than teams based in the west did when travelling to play in the east.

Shift work

Modern work patterns mean some people work shifts throughout the 24-hour period, disrupting their sleep cycle.

Czeisler et al (1982) studied workers at a factory whose shift patterns appeared to cause sleep and health problems. The researchers recommended **21-day shifts** (allowing more time for workers to adapt), and changing shifts **forward in time** (phase delay). After implementing the changes **productivity** and **job satisfaction** increased.

Research on Biological Rhythms has **Limitations**

1) Findings from animal studies can't accurately be **generalised** to humans — humans have greater **adaptability**.
2) Studies that have deprived humans of natural light have still allowed **artificial light**, which may give many of the **benefits** of natural light — this reduces the **validity** of these studies.
3) Things like **individual differences** need further study. Some people are more alert early in the day, and others later on, and the speed with which we **adapt to disruptions** can vary. It's difficult to determine whether a person's lifestyle is a **cause or effect** of their biological rhythms.
4) If we fully understand what causes the problems linked to jet lag and shift work, we can **minimise** or **avoid them**, reducing accidents in work environments. However, there are different ways to deal with these problems, e.g. taking time to **naturally adjust**, or using **drugs** to reduce the effects of sleep deprivation.

Practice Questions

Q1 What is the difference between circadian, infradian and ultradian rhythms?
Q2 Explain what is meant by 'endogenous pacemakers' and 'exogenous zeitgebers'.
Q3 Why does jet lag occur?
Q4 Why is shift work disruptive to biological rhythms?
Q5 Give two criticisms of research on biological rhythms.

Exam Question

Q1 a) Outline the roles of endogenous pacemakers and exogenous zeitgebers in biological rhythms. [10 marks]

b) Discuss research studies that have examined the role of endogenous and exogenous factors in human biological cycles. [15 marks]

"I didn't mean to fall asleep Miss — the melatonin made me do it..."

It's scientific fact that if you're a rock star, your biological rhythm immediately changes to 'Here I Go Again' by Whitesnake. Actually, that's not scientific at all. Nor is it fact. When you can answer the practice questions, and you've had a crack at the essays, think about what your rock rhythm would be... Are you ready? It's 'Here I Go Again', by Whitesnake. Fact.

Sleep States

AQA people, the fun continues here. *We spend about a third of our lives asleep, so it must be pretty important. Amazingly, no one's quite sure why. I reckon I know though — it's because staying in bed all day is brilliant.*

Sleep Can Be Split into Stages of Different Brain Activity

Electroencephalograms (EEGs) measure electrical activity in the brain, and are used to record the stages of sleep.

1) Adults pass through the stages about **five times a night**, with each cycle lasting about **90 minutes**. Who'd have thought we were so busy...
2) As you fall into deeper sleep, brain activity becomes **higher voltage** and **lower frequency**. These are the stages of slow wave sleep (SWS):

   Stage 1 is a bit like deep relaxation, with lowered heart rate, muscle tension and temperature. It's quite easy to wake people up.

   Stage 2 has slower and larger EEG waves, with some quick bursts of high frequency waves called **sleep spindles**.

   Stage 3 has even larger, slower waves.

   Stage 4 has the largest, slowest waves of all, because it's the deepest stage of sleep. Metabolic activity is pretty low in general, and the sleeper is very hard to wake.

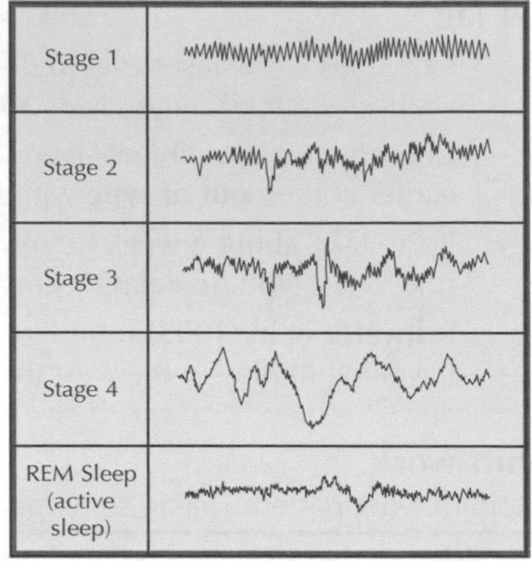

3) After stage 4 the cycle reverses back through stages 3 and 2. A period of **active sleep** occurs instead of stage 1.
4) During the active stage, metabolic activity increases, and the body appears almost paralysed except for **rapid eye movement (REM)**. The EEG pattern is almost like when you're awake. The cycle is repeated about five times during the night, but we only enter stages 3 and 4 in the first two. Periods of REM increase with each cycle.

There are Lots of Different Theories of Sleep

Evolutionary approaches relate to the **environment, evolution** and **survival of the fittest**.

1) **Webb (1968)** suggested that everyday sleep is similar to **hibernation** — sleep conserves energy at times when it's harder to get resources (i.e. at night time). Using energy would be **inefficient**.
2) **Meddis (1977)** suggested that sleep helps keep animals **safe**. By being quiet and still, they are less likely to attract predators (especially at night). However, sleep also makes animals **vulnerable** to predators if discovered.
3) Not sleeping at all would be very advantageous, but as it seems to occur in all animals, it must have an **important function** — although how much sleep animals have **varies**. Animals that **graze** often and must avoid predators **sleep less**, while **predators**, that don't eat as frequently and aren't hunted, **sleep more**.

- The evolutionary approach, focusing on survival and environmental adaptation, is useful for understanding **how and why** behaviours occur. Behaviours have evolved to help survival and adapt us to our environment.
- Evolution occurs over **long periods** so it's hard to test theories about why some behaviours have been **naturally selected**. So, it's difficult to **falsify** them (see p.238), making them **less useful** from a scientific perspective.

Restoration approaches suggest that sleep restores the body's ability to **function**, after being busy during the day.

1) **Oswald (1980)** suggested that SWS/non-REM sleep is for restoring bodily functions linked to **physical activity**, and REM sleep is for restoring **brain functions**.
2) **Horne (1988)** distinguished between two types of sleep: **core sleep**, which is made up of stage 4 SWS (for body restoration) and REM sleep (for brain restoration), and **optional sleep**, which is made up of the other sleep stages. Although optional sleep is not necessary, having it can help to conserve energy.

- It seems that important **brain and body restoration** occurs during sleep. Babies, whose brains are developing, spend more time in REM sleep and release more **growth hormone** during SWS.
- **Shapiro et al (1981)** found that long-distance runners had more SWS after a race, implying that the exercise **increased** the need for bodily restoration.
- However, **Horne and Minard's (1985)** study found that when participants did physical and cognitive activity they fell asleep **more quickly**, but did not sleep for longer. It may be that there was a **reduction** in the amount of **optional sleep** that they had.

Sleep States

Several **Techniques** are Used in Sleep Research

The following equipment and techniques are often used in **sleep laboratories**:

1) Equipment such as **EEGs** measure electrical activity in the brain and provide **quantitative reports** which can easily be compared to others. They have high **reliability** and changes in sleep stages can be easily identified.
2) Other equipment used includes **EOGs** (electrooculograms) which measure the electrical activity of the **eyes**, and **EMGs** (electromyograms) which measure the electrical activity in **muscles**.
3) **Self reports** involve participants keeping a record of their dreams or estimating their length. They're useful for gaining information which couldn't be collected in any other way, but they're limited by the **accuracy of recall**.
4) **Observations** of patterns and directions of **eye movements** can be recorded and related to sleep stages.
5) Variables, such as noise and distraction, are **controlled** to increase the **reliability** of the research. However, research in sleep laboratories creates an **artificial environment**, which may affect the participants' sleep patterns and so reduce **validity**.

Our **Sleeping Patterns Change** During Our **Lifespan**

The **amount** we sleep and our **patterns** of sleep **change** as we get older.

1) The **older** we get the **less** we tend to sleep — babies sleep up to 20 hours a day, whilst most adults average 7-8 hours and people over 50 average only 6 hours.
2) Also, as we get older we tend to have **less REM sleep** — Kleitman (1963) found that newborn babies may spend 8-9 hours every day in REM sleep. Children have less REM sleep than infants, and adults have less than children.
3) Kales and Kales (1974) found that elderly people are more likely to **wake up** several times during their night's sleep than younger people.

Comments

1) Most evidence for changes in sleep patterns comes from laboratory research using **EEG recordings**. These recordings are obtained by attaching **electrodes** to participants. This creates an **unfamiliar sleeping environment** for the participants, which may **disrupt** their usual **sleep patterns**.
2) However, Empson (1989) suggests that after the first night participants **adjust** to the conditions and their sleep is representative of their usual patterns.
3) More research is needed to find out the **reasons** for lifespan changes in sleep. For example, REM sleep in childhood may be linked to brain development.

Practice Questions

Q1 Summarise the four stages of slow wave sleep.

Q2 What is active sleep?

Q3 How does the average amount of sleep that we have every day change over our lifespan?

Q4 Give a limitation of sleep research using EEG recordings.

Exam Question

Q1 a) Outline evolutionary explanations of the function of sleep. [10 marks]

b) Outline restoration approaches to the function of sleep. [10 marks]

c) Evaluate research on the nature and functions of sleep. [5 marks]

REM sleep — not the same as dozing off with your headphones on...

Don't know about you but I'm not looking forward to getting down to six hours sleep a night — talk about falling standards. Bring back the good old days of 20 hours snoozing out of 24. Anyway, seeing as you've got so much more time awake than ever before, I suggest that you put it to good use and learn about the nature, functions and lifespan changes of sleep. Enjoy.

Disorders of Sleep

Again, AQA people only. *There are lots of different sleep disorders — some are common, like insomnia, whilst others are slightly more unusual, like narcolepsy. And then there's sleepwalking — which can lead to all sorts of bizarre situations.*

Insomnia is a Sleep Disorder

1) People with **insomnia** have **difficulty falling asleep**, **difficulty staying asleep**, or **both**.
2) They may feel **sleepy** and **irritable** during the day, with **impaired concentration** — this can affect their daily life and their relationships.
3) Insomnia may be **acute**, lasting a few nights, or **chronic**, lasting for weeks, months or years.
4) Research has suggested that about **10%** of adults may suffer from **chronic** insomnia.
5) There are different types of insomnia:

Primary Insomnia

Primary insomnia is insomnia that **isn't linked** to any existing **physical** or **psychological** conditions. Instead, it may be caused by:

1) **Stimulants**. Stimulants such as caffeine or nicotine increase arousal and can lead to insomnia. This can also lead to a vicious circle of frustration and anxiety.
2) **Disruptions to circadian rhythm**. Jet-lag, shift work and sleeping at irregular times (e.g. staying-up late at weekends) may all disrupt sleep patterns and lead to insomnia.

Secondary Insomnia

Secondary insomnia is the result of existing **physical** or **psychological** conditions. For example:

1) **Physical complaints**. A number of physical complaints such as arthritis, diabetes and asthma can cause insomnia.
2) **Psychological conditions**. A number of psychological conditions, e.g. depression, can cause insomnia.
3) **Stress or anxiety**. Worrying about something causes anxiety (higher bodily arousal), which may in turn cause insomnia. Failure to get to sleep can cause frustration, which creates more anxiety, making it even harder to get to sleep and producing a vicious circle.
4) **Medication**. Some medications may have side effects which disrupt sleep. Also, medications taken to improve sleep may cause problems if their effects are too long-lasting (leaving the person sleepy the next day), or if their effects wear off too early. Some people may become dependent on sleeping pills and suffer even worse insomnia if they stop taking them.

Insomnia is Influenced by Many Factors

An episode of insomnia can be influenced by many factors. For example:

1) **Sleep apnoea**. This is a condition where a person's airways become temporarily **blocked** whilst they are sleeping, causing their **breathing** to be **interrupted**. This **disrupts** their **sleep pattern** — either causing a person to wake up or to move into a lighter stage of sleep. Sleep apnoea is linked to snoring and may be caused by various abnormalities in brain or respiratory functioning. It's also linked to obesity — especially in males.
2) **Personality traits**. Characteristics like being **overly sensitive**, **worrying**, having a very **serious attitude** to life issues and being **overly dependent** on other people can lead to insomnia.
3) **Depression and anxiety**. These increase **emotional arousal** — which may then increase **physiological arousal**, causing insomnia.

Claire broke the news gently — Jake's nap time snoring was the cause of the insomnia epidemic in Class 1.

Research into insomnia is **difficult** as there are **many variables** that can cause or influence the condition. This problem is compounded by the fact that some of the variables are **hard to control**. Much of the research that's been done has produced **correlational evidence** rather than showing cause and effect.

Disorders of Sleep

Sleepwalking is a Sleep Disorder...

Sleepwalking is a disorder associated with **stage 3** and **stage 4** sleep. It affects approximately **15% of children** and **2% of adults**. The causes of sleepwalking are not fully known but it's thought it can be triggered by...

- **Sleep deprivation**, especially in people with a history of sleepwalking
- An **irregular sleep schedule**
- **Stress** or **anxiety**
- Some **drugs**, e.g. anti-psychotics or stimulants

Dauvilliers et al's (2005) study suggests there may be a **genetic component** to sleepwalking as well — they found higher concordance rates for the disorder in identical twins than in non-identical twins.

...and so is Narcolepsy

Narcolepsy is a disorder causing sudden episodes of **day-time sleepiness**, leading to a person falling asleep for a short period of time (seconds or minutes). They may also experience **features** of sleep such as **weak muscles** (**cataplexy**) and **dream-like imagery**. Narcolepsy affects **0.02-0.06%** of the population, most of whom develop the condition in early adulthood. The causes of narcolepsy may include:

- **Reduced levels of hypocretin**. Hypocretin is a chemical that's involved in regulating arousal levels. It's thought narcolepsy may be caused by the body's immune system attacking the cells that produce hypocretin, reducing the body's ability to regulate sleep.
- **Genetics**. Studies have shown a 25-31% concordance rate for the condition between identical twins — this suggests a genetic link. This concordance rate is fairly low, so environmental influences must also be important. It could be that a virus, e.g. that causes measles, may trigger a genetic predisposition to narcolepsy. So a person would need the genetic predisposition for narcolepsy as well as contact with the virus before developing the condition — meaning the cause would be both genetic and environmental.

Alfie might claim it was narcolepsy but he was fooling no-one. They knew a lazy seal when they saw one.

Practice Questions

Q1 What is insomnia?

Q2 What is the difference between primary insomnia and secondary insomnia?

Q3 How can depression influence insomnia?

Q4 List three possible causes of sleepwalking.

Q5 List some possible causes of narcolepsy.

Exam Question

Q1 a) Outline explanations for primary and secondary insomnia. [10 marks]

b) Describe and explain how sleep apnoea and personality traits can influence insomnia. [10 marks]

c) Evaluate the evidence for one explanation for narcolepsy. [5 marks]

Revision — it cures insomnia and induces narcolepsy in one go...

Now stay with it — you need to remember this stuff. It's not too bad really, three sleeping disorders — insomnia, narcolepsy and sleepwalking, with explanations for all of them. Once you've learnt that, you can give yourself a pat on the back, make yourself some cocoa and have a little nap if you like — because you've reached the end of this very short section. Huzzah.

Theories of Perception

This section is for AQA only. *Perception is how we make sense of things around us. Without it the world would be a mish mash of meaninglessness — so it's pretty important. With that in mind, you'd better have a look at some theories...*

Perception is the Process of Giving Meaning to Stimuli

1) Our senses are constantly detecting **stimuli** in the environment around us.
2) The information the stimuli provide has to be **processed** in order to **make sense of it**.
3) This processing is known as **perception**.
4) Theories of how the information is understood are known as **theories of perception**. You need to know about two of them — Gibson's **direct theory** and Gregory's **indirect theory**.

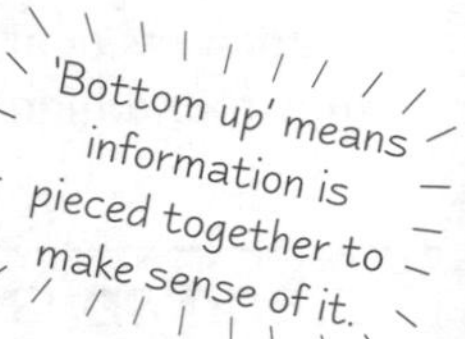

'Bottom up' means information is pieced together to make sense of it.

Gibson's Direct Theory of Perception is a Bottom Up Theory

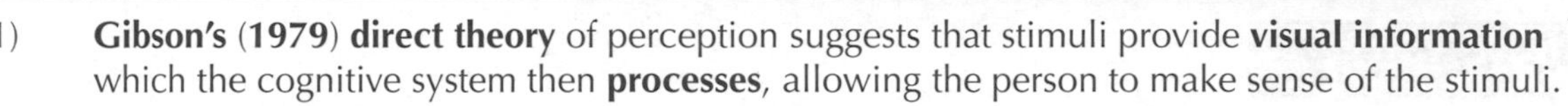

1) **Gibson's (1979) direct theory** of perception suggests that stimuli provide **visual information** which the cognitive system then **processes**, allowing the person to make sense of the stimuli.

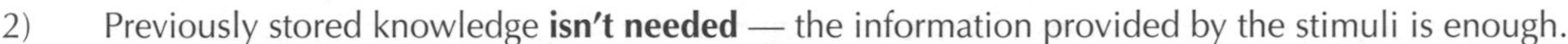

2) Previously stored knowledge **isn't needed** — the information provided by the stimuli is enough.
3) Gibson argues that this is possible because of the large amount of information provided by the **optic array**:

The Optic Array

The optic array is the **pattern of light** that enters the eye, allowing things to be seen. It's a really **complicated** pattern — it's made up of all the light rays reflecting off all the objects and surfaces in view, so it holds **lots of information**. To make things even more complex, it **changes** each time you **move**. The optic array gives rise to **texture gradients, horizon ratios** and **optic flow patterns**. These are all involved in perception.

Texture gradients

Objects that are **far away** take up less of the optic array and are **closer together** than objects that are near. This is known as the **texture gradient**. It provides information on the **depth** and **distance** of objects.

Horizon ratios

Objects that are the **same height** are cut in the **same place** by the horizon, regardless of how far away they are. This is known as a **horizon ratio** and provides us with information on the **size** and **distance** of objects.

Optic flow patterns

As we move, the place we're moving towards appears to be stationary whilst other objects appear to **move past us**. Objects that are **close** to us seem to be moving **quickly**, whilst those **far away** seem to move much more **slowly**. For example, when you travel in a car, signposts and nearby buildings zoom by in comparison to mountain ranges in the distance. This is due to **changes in the optic array** as we move. These are known as **optic flow patterns**. They give us information on the **position** and **depth** of objects.

Although the optic array **changes** when a person **moves**, the information provided by texture gradients, horizon ratios and optic flow remains **constant**. This enables us to perceive the world around us.

4) The optic array explains our perception of the **position** of objects relative to each other. However, it doesn't address how we're able to perceive what objects **are** or how they should be **used**.
5) Gibson proposed that we perceive how an object should be used from the object itself. An object **affords** (offers) **itself** to certain **behaviours**, e.g. a bed affords itself to lying down.
6) The **affordances** of objects can **change** depending on the **circumstances**, e.g. a box might afford itself to storing something or afford itself to being stood on to reach a high object.

Comments on Gibson's Theory

1) Gibson studied perception in real-world situations, so his theory has **ecological validity**. His theory also has **practical applications** — the concept of optic flow has been used to help train pilots.
2) However, the idea of **affordances** has been **criticised**. Many psychologists believe that the uses of some objects can't be perceived without drawing on **stored knowledge** or **experience**.

Theories of Perception

Gregory's Indirect Theory of Perception is a Top Down Theory

'Top down' means perception is steered by context and prior knowledge.

1) **Gregory's (1966) indirect theory** of perception suggests that stimuli often **don't** provide the cognitive system with **enough information** for it to make sense of a situation.
2) This could be because the stimuli are **ambiguous** or because the information they provide is **limited**.
3) Instead, stimuli are treated as **hypotheses** which are tested within different **contexts** using **stored knowledge**.
4) **Visual illusions** provide support for Gregory's theory:

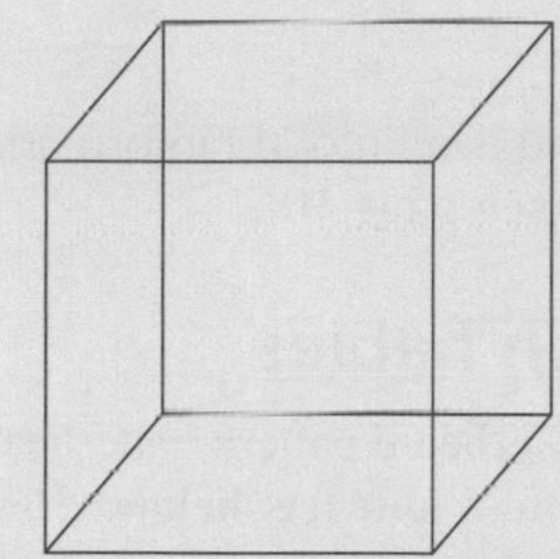

The diagram on the left shows a **Necker cube**. As you look at it your perception of which face is the **front face** changes. Gregory suggests that this is your brain **testing different hypotheses**. As there's **no context** to help you decide which the front face is, your brain continues to switch between them. This **supports** Gregory's theory that stimuli alone don't always provide enough information for the cognitive system to work out what's going on.

Comments on Gregory's Theory

1) There's plenty of evidence to support Gregory's theory — however, it's based on **laboratory experiments** so **lacks ecological validity**.
2) The theory can explain **errors** in perception — for example, those caused by **optical illusions**.
3) However, many psychologists reckon that if perception is based entirely on hypothesis testing we would make **more errors** in perception than we do.

Perception is Probably a Combination of Top Down and Bottom Up Processes

1) Many psychologists believe that perception stems from a **combination** of **top down** and **bottom up** processes.
2) **Bottom up** processes are most likely when the information provided by stimuli is **unambiguous** and **plentiful**.
3) **Top down** processes become more dominant when the amount or the quality of information provided by stimuli is **reduced**. We become more dependent on **stored knowledge** and **past experiences**.
4) When this happens, unconscious 'educated guesses' play a greater part in perception.

Practice Questions

Q1 What is perception?

Q2 Give an example of a bottom up theory of perception.

Q3 What is the optic array?

Q4 What do texture gradients provide information on?

Q5 Which features of the optic array provide information on the size of objects?

Q6 Why does Gregory's (1966) theory lack ecological validity?

Exam Question

Q1 Outline and evaluate Gregory's indirect theory of perception. [25 marks]

Bottom up theory — not the same as bottoms up. That's for after the exam.

Before you get to the celebratory times after finishing exams you need to get through the not-so-great times of learning for the exam. And as part of that, you definitely need to take the time to learn about Gibson's and Gregory's perception theories. So stuff your brain with info on affordances, visual illusions, hypotheses and the like — not forgetting that mysterious optic array.

Development of Perception

Just AQA again. *The odd visual illusion aside, we're pretty good at perception and can make sense of most things most of the time. Hmmm, I wonder if we're born with this skill or if we learn it. Oh yes — it's nature vs nurture time again.*

There Have Been Lots of Studies on The Development of Perception

There's been much debate over whether our perceptual abilities are **innate** (inbuilt) or are **learned** through experience. In other words, whether they're down to **nature** or **nurture**. Studies have been carried out to investigate the development of perceptual abilities such as **depth perception** and **visual constancies**.

Some Studies Suggest Depth Perception is Innate

Depth perception allows us to change a 2D image on the retina (the inner lining of the eye) into 3D information. We do this using cues such as relative size, texture gradients and optic flow patterns (see page 10).

	Gibson and Walk (1960) — depth perception in babies
Method:	A **'visual cliff'** was created using a layer of glass with **two levels** of a checkerboard pattern underneath. The shallow level had the pattern just below the glass, the deep level had the pattern **four feet below**. 36 six-month old babies were placed on the shallow side and encouraged by their mothers to crawl on to the deep side.
Results:	Most babies **wouldn't** crawl on to the **deep side** of the visual cliff.
Conclusion:	Babies can perceive depth so **depth perception** is the result of **nature**, not nurture.
Evaluation:	The **validity** of this study is questionable as the babies were six months old and could have **learnt** depth perception by this age. **Campos (1970)** tested **babies** by measuring their heart rate when they were on different sides of the cliff. He found that the heart rate of two-month old babies (who **couldn't crawl**) was the **same** on both sides, suggesting they didn't perceive any change in depth. Nine-month old babies (who **could crawl**) had a **increased** heart rate on the deep side, suggesting they had learned depth perception, i.e. through **nurture**.

Studies Have Suggested That Visual Constancies are Innate

1) As you look at an object, an image of it forms on the **retina**, allowing it to be seen.
2) The **closer** an object is, the **larger** the image it creates on the retina. However, when the brain interprets the image it's able to identify the object as being closer rather than larger. This is known as **size constancy**.
3) Similarly, when an object is rotated, e.g. a door opening, the **shape** of the image on the retina **changes** but the brain doesn't interpret this as the object changing shape. This is known as **shape constancy**.
4) Size and shape constancy are both **visual constancies** and important perceptual abilities.
5) Several studies have been carried out to determine whether visual constancy is a result of **nature** or **nurture**:

	Slater and Morrison (1985) — shape constancy in babies
Method:	**Newborn** babies were shown a square held at **different angles**. At some angles the image on the retina would be a **trapezium**. Once the baby was familiar with the square they were shown a trapezium **alongside it**.
Results:	The babies were more likely to look at the new **trapezium** than the square.
Conclusion:	Babies can distinguish between the trapezium and the square held at an orientation where it looks like a trapezium. So, babies have an **innate** ability to apply **shape constancy** to objects.

	Bower (1964, 1966) — size constancy in babies
Method:	**Two-month-old** babies were conditioned to look at a **30 cm cube** held **1 m away** from them, by being given a reward each time they looked at it. Once they could do this they were presented with new stimuli. Firstly they were shown a **90 cm cube** held **1 m away**. This would create a **larger** retinal image than the original cube. Then they were shown a **90 cm cube** held **3 m** away, producing the **same size** retinal image as the original. Lastly, the **original 30 cm cube** was held at a distance of **3 m**, producing a **smaller** retinal image than before.
Results:	The babies preferred to look at the **original 30 cm cube** held at a distance of **3 m** than the 90 cm cubes.
Conclusion:	Babies can distinguish between objects of different sizes regardless of the size of the image they create on the retina. So, babies have an **innate** ability to apply **size constancy** to objects.

Development of Perception

Cross Cultural Studies Have Been Carried Out On *Perceptual Abilities*

1) If perceptual abilities are the result of **nature** they're likely to be present in **everyone** regardless of culture.
2) However, if they're the result of **nurture** they're likely to **vary** between people of different cultures.
3) So, **cross-cultural studies** can help to determine whether perceptual abilities are the result of **nature** or **nurture**:

1) The **Müller-Lyer illusion** shows two lines of the **same length** that can appear to be different lengths due to inward or outward facing arrow heads (see diagram on right).
2) **Segall et al (1966)** showed the illusion to a sample of **urban** South Africans and a sample of **rural** Zulus.
3) Most of the urban South Africans identified the line with the **inwardly pointing arrows (a)** as being **longer** than the line with the **outwardly pointing arrows (b)**. The Zulus were **less susceptible** to the illusion, with a high proportion identifying the lines as being the same length.

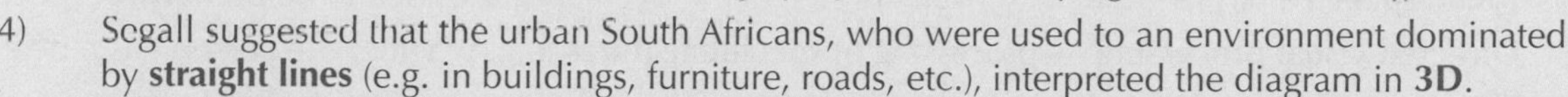

4) Segall suggested that the urban South Africans, who were used to an environment dominated by **straight lines** (e.g. in buildings, furniture, roads, etc.), interpreted the diagram in **3D**.
5) In 3D, **line a** resembles an object receding **away** from the observer (e.g. the inner corner of a room). **Line b** resembles an object projecting **towards** the observer (e.g. the outer corner of a building).

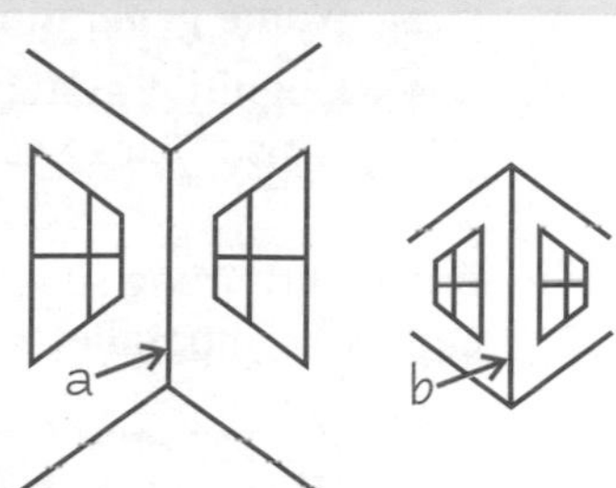

6) As **line a** appears to recede away from the observer the brain interprets it as being **further away** than **line b**.
7) So, the brain interprets **line a** as being **larger** than the image it forms on the retina (**size constancy**) and **perceives** it to be **longer** than **line b**.
8) The **Zulu** people were **less familiar** with buildings made from **straight lines** — their huts were circular. Segall suggested that they saw the lines in **2D**, so didn't apply size constancy and didn't perceive any difference in the length of the lines.

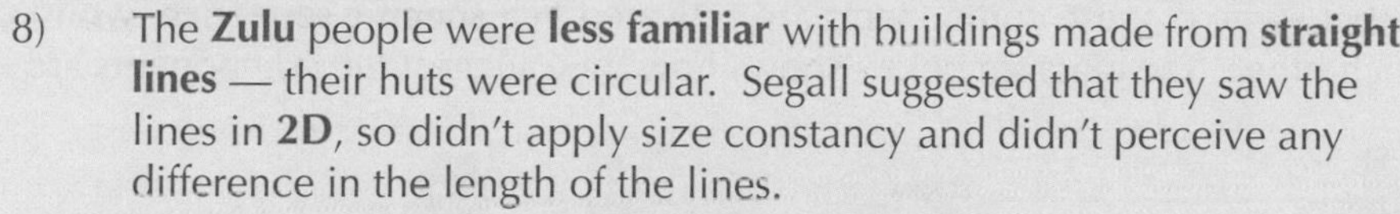

9) He saw this difference in perception across cultures as evidence that perceptual abilities are **developed** in response to the **environment**, i.e. perception is the result of **nurture**.

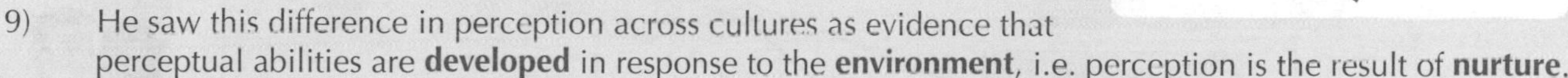

Perceptual Abilities May Result From *Nature* and *Nurture*

1) **Cross cultural studies** (e.g. Segall et al (1966)) and **infant studies** (e.g. Bower (1985) and Slater and Morrison (1985)) can both be useful in studying the development of perceptual abilities.
2) However, the results of these studies **vary** — some suggest perception is **innate** and some suggest it's **learned**.
3) Many psychologists believe that perceptual abilities could be caused by a **combination** of nature and nurture.

Practice Questions

Q1 What did Gibson and Walk's (1960) 'visual cliff' study test?

Q2 What is size constancy?

Q3 How can cross-cultural studies help determine whether perceptual abilities are the result of nature or nurture?

Exam Question

Q1 a) Outline one cross-cultural study into the development of perceptual abilities. [10 marks]

b) Discuss the nature-nurture debate in relation to explanations of perceptual development. [15 marks]

I perceive you might not care whether it's down to nature or nurture...

...however, I also perceive that the examiners don't care that you don't care. I'm perceptive like that. And I perceive that, regardless of your cultural background, your perceptual abilities will lead you to concur. So, in short, learn these pages.

Face Recognition and Visual Agnosia

Still just for AQA. *Of all the clever things we can do, being able to recognise thousands of different faces is surely one of the most useful. So you'd think someone would have come up with a theory of how we do it. And you'd be right.*

Bruce and Young's (1986) Theory Suggests How We Recognise Faces

1) **Face recognition** is an important perceptual ability — allowing us to **form relationships** and **function socially**.
2) It lets us tell the **difference** between thousands of faces, even though they have the **same basic features**, e.g. eyes.
3) We're also able to **identify familiar faces** — those of friends, family or famous people.
4) **Bruce and Young** (**1986**) suggest that the process of face recognition is **different** from recognition of other objects. Their model outlines a number of different **components** involved in face recognition:

- **Structural encoding** — physical features are interpreted to determine **basic information** (e.g. age, gender). This allows a **structural model** of the face to be built up.
- **Expression analysis** — facial features are analysed to work out the person's **emotional state**.
- **Facial speech analysis** — facial movements (e.g. lip movements) are used to help **interpret speech**.
- **Directed visual processing** — processing of **specific features** (e.g. whether the person has a beard).
- **Face recognition units** — these contain information about the structure of **familiar faces**.
- **Person identity nodes** — these contain information known about the **person** (e.g. their job, interests).
- **Name generation** — this helps us to retrieve the **name** of a familiar person and relate it to their face.
- **Cognitive system** — this contains **extra information** (e.g. the context in which a face is likely to be seen). It also helps determine which of the **other components** involved in face recognition are activated.

5) Bruce and Young suggested that some of these components are activated in a **specific sequence**, whilst others can work in **parallel** with each other. The diagram below shows how they suggest the components are linked.

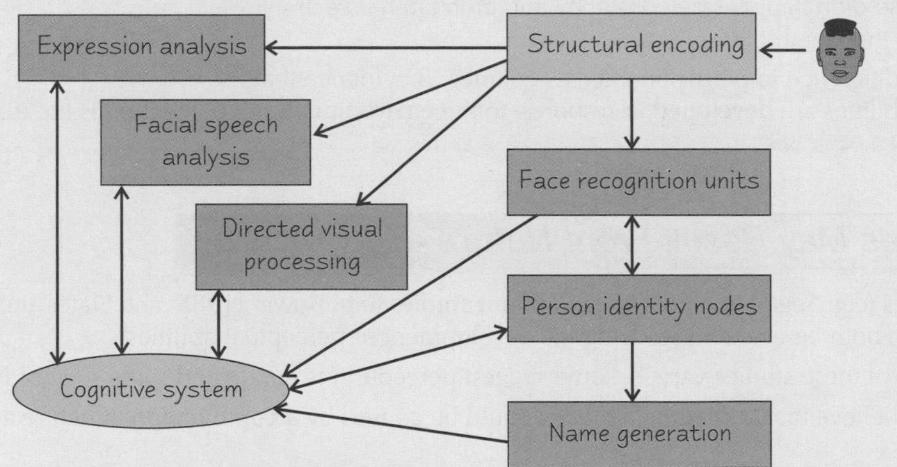

It might well be familiar, but no-one ever seemed to look at Troy's face.

- For example, **structural encoding** is always the **first** component to be activated. After this either **face recognition units**, **facial speech analysis**, **expression analysis** or **direct visual processing** may be activated. These components work in **parallel**.
- However, **person identity nodes** can only be activated **after** the **face recognition units**, and only **after this** can **name generation** be activated. These components work in **sequence**. Makes sense — you can't come up with information about someone until you've realised they're familiar.

The Components Used Depend on Whether the Face is Familiar or Not

Bruce and Young's model proposes that we use **different components** to process **new** and **familiar** faces.

1) They suggest that processing of a **new face** involves **structural encoding**, **expression analysis**, **facial speech analysis** and **directed visual processing**.
2) Recognition of **familiar faces** uses **structural encoding**, **face recognition units**, **person identity nodes** and **name generation**.

Face Recognition and Visual Agnosia

People with Prosopagnosia Have Trouble Recognising Faces

1) **Prosopagnosia** is a condition where people have difficulty **recognising familiar faces**.
2) It's usually caused by **brain damage**, but some evidence suggests that it could also be **congenital** (present at birth).
3) There are **different types** of prosopagnosia, with the most serious forms leaving people unable to recognise their spouse, close family and friends. Some patients can't even recognise their own face.
4) Some studies of prosopagnosia have provided support for Bruce and Young's model of face recognition:

- **Farah (1994)** studied a patient (LH) who developed prosopagnosia as a result of **brain damage** caused by a **car crash**.
- Along with a control group of participants who didn't have prosopagnosia, he was shown pictures of **faces** and pairs of **spectacles** and then given a **recognition memory test**.
- LH performed **as well** as the control group in recognising **spectacles** but much **worse** than the control group in recognising the **faces**.
- This suggests that prosopagnosia is caused by damage to the area of the brain involved in **face recognition** but not **object recognition**.
- This supports Bruce and Young's proposal that face recognition and object recognition are **separate processes**.

- **Kurucz and Feldmar (1979)** saw a patient with prosopagnosia who was **unable** to **identify familiar faces** but could interpret the **emotional state** of the person.
- This suggests that recognition of familiar faces and interpretation of emotional states are processes that work **independently** of each other.
- This supports Bruce and Young's concept of expression analysis and face recognition units as **separate components** that work in **parallel** with each other — one can be functional even if the other isn't.

5) These case studies suggest that the various types of prosopagnosia are caused by problems with one or more of the components of Bruce and Young's model. For example, the patient in Kurucz and Feldmar's study would have suffered damage to **face recognition units** or **person identity nodes** but **not** to the **expression analysis component**.

There's Some Evidence That Bruce and Young's Model Isn't Correct

Some studies suggest that Bruce and Young's model **isn't accurate**. For example:

1) **de Haan et al (1991)** found that when given the names and faces of famous people, a patient with amnesia was able to correctly match **88%** of the **faces** to the **names** even though they couldn't give any other information about the person.
2) This doesn't support Bruce and Young's model — the study suggests that activation of **face recognition units** was followed by **name generation**, bypassing **person identity nodes** entirely.

Practice Questions

Q1 What is the role of expression analysis in Bruce and Young's (1986) theory of face recognition?

Q2 Which components of Bruce and Young's (1986) model contain information about familiar faces?

Q3 What is prosopagnosia?

Exam Question

Q1 a) Outline Bruce and Young's (1986) theory of face recognition [15 marks]

b) Using case studies, describe the evidence in support of Bruce and Young's theory. [10 marks]

Prosopagnosia's not so bad — there are some faces you want to forget...

So, final two pages for this section. Best to go out with a flourish and learn them really well I think. Especially as there's only ONE theory here. I'm unbelievably kind to you when you think about it. Anyway, enough about me. You need to learn Bruce and Young's theory and the info on prosopagnosia, including the case studies. And then you're done with perception.

Formation, Maintenance and Breakdown

AQA people only. Relationships are a bit of a song and dance at the best of times. But learn these pages and you'll be able to explain — WITH evidence — why you went off on one when Kevin nicked one of your chips without asking.

We Might Form Relationships for **Selfish Reasons**

1) **Reward/need satisfaction theory** states that we form friendships and relationships to receive **rewards** or **reinforcement** from others.
2) Relationships provide **rewards** (approval, sex, status, love, money, respect, agreement with our opinions, smiling, information, etc.) that satisfy our **social needs** (for self-esteem, affiliation, dependency, influence, etc.)
3) So, in terms of operant conditioning, being in a relationship is **positively reinforced** because it is rewarding.
4) **Byrne and Clore's (1970)** Reinforcement-Affect theory suggests that both **operant** and **classical conditioning** play a part in relationships. The theory states that we **learn** to associate people with **positive or enjoyable situations**, even if they are not **directly rewarding** us in these instances.

Economic Theories Consider Relationships to be a **Trading Process**

1) **Social Exchange Theory** (Thibaut & Kelley, 1959) suggests that people try to **maximise rewards** (e.g. attention, self-esteem, happiness) from a relationship and **minimise costs** (e.g. time, effort, emotional support).
2) If the relationship is to continue, then the rewards must not be **outweighed** by the costs — we should end up in **profit**. So, relationships are formed using a sort of 'cost-benefit' analysis.
3) But if we are striving to **get more** and **give less**, this may result in an **unequal relationship**.

1) **Equity theory** suggests that people expect relationships to be **fair and equal**.
2) They want to receive rewards from relationships that are **in balance** with the rewards they provide for the other person.
3) If a relationship is unequal or unfair then it produces **discomfort and distress** in both partners, even if you are the one getting more and giving less.
4) The disadvantaged person may try to **make things fairer** if it seems possible.

"This doesn't seem very fair."
"Well... it is, so keep pushing."

Relationships can be **Perceived Very Differently**

People within a relationship may have different feelings about the relationship and have different levels of satisfaction.

Hatfield et al (1979) asked newlyweds to assess what they and their partner **contributed** to the relationship and their level of **contentment** with the marriage:
- The least satisfied were those who were **under-benefited** (unhappy about giving the most).
- The next least satisfied were those who were **over-benefited** (perhaps they felt a bit guilty about giving the least). Equal relationships were the **most satisfactory**.

But there may be sex differences in how we feel about unequal relationships. **Argyle (1988)** found that:
- Over-benefited **men** were almost as satisfied as those in equitable marriages.
- Over-benefited **women**, however, were much **less satisfied** than women in equal relationships.

Theories of relationship formation can also give an insight into **relationship maintenance**.
- A relationship in which your needs are satisfied would be important for you to **protect and maintain**.
- In the same sense, equity theory says that people in an unbalanced, unfair relationship may **attempt to change things** in order for the balance to be restored.

Formation, Maintenance and Breakdown

A Range of Factors can Influence the **Breakdown of a Relationship**

These are some common reasons for the breakdown of a relationship:

- **dissatisfaction** or **boredom** with the relationship
- **breaking agreed rules** (e.g. being faithful, confidentiality)
- **interference** from other relationships (e.g. family or friends)
- **abuse** (e.g. violence, drugs, alcohol)
- an attractive **alternative relationship** exists
- costs **outweigh** benefits
- **conflict** or **dispute** (e.g. over finances)
- **jealousy** over a real or imagined rival

Theories Suggest Relationships **End in Stages**

Lee (1984) conducted interviews with over 100 couples who had broken up.
He identified **five stages** in the process of the breakdown of a relationship:

1) **Dissatisfaction** in one or both partners
2) **Exposing** the dissatisfaction and identifying problems
3) **Negotiating** the exposed problems
4) **Resolution** — attempting to solve problems
5) **Termination** of the relationship if no resolution

Not all couples went through **all the stages**. It seems that less intimate relationships may progress to the termination stage **more quickly**. Stronger relationships took **longer** to go through the stages and took longer to get over.

Duck (1988) developed a **four-phase model** of the ending of an intimate relationship.

1) **Intra-psychic** phase — inside the head of **one person**. One partner becomes **dissatisfied** with the relationship.
2) **Dyadic phase** — between **two people**. The other partner is told about the dissatisfaction.
3) **Social phase** — beyond the couple. The break-up is **made public** to friends and family. **Implications** are discussed (e.g. care of children). The relationship **can still be saved** here (e.g. intervention of family, external marital support).
4) **Grave-dressing phase** — finishing the relationship completely. The ex-partners organise their lives post-relationship. They tell their own version of the break-up and of their current relationship with their ex.

However, the theories don't take **individual differences** into account and **research evidence** suggests these models don't show how **complex** relationship dissolution can be.

- **Rusbult and Zembrodt (1983)** said some people in relationship breakdowns **actively lead** the process (to resolve the problems or speed up the ending). Others are **passive** (believing things will resolve themselves).
- **Akert (1992)** said people who do the breaking up are **less likely** to be upset and show physical symptoms (e.g. loss of appetite and sleep) — not surprising really.
- Finally, these theories don't take **cultural differences** in relationships into account (see page 21).

Practice Questions

Q1 List some needs and rewards provided by relationships.

Q2 Give three examples of reasons for the breakdown of a relationship.

Q3 What are Lee's five stages of relationship breakdown?

Q4 Describe the dyadic phase of Duck's model.

Exam Questions

Q1 Outline and evaluate two or more theories of relationship formation. [25 marks]

Q2 Discuss research (theories and/or studies) relating to the dissolution of relationships. [25 marks]

People might try and tell you that a relationship is the best kind of ship...

... but that's clearly a lie. The best kind of ship is probably like that one out of Pirates of the Caribbean. It had cannons. And pirates. But I doubt psychologists are cut out for the high seas. Duck might cope, I suppose. Now, make sure you can describe the main theories concerning the formation and dissolution of relationships, and then we can quack on...

Reproductive Behaviour

These pages are just for AQA. *If you've ever wondered why we find certain characteristics attractive in people, or why parents put so much time and effort into bringing kids up, then you've come to the right pages. All will be revealed...*

Sexual Selection Explains Certain *Reproductive Behaviours*

1) Within a species there are certain **characteristics** that make individuals **attractive** to potential mates.
2) For example, female peacocks find the **long**, **brightly coloured tails** of male peacocks attractive.
3) Males with very brightly coloured tails are more noticeable to **predators**. Those with very long tails find it **difficult to escape** from predators. So, long, brightly coloured tails **reduce** male peacocks' **chances of surviving**.
4) However, as female peacocks are **attracted** to this feature, males with long, brightly coloured tails have a **higher chance of reproducing** and passing their genes on to the next generation than other males.
5) This means that the characteristic **evolves** in the species even though it reduces the survival chances.
6) This evolution of characteristics which are attractive to potential mates is known as **sexual selection**.
7) In **humans**, characteristics affecting attractiveness include **physical** and **mental health** and some **physical features**.
8) These influence potential mates as they indicate ability to **reproduce** and **provide for offspring**.

There Are *Different Types* of *Sexual Selection*

Intrasexual selection

Intrasexual selection takes place when males compete (often aggressively) and the winner is rewarded with the female. The female is **passive** in this process — she doesn't choose her own mate.

Intersexual selection

Intersexual selection takes place when males compete for the **attention** of a female. The female plays an **active role**, choosing her mate.

Sperm Competition is a Form of *Intrasexual Selection*

1) Short's (1979) **Sperm Competition Theory** suggests that males are motivated to ensure that their sperm is **successful in fertilisation** and compete against other males to make this happen.
2) In **humans** this has resulted in men evolving to release **large amounts** of sperm during ejaculation.
3) This is a form of **intrasexual selection** and increases the likelihood of **successful fertilisation**.

Buss (1989) Carried Out *Cross Cultural Research* Into *Intersexual Selection*

Buss (1989) — gender differences in mate selection

Method: **Questionnaires** were used to collect data from over 10 000 men and women from 37 different cultural groups. The questionnaires covered **demographic information** such as age, gender and marital status. They also asked about preferences for variables such as marriage, age differences and characteristics in a mate (e.g. intelligence, sociability and financial prospects).

Results: **Women** valued variables associated with **gaining resources** (e.g. money, safe environment) more highly than men. **Men** valued variables associated with **reproductive capacity** (e.g. youth) more highly than women.

Conclusion: Historically, women have had limited access to the **resources** needed to provide for themselves and their offspring. So, they've evolved to select mates who can **provide** these resources. Men have been limited by access to **fertile women**, and so have evolved to be attracted to women with a high likelihood of **reproducing**.

Evaluation: The study supports an **evolutionary explanation** of gender differences in sexual selection. **Similar findings** were found across a range of **different cultures**. However, it **wasn't** a truly **representative** study as it was hard to include rural and less educated populations. The study also didn't take **social influences** on mate selection into account. For example, changes in society mean that women in many cultures are now able to provide for themselves and their offspring, and aren't as dependent on men for resources.
Also, **homosexual relationships** aren't explained, as reproduction isn't a goal in same-sex relationships.

Reproductive Behaviour

Parental Investment** Can be Explained in Terms of **Evolution

1) **Parental investment** refers to any **time**, **effort** and **energy** that a parent puts towards the **conception**, **gestation** and **rearing** of a child that **reduces** their ability to invest in **other offspring**.
2) In species where gestation is **short** and offspring become independent **quickly**, **less** parental investment is needed.
3) However, in **humans**, parental investment is **more demanding** — gestation takes nine months and children don't become independent for many years.
4) There are a number of **evolutionary factors** that affect parental investment. For example:

Sex differences

1) Parental investment in humans shows **sex differences**.
2) Men only need to be involved at **conception** whilst women also have to invest during **pregnancy**.
3) There are differences when the offspring is born too, e.g. women have to invest in **breast-feeding**. Historically, men provided **protection**, **shelter** and other **resources** (e.g. food) whilst women invested more time and energy in the **day-to-day care** of children.
4) The **number of children** women can have is **limited** so they're likely to invest **heavily** in the survival of each one. Men can have many more children so investment in each individual is **less important**.
5) Trivers (1972) suggests the sex that invests **most** in the offspring (usually females) will **discriminate** when choosing a mate. The sex that invests **least** (usually males) will **compete** more for the higher investing mates.

Parent-offspring conflict

1) It seems sensible that parents should produce **lots of offspring** to help the species survive.
2) However, spending time nurturing children has **costs**. For example:
   - **Pregnancy** and **lactation** make physical demands on the mother.
   - **Looking after** and **providing** for young children is demanding.
   - **Multiple pregnancies** and **pregnancies in later life** can have health implications for the mother.
3) These conflicts between the needs of the parent and those of the children are known as **parent-offspring conflict** — they suggest that parental investment may be better spent on a **smaller** number of children.
4) This is becoming more common as **infant mortality** rates decrease, and advances in birth control mean that many people have access to **contraception** — making it easier to **control reproduction**.
5) This is one example of how reproductive behaviour has changed over time as **societies change**.

Practice Questions

Q1 List some characteristics that influence attractiveness in humans.

Q2 What is meant by parental investment?

Q3 Give an example of a cost of spending time nurturing offspring.

Exam Question

Q1 a) Outline the relationship between sexual selection and human reproductive behaviours. [10 marks]

b) Discuss the influence of sex differences and parent-offspring conflict on parental investment. [15 marks]

Research into sexual selection — sounds like a very dodgy excuse to me...

So it turns out that parent-offspring conflict is nothing to do with rows about what time you got in last night. It's a proper psychological term, and it's one that you need to know — along with sex differences, parental investment and sexual selection. Once you've got those straight you'll be able to wow those examiners with your reproductive knowledge.

Adult Relationships

Still for AQA people only. *We form relationships with people throughout our lives. The relationships we form when we're young and the ones we see around us can affect our own ability to form successful adult relationships.*

Hazen and Shaver (1987) Linked Attachment Theory to Adult Relationships

1) **Childhood** experiences can influence **adult relationships** as they provide **examples** of how to behave.
2) **Hazen and Shaver** (**1987**) noticed similarities between the attachments infants form with their caregivers and the behaviour shown by adults in romantic relationships.
3) They investigated the link between the **attachment type** individuals showed as children and the way they felt about **adult relationships**:

	Hazen and Shaver (1987) — attachment and adult relationships
Method:	Descriptions of three attitudes towards adult relationships were published in a newspaper. These attitudes were based on **Ainsworth et al's attachment types** (see p.182). Readers were asked to choose the attitude that best suited them. They were also asked to describe their relationships with their own caregivers.
Results:	The **attachment type** that an individual had shown as a child was **significantly related** to how they felt about **adult relationships**. Those who showed a **secure** attachment type in childhood were more likely to enjoy **secure** relationships as an adult. Those with an **anxious-avoidant** attachment type in childhood were more likely to find it **difficult to trust people** in adult relationships. Those with an **anxious-resistant** attachment type in childhood were more likely to feel **anxious** in adult relationships and find it hard to get others as close to them as they wanted.
Conclusion:	Relationships formed with parents during childhood affect relationships in adulthood.
Evaluation:	The study was based on **self-report data** which is **subjective** and therefore may be **unreliable**. The data was also **retrospective**, further reducing the reliability of the study. Also, because the study relied on people replying to a newspaper article, the sample might not be **representative** of the whole population.

Parental Divorce Can Also Affect Adult Relationships

1) Many studies show that people who experienced **parental divorce** during childhood have **more negative attitudes** towards relationships than those who didn't experience parental divorce.
2) These negative attitudes include being **less optimistic** about having a successful relationship, feeling **less trustful** of partners, having a **more favourable attitude** towards **divorce** and a **more negative attitude** towards **marriage**.
3) Silvestri (1991) found that having **divorced parents** significantly increased an individual's **own chances** of getting divorced. Johnston and Thomas (1996) suggest that this could be because individuals model their adult behaviour on their parents' behaviour.
4) Alternatively, it could be a result of **learnt negative behaviour**, **disruption** caused by family tension, or **separation** from a parent or siblings during normal child developmental stages.
5) If one parent is absent the child doesn't have a **template** on which to model their own adult relationships. Franklin et al (1990) found that this can create problems with children's future adult relationships.
6) Not all children of divorced parents go on to have unsuccessful adult relationships. There are many factors which can influence the long-term effects, e.g. **quality of relationship** with parents and **support after divorce**.
7) This research can be used to **minimise** the **effect of divorce** on children.

Peer Interaction in Adolescence Develops Skills For Adult Relationships

1) Arnett (2007) suggests that friendships with **peers** during childhood and adolescence give opportunities to develop the **skills** needed to form **successful adult relationships**. These include how to **resolve conflict** and how to take on different **roles** needed in relationships.
2) Collins and van Dulmen (2006) support this theory and also suggest that relationships with peers give individuals the opportunity to learn **behaviours** and **expectations** involved in relationships.
3) So, experiences during childhood and adolescence influence the **quality** of adult relationships.

Adult Relationships

Different Cultures have Different Attitudes to Relationships

Western societies tend to be **individualist** and **Eastern** societies tend to be **collectivist**.

1) A **collectivist** society sees the individual as part of an **interdependent social group**. Obligations to others and the good of the group are very important.
2) Relationships are more likely to be **non-voluntary** (e.g. arranged marriages), where marriage joins **families** as well as individuals. Extended families are more likely to **live together**, providing support for each other.
3) In Western societies, the emphasis is on the **individual's** freedom, achievements and rights. So relationships are formed for individual happiness and are mostly **voluntary**, where a person chooses their partner for themselves.

The Attitudes and Values of Cultures Affect Relationships

Hsu (1981) stated that Western cultures value **change** and **new things**, but that Eastern cultures value **ancestry**, **history** and **continuity**. **Values** affect relationships in different parts of the world.

Duration

- Relationships are more likely to be **permanent** in non-Western cultures.
- In Western societies, we are more likely to split up and have **new relationships**.

Marriage

- Arranged marriages are often associated with collectivist cultures, and involve **whole families**. Arranged marriages also seem to have more **stability** than those based on 'romantic love'.
- However, **De Munck (1996)** found that in a Sri Lankan community with an emphasis on arranged marriages, **romantic love** was still considered when choosing a partner.
- **Ghuman (1994)** stated that arranged marriages were **common** among Hindus, Muslims and Sikhs in Britain, but **Goodwin (1997)** found that only **9%** of Hindu marriages he studied were arranged.
- **Levine et al (1995)** found a higher percentage of people from **collectivist** societies would marry a person with the **right qualities** whom they didn't love, compared to members of **individualistic** societies.

Divorce

- **Goodwin (1999)** calculated the US divorce rate to be **40-50%**.
- However, the Chinese regard divorce as shameful to the **families involved** as much as the divorcing couple — **fewer** marriages end in divorce. This is beginning to change though, as a result of **westernisation**.

Barry got his family's seal of approval before agreeing to anything.

Practice Questions

Q1 Describe the effect of parental divorce on a person's attitude towards adult relationships.

Q2 Give an example of a skill used in peer relationships that can also be used in adult relationships.

Q3 List some differences between trends in relationships in individualistic and collectivist cultures.

Exam Question

Q1 a) Discuss the influence that childhood experiences may have on adult relationships. [10 marks]

b) Discuss research relating to cultural differences in relationships. [15 marks]

I'm the anxious-resistant-avoidant type when it comes to exams...

Just like 40-50% of US marriages, you've reached the end of the road — or at least the end of the section. The key things to learn here are how childhood experiences affect adult relationships, and how relationships vary between cultures. Which is basically everything on these pages. Apart from Barry and the seals — you don't have to learn about him. He's very strange.

Social Theories of Aggression

These pages are just for AQA. *This section is all about aggression — GRRRR! Eeek, I scared myself a bit there.*

Deindividuation *Theory Says Being* ***Anonymous*** *Encourages Aggression*

One **social psychological** theory of aggression suggests we're **disinhibited** when we're an **anonymous** part of a **crowd**. People may feel less **personal responsibility** and less fear of **public disapproval** when they're part of the group. **Festinger et al (1952)** coined the term **deindividuation** to describe this state.

Aggression is behaviour intended to harm — including physical and psychological harm.

There's some **real-world evidence** for this effect:

1) **Mullen (1986)** analysed newspaper reports of **lynch mob violence** in the US. The **more people** there were in the mob, the **greater** the level of violence.
2) **Mann (1981)** analysed 21 reports of **suicides** and identified ten cases where a crowd had **baited** the person threatening suicide (e.g. shouting 'jump'). Baiting was more likely to happen **at night**, when the crowd was **at a distance** and when the crowd was **large** (more than 300 people).

Research studies have also supported deindividuation:

1) **Zimbardo (1969)** showed that **anonymity** affects behaviour. Participants in his study believed they were administering **shocks** to another participant in a learning experiment. **Individuated** participants wore normal clothes, large name badges and were introduced to each other. **Deindividuated** participants wore coats with hoods, were instructed in groups and weren't referred to by name. The **more anonymous** participants administered more and longer shocks.
2) **Diener et al (1976)** observed 1300 trick-or-treating children in the US. If they were **anonymous** (in costumes, masks or large groups) they were **more likely** to steal money and sweets.

This evidence supports the idea that deindividuation **increases** aggression. But there are also examples of it having **no effect** or even **reducing** aggression. For example, individuals in crowds at religious festivals often express goodwill to others. It could be that being in a group means that you **conform to group norms**. If group norms are **prosocial**, the individual may behave that way too.

Social Learning Theory *Says* ***Experience*** *Explains Aggressive Behaviour*

Social learning theory says behaviours are learnt in two ways:

1) **directly** through **reinforcement** (i.e. reward and punishment).
2) **indirectly** by seeing others being rewarded or punished for behaviours (**vicarious learning**).

Bandura (1965) conducted the **Bobo Doll Experiment** to investigate whether **aggressive behaviour** can be learnt through reinforcement and punishment.

A Bobo doll is an inflatable figure with a weight in the bottom.

Bandura (1965) — Bobo Doll Experiment

Method: In a **controlled observation** with an **independent measures** design, children watched a video of a male or female model behaving aggressively towards a Bobo doll. Their behaviour was distinctive — e.g. they used a hammer or shouted certain things. The children either saw the model being told off (**punished**) or being rewarded with sweets (**reinforced**). In a **control condition**, the model was neither rewarded nor punished. The children were then allowed to play in a room of toys, including the Bobo doll.

Results: Children who'd seen the model being rewarded and those in the control condition imitated **more** aggressive behaviours than those who saw the model being punished.

Conclusion: Children learn aggressive behaviour through **observation** and **imitation**, particularly if it's rewarded.

Evaluation: The models used distinctive actions that the children were unlikely to produce spontaneously, meaning that Bandura could be sure that **imitation** was taking place. However, the conditions were pretty **artificial** — it's unlikely that children would see adults behaving aggressively towards toys in real life, so the study lacks **ecological validity**. The study also didn't consider the differences between **playfighting** and aggression towards other people. The **previous** behaviour of the children wasn't considered, and no **follow-up** was done to see if the aggressive behaviour was long-term.

Institutional Aggression

Institutional Aggression is Often Seen as *Acceptable*

Aggression doesn't always involve red faces, bulging eyes and throbbing veins. It can be calm, organised, and even respectable. Certain groups in society are actually relied on to show aggression, so the rest of us don't have to...

Aggression in the police force

To uphold the **rules** and **norms** of society the police are allowed to use aggression against people breaking the law. In this situation, aggression can be seen as a **prosocial behaviour** and many people think the threat of police aggression is critical in maintaining order in society. To make sure their aggressive behaviours are **controlled** and **appropriate** to the situation police officers have to go through training — uncontrolled police aggression or abuse of police power isn't tolerated by society. The **Independent Police Complaints Commission** helps make sure that police aggression is controlled and appropriate by holding police officers accountable for their actions.

Aggression in the military

Wars are usually started and coordinated by **politicians**. Their motivations may be very different to those of the soldiers who join up to fight. For example, a soldier may join the military in order to become part of a **group** and feel a **sense of belonging**, leading to increased **self-esteem**.

Aggression, or the threat of aggression, is an important feature of a soldier's job. However, like in the police force, the aggression needs to be **controlled** and used for **specific purposes** only. For this reason soldiers receive training on **when** to behave aggressively and what **types** of aggression are appropriate. For example, the use of guns to return enemy fire is deemed acceptable, but violence towards prisoners and innocent civilians is not.

However, organised aggression isn't always respectable or accepted by society.
Terrorist groups are an example of aggressive organisations that **aren't** tolerated by society.

Aggression in terrorist groups

People who join **terrorist organisations** may be motivated by a wide range of reasons, including the sense of belonging that comes with joining a group. Many join believing it will bring them certain **benefits**, e.g. young Palestinians living in poverty are often recruited as suicide bombers with the promise of glory in the afterlife. The difference between military organisations and terrorist groups is **relative**, depending on who the target of aggression is — enemy soldiers or civilians.

Practice Questions

Q1 What does deindividuation mean?

Q2 Outline a laboratory experiment that linked deindividuation and aggression.

Q3 Give two criticisms of Bandura's (1965) Bobo Doll experiment.

Q4 Give two examples of institutional aggression.

Q5 Give three reasons why an individual might decide to join the army and fight for their country.

Exam Question

Q1 a) Outline two social psychological theories of aggression. [9 marks]

b) Evaluate the theories of aggression outlined in part (a). [16 marks]

That wasn't aggression — my fist slipped... And then so did my foot...

It doesn't seem at all surprising that a small child will mimic behaviour that they've recently seen, especially if there's been no harmful outcome of the behaviour they witnessed. But is hitting a doll the same as hitting another child because you've seen someone on TV doing it... Hmm, not too sure about that one — it's a really big jump, and not something you can easily test.

Biological Explanations of Aggression

Still AQA only here. *Aggression is a tendency that humans share with almost all other species of animals, as anyone who has tried to give a cat a bath will know. It's an ancient response that can be partially explained by our biology.*

There Are **Genetic Influences** Underlying Aggression

1) Species of various animals have been **selectively bred** to produce highly **aggressive** individuals — e.g. Doberman dogs were originally bred by humans to behave aggressively towards intruders so they can be used as guard dogs.
2) This ability to select the most aggressive dogs and breed them together to give **new generations** with the **same** aggressive tendencies suggests that there are specific **genes** that determine levels of aggression.
3) In humans, evidence for a genetic component to aggression comes from **twin studies** and **adoption studies**, where **criminality** is used as a measure of aggression.

Christiansen (1977) — Twin study into aggression

Method: A **concordance analysis** of all 3586 pairs of **twins** born between 1881 and 1910 in a region of Denmark was conducted. From this sample, **926** individuals were registered by the police for **criminal activity**. **Identical (MZ)** and **non-identical (DZ)** twins were compared for the rate at which **both** twins of the pair were registered.

Results: **Male MZ twins** showed **35% concordance** for criminality, compared to the **12% concordance** shown between **DZ twins**. **Female MZ** twins showed **21% concordance** compared to **8%** for **DZ** twins.

Conclusion: There's a **genetic component** to aggressive behaviour.

Evaluation: Genetics can't be the only factor, as the concordance rate for MZ twins (who share all of their genetic material) wasn't 100%. In previous twin studies, **samples** have been used where at least one twin had committed a crime. This gave **inflated** concordance rates. However, by studying **all** the twins born in a specified time frame, this study gives a more **representative** rate of concordance. As with all twin studies, **shared environment** for MZ twins is a **confounding variable**.

Mednick et al (1984) — Adoption study into aggression

Method: A **concordance analysis** of 14 427 Danish **adoptees** was conducted. Rates of concordance for **criminality** between the adoptees and their **adopted** and **biological parents** were compared.

Results: **13.5%** of adoptees with parents (adoptive or biological) **without** a criminal conviction had a criminal conviction themselves, compared to **14.7%** of adoptees with at least one criminally convicted **adoptive** parent, **20%** of adoptees with at least one criminally convicted **biological** parent, and **24.5%** of adoptees with at least one convicted adoptive **and** one convicted biological parent.

Conclusion: A **genetic link** is supported. However, the **concordance rates** are quite **low**, suggesting that there are **other** factors that lead to criminality.

Evaluation: Adoption studies allow **separation** of the genetic and environmental influences. However, criminal convictions may not be a **valid indicator** of aggression — the convictions could have been for non-violent crimes. Also, just because a person has not been **convicted** of a crime does not necessarily mean that they have never committed one.

Areas of the **Brain** Have Been Linked to Aggression

Different areas of the **brain**, including the **temporal lobe** and the **limbic system**, have been linked to different forms of aggressive behaviour. One part of the limbic system, the **amygdala**, has been found to have a particularly strong connection to aggression. Animal studies have shown that **electrical stimulation** of different parts of the amygdala can either **cause** or **reduce** aggression. **Lesions** to the amygdala have been found to cause cats to **attack**, but caused dogs to become **more submissive** and **less aggressive** — they needed **more stimulation** to provoke a response.

There is some evidence for the role of the amygdala in **human** aggression too. **Charles Whitman**, a sniper who killed 14 innocent people and wounded 31 others, left a note that pleaded for his brain to be examined after death for possible dysfunction. An autopsy showed that he had a **temporal lobe tumour**, pressing on his amygdala.

Biological Explanations of Aggression

Hormones *May Also Be Involved in Aggression*

High levels of **testosterone** (an androgen) are linked to aggression.

1) Levels of testosterone have been **compared** in **males** and **females**, and in **violent** and **non-violent** criminals.
2) **Males** in general, and **violent criminals** in particular, have **higher** levels of testosterone. This may explain their higher levels of **aggression**.
3) However, there's a problem with establishing **cause and effect** — this data is only **correlational**. Another factor could be causing aggressive behaviour, or it could be that being aggressive raises levels of testosterone.

Cindy wasn't the aggressive type, but if she ever saw that hairdresser again...

Van Goozen et al (1994) studied the effects of testosterone **directly**. This avoided having to depend on correlational data, which made it easier to establish cause and effect.

Van Goozen et al (1994) — Aggression in sex-change participants

Method: In a **repeated measures** design, 35 female-to-male and 15 male-to-female transsexuals completed **questionnaires** to assess **proneness to aggression**. They completed the questionnaires before and after receiving hormone treatment to 'change' their sex. Female-to-male transsexuals were given testosterone (an androgen) and male-to-female transsexuals were given anti-androgens. Treatment lasted 3 months.

Results: **Female-to-male** transsexuals reported an **increase** in aggression proneness, whereas **male-to-female** transsexuals reported a **decrease**.

Conclusion: Levels of **testosterone** determine the likelihood of displaying **aggressive behaviours**.

Evaluation: By controlling levels of testosterone **experimentally**, the **direction** of cause and effect between testosterone and aggression can be established. However, **self-report** measures of aggression were used, which are subjective and so may not be valid. The participants may have been conforming to **stereotypes** of their new gender roles by expressing an increase or decrease in aggression.

Practice Questions

Q1 Give two possible biological causes of aggression.
Q2 Outline the conclusion of the study by Christiansen (1977).
Q3 Describe the method used in the study by Mednick et al (1984).
Q4 Which parts of the brain have been linked to aggression?
Q5 Which hormone has been linked to aggression?
Q6 Give one advantage and one disadvantage of the method used in the study by Van Goozen et al (1994).

Exam Question

Q1 a) Outline the role of hormones in aggression. [9 marks]

b) Discuss the genetic explanation for aggression. [16 marks]

Pardon me for being aggressive — it was not me, it was my amygdala...

Not quite as snappy as the original, but I still have high hopes that it'll catch on. It's quite surprising that biological parents have more influence on criminal behaviour than the adoptive parents you've grown up with. But, as the study pointed out, the concordance rates are still quite low, so there must be other factors involved — e.g. your friends and where you live.

Aggression as an Adaptive Response

Last two pages for AQA only. *Aggression often (though not always) serves a purpose. That doesn't give you licence to go stomping around though — it's not big and it's not clever. Speaking of clever, you'd best get on and learn this stuff...*

There's an **Evolutionary Explanation** For Aggression

Lorenz proposed a theory of aggression based on **animal behaviour**. He used the idea of **natural selection** (that only the best adapted will survive and pass on their genes) to explain how the behaviour of animals is shaped. Lorenz suggested his theory could also be applied to **humans**.

1) Aggression is an **innate tendency** that's triggered by **environmental stimuli**.
2) Aggression is an **adaptive response**. An individual will be more likely to pass on their **genes** if they're able to gain the **upper hand** in competition for food, mates or territory.
3) Aggression is **ritualised**. A behaviour won't be passed on in the genes if it gets an animal **killed** before it produces offspring. So, there are ritual behaviours in place to stop confrontations being fatal, e.g. wolves end a fight by the loser exposing his jugular vein as a sign of **submission**. This puts the winner in prime position to kill their rival, but in fact the winner takes no further action. If animals were **routinely killed** during everyday power struggles or mating contests, it's likely the species would become **extinct**.

Lorenz's theory has been **criticised** on the fact that aggression **isn't always** adaptive and ritualised — there are many species that **do** fight to the death. Also, the relevance of the theory to **humans** is limited, as **cultural** influences are highly influential in the expression of aggression, e.g. a person's religious beliefs may shape their actions, as may the availability of weapons or the occurrence of war. However, an **evolutionary** approach may be relevant in explaining **some** aggressive human responses.

Jealousy is Aggression to **Deter a Partner's Infidelity**

Tony didn't see it as infidelity, more a service to mankind — genes as good as his should be passed on.

1) In a survey by **Kinsey (1948)**, **50%** of married **men** and **26%** of married **women** reported having had sex with somebody else while married.
2) Infidelity can be seen as an **evolutionary adaptive strategy** for a man to increase the **quantity** of offspring carrying his genes, and for a woman to improve the **quality** of her offspring.
3) However, it's obviously **not** in the **genetic interests** of their **partners** to be cheated on — it won't be their genes being passed on to the next generation.
4) Indicators that a partner is being unfaithful often lead to **jealous rage**. Jealousy has been explained as a product of **evolution**, although this response is triggered **differently** in each sex.

	Buss et al (1992) — Sex differences in jealousy
Method:	This was a **cross-cultural questionnaire study**. Participants were presented with the **hypothetical scenario** that someone they were in a serious, committed romantic relationship with had become interested in someone else. They were asked what would distress them more — imagining their partner forming a deep **emotional attachment** to that other person, or enjoying passionate **sexual intercourse** with the person.
Results:	Across all studies, **more men** than women reported **sexual infidelity** to be most upsetting. On average, **51%** of the men versus **22%** of the women chose this to be more distressing than **emotional infidelity**.
Conclusion:	Men's jealousy is innately triggered by the threat of uncertainty over the **paternity** of children produced within the relationship. However, women are more threatened by **emotional involvement** as it could mean being left for another woman, and so reducing the resources available to her children.
Evaluation:	The fact that the evidence was **consistent** across **different cultures** suggests that these different responses are **innate** rather than learned. However, the fact that the questionnaires were based around a **hypothetical** situation, and the responses available to the participants were **multiple choice**, means that the **validity** of the results is questionable — they may not accurately reflect what participants would actually do if they found themselves in that situation.

Aggression as an Adaptive Response

***Groups* May Behave *More Aggressively* Than Individuals**

There are many examples where individuals in a **group** behave far **more aggressively** than they would if they were on their own — for example, in a football crowd, a lynch mob or a riot (also see page 22).

Collective Unconscious Theory

LeBon (1895) came up with **collective unconscious theory** as an explanation of group aggression. According to LeBon, there are **four situational factors** that determine behaviour in a crowd situation:

1) A heightened state of **suggestibility** — people go along with suggestions made in an authoritative manner when they're caught up in the chaos of a crowd.
2) **Social contagion** — this is the process by which irrational moods, feelings and ideas (e.g. aggression) pass through a crowd. Emotional intensity within individuals in a crowd increases as they interact.
3) **Impersonality** — an individual who's recognised as being part of the 'enemy' group (e.g. the police in a riot) is perceived as having all the traits that are hated about that group, rather than as an individual person.
4) **Anonymity** — the feeling that you can't be personally identified in a crowd situation allows people to lose responsibility for their actions and act without inhibitions.

However, this theory is **limited** by the way it concentrates on the **irrational** and **unruly** aspects of crowd behaviour. It also can't explain **why** crowds choose one course of action over another.

Emergent Norm Theory

Turner and Killian (1972) disagreed with LeBon's idea that individuals in a crowd become an unruly and irrational mob. They believe that crowds are **rational** and governed by **norms**. People who act in a distinctive way become '**leaders**' and it becomes the norm to behave in the same way. For example, people in a crowd conform to the pattern set by the first people to respond to a situation — such as by applauding, booing or throwing tomatoes at the end of a performance.

Orum (1972) — Evidence for the emergent norm theory

Method: This was a **case study** of behaviour shown during the **American race riots**.

Results: Sit-ins, picketing and boycotting were directed at buildings perceived to be **discriminative**. Buildings that provided equal access services were **spared**.

Conclusion: The aggression of the crowd was caused by a sense of **injustice**. This led to the **emergence of a norm** that set **limits** to the crowd's actions.

Evaluation: Case studies provide a detailed, contextualised account of the subject in question. However, it may **not** be **valid** to generalise the findings to all accounts of group aggression. For example, not all groups will be as specific in selecting the targets of their protests.

Practice Questions

Q1 What is meant by ritualised aggression?

Q2 Describe the findings of the study by Buss et al (1992).

Q3 List the four factors that determine crowd behaviour, according to LeBon (1895).

Exam Question

Q1 a) Describe one explanation for the group display of aggressive behaviour in humans. [5 marks]

b) "Aggression is an adaptive response." Discuss this statement. [20 marks]

Forget infidelity — it's people with no exams that send me into a jealous rage...

The point to remember about evolutionary arguments is that a modern man or woman probably wouldn't have an affair in order to spread their genes about or improve the quality of any offspring. But these may be deeply buried motives that have been passed down from their early ancestors and still affect their behaviour today, even if they're not aware of it. Spooky.

Factors Influencing Eating Behaviour

These pages are just for AQA people. *In fact, this whole chapter is just for AQA. And it's all about food and eating, so if you're feeling peckish I suggest you go and make yourself some toast before you start reading.*

Cultural Influence *Affects Attitudes Towards* ***Food*** *and* ***Size***

In the UK today we tend to assume that you have to be **skinny** to be **beautiful**. But that's actually quite a **recent** idea.

1) Throughout human history, being **voluptuous** (curvy) was considered an attractive trait in a potential partner — it signalled **health** and access to **plentiful resources** in times of scarcity. People were proud to gorge themselves on food and drink because it signalled their **wealth** and **status**.
2) However, in the last 40 years the '**supermodel**' and '**size zero**' figure has become popular in Western culture. Highly profitable diet, exercise and surgery industries have sprung up as a result of this popularity.
3) In many other places big is **still** seen as best though — for example, in many **African** cultures plump females are regarded as wiser and more fertile, in **Asian** cultures weight is often still linked to affluence and success, and **Pacific Islanders** (Hawaiians/Samoans) equate large physical size in both genders with beauty and status.

Food is also an important part of many **religions**:

1) Some **fast** to show devotion (e.g. **Muslim** Ramadan).
2) Some **feast** to celebrate important events (e.g. **Christian** Christmas).
3) Some **forbid** certain foods (e.g. **Judaism** — pork isn't eaten).
4) Some incorporate food in **rituals** (e.g. **Catholicism** — communion wafers).

Different cultures attach different **meanings** to foods and eating forms a major part of many **celebrations** and **ceremonies** worldwide. Imagine birthdays without cake, or Christmas without sprouts...

Attitudes to Food Can Be Affected By ***Mood***

Anyone who has been unable to eat when **stressed** or who has 'pigged out' on junk food when they're feeling **down** will know that mood and food are **linked**.

1) A reduced appetite or bad diet, caused by a lack of motivation, is a common symptom of **depression**.
2) If you don't have the **energy** to prepare healthy meals you might be more likely to resort to unhealthy pre-packaged ready meals and quick snacks.
3) Some people may impulsively '**comfort eat**' or **binge eat** in the hope that a quick indulgence will make them feel better — usually choosing foods high in carbohydrates, fat, sugar and salt to provide that quick 'hit'.
4) This can lead to a **vicious cycle** of mood swings caused by unnatural highs and lows in blood sugar levels, which trigger further cravings.

Psychologists are currently investigating the role **emotional intelligence (EI)** plays in the relationship between mood and eating behaviour. They believe that people with a **high level** of personal EI make better food choices and are less likely to use food to regulate their mood. These people are also less likely to find that their appetite is affected (reduced or increased) by **stress**.

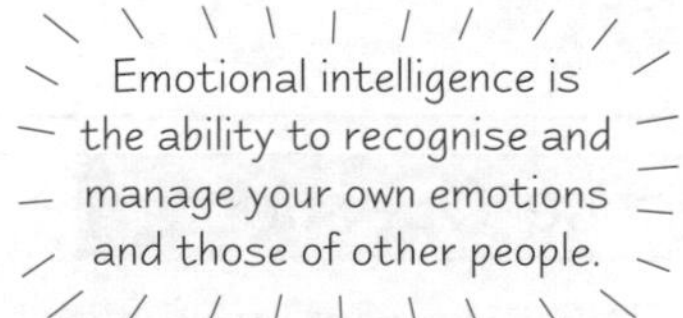

Emotional intelligence is
the ability to recognise and
manage your own emotions
and those of other people.

Health Concerns *Can Affect* ***Eating Behaviour***

Health concerns (e.g. high blood pressure) can affect what and how much we eat. However, eating healthily can become an **obsession** for some people:

Orthorexia is an **eating disorder** where people survive on a **highly restricted diet** to try and avoid anything they think might be 'unhealthy'. This can range from pesticides, herbicides, artificial additives or genetically modified ingredients to fats, animal products, or anything except raw fruit and vegetables. In extreme cases this can lead to **malnutrition** or even **death**.

More familiar examples of eating disorders include **anorexia** and **bulimia** (see p.32–35). Sometimes these can begin with a desire to lose weight and be more **healthy**, which then gets out of hand and becomes a dangerous **obsession**.

Factors Influencing Eating Behaviour

Dieting Doesn't Always Lead to *Weight Loss*

It's not as easy as just going on a diet and watching the weight drop off. Whether a person **succeeds** in losing weight depends on things like motivation, willpower, genetics, lifestyle and medical conditions (e.g. diabetes or thyroid problems). Other factors include:

Support and Encouragement

1) Eating is often a part of **social interaction**, so many experts think dieting should be too.
2) Informing friends and family of weight loss goals should help reduce the **temptations** of food and encourage **positive reinforcement** (and punishment) from others. Lots of dieters also join a weight loss group or diet with a friend or partner to maintain **motivation**.
3) But this approach doesn't work for everyone — some people find constant monitoring by others stressful and use **secretive binge eating** as a defence mechanism.

They were meant to be on a diet, but Mike sensed that his wife's resolve had slipped.

Physiological Changes Due to Dieting

1) Your body has evolved to cope with **chronic food shortages** by lowering your metabolic rate and protecting fat stores in times of **starvation**. Extreme dieting triggers this response.
2) If you then return to normal eating you end up with **more excess calories** than before which are then converted to fat. To overcome the feeling of deprivation during the diet people often also **overeat** afterwards, which gives an even bigger weight gain.
3) You may then start **another**, even more restrictive diet to undo the weight gain. But this will just reduce the metabolic rate **further** and so the pattern of **'yo-yo' dieting** continues.

Polivy and Herman (1975) — Psychological effects of dieting

Method: In a study with an independent measures design, samples of **dieting** and **non-dieting** students were placed in three **'pre-load'** conditions — drinking either one or two glasses of milkshake or nothing at all. They were then given unlimited supplies of ice cream.

Results: The non-dieters ate **less** ice cream the more milkshakes they had drunk. The dieters ate **more** ice cream the more milkshakes they had drunk.

Conclusion: Drinking the milkshake had damaged the dieters' determination — they gave in to total indulgence after failure. This is known as **'the counter-regulation effect'**.

Evaluation: These findings **support** what we already know about dieting (the 'diet starts tomorrow' mentality). **Follow-up studies** have found that many people have an 'all-or-nothing' mentality to dieting — if they break the diet they tend to see it as immediate failure and so eat as much as they like.

Practice Questions

Q1 Explain why a fuller figure has traditionally been considered attractive in many cultures.

Q2 Suggest a reason why dieting might fail.

Q3 Describe a physiological effect of dieting.

Exam Questions

Q1 Discuss the factors that affect eating behaviour and attitudes to food. [25 marks]

Eating behaviour — now that's the kind of study I'd volunteer for...

There's now such pressure on people, especially women, to look slim in order to feel attractive that it's hard to believe it's all just down to fashion. But from an evolutionary point of view the old-fashioned preference for a curvier figure makes more sense. This showed you had the physical resources to grow and provide for a baby successfully.

Biological Explanations of Eating Behaviour

These pages are for AQA only. *There are biological reasons for why you feel hungry or full at different times.*

Neural Mechanisms *Control Eating and* ***Satiation***

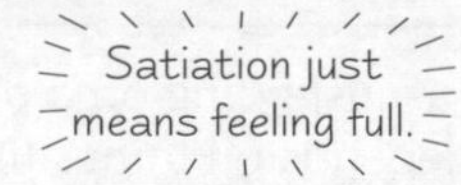

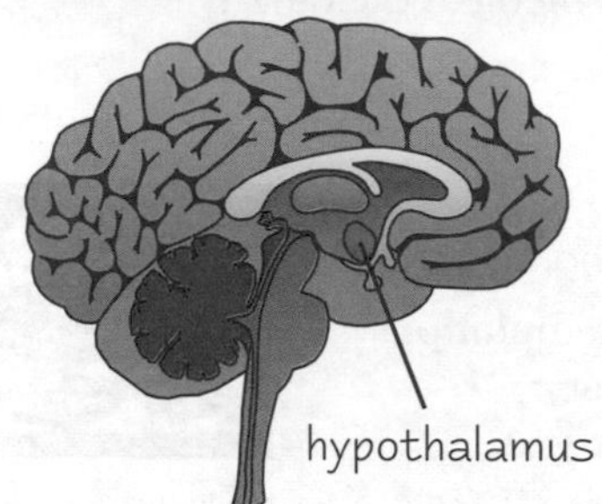

Satiation just means feeling full.

1) The **hypothalamus** is a gland in the brain responsible for **homeostasis** (keeping conditions in the body constant).
2) It helps to **regulate** things like temperature, circadian rhythms and intake of food and drink.
3) The **ventromedial nucleus (VMN)** and the **lateral nucleus (LN)** are the parts of the hypothalamus that are thought to be involved in **food regulation**.

The ***Ventromedial Nucleus*** *is the* ***Satiety Centre***

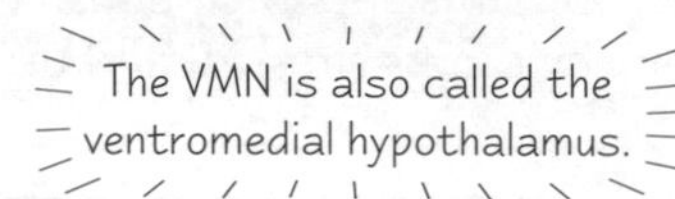

The VMN is also called the ventromedial hypothalamus.

1) Satiety is the **unconscious physiological process** that **stops** you eating.
2) The **VMN** provides the signal to stop eating when it picks up **hormonal messages**. For example, when food is being digested the level of the hormone CCK in the bloodstream is high. This stimulates receptors in the VMN.
3) Experimental **electrical stimulation** of the VMN has been shown to **reduce food intake**.
4) Malfunctions in the VMN may cause **obesity**. This was demonstrated by Baylis et al (1996).

	Baylis et al (1996) — VMN lesioning in rats
Method:	Two **symmetrical lesions** (injuries) were made in the VMN of eight male and five female rats. Their body weight was later compared with **age-matched controls**.
Results:	The rats with lesions in their VMN had become **obese**, while the control rats had not.
Conclusion:	Lesions in the VMN cause **hyperphagia** (overeating) and obesity, so the VMN must play a role in satiation.
Evaluation:	This was a very **small sample** using only one breed of rat, so the findings can't be generalised. Also, **other tissues** surrounding the VMN might have been damaged when the lesions were created, so it might not necessarily just be the VMN that is involved.

The ***Lateral Nucleus*** *is the* ***Hunger Centre***

1) When the body's blood sugar level drops, homeostatic responses kick in to help restore the **equilibrium**.
2) **Receptors** in the LN detect the drop in blood sugar. This then causes neurons to fire that create the sensation of hunger.
3) The person is driven to eat and blood glucose levels increase. Receptors then send a hormonal message to the **VMN** to give the sensation of fullness (see above).

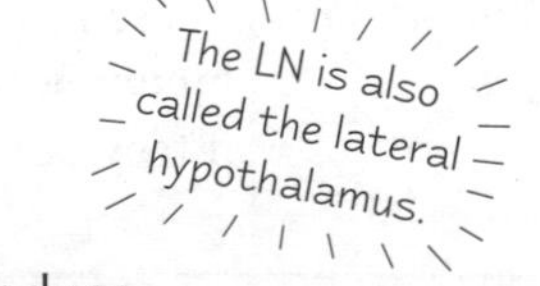

The LN is also called the lateral hypothalamus.

Damage to the LN can reduce food intake. For example, chemical lesions are known to produce **aphagia** (failure to eat). However, as with VMN studies, there may be **methodological problems** muddying the water.

	Winn et al (1990) — LN lesioning in rats
Method:	The toxin **NMDA** was used to make **lesions** in the LN of rats. A small dose (lesions in **LN only**) and a large dose (lesions spread to **adjacent areas**) condition was used, and there was also a **control group**.
Results:	Rats that had the small dose of NMDA showed **no changes** in their eating behaviour after a brief recovery period. However, rats that had the large dose showed **long-term deficits** in their eating behaviour.
Conclusion:	Damage to the **hypothalamus** impairs feeding responses, but the LN may **not** have as much of an effect as previously thought.
Evaluation:	This research is useful as it shows that the localisation of brain function is **more complex** than originally thought. However, this was an **exploratory study** to test whether NMDA was an effective toxin for use on the hypothalamus and wasn't originally intended to investigate hunger. Therefore, all the relevant variables may not have been controlled, reducing the **reliability** of the results.

Biological Explanations of Eating Behaviour

*There Are **Evolutionary** Reasons For **Food Preferences***

People need food to **survive** and throughout history it's been a driving force for **evolution**. This can help explain why so many people would rather have a chocolate eclair than a slice of grapefruit.

Why we like sweet stuff...

- **Harris (1987)** found that **newborn babies** have a preference for sweet things and dislike bitter things.
- These preferences and dislikes are **universal**, suggesting a **genetic** (therefore evolutionary) explanation.
- Early mammals were **frugivores** (ate mainly fruit). Sweet food now triggers the release of the pleasure-inducing brain chemical **dopamine** which acts as a reinforcer.
- Most **poisons** have a strong bitter taste — so our dislike of this type of taste could be a **survival reflex**.

Why we prefer food that's bad for us...

- **Burnham and Phelan (2000)** suggest that a preference for **fatty foods** would have helped our ancestors survive in times of **food scarcity** — these foods are full of energy-giving **calories**.
- Even though food is no longer scarce, we're still programmed to stuff ourselves with burgers and cakes when they're available in order to **build up fat reserves** in case there's ever a shortage. Again, **dopamine** may act as a reinforcing reward.

Why we like our meat spicy...

- **Sherman and Hash (2001)** analysed almost 7000 recipes from 36 countries and found that **meat** dishes contained far more **spices** than **vegetable** dishes. They hypothesised that this was because spices have **antimicrobial** properties — meat is more vulnerable to being infested with bacteria and fungi than vegetables are.
- This may also explain why people in **hot climates** tend to eat **more** spicy food — microbes grow faster in warmer conditions.

For the ultimate dopamine hit Jessie liked to take her sugar neat.

Why we won't eat green bananas or mouldy bread...

We've learned to avoid food that seems **unripe** or **mouldy**. Knowledge passed on from other people as well as our own experiences tell us that good food means life and bad food means death (or at least a dodgy tummy and wasted energy).

Practice Questions

Q1 Describe the function of the hypothalamus in eating behaviour.

Q2 How do Burnham and Phelan (2000) explain our preference for fatty foods?

Q3 Explain how Darwin's theory of natural selection can be applied to food preferences.

Exam Question

Q1 Describe and evaluate research studies into hunger and satiation and explain what they tell us about the neural mechanisms involved. [25 marks]

I can't help it — I've evolved to eat cheesecake...

This explains the mystery of why people seem to love chips, kebabs and anything bad, and shudder at the thought of broccoli and spinach. Our ancestors would be surviving on plants and thinking themselves lucky, and now and again having a big blow-out on a dead mammoth to keep them going through the lean times. Mmmm, barbecued mammoth. My favourite.

Anorexia Nervosa

Still AQA, going it alone. *Lots of people are worried about their weight, but for some this preoccupation leads to really serious health problems. Disorders like anorexia nervosa have become more common over the past couple of decades.*

Anorexia Nervosa Leads to Significant *Weight Loss*

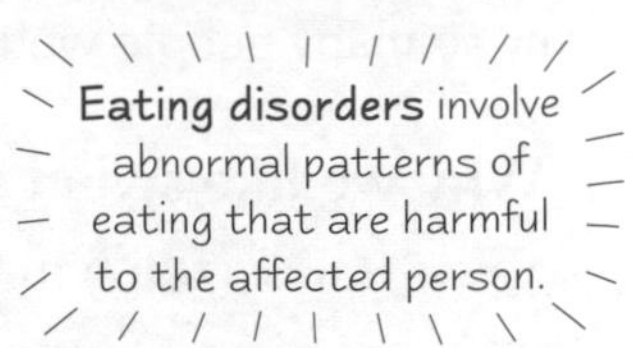
Eating disorders involve abnormal patterns of eating that are harmful to the affected person.

Anorexia nervosa is one of the most common eating disorders in the UK. About **90%** of cases are **females** aged **13–18** years old. About **1 in 250 females** and **1** in **2000 males** in the UK between **15 and 30** suffer from anorexia. It involves a dramatic reduction in the amount of food eaten, leading to significant **weight loss**.

The **DSM-IV** (the main diagnostic manual for mental disorders) describes four main characteristics of anorexia:

See page 72 for more about the DSM.

Low weight — anorexia is characterised by a refusal to maintain a normal body weight. This is usually classified as consistently weighing **less than 85%** of the expected weight for their build, age and height.

Body-image distortion — people with anorexia have **distorted self-perception**. They believe they're overweight even when very thin, judge themselves based largely on their weight and refuse to accept the seriousness of their condition.

Anxiety — anorexics are very **fearful** of gaining weight or getting fat even when they're seriously underweight.

Amenorrhoea — females usually **stop menstruating** due to their low body weight. Missing **three consecutive periods** is a clinical characteristic of the disorder.

There Are *Biological Explanations* For Anorexia Nervosa

Genetic Explanations Have Been Suggested

	Holland et al (1988) — concordance rates in twins
Method:	**Concordance rates** (extent to which twins share the same traits) were studied in 45 pairs of twins. At least one twin of each pair had been diagnosed as having anorexia nervosa — the study examined how often the other twin also suffered from the disorder.
Results:	The concordance rate was **56%** for **identical** (MZ) twins and only **5%** for **non-identical** (DZ) twins.
Conclusion:	Anorexia has a **genetic basis**.
Evaluation:	Identical twins share 100% of their genetic material, so **other factors** must also be involved in causing anorexia nervosa as the concordance rate was only **56%**. The higher concordance in MZ twins could be due to **environmental** rather than genetic factors, as looking the same may lead to more shared experiences.

Neural Causes Have Also Been Investigated

1) Researchers have suggested that anorexia nervosa may be due to **damage to the hypothalamus**, specifically the **lateral nucleus** (the area of the brain responsible for controlling hunger, see page 30). Lesion studies show that damage to this area can produce **aphagia** (a failure to eat) in animals, and recent research suggests that anorexics have **reduced blood flow** to this area. But it hasn't yet been proven whether this is a **cause** or an **effect** of the disorder.
2) Anorexics often also have **abnormally high levels** of the neurotransmitter **serotonin** and this causes abnormally high levels of **anxiety**. Serotonin production is stimulated by biological components (amino acids) in **food**, so starvation may actually make anorexics feel better. But again, it's not clear whether these serotonin levels are a **cause** or an **effect** of the disorder.

Anorexia Nervosa

The **Psychodynamic Approach** Suggests **Unconscious** Motivations

1) **Anorexia nervosa may be a reaction to sexual abuse.**

   If a person is sexually abused they may then **loathe their body** for appearing attractive to an abuser — anorexia nervosa is a way to help **destroy the body** and so make it less attractive to others.

2) **Anorexia nervosa may reflect a reluctance to take on adult responsibilities.**

   Anorexia nervosa prevents females developing **breasts or hips** — instead of gaining a womanly shape they **remain physically childlike** and so are able to remain **dependent** on their parents for longer.

3) **Anorexia nervosa may reflect low self-esteem.**

   Very low self-esteem may cause a person to believe their needs (in this case food) to be **wrong** in some way, or that they're **not worthy** of having food. They then **deny themselves** food.

4) **Anorexia nervosa may be a battle against controlling parents.**

   Bruch (1978) found that parents of anorexics tend to be **domineering**. Anorexia might be an attempt to regain some **control** by manipulating the one thing they have control of — their body.

Remember though — it's hard to find **empirical evidence** for theories like these, and there are many **counter arguments**, e.g. not everyone with anorexia nervosa has experienced sexual abuse or has controlling parents.

The **Behavioural Approach** Suggests **Conditioning** May Be the Cause

Classical conditioning

Leitenberg et al (1968) claimed that anorexia nervosa could be a result of someone learning to associate **eating** with **anxiety** — often to **phobic proportions**. Losing weight helps to **reduce** that anxiety.

Operant conditioning

Praise and admiration for initial weight loss acts as **positive reinforcement** for more extreme food avoidance. A constant feeling of **hunger** then acts as a **reward** in itself. **Gilbert (1986)** reported that anorexics experience pleasure and pride as a result of not eating. The **guilt** associated with eating is lessened (**negative reinforcement**), as well as the fear that their weight will attract negative attention (**punishment**).

Practice Questions

Q1 Outline the clinical characteristics of anorexia nervosa.

Q2 Explain how Holland et al's (1988) study provides evidence for a genetic explanation of anorexia nervosa.

Q3 Describe two psychodynamic explanations of the possible causes of anorexia nervosa.

Q4 Explain how operant conditioning may play a role in the development of anorexia nervosa.

Exam Question

Q1 a) Describe one biological explanation for anorexia nervosa. [5 marks]

b) Outline and evaluate psychological explanations for anorexia nervosa. [20 marks]

Anorexia nervosa isn't as recent a problem as you might think...

...in fact, it was first diagnosed in 1868 by William Gull. And although it's most common in teenage girls, it can affect all kinds of different people from all walks of life. It's probably caused by a mixture of the factors listed on these pages and each individual case will be different. Sufferers are often just as confused by their motivation as everyone else.

Bulimia Nervosa

You can ignore these pages if you're not doing AQA. *Bulimia nervosa is another type of eating disorder that's common in the UK. Sufferers don't starve themselves but can still have serious health problems due to the condition.*

Bulimia Nervosa *Follows a Pattern of* ***Binge Eating*** *and* ***Purging***

Bulimia nervosa involves a pattern of binge eating followed by some kind of purge so that weight isn't gained — for example by inducing vomiting, doing excessive exercise or using laxatives. So, the person's weight fluctuates but stays within a normal range.

The **DSM-IV** (the main diagnostic manual for mental disorders, see p.72) describes five main characteristics of bulimia:

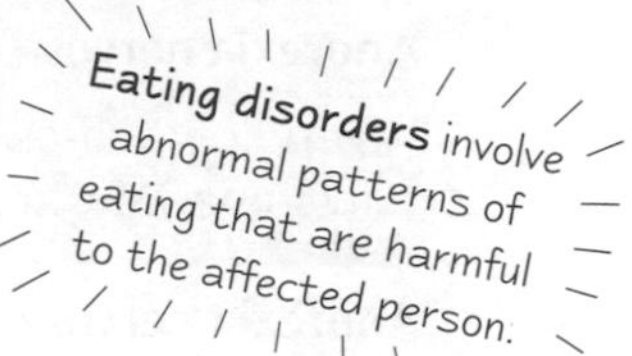

Eating disorders involve abnormal patterns of eating that are harmful to the affected person.

Bingeing — eating a large quantity of food in a short time frame. During a binge the person feels **out of control**, i.e. they can't stop themselves from eating.

Purging — after **bingeing** the person tries to **prevent weight gain**. This may involve vomiting, using laxatives, not eating for a long period of time or excessive exercise.

Frequent bingeing and purging — the binge-purge cycle needs to have been repeated about **twice a week** for at least **3 months** before a diagnosis of bulimia is given.

Distorted self-evaluation — people suffering from bulimia judge themselves based largely on their **body shape** and **weight**.

Separate condition to anorexia — bulimia isn't just a feature of anorexia, it can exist as a condition **on its own.**

There Are ***Biological Explanations*** *For Bulimia Nervosa*

Concordance rates are the extent to which twins share the same trait.

Genetic Explanations *Have Been Suggested*

Kendler et al (1991) studied over 1000 pairs of twins where at least one twin had bulimia nervosa and found **concordance rates** of **23%** in **identical** twins and **9%** in **non-identical** twins. Although this suggests **genetics** may play a part in bulimia nervosa, it can't be the full story. As identical twins share all of their genetic material, a concordance rate of 100% would be expected if genetics were the only factor.

Neural Causes *Have Also Been Investigated*

	Kissileff et al (1996) — The role of cholecystokinin (CCK)
Method:	25 people with bulimia nervosa and 18 **controls** were asked to binge eat (i.e. eat as much as they could in one sitting).
Results:	The participants with bulimia nervosa consumed an average of **3500 calories** whereas the controls only managed **1500 calories** on average. The participants with bulimia nervosa were also found to have **depressed levels of CCK** (a hormone related to satiety, see page 30).
Conclusion:	Depleted levels of CCK allowed bulimic patients to carry on eating without feeling full.
Evaluation:	This would seem to fit with the **enhanced appetite** that many bulimics report and their pattern of overeating. However, a lot of the research into the effects of CCK on satiety is based on **animal models**, so there's no guarantee that the same findings apply to humans. The study also used a fairly **small sample size**, so it might not be valid to generalise the results to the whole population.

It's also been found that bulimics often have **abnormally low levels** of the neurotransmitter **serotonin** leading to bouts of abnormally **low mood**. Serotonin production is stimulated by biological components (amino acids) in **food**, and so overeating may actually make bulimics feel temporarily better — although it later leads to guilt and purging.

Bulimia Nervosa

The **Psychodynamic Approach** Says Bulimia is a **Defence Mechanism**

1) **Bulimia nervosa may be a reaction to sexual abuse.**

The binge-purge cycle helps to express **self-disgust** for attracting an abuser by punishing the body. **Wonderlich et al (1996)** interviewed 1099 American women and found a **correlation** between childhood sexual abuse, dissatisfaction with appearance and bulimia. 16-33% of cases of significant bulimia could be attributed to sexual abuse in childhood.

2) **Bulimia nervosa may be a result of emotional damage caused by poor relationships with parents.**

According to **Halmi (1995)**, bulimics often **mistake** their emotions for **hunger**, as poor parental relationships stunted their ability to **distinguish** between internal **needs** and **feelings**.

3) **Bulimia nervosa may be a defence mechanism to help guard against trauma.**

Bulimia is often **triggered** by a specific **traumatic event**, e.g. a divorce or long-term illness. Bulimics may try to **block out** unhappy feelings by indulging in overeating.

Theories from the psychodynamic approach are difficult to find **empirical evidence** for, and there are many **counter arguments**. For example, not everyone with bulimia has experienced sexual abuse or suffered a trauma that could be pinpointed as a trigger.

The **Behavioural Approach** Suggests Bulimia is **Learned**

Operant conditioning

Bulimics often have **poor eating habits** before they develop the disorder fully, e.g. they often reduce their food intake as part of a diet, then overeat to compensate for their deprivation. Both of these behaviours would bring about **positive reinforcement** — praise for weight loss and satisfaction from indulgence. However, overeating may lead to **anxiety** (a **punishment**) which is then reduced by purging (**negative reinforcement**). This makes the purging behaviour more likely to happen again.

Social learning theory

Hamilton and Waller (1993) found that bulimics **overestimated** their own size and shape after seeing **fashion magazine photos**. **Rodin (1991)** found that they often had **mothers** who also had the disorder, or who constantly dieted. This would suggest that exposure to **models** who are positively reinforced for their weight loss may lead to **imitation**.

Practice Questions

Q1 Outline the clinical characteristics of bulimia nervosa.

Q2 Explain why Kendler et al's (1991) study does not offer a complete explanation of bulimia nervosa.

Q3 How does social learning theory explain why some people suffer from bulimia nervosa?

Exam Question

Q1 Outline and evaluate one biological and one psychological explanation of bulimia nervosa. [25 marks]

Bulimia nervosa was only recognised as a condition in 1979...

...but it can have really serious health effects — for example, those who purge by vomiting (which accounts for 75% of people with the condition) can get peptic ulcers, become dehydrated and suffer from electrolyte imbalances. Electrolyte imbalances are especially worrying as they can lead to an irregular heartbeat that can prove fatal. Not good at all.

Obesity

Just for AQA. *It might seem odd at first to include obesity in a section on eating disorders — but overeating to the point of being clinically obese certainly counts as an abnormal eating pattern that's harmful to the person affected.*

Obesity is When Someone Has an **Abnormally High Body Mass Index**

1) A person is classed as obese if they have a **BMI** (body mass index) of **30 kg/m² or higher**. This is about 20% above normal for their height and body frame, i.e. they're carrying too much adipose (fatty) tissue.
2) Obesity is generally caused by a person **taking in more calories** (food) than they **burn off** (by exercise), but there are some genetic conditions and medications that can increase the risk of obesity.
3) It's estimated that by 2050 over half of the people in the UK will be obese. This is pretty worrying when you consider that it's already one of the leading **preventable** causes of death worldwide — it increases the risk of **illnesses** like heart disease, diabetes and cancer.
4) The most effective way to treat obesity is with a **sensible diet and plenty of exercise**. However, increasingly people are turning to quick fixes — 'miracle' pills or surgery such as stomach stapling, gastric band fitting or gastric bypass surgery.

Body mass index is a measurement of height relative to weight. A normal BMI is between 18.5 and 25.

Exercise is the best way to combat obesity, but that still didn't excuse Kristy's outfit.

Obesity Can Have **Biological Explanations**

Some studies have shown that there is a **genetic** element to obesity.

Stunkard et al (1986) — Adoption studies and obesity

Method:	The weight of 540 **adult adoptees** from Denmark was compared with that of both their **biological and adoptive parents**. The adoptees were split into 4 weight classes — thin, median, overweight and obese.
Results:	There was a **strong relationship** between the weight of the adoptees and that of their biological parents. There was **no relationship** between the weight of the adoptees and their adoptive parents in any of the weight classes.
Conclusion:	Genetic influences have an important role in determining adult weight, whereas **environment** seems to have **little effect**.
Evaluation:	This finding is **supported** by other biological versus adoptive relative research and even by some **twin studies**. However, it's probably too **reductionist** to say that genetics alone are responsible for obesity. Also, the participants were all from Denmark, so the results **can't be generalised** to the whole population.

In some cases obesity is caused by a **chemical** problem.

Montague et al (1997) — Leptin's role in obesity

Method:	Two severely obese children (male and female cousins) were studied — a large proportion of their total body weight was made up of **adipose (fatty) tissue**.
Results:	A **mutation** on the part of their DNA responsible for controlling their supply of **leptin** was found — they didn't produce enough leptin. Leptin is a protein produced by adipose tissue to signal that **fat reserves** in the body are **full**.
Conclusion:	Their leptin deficiency had caused the children's obesity. They did not have enough of this chemical to **suppress appetite** in the normal way.
Evaluation:	A number of trials in which obese patients were given doses of leptin have had **very little success**. Research now suggests that most people with obesity in fact have **high levels** of leptin — they're just **resistant** to its effects. This was a **case study** of only two children, so although it revealed a lot about their particular situation, the findings **weren't relevant** to the majority of obese people.

Obesity

The **Psychodynamic Approach** Links Obesity With **Emotional Conflict**

1) **Obesity may be the result of an oral fixation.**

   It's been suggested that obese people experienced trauma at the **oral stage** of psychosexual development, and so developed a fixation there. This means that they derive **pleasure from food** and are **unable to delay gratification**, as they're ruled primarily by the **id** (the pleasure principle).

2) **Obesity may reflect a lack of coping skills.**

   Lots of people binge eat as a result of **stress** — it's a form of **denial** used to escape negative feelings that the person **can't cope** with.

3) **Obesity may be due to our thanatos instinct (death drive).**

   Psychodynamic psychologists believe that attempting to eat ourselves to death reflects the unconscious human **desire for self-destruction.**

4) **Parental overfeeding may be a reaction to trauma.**

   Parents who have experienced the **death of a child** are sometimes prone to **overfeeding** remaining or subsequent children to the point of morbid obesity. They feel **unable to deprive** the child of anything.

Psychodynamic theories are difficult to find **empirical evidence** for. Also, there are many **counter arguments**. For example, not everyone who is obese has parents who experienced a trauma.

The **Behavioural Approach** Suggests Obesity is **Conditioned**

Children learn from an early age to **associate** eating with happiness (i.e. classical conditioning) for several reasons:

1) Parents or teachers may use food to **reinforce good behaviour**, e.g. sweets as **rewards**.
2) Parents may **praise** children for clearing their plate or **punish** them for wasting food at mealtimes.
3) Advertisers use **brightly coloured** packaging, friendly **characters** and **free gift** giveaways.
4) **Celebrations** are always accompanied by food, e.g. birthday parties.

As adults they may then overeat to try to recapture these happy emotions (**positive reinforcement**) or to remove a negative state such as sadness, anger or boredom (**negative reinforcement**). So, operant conditioning is also in effect.

Practice Questions

Q1 Outline the clinical characteristics of obesity.

Q2 Why did Stunkard et al (1986) reject environmental factors as causes of obesity?

Q3 What did Montague et al's (1997) study suggest as a possible cause of obesity?

Q4 Explain why parents may overfeed children.

Q5 Describe how operant conditioning can cause obesity.

Exam Question

Q1 a) Outline one or more biological explanation(s) for obesity. [9 marks]

b) Evaluate one or more psychological theories of obesity. [16 marks]

So it could be your genes stopping you fitting into your jeans...

Hmmm, this chapter has given me some food for thought and no mistake. In fact, my thoughts have been full of nothing but food. Too little, too much, too much rapidly followed by too little — eating can be a complicated business and trying to explain it isn't straightforward either. As usual, a single, simple explanation just won't cut it. Terribly sorry about that.

Psychological Influences on Gender

This section is for AQA only. *You'd think gender would be straightforward — you're either masculine or feminine. But that would make an insultingly easy exam question. And no-one likes to be insulted. So there's a bit more to it...*

Cognitive Developmental Theory Suggests Ideas on Gender **Change With Age**

1) **Gender** is the way someone acts and identifies themselves — the behavioural characteristics that make a person **masculine** or **feminine**.
2) **Cognitive developmental theory** was first proposed by Piaget. It suggests that children's thoughts and views on the world **change** as they develop.
3) Many theories use Piaget's ideas to explain how ideas about **gender** change with age.

For more on Piaget's cognitive developmental theory see p.50.

Kohlberg (1966) Developed a **Theory of Gender Consistency**

1) **Kohlberg's** (**1966**) theory of **gender consistency** is part of his wider cognitive developmental theory. It identifies **three stages** of gender development:

   - **Gender identity** — the child is aware that they're **male** or **female**, but think their gender might **change** (e.g. by wearing opposite sex clothes). This stage usually occurs between the ages of 2 and 3½ years old.
   - **Gender stability** — the child realises that their gender will remain **fixed** over **time** (e.g. boys will become men). However, they may think that gender can **change** in **different situations** (e.g. when doing an 'opposite-sex activity'). This stage usually occurs between the ages of 3½ and 4½.
   - **Gender consistency** — the child is aware that gender remains fixed in **different situations** (e.g. cross dressing doesn't change gender). This usually occurs between the ages of 4½ and 7.

2) There is some evidence for Kohlberg's theory. For example, **McConaghy's** (**1979**) study showed that children in Kohlberg's **gender stability** stage determined the gender of dolls by their **clothing** rather than their genitals. This suggests they believe that when the situation (e.g. clothing) changes, gender does too.
3) Munroe et al's (1984) study found the same stages in children from **different cultures**.
4) However, Kohlberg's theory has been criticised for ignoring the effects of **social influences** and **conditioning**. Also, it describes what happens, but doesn't explain **why**.

Martin and **Halverson (1981)** Developed the **Gender Schema Theory**

1) Martin and Halverson's gender schema theory **combines** cognitive developmental theory and social learning theory to suggest how **gender stereotyping** helps children learn what is and what isn't appropriate for their gender.
2) It proposes that, by the age of **three**, children have developed a **basic gender identity**. They also have a **gender schema** which contains the child's ideas about **gender appropriate behaviour**.
3) Through **observation**, children continue to learn gender appropriate behaviours and **add** them to their schema.
4) A child's gender schema is based on the concept of an **in-group** and an **out-group**:

   - Activities, objects and behaviours associated with their **own sex** are seen as **in-group**. Those associated with the **opposite sex** are **out-group**.
   - So, for example, a boy might **label objects** such as cars and trousers as in-group and objects like dolls and skirts as out-group.
   - Through reference to their **in-group/out-group schema**, children will show a **bias** towards **in-group** behaviours.

5) Having a gender schema can help children to manage all the information that they're exposed to. They can focus on **processing** information related to their **in-group** and **filter out** information related to their **out-group**.
6) However, there are also **disadvantages** — reinforcing stereotypical gender roles can discourage children from showing interest in things related to their out-group. This can limit their opportunities and lead to **discrimination**.
7) There is some evidence to support gender schema theory. For example, **Bradbard et al** (**1986**) gave children unfamiliar toys and found they were more likely to play with them (and remember them) if they were described as being for their **own gender** rather than the other.
8) As children get older they are capable of **more complex cognition** and understand that their gender doesn't limit them rigidly to in-group objects and behaviours.

Psychological Influences on Gender

People Who *Don't Fit* Gender Stereotypes Show *Psychological Androgyny*

1) **Bem (1974)** developed a self report questionnaire known as the **Sex Role Inventory**. It aimed to measure the mix of stereotypically masculine and feminine traits present in an individual.
2) Individuals rate how likely they are to display certain **character traits**, e.g. shyness. Those who score highly for both masculine and feminine traits are said to be **psychologically androgynous**.
3) Bem suggests that androgyny is **advantageous** in society as it means people have the traits needed to cope with a **range of situations**. Those who score highly on only one scale have a more limited range of skills.
4) Several studies suggest that **environmental factors** are the cause of psychological androgyny. For example:

- Weisner and Wilson-Mitchell (1990) compared children raised in families that put an **emphasis** on traditional gender roles with children raised in families that actively **downplayed** traditional gender roles.
- They found that androgyny was **higher** in children who had been encouraged to **ignore** traditional gender roles.

Gender Dysphoria is Also Known as *Gender Identity Disorder*

1) **Gender dysphoria** is a mental disorder which causes a person to feel that they're **biologically** one gender but **psychologically** the other — they feel that they're trapped in the wrong body.
2) For example, a boy may behave **effeminately**, want to wear **female clothes** and have a **baby**.
3) Some studies have indicated that gender dysphoria could be caused by **parental psychiatric problems** or **absent fathers**. For example, Rekers and Kilgus (1997) studied families where offspring had gender dysphoria and found that:

- **80%** of the gender dysphoria sufferers had **mothers** with **mental health problems**.
- **45%** had **fathers** with **mental health problems**.
- **37%** of sufferers had **absent fathers** (or no male role model).

4) However **not all** children who experience these problems during childhood go on to develop gender dysphoria — so there must be **other explanations**.

Practice Questions

Q1 Give the three stages of gender development outlined in Kohlberg's (1966) theory of gender consistency.

Q2 According to Martin and Halverson's (1981) gender schema theory, what is an in-group?

Q3 Why did Bem consider psychological androgyny to be advantageous?

Exam Question

Q1 a) Discuss Martin and Halverson's (1981) gender schema theory. [15 marks]

b) Outline one explanation for gender dysphoria, including relevant research. [10 marks]

In-group, out-group, shake-it-all-about group...

Told you there was more to it — but it shouldn't be too bad to learn. It's just Kohlberg's theory (which is pretty simple) and gender schema theory (which there's a bit more to, but nothing to make your head spin). Then psychological androgyny (which could be good for you) and gender dysphoria (a.k.a. gender identity disorder). And then you're done (yay).

Biological Influences on Gender

Once again, just AQA. Biological factors influence gender. No surprises there — the title gives that one away. You need to know what these factors are and how they influence gender. Luckily, these two pages are here to help you out.

Gender Development is Affected by Genes and Hormones

Males and Females Have Different Sex Chromosomes

1) **Females** have a **pair of X** chromosomes — XX. So all ova contain an X chromosome.
2) **Males** have **one X** chromosome and **one Y** chromosome — XY. This means sperm may contain either an X chromosome or a Y chromosome. It's the **Y chromosome** that leads to **male development**.
3) If an ovum is fertilised by a Y carrying sperm, the offspring will be **XY** (**male**). If an ovum is fertilised by an X carrying sperm the offspring will be **XX** (**female**). Which sperm fertilises the ova is determined by chance.
4) Some humans are born with **variations** in the standard sex chromosome pattern. Studies of people with such variations indicate that **gender differences** can be caused by **different sex chromosomes** in males and females.

Sperm and ova only contain one sex chromosome.

For example, in **Klinefelter's syndrome** males are born with **XXY sex chromosomes** — they have an **extra X chromosome**. Males with this syndrome are **sterile** and tend to be **less muscular** and have **less facial and body hair**. They can have problems using **language** to express themselves and may have trouble with **social interaction**.

Males and Females Have Different Hormone Levels

1) The major male and female hormones are **androgens** and **oestrogens**.
2) Both types of hormone are present in males and females, but in very **different amounts**.
3) **Men** produce more **testosterone** (an androgen) each day than females, and **females** produce more **oestrogens** than males.
4) However, some humans produce **smaller** or **larger** quantities of these hormones than normal.

For example, sometimes people are born with much more **testosterone** than normal — a particular form of a syndrome called **CAH**.

1) This form of CAH can cause **early sexual development** in males, but doesn't have much of an effect otherwise.
2) The **behaviour** of **girls** with this type of CAH tends to be **masculinised** — they have a preference for playing with boys' toys and enjoy 'tomboyish' activities.
3) **Physically**, girls tend to look more **masculine**. Their **growth** is fast and **puberty** can happen early.
4) CAH can also cause **physical abnormalities** such as **ambiguous genitalia**. This can make it difficult to tell whether someone is **male** or **female** at birth.

5) Case studies of conditions like this suggest that the effect of **testosterone** on the **developing brain** is responsible for the **differences in gender behaviour**.

There are Evolutionary Explanations For Differences in Gender Roles

Gender roles are the behaviours seen as **appropriate** for one sex and not the other. For example, traditional gender roles would include men being the breadwinner and women staying at home to bring up the children. Many psychologists believe that gender roles originally developed through **evolution**. For example:

1) **Shields** (**1975**) suggests that men and women evolved to have roles that **complemented** each other — dividing the behaviours necessary for survival.
2) **Buss** (**1995**) suggested that the different behaviours shown by men and women are the result of different **reproduction strategies**. For example, Trivers (1972) suggests that women invest more in offspring than men do and so discriminate more when choosing a mate. This could lead to some stereotypically female behaviours, e.g. coyness. In contrast, men have to compete for mates so demonstrate more aggressive behaviours.

Timmy hoped his dad would give up on traditional gender roles soon — he was taking a pounding.

Biological Influences on Gender

The **Biosocial Approach** Can Explain **Gender Development**

The **biosocial approach** explains gender development as a result of both **biological** and **social factors.** **Money and Ehrhardt's (1972)** biosocial theory of gender has two main aspects:

1) During **foetal development**, **genetics** and **physiological changes** (such as the inheritance of an X or Y chromosome and the presence of hormones like testosterone) lead to the development of male or female **physical characteristics.**
2) Once the baby is **born** people **react differently** to it depending on its **gender** — it's given a **social label**. This labelling means that males and females are treated differently from birth and learn different attitudes and behaviours as a result — they are **socialised** in different ways.

Money and Ehrhardt suggest that the **social labelling** of infants and children has a **greater influence** on their behaviour than physiological differences do.

Money and Ehrhardt identified **18 months** to **3 years** of age as the critical period for **gender role development**:

1) They studied girls who had been incorrectly labelled as **male** at birth (as they had a form of **CAH**).
2) Until the disorder was diagnosed, the girls had been **raised as boys**. They then underwent gender reassignment surgery and were treated as **girls**.
3) The study found that those who received surgery **before** the age of 3 were able to adapt to their new gender **easily**, whilst those who received surgery **after** the age of 3 had much more **difficulty**.

Smith and Lloyd (1978) investigated differences in behaviour towards male and female babies:

Smith and Lloyd (1978) — Behaviour towards male and female babies

Method: A sample of women were asked to play with an **unfamiliar baby**. A variety of toys were available for them to use. A number of babies were used in the experiment — some were **male** and some were **female**.

Results: Participants were likely to offer **gender stereotyped toys** to the baby they played with. They also used **different verbal communication styles** depending on the given gender of the child. Boys were given encouragement for **motor activity**, girls were more likely to be spoken to **calmly** and in a **soothing manner**.

Conclusion: People's behaviour towards babies alters depending on the babies' **gender**.

Evaluation: This study provides support for the **biosocial theory**, showing that people react differently to boys and girls. This imposes different ideas of what it is to be a boy or a girl on the baby, i.e. they are **socialised differently** and so learn to behave according to a particular gender role. However, it's possible the participants might have shown **demand characteristics** — they could have worked out the purpose of the experiment and acted to fit in with it.

Practice Questions

Q1 Which chromosome leads to development of male features?

Q2 Name the major male and female hormones.

Q3 Explain what is meant by gender roles.

Exam Question

Q1 a) Outline the roles of hormones and genes in gender development. [10 marks]

b) Discuss the biosocial approach to gender development. [15 marks]

So, your gender is influenced by biology — never saw that one coming...

Ah, hormones. They're always popping up as reasons for this, that or the other. Maybe they're why you're feeling so restless and depressed now. No... wait... that would be the revision. Anyway, biological influences on gender — genes, hormones, and evolutionary factors. Read about them, learn about them, write about them in the exam, get top marks. Simple.

Social Influences on Gender

These pages are for AQA only. *Like most things in psychology, gender is influenced by social factors. These include the way that family and friends behave, the media, the school you go to and the culture you grow up in. Read on...*

Parents** and **Peers** Can Influence **Gender Roles

1) **Social learning theory** suggests that we learn by **observing** and **copying** the behaviour of people around us.
2) This learning can be **passive** (when the behaviour is simply watched and copied) or it can be **active** (when the behaviour is reinforced by rewards or discouraged by punishments).
3) **Gender typical behaviours** can be learnt this way, with males copying the behaviour of other males and females copying behaviour of other females. For example, girls may imitate the behaviour of their mothers — the behaviour becomes part of their idea of the female gender role.
4) There's also evidence that parents and peers **react differently** to children depending on their gender:

Parents

- Rubin et al (1974) found that fathers used words like '**soft**' and '**beautiful**' to describe newborn **daughters** and '**strong**' and '**firm**' to describe **sons**.
- Culp et al (1983) found that women treated babies differently according to how they were dressed — **talking** more to those dressed as **girls** and **smiling** more at those dressed as **boys**.
- Hron-Stewart's (1988) study found that adults were **quicker** to comfort a crying baby **girl** than a crying baby boy, expecting boys to be hardier and braver. Also, mothers were more likely to help a **daughter** complete a task than a son.

Peers

- Maccoby and Jacklin (1987) found that children as young as three prefer **same-sex playmates**. Maccoby (1990) found that when children organise their own activities they tend to segregate themselves according to their **gender**.
- Serbin et al (1984) suggest that girls try and influence situations by **polite suggestion** whilst boys use **direct commands**.
- Lamb and Roopnarine's (1979) study of nursery behaviours found that children **encouraged** gender appropriate behaviour and **criticised** gender inappropriate behaviour.

5) The different behaviours that girls and boys observe and experience can lead to development of gender roles.

*The **Media** Can Also Influence **Gender Roles...***

TV, **films**, **magazines** and **computer games** usually show **gender stereotypical behaviour**. Several studies have shown that the behaviour displayed in these media can influence gender roles. For example:

1) Some studies have shown that the **more TV** a child watches the **more stereotypical** their views on gender are.
2) Williams (1986) carried out a two year **natural experiment** in Canada. He looked at the effect of introducing TV to a town (Notel), by comparing it to a nearby town that already had TV (Multitel). At the start of the experiment, gender stereotyping was much greater in Multitel than Notel. Williams found that gender stereotypes of Notel children **increased** and became more like those of Multitel children after the introduction of TV.

*...and So Can **Schools***

1) The attitude of **schools** and **teachers** can influence gender roles.
2) For example, if teachers hold gender stereotypes this may influence their beliefs about the **abilities** and **preferences** of girls and boys.
3) Bigler (1995) compared students in classes that were **divided by gender** with students in classes where gender **wasn't emphasised**. Students divided by gender were more likely to have **stronger gender stereotypes** and a stronger belief that all males are similar and all females are similar.

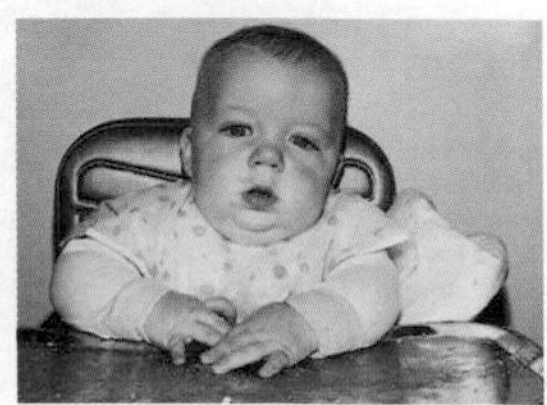

Boris tried not to conform to the stereotype of the 'cute baby'. Everyone agreed it was a great effort.

Social Influences on Gender

There's Been **Cross-Cultural Research** Into **Gender Roles**

1) **Cross-cultural research** has been carried out to identify how gender roles differ between cultures.
2) Cross-cultural research can also help us to understand the **causes** of gender roles — if roles are **similar** in different cultures it suggests a **biological** explanation. However, if they **vary** between cultures a **social** explanation of gender roles is more likely.

- Whiting and Edwards (1988) observed the behaviour of children in the USA, Mexico, Japan, India, the Philippines and Kenya.
- They found that gender behaviour was very **similar to Western stereotypes** and that there were clear differences between **male** and **female** behaviour.
- For example, girls were more **caring** than boys, and boys were more **aggressive** than girls.
- In societies where children were expected to work to contribute towards the family, there were further gender differences. Girls were more likely to look after **younger siblings** and do **domestic work**, whilst boys were more likely to look after **animals** and were less likely to work within the home.

Responsibility for **Childcare** May Determine **Gender Roles**

1) Katz and Konner (1981) looked at **80 different cultures** — they found that in **90%** of them **women** had the main responsibility for child rearing.
2) This **gender division** has implications for men and women in terms of **occupation**, **finance** and **mobility**.
3) D'Andrade (1966) looked at information from **224 societies** to investigate what **types of tasks** and jobs were performed by males and females. He found that:

- **Men** were more likely to **travel further** from the home, and be involved in **weapon making**, **metal work** and **hunting**.
- **Women** were more likely to **make** and **repair clothes**, **prepare** and **cook food**, and **make objects** for use in the **home**.

4) Segal (1983) suggested that the differences in **activities** associated with gender roles are related to the differences in **involvement in childcare**.

Max was slightly hurt by his sisters' reaction to his offer of looking after the baby.

Practice Questions

Q1 What did Rubin et al (1974) discover about the way fathers describe their newborn children?
Q2 What did Maccoby and Jacklin (1987) find from their study on the type of playmates children prefer?
Q3 Which students in Bigler's (1995) study had the strongest gender role stereotypes?
Q4 How can cross-cultural research help us to understand the causes of gender roles?
Q5 Outline the activities associated with males and females in the D'Andrade (1996) study.

Exam Question

Q1 a) Discuss how parents and peers may influence gender roles. [10 marks]

b) Describe and discuss cross-cultural research into gender roles. [15 marks]

A whole town with no TV. Not a single one. In Canada. In 1986. Scary.

It seems everyone's plotting to force us into gender roles and turn us into stereotypes — parents, friends, teachers and the media. There's no getting away from it. I say we fight back. We could start off by getting rid of TVs. We'll just chuck 'em out — it's proven to work and then we'll be free. Life with no TV, it'll be great. Hmmm... maybe gender roles aren't so bad...

Theories of Intelligence

This section is for AQA only. *You might have thought intelligence was pretty straightforward — if you do well in your exams you're smart, if you don't you're not. Turns out it's not that simple — there are several theories of intelligence...*

The Learning Approach Suggests Intelligence is Developed by Reinforcement

1) The **learning approach** to intelligence suggests intelligent behaviours are developed through **conditioning**.
2) For this to happen there needs to be an initial **change in behaviour** that's then **rewarded**. This is known as **reinforcement** and encourages the person to **repeat** the behaviour.
3) For example, Skinner taught pigeons to play ping-pong by providing **positive reinforcement** in stages — for standing on the court, then for touching the ball, then for hitting it correctly, etc.
4) Intelligent human behaviours, e.g. **driving a car** or **writing**, can be learnt in the same way.

Comments

- This approach has been criticised for being **reductionist** (see page 245) — it ignores other aspects of intelligence, e.g. the biological approach.
- More understanding is needed of what **cognitive abilities** are involved in intelligence and what **biological** and **environmental factors** influence individual differences in intelligence.

The Psychometric Approach Focuses on Intelligence Testing

1) The **psychometric approach** involves measuring intelligence to produce an **intelligence quotient** (**IQ**) **score**.
2) This is done through **intelligence tests** that are focused on mathematical ability and abstract, logical reasoning.
3) Spearman (1904) found that people who did well on **one** kind of test, e.g. arithmetic, usually did well in **other** kinds of tests, e.g. spatial reasoning. In other words, their test scores showed a **positive correlation**.
4) So, he proposed that everyone has a **general intelligence** that's **genetically determined** and **unchangeable**. He termed this '**g**'. He also suggested that people develop **specific abilities**, '**s**', which are influenced by **learning**. This can explain why, for example, some people are better at maths than at English.

Comments

- Thurstone (1938) argued **against** the concept of g, claiming that there are **7 independent groups** of primary mental abilities (e.g. numerical, verbal, spatial) rather than one general intelligence.
- There are many issues with the use of IQ tests. Many things, e.g. musical ability, are **difficult to measure**. Also, tests may be **culturally biased** (see pages 242-243).
- **Developmental factors** are not considered by the psychometric approach — **g** may be influenced by **education** and **nutrition**, which could promote or impair the development of intelligence.

The Information Processing Approach Focuses on Cognitive Processes

1) The **information processing approach** to intelligence focuses on the use of a **set** of **cognitive processes**.
2) **Sternberg** (**1985**) suggested that these underlie intelligence and can be split into **three components**:
   - **Metacomponents** — planning and control processes used in problem solving and decision making.
   - **Performance components** — processes that allow us to carry out actions, e.g. memorising, calculating, etc.
   - **Knowledge acquisition components** — processes used to learn new information.
3) Sternberg proposed that these three components are **universal** and apply to **three aspects of intelligence**:
   - **Analytical intelligence** — the ability to solve problems, see solutions, monitor and plan.
   - **Creative intelligence** — the ability to react to stimuli and develop ideas, either new or familiar.
   - **Practical intelligence** — the ability to adjust to different environments and contexts.

   These three kinds of intelligence make up **Sternberg's triarchic model of intelligence**.

Comments

- Sternberg's model allows for the influence of both **internal** and **external factors** on intelligence.
- It also addresses intelligence in relation to **practical**, **real-life scenarios** rather than just academic contexts.
- However, Gottfredson (2003) argues that Sternberg's concept of practical intelligence is **faulty** — it simply represents a set of skills developed to cope with a particular environment, rather than a kind of intelligence.

Theories of Intelligence

Gardner's (1985) Theory Identifies Seven Kinds of Intelligence

1) Traditionally, intelligence has been seen as a **single concept**, emphasising verbal, logical and mathematical skills.
2) Gardner's theory of **multiple intelligences** suggests that we have **several different kinds** of intelligence. These each involve different cognitive structures so are **independent** of each other, although they do interact.
3) So, a person could have a **high level** of ability in **some areas** of intelligence, but a **low level** in **other areas**.
4) Gardner identified **seven** kinds of intelligence:

- **Logical-mathematical** — ability in mathematics and logical and abstract reasoning.
- **Verbal-linguistic** — speaking, reading, writing and the ability to learn languages.
- **Visual-spatial** — ability in mental visualisation and art.
- **Musical** — abilities relating to sound, rhythm and tone.
- **Bodily kinaesthetic** — use of body, e.g. athletic and dance ability.
- **Intrapersonal** — associated with self-understanding, feelings, motivations and objectives.
- **Interpersonal** — social skills, empathy and ability to cooperate with others.

5) In 1997, Gardner added an **eighth** kind of intelligence to his model — **naturalistic intelligence**. People with high naturalistic intelligence are able to relate well to **nature** and **animals**.

Comments on Gardner's Theory

- Gardner's theory is based on a **range** of **research methods**, including psychometric tests and case studies of people who have low IQ scores but high ability in particular kinds of intelligence. For example, Horwitz et al (1965) found that some people who were considered to have low intelligence could rapidly calculate the day of the week that a particular date fell on.
- The concept of multiple intelligences can be **applied to education**. This would give a **broader approach** than the traditional emphasis on verbal and mathematical skills. It can also help teachers to understand the best ways for different students to **learn** things.
- The theory has been criticised because some aspects are **vague**, e.g. intrapersonal and musical intelligence are **difficult to define**. They're also **difficult to measure precisely**.
- Also, some people believe that some of the types of intelligence identified by Gardner are really just names for **talents** or **personality traits**, rather than a kind of intelligence.

Practice Questions

Q1 Give a problem associated with IQ tests.

Q2 In the psychometric approach to intelligence what does 'g' represent?

Q3 Give the three aspects of intelligence identified in Sternberg's (1985) theory.

Q4 Which of Gardner's multiple intelligences is associated with the ability to learn languages?

Q5 Give one criticism of Gardner's (1985) theory of multiple intelligences.

Exam Question

Q1 a) Outline the information processing approach to intelligence. [10 marks]

b) Describe and evaluate Gardner's (1985) theory of multiple intelligences. [15 marks]

Idle-slacker intelligence — the ability to do nothing, common in students...

Who'd have thought there were so many different kinds of intelligence. I wonder what they'll come up with next — maybe the ability to put together great outfits, or a high potential for buying exceedingly good birthday presents, or intelligence in the area of competitive eating perhaps. Tell you what is impressive though, those ping-pong playing pigeons. Marvellous.

Animal Learning and Intelligence

Also just for AQA people. *So, humans have varying levels of intelligence and are able to learn — even though it might not feel like much is going in sometimes. These pages look at other animals and whether they're able to learn.*

Classical Conditioning Involves Reflexive Responses

Classical conditioning occurs when a stimulus produces a response in an organism because it's become **associated** with **another** stimulus which normally produces that response. Animals can be classically conditioned.

Example

When dogs see food, they salivate. This is an automatic, unlearned response — a **reflex**. The food is an **unconditioned stimulus** (UCS) and salivation is an **unconditioned response** (UCR). **Pavlov (1927)** studied laboratory dogs that **always** received their food after a **bell** was rung. After a while the dogs would salivate when the bell was rung (before getting the food) as they **associated** the bell with food. The bell had become a **conditioned stimulus** (CS), and salivation had become a **conditioned response** (CR).

The principles of classical conditioning are:

1) **Generalisation** — when stimuli similar to the original CS (e.g. a bell with a different pitch) produce the CR (e.g. salivating).
2) **Discrimination** — when stimuli similar to the original CS don't produce the CR. This can be achieved by withholding the UCS (e.g. food) when the similar stimulus is used. The animal will begin to discriminate between the CS and the similar stimulus and will only respond to the CS.
3) **Extinction** — when the CR (e.g. salivating) isn't produced as a result of the CS (e.g. bell). This happens when the CS is repeatedly presented without the UCS (e.g. food) following it.
4) **Spontaneous recovery** — when a previously extinct CR is produced in response to the CS. This happens when the CS is presented again after a period of time during which it's not been used.
5) **Higher order conditioning** — when a new CS (e.g. a light) produces the CR because the animal associates it with the original CS. This can be achieved by consistently presenting the new CS before the original CS.

Operant Conditioning Involves Voluntary Behaviours

Operant conditioning occurs when organisms learn to associate **particular behaviours** with **particular consequences**. **Positive** consequences encourage them to **repeat** the behaviour, **negative** consequences discourage them from repeating the behaviour. Operant conditioning can involve **positive reinforcement**, **negative reinforcement** or **punishment**:

- **Positive reinforcement** — the behaviour produces a positive outcome, e.g. food, so the behaviour is reinforced.
- **Negative reinforcement** — the behaviour removes a negative stimulus, e.g. pain, so the behaviour is reinforced.
- **Punishment** — the behaviour is punished, e.g. electric shock, deterring the animal from repeating the behaviour.

Operant conditioning can be used to teach animals certain behaviours:

Example

Skinner (1938) studied laboratory rats to see if they could learn behaviour through operant conditioning. He placed the rats in boxes containing a lever. Pushing the lever provided the rat with food pellets — a **positive consequence**. Over time, the rats pushed the lever more frequently as they **associated** the behaviour with the reward of food.

Comments

1) Most research into conditioning has involved **laboratory experiments**. This **reduces ecological validity** so the results can't be **generalised** to real-life. More **field research** would be useful.
2) Different **species** have different **capacities** for learning by conditioning. Some may also learn by simple observation, with no reinforcement involved.
3) **Genetics** seem to **influence** and **limit** what different species can learn by conditioning. For example, Breland and Breland (1951) gave food to pigs when they carried wooden coins (in their mouths) to a 'piggy bank'. However, they started to drop them on the floor and push them towards the bank with their snout (showing an **instinctive** foraging behaviour), so taking longer to get the food.

Animal Learning and Intelligence

Non-human Animals May Show Some Kinds of *Intelligence*

Self-recognition, **social learning** and **Machiavellian intelligence** are all seen as evidence of intelligence.

Self-recognition

Self-recognition may be assessed by the **mark test** — an animal is anaesthetised and red dye is put on its forehead. Later, the animal is placed in front of a mirror. If it touches the mark on its head it provides evidence that it **identifies** the image in the mirror as **itself**. A few animals, e.g. chimpanzees, have shown self-recognition. However, Heyes (1994) claims that this doesn't prove that they're self-aware in the same way that humans are.

Machiavellian Intelligence

Machiavellian intelligence is the ability to **manipulate social situations** to reach a goal. For an animal to do this it needs to have **theory of mind** — an ability to imagine the world from the perspective of **others**. Theory of mind allows animals to attribute behaviour to intentions, beliefs and feelings, and enables them to **deceive** others.

Woodruff and Premack's (1979) laboratory experiment

Method: Chimpanzees watched as a trainer placed food under one of two containers, both of which were out of their reach. One of two trainers then entered. One trainer wore a green coat, the other a white coat. If the chimps were able to guide the **green-coated** trainer to where the food was, they were **given the food**. If they guided the **white-coated** trainer to the food, the trainer **kept the food**. However, if the white-coated trainer **did not** find the food, it would be given to the chimp.

Results: After repeating the test several times, all of the chimps learned to guide the green-coated trainer to the food. Some of the chimps **intentionally deceived** the white-coated trainer, pointing to the opposite container to where the food was, whilst the rest **withheld information** about the location of the food.

Conclusion: Chimps have **theory of mind** and are able to **deceive**.

Evaluation: The chimps may have learnt to guide the green-coated trainer to the food through **conditioning** (with food acting as a **positive reinforcer**) rather than actively attempting to deceive the white-coated trainer. This doesn't require a theory of mind so wouldn't be an example of Machiavellian intelligence.

Social Learning

Social learning occurs when an animal **copies** behaviour that it sees another animal receive a **benefit** from. This is known as **vicarious reinforcement**. Kawai's (1965) **naturalistic observations** of macaque monkeys showed that one of them started to wash potatoes in the sea before eating them. Other monkeys soon seemed to **imitate** this. However, Nagell et al (1993) suggest that animals may just notice environmental features that others are **interacting** with, so also **explore** them and learn by **trial and error**.

Practice Questions

Q1 Outline Pavlov's (1927) experiment on classical conditioning in dogs.

Q2 What is spontaneous recovery?

Q3 What is Machiavellian intelligence?

Exam Question

Q1 a) Outline theories of simple learning in non-human animals. [10 marks]

b) Discuss evidence for intelligence in non-human animals. [15 marks]

I can't come out — I'm conditioning my hair...

So animals are able to learn things — nothing new there. After all, you can train parrots to talk and horses to jump, not to mention all the stuff that guide dogs learn. Don't know why everyone gets so excited about Pavlov's slobbery dogs.

The Evolution of Intelligence

Still AQA only. *Many animals are bigger, stronger or faster than humans but appear to be less intelligent. Many factors may explain why humans are more intelligent than other species, and why intelligence varies between individuals.*

Evolutionary Factors May Have Affected the Development of Intelligence

1) **Darwin's** (1859) theory of **natural selection** suggests that characteristics that increase an animal's chances of **surviving** and **reproducing** are likely to be passed from one generation to the next.
2) If **intelligence** is **beneficial** to survival, the **most intelligent** members of a population are the **most likely** to **survive** and **reproduce**. This gives rise to **intelligent offspring**, who are also likely to survive and reproduce.
3) In this way the species **evolves** over time to become **more intelligent**.
4) Humans are a **highly intelligent species**. This suggests that intelligence is a characteristic that's been **beneficial** to the survival of humans and has **evolved** through **natural selection**.
5) **Several factors** may have contributed to the evolution of human intelligence. For example:

1) *Ecological Demands*

1) The **ecological demands** of the environment may have stimulated the development of intelligence.
2) For example, a hunter-gatherer or foraging lifestyle requires **memory** and **navigational skills**, so higher intelligence levels would be beneficial for survival.

2) *Social Complexity*

1) Humans are **social animals**. Living in **groups** could have contributed to the development of intelligence.
2) The **social complexity** of group living may help survival, e.g. by giving **protection** from predators and **cooperation** when hunting. However, social living also creates **competition** and **conflict**, e.g. for a mate.
3) Successful social living is more likely if animals are **intelligent** and have **theory of mind**, allowing them to understand others' intentions and feelings. This also allows for **Machiavellian intelligence** — where individuals and groups can deceive others for their own advantage.
4) There is some evidence that **social complexity** and **intelligence** are **linked**:
   - Other animals considered to be intelligent, e.g. **primates** and **dolphins**, also live in social groups.
   - Cosmides and Tooby (1992) found that people are better at solving logical problems if they are put in terms of **everyday social situations**, rather than presented in an abstract form. This suggests that intelligence may have evolved to deal with **social situations**. However, it's not clear which evolved first — intelligence or group living.

3) *Brain Size*

1) Jerison (1973), found a **positive correlation** between **body size** and **brain size** in animals. However, humans have brains **seven times larger** than expected for a mammal of our size.
2) Early hominids had a brain size of about 600 cubic centimetres. This remained relatively constant for 1.5 million years before **doubling** in size over the last 0.5 million years.
3) This is despite the fact that larger brains require **more energy** and make **childbirth** more **difficult** and **dangerous**.
4) However, these evolutionary costs are **balanced** by **increased intelligence**. Higher intelligence requires **more brain cells** and possibly **more specialised brain areas** — and so **bigger brains** evolved.
5) Research on brain size as a proportion of body size **supports** this theory. Willerman et al (1991) used MRI scanning to measure the brain size of college students. Those with **higher IQ scores** had **larger brains** (proportionate to body size). However, a limited, unrepresentative sample was used, meaning that it's hard to generalise the results. Also the type of IQ test may have had an effect on the results.

The Evolution of Intelligence

Intelligence Test Performance is Influenced by *Genetics* and the *Environment*

1) There's a lot of debate about the role **genetic** and **environmental factors** play in intelligence test scores.
2) Closely related people, e.g. siblings, tend to have more highly correlated IQ scores than less closely related people, e.g. cousins.
3) Bouchard and McGue (1981) did a meta analysis of 111 studies and found that the people with the **highest** IQ correlations were **identical** twins reared **together**. They showed a correlation of **0.86** compared to **0.6** for **non-identical** twins reared together. This suggests that intelligence is influenced by **genetics**.
4) However, **environmental factors** must influence intelligence to some extent otherwise the identical twins would show a correlation of **1**.
5) Another way of testing for genetic influences is to **compare** the correlations **adopted children** show with their **biological** and **adoptive relatives**. A **higher correlation** with their **biological relatives** than with their adoptive relatives (whose environment they share) suggests a strong **genetic** link.
6) But Schiff et al (1978) found that children from lower socio-economic backgrounds who were adopted into families with higher socio-economic status showed **higher IQs** than their **biological relatives**. This suggests that intelligence is affected by **environmental factors**.
7) Also, Bouchard and McGue (1981) found that identical twins reared **apart** showed a **lower correlation** in IQ scores (0.72) than identical twins reared together. This supports the theory that environmental factors affect IQ.
8) So, genetics and environmental factors are **both important** in IQ test performance, and probably **interact**. For example, variations in intelligence caused by genetics could be **compounded** or **reduced** depending on the **environment** (e.g. quality of nutrition or education).

Comments

1) Different studies have used **different kinds of IQ test**, making **comparisons** difficult.
2) Closer relatives often share **more similar environments** (e.g. the same home) than more distantly related people. This makes it difficult to separate genetic influences from environmental influences.

Intelligence is Linked to *Culture*

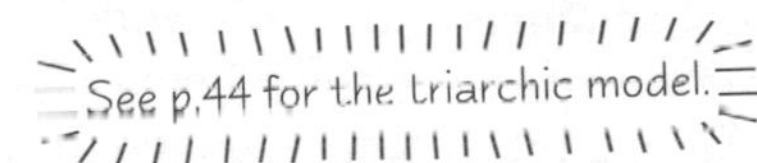
See p.44 for the triarchic model.

1) Sternberg's (1985) **triarchic model** of intelligence suggests that intelligence is shown by successfully adapting to the **physical** and **social demands** of the surrounding environment.
2) Sternberg et al (2001) found that some Kenyan children knew a huge amount about **herbal medicines** but didn't perform very well on normal **IQ tests**.
3) So intelligence must be understood in relation to the **culture** that a person lives in.
4) In some cultures the ability to **pass exams** could be seen as evidence of intelligent behaviour, whilst in others the ability to **hunt** has greater value.
5) Any **intelligence testing** that's carried out must take these differences into account.

Some behaviour isn't considered intelligent in any culture.

Practice Questions

Q1 List three evolutionary factors that may have contributed to the development of human intelligence.

Q2 How can group living help survival?

Q3 Give one piece of evidence that suggests that genetics influences intelligence.

Exam Question

Q1 a) Discuss the role of at least two evolutionary factors in the development of human intelligence. [15 marks]

b) Evaluate the roles of genetic and environmental factors associated with intelligence test performance. [10 marks]

Evolution of intelligence — feels like mine is going the other way...

That's the last pages on intelligence done — learn this stuff and you'll have this very clever topic wrapped up. The key things here are the development of human intelligence and the whole genetic vs environmental factors issue. Learn and enjoy...

Development of Thinking

It's a bright and shiny new section, and it's all for AQA. *Doesn't that make you feel special AQA people... It's all about thinking, and how your thinking develops as you get older. As you might be learning to expect by now, there are a lot of different theories about this. And I bet you want to know all about them. Well, as luck would have it...*

Piaget Proposed That **Cognition** Progresses in **Stages**

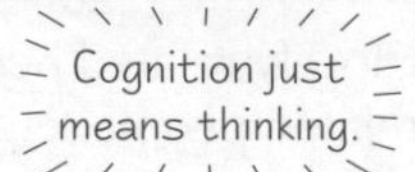
Cognition just
means thinking.

Piaget said that we're all born with the **basics** to allow **cognitive progression** — reflexes and senses. He reckoned that more **complex** abilities become possible as children move through **stages of development** as they get older:

Sensorimotor stage (0–2 years)	The child's knowledge is limited to what their senses tell them when they're exploring their surroundings. This exploration brings about an understanding of the concept of object permanence (if you put a towel over a toy, the toy is still there).
Preoperational stage (2–7 years)	The child has some language now, but makes logic mistakes — e.g. cats have four legs, so everything with four legs must be a cat. They typically can't do the three mountains task (see below) or conservation tasks (see next page). Children at this stage show egocentrism, irreversibility and centration (see below).
Concrete operational stage (7–11 years)	The child's use of logic improves and they can do conservation tasks. They no longer show egocentrism, irreversibility and centration but can't yet use abstract reasoning (reasoning in their head).
Formal operational stage (11+ years)	The child is much more advanced now, and can use abstract reasoning in problem solving. They can also use hypotheses and theoretical principles, and deal with hypothetical situations.

1) Piaget used the idea of **schemas** a lot in his work. A schema contains all the information you **know** about an object, action or concept — e.g. the schema of a human face has two eyes, a mouth and a nose, and the schema of riding a bike contains all the movements you'd need to make.
2) Schemas help you to **organise** and **interpret** information — new experiences are taken into our schemas (**assimilated**) and are **accommodated** by them. Accommodation just involves altering existing schemas.
3) Piaget reckoned that children try to find a **balance** between assimilation and accommodation during cognitive development.

Piaget Used the **Three Mountains Task (1956)** as Evidence for His Theory

1) Piaget built a **3-D model** of **three mountains** (well, he was from Switzerland).
2) The mountains had different **landmarks** on them — e.g. one had a cross on it, and another had a house.
3) Piaget put a small doll on one of the mountains and then showed children photos of the mountains taken from **various angles**. The children were asked to pick the photo that matched what the **doll** could see.
4) He found that children at his **preoperational stage** (2–7 years old) picked the photo taken from their **own perspective**, rather than the one taken from the **doll's perspective**.
5) He concluded that children at this stage were unable to put themselves in the doll's shoes.

Piaget used this and other experiments as evidence that children at his preoperational stage have the following qualities:

1) **Egocentrism** — they can only view the world from their **own viewpoint**. They're not sensitive to the fact that others may have **different** views or thoughts (as demonstrated by the three mountains task).
2) **Irreversibility** — they don't understand that you can undo an action (e.g. that you can reform a sausage-shaped piece of clay into its original ball shape).
3) **Centration** — they focus on small aspects of a task, not the task as a whole.

Development of Thinking

Piaget Showed How *Other Skills* Develop in *Later Stages*

Understanding of conservation

1) **Conservation** is the understanding that a **set quantity** stays the **same**, even if it **looks** different. For example, if liquid is poured from a short, fat glass into a tall, thin glass, the amount of liquid is still the same. Another example is counters in a row — two rows of five counters both have the same number of counters, even if the counters in one row are spaced out so that it looks longer.
2) Children at the **concrete operational stage** can **correctly identify** that the amount of liquid or the number of counters stays the same even after they've been rearranged. But children at the **preoperational stage** will say that the spaced out row contains **more** counters or the tall glass **more** liquid.
3) However, **McGarrigle and Donaldson (1974)** found that if a puppet (Naughty Teddy) **'accidentally'** knocked the counters so that the row looked longer, even younger children at the **preoperational stage** said that the number of counters was the **same**. This suggests that they **did** understand conservation.

The four beaker problem

1) **Piaget and Inhelder (1956)** gave children four beakers, each containing a colourless liquid. When two of the liquids were mixed the liquid turned yellow. Children had to work out the **right combination**.
2) Children at the **formal operational stage** used **systematic testing** of different mixtures to find the answer, whereas children at the **concrete operational stage** used a **random** approach.
3) However, some researchers have argued that **not everybody** gets to this stage of systematic hypothesis testing, so it might not be a **universal** stage of development.

There's Evidence *For* and *Against* Piaget's Stages of Cognitive Development

1) There's **cross-cultural similarity** in the stages — studies have suggested that children of all backgrounds progress through the stages in the same way, which provides **support** for Piaget's theory.
2) Piaget **underestimated abilities** at each age — for example, the experiment with Naughty Teddy showed that preoperational children **can** in fact understand the concept of conservation.
3) He said that **practice** and **teaching wouldn't** speed up progression through the stages but this isn't true — it's been found that teaching **can** help to move children on through the stages.
4) Piaget didn't think that **language** was important in cognitive development. He thought you needed **cognitive development first** in order to allow language to develop. But other theorists, such as **Vygotsky**, take a different view on this, as you'll find out on the next page...

Practice Questions

Q1 Name Piaget's four main stages of cognitive development.

Q2 How is the preoperational stage different from the concrete operational stage?

Q3 Did McGarrigle and Donaldson's (1974) experiment provide evidence for or against Piaget's theory?

Q4 Give two criticisms of Piaget's theory.

Exam Question

Q1 Describe and evaluate Piaget's theory of cognitive development. [25 marks]

Naughty Teddy! You've wrecked my theory...

Piaget's stages were an attempt to explain how children's understanding of the world changes as they develop, and the stages do help to show this. The trouble with any stage theory is that they tend to overestimate any differences between stages, and underestimate differences between individuals within the same stage. Oh well, nothing's perfect I suppose...

Development of Thinking

It's AQA again here. *Some more theories on cognitive development coming up — over to you, Vygotsky and Bruner.*

Vygotsky Reckoned **Culture** Plays a Big Part in **Cognitive Development**

1) **Vygotsky** said there were two types of mental function — **elementary** and **higher**. Elementary functions can be thought of as **innate reflexes**, **sensory abilities** and certain types of **memory**. Higher functions include more complex tasks like **language comprehension** and **decision-making**.
2) **Social** and **cultural factors** play a necessary part in moving from one type of functioning to the other — it's the influence of **others** around you that drives cognitive development.
3) One of Vygotsky's ideas was the **zone of proximal development**. This is the difference between the problem solving a child can do on their **own** and the problem solving they can do with a **more able peer** or **adult**.
4) If your teacher has an idea of what your **potential** is, they can help you reach it by pushing and guiding. So it's **interaction** with the teacher that's important (unlike Piaget's idea that progression happens on its own).
5) Instruction is **social** and driven by the teacher using **language** and **cultural** influences. The intention is to help the child to be **self-regulated** and responsible for their own learning.

Language is Also Important in Cognitive Development

Vygotsky suggests that **language** is a **driving influence** on cognitive development:

1) Children first learn language as a means to **communicate** with caregivers. It's also a tool that allows adults to communicate **social** and **cultural information** to children.
2) As the child grows older they use language not only to communicate but also to **guide** their **behaviour** — they use **self-talk** (talking out loud) to **regulate** and **direct** themselves.
3) This self-talk eventually becomes **internalised** and becomes silent **inner speech**. At this point the child has developed two very different forms of language — **inner speech** and **external oral speech**.
4) **Oral speech** is used socially for **communication**, whilst **inner speech** is a **cognitive tool** that allows individuals to **direct** and **monitor** their **thoughts** and **behaviour**.
5) If someone finds a task difficult they may re-employ **self-talk** to exert greater **control** over their thoughts.

Vygotsky Also Came Up With **Stages of Development**

Vygotsky's stages **aren't as rigidly defined** as Piaget's — they're broader areas of development (without specified ages) giving an idea of the stages children go through as their thinking matures (**concept formation**).
He came up with these 4 stages after studying how children of various ages went about solving a problem:

1) **Vague syncretic** — **trial and error** methods are used, with **no understanding** of the underlying concepts.
2) **Complex** — use of **strategies** begins but they're **not** used successfully.
3) **Potential concept** — successful strategies are used but only **one at a time**.
4) **Mature concept** — **lots** of strategies used at the same time. Thinking becomes **mature** and **developed**.

Vygotsky's Theory Has **Strengths** and **Weaknesses**

Vygotsky carried out **very few studies** whilst coming up with his theory. However, other people have carried out studies that have provided evidence that **supports** Vygotsky's theory:

1) **Gardner and Gardner (1969)** found that with **instruction** animals can reach **higher levels** of functioning. This is evidence for the role of **culture** in learning.
2) **Chi et al (1989)** showed that pretending to **talk to the author** as you read (self-explanation) can help increase understanding. This is evidence for the use of **speech in thought**.
3) **Berk (1994)** found that children who used **more self-talk** when solving maths problems did better over the following year. This is evidence for the use of **self-talk** in problem-solving.

Another strength is that the theory can be **successfully applied to education** (see page 54). However, a **major criticism** is that the theory over-emphasises social and cultural factors in intelligence and **ignores biological factors**.

Development of Thinking

Bruner's Theory Focuses on **Representations of Knowledge**

Bruner (1966) claimed that our brains use three **modes of representation** for knowledge:

1) **The Enactive Mode** — at first, knowledge is only in the form of **physical actions**, i.e. learning by doing. For example, a baby's knowledge of a rattle would involve how to hold and shake it. Later, this mode is used to represent knowledge such as how to swim. So, knowledge just involves '**muscle memory**'.

2) **The Iconic Mode** — at 2–6 years we begin to also store knowledge in the form of **mental images** involving different senses like vision, smell and touch. For example, our knowledge of what an apple is includes what it looks like and tastes like.

3) **The Symbolic Mode** — from about 7 years old we develop the ability to think in **symbolic ways** — we can store things as words and numbers. Language and thinking become strongly linked, e.g. we use language to talk about experiences. This allows us to **mentally manipulate** concepts and ideas, and to think in **abstract** ways.

Like Vygotsky, Bruner thought that **language** was very important for cognitive development. So, **language instruction** might help achieve understanding. However, **Sinclair-de-Zwart (1969)** found that although language appropriate for **conservation tasks** could be taught to children who couldn't conserve, most were still **unsuccessful** at the conservation tasks. Further development seems to be necessary before the next stage can be reached.

There is Some **Evidence** to **Support** Bruner's Theory

Bruner and Kenney (1996) — Iconic and symbolic thinking

Method: Children aged 5–7 were shown a grid with an arrangement of different sized glasses on it. These were removed and the children had to **replace** them as they had been (requiring **iconic thinking**), or **rearrange** them, e.g. in a mirror image (requiring **symbolic thinking**).

Results: **All** the children **replaced** the glasses correctly, but only the **older** children could **rearrange** them. Children without the appropriate language to talk through the problem were only able to do the **replacement task**.

Conclusion: Mental manipulation of ideas requires **symbolic representation**, and children must have progressed to the **symbolic mode** of cognitive development in order to think in this way. Language is important for more complex thinking.

Evaluation: This was a **laboratory experiment** so there was **good control over variables**. However, all the study really showed was that **older** children can manage more **complex tasks** — so, this could also be used as support for Piaget or Vygotsky's theory.

Practice Questions

Q1 According to Vygotsky, what is inner speech used for?

Q2 Give two pieces of evidence that support Vygotsky's theory of cognitive development.

Q3 What is the difference between iconic and symbolic representation?

Q4 What did Bruner and Kenney conclude from their 1996 experiment?

Exam Question

Q1 a) Outline one theory of cognitive development. [9 marks]

b) Evaluate the theory of cognitive development outlined in (a). [16 marks]

I like Bruner's theory best — he's the easiest to spell...

I wonder how many different spellings of Vygotsky's name crop up on exam papers... Quite a few, I imagine. If you're like me and struggle to remember how to spell your own name, it's worth taking the time to learn it now. Vygotsky, that is — not your name. If you really can't spell that by now I doubt you'll ever be able to. Sorry to be the one to break it to you.

Applying the Theories to Education

You only need to learn these two pages if you're doing AQA. *Psychologists don't spend their valuable time carrying out experiments and coming up with theories just for fun, you know. They can have practical applications, such as using ideas about cognitive development to improve education — which, funnily enough, is the next thing you need to learn...*

Piaget's Theory Has Implications for Education

Piaget's theory suggests a **child-centred approach** to education, in which children can learn for themselves through their own experience. It can be applied to find ways to help children **learn** more effectively:

1) **Learning by discovery** — according to Piaget, when children encounter new experiences that their current **schemas** can't deal with adequately, they develop new schemas through the process of **accommodation** (see page 50). This implies that providing opportunities to **actively** experience new things in a stimulating classroom with lots of **different** resources will help promote cognitive development.
2) **Readiness** — Piaget claimed that development is limited by the process of **maturation**. So, children **can't** learn particular kinds of knowledge until they're **ready** to develop the necessary schemas. For example, a child at the **preoperational** stage isn't ready to understand conservation of volume.
3) **Appropriate materials** — teachers must provide **appropriate challenges**, e.g. **preoperational** children should be given **concrete examples** of new ideas to help their understanding. Teachers must also be sensitive to **developmental differences** between students, because some children mature and learn more quickly than others.

The Plowden Report (1967)

The Plowden Report reviewed **primary level** education and made **recommendations** for UK schools. The report included research and surveys. Some of the recommendations it made were based on **Piaget's theory**. For example, Piaget's ideas about **discovery learning**, **readiness** and a **set sequence** of developmental stages were used in the report. However, Piaget's theory **isn't** now as widely accepted as it once was. It's now known that children generally have **more abilities** than Piaget claimed, e.g. **operational** thinking may develop **earlier** than Piaget suggested.

Vygotsky's Theory Emphasises Social Interaction

Vygotsky's theory is a **teacher-guided approach** and suggests that **interactions** with others are important in learning. In other words, **other people** are needed to stimulate cognitive development. For example, **scaffolding** is an important concept developed from Vygotsky's theory where other people assist a child's cognitive development:

- **Scaffolding** is when a **teacher**, another **adult** or a **more cognitively advanced child** acts as an **expert** to guide the child.
- They do this by making suggestions or doing demonstrations to provide a **framework** by which the child learns to do a task.
- At first the child might need lots of help, but as they learn **less help** is needed and they can carry on learning **independently**.
- For scaffolding to work it needs to take place within the child's **zone of proximal development** (**ZPD**) (see p.52).

Prof. Telfer's trainee teachers suddenly realised he didn't know what he was talking about.

	Wood et al (1976) studied scaffolding
Method:	**Thirty** children aged 3–5 were given the task of building a model and were **observed**. A **tutor** gave help to each child according to how well they were doing — the help was either in the form of showing or telling.
Results:	Scaffolding allowed the children to complete a task they **wouldn't** have been able to do alone. The **effectiveness** of the scaffolding was influenced by various factors, e.g. how the tutor **simplified** the task, and how they helped them **identify important steps**. **Showing** was used most when helping **younger** children, whilst **telling** was used more with the **older** children. Also, the **older** the child was the **less** scaffolding was needed for them to complete the task.
Conclusion:	Scaffolding **can** be helpful but consideration needs to be given to **maximise** its effectiveness.
Evaluation:	This study had fairly **good ecological validity**, but there was less control over variables, **reducing reliability**.

Applying the Theories to Education

Bruner Proposed a Spiral Curriculum

Bruner (1966) agreed with Vygotsky that **social interaction** is important for cognitive development, and he made some important suggestions for education:

1) **The Spiral Curriculum** — although a child's age and level of development will **limit** what they can learn, Bruner argued that even difficult concepts can be introduced at an appropriate level from an **early age**. As the child grows the concept can be **repeatedly revisited**, each time in more depth — this will achieve a more complete and in-depth understanding. In this way, children can **build up** their knowledge, and the earlier learning should make the later learning **easier**.

2) **Motivation** — Bruner argued that children are more motivated to learn if they have an **intrinsic interest** in what they're studying. This is **more of an incentive** than external motivations like getting good marks. So teachers should encourage an **active interest** in topics and aim to come up with engaging ways to teach them.

3) **Language** — by **discussions** in class, children can learn about **other perspectives**, and achieve **deeper understanding**.

4) **Discovery Learning** — Bruner emphasised that children should not just learn facts, but should learn by **exploring** and **discovering** facts. This also helps them to learn about the **process** of acquiring knowledge.

Bruner's ideas have been very influential — for example the use of a spiral curriculum is now quite common.

Application of Theories to Education May Need to Be Reviewed

1) Although theories of cognitive development have been **usefully applied** to education, there are often **practical difficulties** involved. For example, it can be very time-consuming to continually assess the ZPD of all the children in a class. Also, providing enough appropriate challenges and finding appropriate expert peer tutors can be a problem.

2) As **more research** is done and **theories develop**, the implications for education need to be regularly reviewed. For example, **Sylva** (**1987**) has suggested that Piaget's learning by discovery is **not** actually always the most effective approach and that his theory should not be relied on so heavily.

Archie suspected that his peer tutors were neither expert nor appropriate. He was no fool.

Practice Questions

Q1 What is meant by 'discovery learning'?

Q2 How is Vygotsky's approach to education different from Piaget's 'child-centred approach'?

Q3 What is involved in 'scaffolding'?

Q4 What is meant by a 'spiral curriculum'?

Q5 Why might applications of cognitive theories to education need to be regularly reviewed?

Exam Question

Q1 Outline and evaluate the application of theories of cognitive development to education. [25 marks]

A spiral curriculum — just going round and round in circles...

I'm pretty sure I experienced a spiral curriculum when I was at school. About twice a year in biology lessons they'd make us put a piece of pondweed in a beaker of water and count the bubbles. I never actually found out why though, so I'm guessing something went a bit wrong there. They should probably think about reviewing that approach, in my opinion.

Development of Moral Understanding

These pages are just for AQA people. *Hmmm, moral development. Being good, being bad. Would it be morally wrong to skip these pages and go and watch some TV instead? Well, you'll never know unless you read them...*

Kohlberg Thought That Moral Understanding Progresses in Stages

1) Kohlberg argued that your **moral understanding increases** as you grow older because at each stage you take more and more of the **social** world into account.
2) He investigated this idea using a **moral dilemma** story called **'Heinz's dilemma'**. Heinz had to choose whether or not to break into a shop to steal expensive drugs to cure his dying wife.
3) He used a sample of **72 boys** aged 10, 13 and 16 and later **repeated** the experiment with younger boys.
4) Kohlberg was interested in **how** participants **justified** the action they chose for Heinz, rather than whether they thought he should steal the drugs or not.

He used his findings to come up with **three levels** of moral understanding — **preconventional morality**, **conventional morality** and **postconventional morality**. Each of these levels is made up of **two stages**:

Preconventional morality

Stage 1 — Punishment and obedience orientation

Reasons for behaviour aren't taken into account. The only reason for not doing something is because you'll be **punished**. For example, Heinz shouldn't steal the drugs because he'll go to jail.

Stage 2 — Instrumental purpose orientation

Morality is based on meeting your **own interests** and getting what you **want**. For example, Heinz should steal the drugs because otherwise his wife will die and he'll be upset.

Conventional morality

Stage 3 — Morality of interpersonal cooperation

You try to live up to the **expectations** of people who are **important** to you. Behaviour that improves your relationship with these people is seen as moral. For example, Heinz should steal the drugs as his family and friends would expect him to do everything he can to save his wife.

Stage 4 — Social-order orientation

Moral behaviour is behaviour that fits in with **social norms**, **obligations** and **rules**, e.g. following the law. Morality is seen in the context of society as a whole. For example, Heinz shouldn't steal the drugs because it's against the law, and laws should always be followed.

Postconventional morality

Stage 5 — Social-contract orientation

Laws are seen as **flexible** in certain situations, and not all of **equal importance**. Laws are only followed if they contribute towards the welfare of others. For example, Heinz should steal the drugs — although stealing is against the law, it's better to steal than to let his wife die.

Stage 6 — Universal ethical principles

You've developed your own set of **abstract moral principles** that you follow above those laid down by the law. For example, Heinz should steal the drugs as human life has a higher value than personal property.

Other Researchers Have Studied Kohlberg's Findings

Other researchers have reviewed and evaluated Kohlberg's work:

1) **Sobesky** (**1983**) found that using **different versions** of Heinz's dilemma (i.e. different consequences for Heinz and his wife of Heinz stealing or not stealing) **changes the response** of the reader. So an individual's response **isn't fixed** depending on the stage of moral development they're at, but changes according to the **situation**.
2) The theory is **sex-biased**. Most of Kohlberg's work was carried out on **US males**, so his findings may not apply to other groups. Gilligan claimed that the theory was **androcentric** and focused too much on male-oriented ideas about **justice** rather than also taking into account **other moral approaches** that might appeal more to women.
3) **Hart and Fegley** (**1995**) found that some morally-driven people are **not** motivated by duty or by right and wrong, as Kohlberg suggested — some people are motivated to behave morally because it makes them **feel good**.

Development of Moral Understanding

Eisenberg's Theory Concerns *Prosocial Reasoning*

1) **Eisenberg (1986)** studied **prosocial reasoning**, i.e. how we think about doing good or positive things for other people, such as being kind, helpful or generous.
2) This differs from **Kohlberg's** focus on **moral reasoning** and moral dilemmas, which often concerned **anti-social** behaviours, like stealing.
3) However, like Kohlberg, Eisenberg used a **story-telling method** to study the development of prosocial reasoning from preschool age to early adulthood. For example:

> Eisenberg told children a story about a girl on her way to a birthday party who meets another child who's hurt their leg. If she stops to help them she'll be late for the party and miss the food and games. Eisenberg asked the children what the girl should do.

4) From the children's answers, Eisenberg developed a sequence of **developmental stages** or **levels**:

- **Hedonistic** — children are **selfish**, only concerned with achieving their own goals or acting for their own personal benefit.
- **Needs-orientated** — children acknowledge that help is needed, showing **concern** but **not empathy** for others.
- **Approval-orientated** — children express **stereotyped** views of what their society and culture considers good and bad. They're also motivated to behave prosocially to gain approval from others.
- **Empathetic** — children show some **empathy** for how others are feeling and can take their perspective. They also feel **guilt** for failing to help others.
- **Partly internalised principles** — children show some indication that **norms** and **values** of prosocial reasoning are being **internalised**. However, the reasoning can't always be properly explained.
- **Strongly internalised principles** — the norms and values are more clearly seen and more strongly adhered to. Actions concerning rights and responsibilities can be **fully justified**. Issues of **self-respect** and living up to **personal moral values** are also taken into consideration.

Fred had been waiting for help for hours. He wouldn't be volunteering for any more studies.

5) Eisenberg has reported that the stages she identified are found to some extent in other **cultures**, e.g. Italy and Poland. This **cross-cultural similarity** provides support for the theory.
6) Although Eisenberg's stages may **overlap** with Kohlberg's, her theory is still valuable because of its focus on prosocial reasoning — this may develop at a **different rate** from moral reasoning.

Practice Questions

Q1 List Kohlberg's six stages of moral understanding.

Q2 What did Sobesky (1983) find when he studied Kohlberg's dilemmas?

Q3 What is meant by prosocial reasoning?

Q4 List the six main stages outlined in Eisenberg's (1986) theory of prosocial reasoning.

Exam Question

Q1 a) Outline one or more theories of moral understanding and/or prosocial reasoning. [9 marks]

b) Evaluate the theories of moral understanding and/or prosocial reasoning outlined in (a). [16 marks]

Forget the kid with the bad leg, I want cake, give me the CAKE...

That will sound all too familiar to those of you acquainted with a two-year-old, or anyone else stuck at the early stages of moral development for that matter. Anyway — cake tantrums aside, you need to learn about Kohlberg's theory of moral understanding and Eisenberg's theory of prosocial reasoning before you move on. Go on, you know it's the right thing to do...

Development of Social Cognition

AQA only. Social cognition is about understanding about yourself and others, and being able to see things from other people's perspective. So, for example, I know that I'm awesome and that you're probably not having much fun right now...

A Sense of Self Develops During Childhood

Having a **sense of self** includes things like:

- being able to **distinguish** between self and others, and referring to each with **appropriate language**
- having knowledge of our **experiences**, **abilities**, **motivations**, etc.
- having ideas about **body image**

Important stages during development include:

1) **Existential self** — from about three months old we learn to **distinguish** self from non-self, and find out that we exist separately from other things. The development of **object permanence** (see p.50) may help this.
2) **Categorical self** — from about two years old we start to use language to **describe ourselves**, using culturally defined categories, e.g. age, male/female, tall/short, etc. We are also described by **other people** in this way, which can influence our idea of ourself. For example, describing a child as 'clever' or 'naughty' could influence their **self-esteem**.
3) **Identity crisis** — **Erikson (1968)** claimed that during **adolescence**, when going through body changes and starting to make plans for the future, we may **try out** different roles until we find our true identity.

Having a sense of self also involves being able to see yourself as **others** see you. This requires some understanding of the minds of others, and being able to see things from **their perspective**.

Theory of Mind (ToM) is About Understanding Other People's Minds

Humans have a unique ability to **cooperate** and carry out **complex interactions**. It's thought this is possible because we have a **theory of mind**. This involves **understanding that we and others have minds** with knowledge, feelings, beliefs, motivations, intentions, etc. We can **explain** and **predict** other people's behaviour by making inferences about their mental states. This includes the knowledge that others may have **false beliefs** about the world.

Baron-Cohen et al (1985) — theory of mind in autistic children

Method: Three groups of children were studied — children with autism with an average age of 12 years, children with Down's Syndrome with an average age of 11 years, and 'normal' children with an average age of 4 years. The experiment used two dolls — Sally had a basket, Anne a box. Children were asked to name the dolls (the **naming question**). Then Sally was seen to hide a marble in her basket and leave the room. Anne took the marble and put it in her box. Sally returned and the child was asked, 'Where will Sally look for her marble?' (**belief question**). The correct response is to point to the basket, where Sally believes the marble to be. They were also asked, 'Where is the marble really?' (**reality question**) and 'Where was the marble in the beginning?' (**memory question**). Each child was tested twice, with the marble in a different place the second time.

Results: **All** of the children got the **naming**, **reality** and **memory** questions correct. In the **belief** question, the children with Down's Syndrome scored **86%**, the 'normal' children **85%**, but the children with autism scored **20%**.

Conclusion: The findings suggest that autistic children have an **under-developed theory of mind**, sometimes called **mind-blindness**. They seem unable to predict or understand the beliefs of others.

Evaluation: Dolls were used throughout the study, causing it to lack **ecological validity**. Also, children with autism may in fact have a more highly developed theory of mind and understand that dolls don't have beliefs. Repeating the study by acting out the scenes with **humans** might show an increase in ability on the tasks. However, **Leslie and Frith (1988)** did a similar study with real people and not dolls and found the same pattern of results.

Most children develop ToM at around **four** years old. However, the kind of questions asked in Baron-Cohen et al's false belief task may be difficult for younger children to understand. It seems that **three-year-old** children can pass some versions of the test, so theory of mind may actually develop **earlier**.

There's also disagreement about the **development** of ToM. It may have an **innate** basis, but **nurture** and **experience** are also likely to be important in its development.

Development of Social Cognition

Understanding Others Involves **Perspective-taking**

One aspect of having a ToM is understanding that other people's **perspectives** can differ from your own. Children gradually become more skilful in their **perspective-taking ability**. **Selman (1980)** studied children's perspective-taking ability by analysing their responses to stories presenting dilemmas. For example:

> Selman told children a story about a girl who could rescue a friend's cat by climbing a tree. However, she'd promised her father that she wouldn't climb trees. Selman asked the children if she should be punished if she did climb the tree.

Like all little girls, Molly had perfected the "who, me?" look. She knew Daddy wouldn't mind about the tree.

From the children's answers, Selman identified **five** kinds of **perspective-taking**:

1) **Undifferentiated and Egocentric** — up to about six years of age, children can separate **self** and **other**, but in a physical sense only. They don't perceive any psychological differences, seeing the other person in the same way they see an object.

2) **Differentiated and Subjective** — from five to nine, children understand that other people have **different perspectives** because they have access to **different information** (i.e. know different things). However, only their own perspective is seen as important and they can't take the perspective of the other person.

3) **Second-Person and Reciprocal** — between seven and twelve, children can put themselves in someone else's shoes and view a situation from **another's perspective**. They also realise that other people can do the same.

4) **Third-Person and Mutual** — between ten and fifteen years old, children develop the ability to take the perspective of a **third impartial person** who's viewing an interaction between other people.

5) **In-Depth and Societal-Symbolic** — from about fourteen, children understand that **third-party perspectives** can be influenced by factors such as **social or cultural values**. They can see a situation from a variety of different perspectives, e.g. moral, legal, etc.

As children go through these stages they become better able to understand that other people have different perspectives, and can use information to put themselves in other people's shoes.

Selman's ideas about perspective-taking can have **practical applications** in **education**. For example, using **multi-cultural** materials and having **class discussions** can expose children to different perspectives. This may help to promote their perspective-taking ability.

Practice Questions

Q1 Explain what is meant by 'existential self', 'categorical self' and 'identity crisis'.

Q2 How does Baron-Cohen et al's false belief task show whether or not a child has a theory of mind?

Q3 How did Selman study perspective-taking ability?

Q4 Name Selman's five stages of perspective-taking.

Exam Question

Q1 a) Describe theories of the development of a child's sense of self. [9 marks]

b) Discuss the development of children's understanding of others, including perspective-taking. [16 marks]

Actually, I took the marble while your back was turned and swallowed it...

One of my friends at school definitely went through that identity crisis thing. He started out as an emo kid, suddenly went really sporty and obsessed with football, and then for a term or two he seemed to think he was a rapper. He also spent nearly a whole year dressing like a cowboy. I think he's settled down now though — last I heard he was an accountant.

The Mirror Neuron System

Last two for AQA only. Here comes the science bit — all about the biological basis for social cognition.

Social Cognition Has a Biological Basis

1) **Neurons** (**cells**) in the cerebral cortex are organised into **four** main areas: the **frontal**, **temporal**, **parietal** and **occipital** lobes.
2) Different processes, such as **visual perception**, involve one or more of these lobes. Some areas of the brain seem to have very specialised roles in **cognition**.
3) It seems likely that many of our sophisticated **social** abilities, such as **theory of mind**, also involve complex brain mechanisms — these may have **evolved** as our brains and intelligence grew. Abilities like this could have been stimulated by our complex **social living** (see page 48).
4) Attempts have been made to **connect** findings from neuroscience and social psychology and combine them into more complete theories — this is known as **social neuroscience**.

Mirror Neurons Respond to the Actions of Others

Mirror neurons are brain cells that are involved in **performing** an action, such as holding a cup. However, they're **also** active when you **observe** someone else doing the same action. So, whether you're actually holding a cup, or only observing someone else holding a cup, particular mirror neurons will be **active**.

	Di Pellegrino et al (1992) — recording neuron activity
Method:	**Electrodes** were inserted into individual neurons in the **premotor cortex** of macaque monkeys. When the monkeys reached for food, the **activity** in the neurons was recorded.
Results:	The neurons were **active** when the monkeys reached for food, but also, unexpectedly, active when they observed **someone else** reach for food.
Conclusion:	This was the **first** study to provide evidence for the existence of **mirror neurons**. Although the function of mirror neurons is not yet clear, they may help in understanding observed behaviour.
Evaluation:	The experiment was **not** designed to study mirror neurons, so the information gathered about them was **limited**. Also, this experiment involved inserting electrodes into animals' brains, which raises **ethical issues**.

It's hard to record the activity of individual neurons in the brains of **humans**. So, studies have been done using brain scanning techniques such as **functional Magnetic Resonance Imaging** (fMRI), which analyse **brain activity** during particular kinds of behaviours. For example, Iacoboni et al (1999) found that there are areas of the **frontal** and **parietal cortex** that are active when people carry out and observe actions.

Mirror Neurons May Be Important for Social Cognition

Neurons that are active both when **you** do something and when you see **other people** do the same thing may help you **understand** the behaviour of others.

	Fogassi et al (2005) — Mirror neurons and intentions
Method:	The activity of **41 mirror neurons** in 2 macaque monkeys were recorded as they observed a person pick up an apple as if to eat it, or pick up the apple and place it in a cup.
Results:	**Different** groups of neurons responded to the two outcomes (eat or place). Also, some neurons fired after the apple was picked up but before the second action (eat or place) was carried out.
Conclusion:	Different patterns of response link with different **behavioural objectives** and some neurons seem to predict the **intention** of actions. So, mirror neurons may help to **understand** and **predict** the behaviour of others.
Evaluation:	Animals may behave differently under lab conditions, meaning the experiment has **low ecological validity**. Also, the experiment was carried out on monkeys so it's difficult to **generalise** the results to humans — neurons in humans may not respond in the same way.

Experiments with **humans** using **fMRI** show that brain areas that are active when we feel particular emotions (e.g. happiness or pain) are also active when we see others feel the same emotion. This supports suggestions that mirror neurons may be involved in **empathy**.

The Mirror Neuron System

There's a Lot of **Debate** About the **Role** of Mirror Neurons

1) The **function** and **importance** of mirror neurons is not yet fully understood. For example, they may be involved in **imitation** — but macaque monkeys (which have mirror neurons) have a **limited ability** for imitation learning.
2) A connection between mirror neurons and **theory of mind** (**ToM**) has also been debated. However, mirror neurons are found in monkeys that **don't** seem to have ToM in the same way that humans do. Also, **fMRI research** shows that ToM tests activate brain regions that **aren't** generally thought to be part of the mirror neuron system. It may be that mirror neurons can be involved in **learning by imitation**, but that the development of ToM involves **more** than this.
3) More needs to be learnt about the **development** of mirror neurons. **Falck-Ytter** (**2006**) reckoned that mirror neurons start to develop during the **first year** of life. However, **Meltzoff and Moore** (**1977**) found that human infants can imitate facial expressions **soon after birth.** This could either suggest that mirror neurons have an **innate** basis, or else that imitation **doesn't** necessarily involve mirror neurons.

Social Neuroscience Has Raised **Important Issues**

Jake knew what went on in those labs and was holding Dr. Anwar's dog hostage until Maeve was returned to him safely.

1) **Social neuroscience** is **inter-disciplinary** — it involves both **biological** and **social** concepts and theories. These different types of theories may **mutually inform** each other — biological research can help understand social processes better, and vice versa. So, instead of being **reductionist** (p.245), we can understand behaviour at different levels of explanation.
2) This approach may bring important **insights** into human **social cognition** (e.g. the basis of **empathy**). Also, conditions such as **autism** (p.190-191) might be better understood.
3) Animal experiments involve invasive methods, e.g. inserting electrodes into the brain — this raises **ethical issues** (see p.220).

Practice Questions

Q1 What are mirror neurons?

Q2 How have mirror neurons been studied in animals and in humans?

Q3 Who first identified mirror neurons?

Q4 Outline a piece of evidence supporting the idea that mirror neurons may be involved in empathy.

Q5 Why is social neuroscience a particularly valuable new field of research?

Exam Questions

Q1 Discuss the development of social cognition, including the role of the mirror neuron system. [25 marks]

Q2 Outline and evaluate research on the role of the mirror neuron system. [25 marks]

OK, he's picking up the cup — ready neurons... aim... and fire...

This is an interesting little topic to end the section with — it's all fresh and new and nobody knows quite what's going on. There are new ideas springing up and being shot down all over the place. And to think, if a monkey hadn't happened to look over and see someone picking up some food, these pages might never have existed. What a loss that would've been.

Clinical Psychology

This is just for Edexcel. *It's quite a nice section really — clinical psychology is all about diagnosing and treating mental disorders, so the researchers here are actually trying to help people. Almost brings a tear to your eye, doesn't it...*

Clinical Psychologists Explain and Treat Mental Illness

1) Clinical psychology focuses on studying, explaining and treating **emotional** or **behavioural disorders**.
2) Clinical psychologists assess patients using **interviews**, **observations** and **psychological tests**. They then help patients work through their problems, e.g. using talk therapies.
3) Researchers gather **primary** and **secondary data** to improve understanding of mental disorders. Clinicians then apply this to **individual cases** to help them establish a clear **diagnosis** and decide upon the correct **treatment** for each individual.

- **Primary data** — information collected during the researcher's direct observations of a patient, e.g. test results, answers to questionnaires, observation notes.
- **Secondary data** — information collected from other studies. This data can be used to check the validity of studies, or used to prove or disprove a new theory.

Clinical Psychology Uses Twin Studies

1) **Twin studies** are used to find out if **genetic factors** influence the development of mental disorders.
2) They involve looking at **concordance rates** — the **chance** that both twins will develop the mental disorder.
3) **Identical** (**MZ**) twins share all their genetic material, and **non-identical** (**DZ**) twins share around half. So, if both MZ twins are **more likely** to develop schizophrenia (a higher concordance rate) than both DZ twins, it can be assumed that schizophrenia has a **genetic** cause. However, it can't be the full story unless concordance rates are **100%** in MZ twins.

There's more on schizophrenia and twin studies on p.68.

Gottesman and Shields (1966) — schizophrenia in twins

Method: Hospital records for the previous 16 years were examined to identify people with schizophrenia who had a **twin**. Around 40 sets of twins agreed to take part in the study, which was a **natural experiment** using **independent measures**.

Results: The concordance rate was about **48%** for **MZ** twins and about **17%** for **DZ** twins. The exact figures vary depending on the type of schizophrenia, but overall, MZ twins had a much higher concordance rate than DZ twins.

Conclusion: As the results for MZ twins are much higher, this suggests a **genetic cause** for schizophrenia.

Evaluation: The results for MZ twins don't show 100% concordance, which means that there must be **other important factors** that influence schizophrenia. Although the researchers had a large amount of data covering a long period of time, it's unlikely the study could be **replicated** until new data existed.

Twin Studies Have Strengths and Weaknesses

Strengths

- **Rich data** — researchers have the opportunity to study **rare phenomena** in a lot of **detail**.
- **Unique cases** — existing theories can be challenged, and ideas for future research can be suggested.
- **High ecological validity** — the variables aren't manipulated so the findings should be **true to real life**.

Weaknesses

- **Causal relationships** — the researcher **doesn't** have much **control** over the variables, so the findings could be the result of an extraneous variable. This means that it's **difficult** to establish **cause and effect**.
- **Generalisation** — only using a **single case** means it's difficult to generalise the results to other people.
- **Ethics** — it can be difficult to get **informed consent** if the subjects have a **mental disorder**.
- **Opportunities** — identical twins are quite **rare**, so there aren't very many research opportunities, and sample sizes are usually pretty small.

Clinical Psychology

Clinical Psychology Uses *Animal Studies*

Animal studies are used in clinical psychology because they allow researchers to carry out tests that couldn't be done on humans. However, there are still ethical issues — see page 220.

Lipska et al (1993) — schizophrenia in rats

Method:	This was a **laboratory experiment** that involved making lesions in rats' brains to see if they developed schizophrenia-like symptoms. Areas of the hippocampus associated with schizophrenia were damaged using an injection of ibotenic acid a week after the rats were born.
Results:	The rats with a damaged hippocampus developed schizophrenia-like symptoms as their brains matured, e.g. hyperactivity, memory problems and a lack of response to rewards.
Conclusion:	Damage to the hippocampus can lead to the onset of schizophrenia-like symptoms, which suggests that the hippocampus plays a role in the development of schizophrenia.
Evaluation:	The variables in this experiment were tightly controlled, which means that it should be possible to establish **cause and effect** — the rats wouldn't have developed these symptoms if their brains hadn't been damaged. However, it's difficult to know how many symptoms of schizophrenia the rats were actually experiencing, because you can't establish whether they were having hallucinations or delusions.

Animal Studies Have *Strengths* and *Weaknesses*

Strengths

- **Ethics** — researchers can conduct experiments on animals that they **couldn't** do on **humans** because of **ethical restraints**, e.g. lesion studies. This means that clinical psychologists can investigate the **causes** of **mental disorders**, e.g. the effects of particular chemicals or social deprivation. They also don't need to get the animal's informed consent or worry about deception.
- **Speed of reproduction** — most animals reproduce much more **quickly** than humans, so it's quicker and easier to carry out **longitudinal studies** of **genetic influence**, e.g. to see whether schizophrenia has a genetic cause.
- **Detachment** — it's easier for researchers to be **impartial** with animal participants than with humans, so the results are more likely to be **objective**.

Weaknesses

- **Qualitative differences** — humans and animals are qualitatively different, so there are **problems** with **generalising** the results from animal studies to humans. Substances can have different effects on different animals, e.g. **morphine** has a calming effect on humans, but it causes manic behaviour in cats.
- **Language** — animals don't have **language**, which is a vital part of human behaviour. In clinical psychology this means that animals **can't describe** their **symptoms**, so it's difficult to know whether they're experiencing any mental abnormalities.

Practice Questions

Q1 Outline the aims of clinical psychology.

Q2 What's the difference between primary and secondary data?

Q3 Outline one advantage of twin studies.

Exam Question

Q1 a) Describe one research method used in clinical psychology. [4 marks]

b) Evaluate the research method outlined in (a). [5 marks]

Twin study — like a normal study but with two desks...

Just when you thought there couldn't possibly be any more different types of psychology, clinical psychology had to go and rear its ugly head. Woe is you. Although, to be honest, I've got limited sympathy. If you really thought that there weren't any other types of psychology then you obviously haven't been paying much attention. And we can't have that, can we...

Definitions of Abnormality

Just Edexcel here. *Some really quite brainy psychology types have been trying to define abnormality for years, and they don't seem to have quite got there yet. More for us to learn, I'm afraid. These things are sent to try us...*

Abnormality Can Be Defined as *Deviation* From *Statistical Norms*

The concept of deviation from the majority can be expressed **statistically** in terms of the **normal distribution**.

1) When you test a **large sample** of people, you get a wide spread of data which can be **collated** on a **graph**.
2) The scores that occur most often (the **statistically common behaviours**) are defined as **normal**, while **statistically infrequent behaviours** are considered to be **abnormal**:

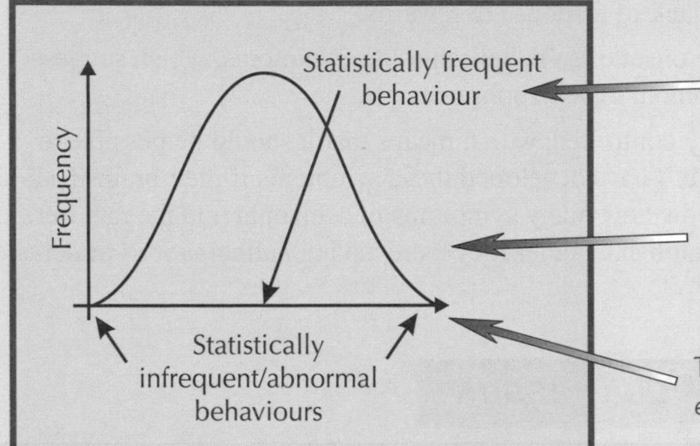

Not all traits show a normal distribution.

People who behave in the 'average' way make up the middle of the bell-shaped curve.

Those people who behave 'abnormally' make up the tail ends of the bell curve — this behaviour is rare (statistically infrequent).

This axis shows a numerical measure of the behaviour, e.g. the number of hand washes per week.

3) This definition of abnormality works well for characteristics which can be **quantified**, e.g. **intelligence**, which has been measured using **IQ tests**. You can then see if someone has an abnormally high or low IQ.

There are *Problems* with this Definition of *Abnormality*

There are **problems** with defining abnormality simply in terms of statistical infrequency:

1) There's **no distinction** between **rare, slightly odd** behaviour and **rare, psychologically abnormal** behaviour.
2) There's **no definite cut-off point** where normal behaviour becomes abnormal behaviour.
3) It doesn't take account of the **desirability of behaviour**, just its frequency. For example, a very high IQ is abnormal, as is a very low one, but having a high IQ is desirable whereas having a low IQ is undesirable.
4) It's difficult to **quantify** something **subjective**, like a person's **mental state**. For example, people might **report** their depressive symptoms differently, or receive different diagnoses depending on the clinician's **opinion**.
5) It can be argued that even something that seems **objective**, like an IQ score, is actually subject to bias. It's just one way to measure intelligence, so it doesn't necessarily define intelligence objectively.
6) Some behaviours that are considered psychologically abnormal are quite common, e.g. mild depression. **Hassett and White (1989)** argue that you cannot use statistical infrequency to define abnormality as it leads to some disorders not being classed as anything unusual.
7) It doesn't take **cultural differences** into account. For example, people from **non-western** cultures might perform less well in an IQ test because they're less familiar with the format. However, this doesn't necessarily mean they're less intelligent.
8) Some behaviours (e.g. having hallucinations) might be **statistically common** in some cultures, but **statistically infrequent** in others. If a person **moves** into a culture where their behaviour is statistically infrequent, they can instantly become '**abnormal**', even though they weren't considered to be before.
9) Definitions of abnormality can **change** over **time**, e.g. homosexuality was classified in the DSM (see p.67) as a **disorder** until 1973. However, the diagnosis was **dropped** because it was found that homosexuality **wasn't** as **infrequent** as previously thought, and that homosexuals don't differ from heterosexuals in terms of **psychological well-being**.

Definitions of Abnormality

Abnormality *Can be Defined as* ***Deviation*** *From* ***Social Norms***

1) Every society has a set of **norms** that it operates by — behaviour that's considered **acceptable** by the majority.
2) According to this definition, people who **deviate** from these norms can be considered **abnormal**.
3) So, abnormality is a **socially constructed label** and people who show 'abnormal' behaviours are usually treated differently, e.g. controlled.
4) Unlike the statistical model, this definition distinguishes between **acceptable** and **unacceptable** behaviour.

Rosenhan and Seligman (1989) outlined **seven** features that indicate abnormal behaviour:

- **Suffering** — for some disorders (e.g. anxiety) the individual reports experiences of suffering and distress.
- **Maladaptiveness** — behaviour that prevents the individual performing tasks and social roles.
- **Vividness and unconventionality** — behaviour that's different to what would be expected in a situation.
- **Unpredictability and loss of control** — behaviour that's uncontrolled, unpredictable and inappropriate.
- **Irrationality and incomprehensibility** — behaviour that doesn't have a rational reason behind it.
- **Observer discomfort** — behaviour that makes other people feel uncomfortable.
- **Violation of moral and ideal standards** — behaviour that doesn't fit in with the morals of society.

There are ***Problems*** *with this Definition of* ***Abnormality***

One of the problems with defining abnormality in terms of social norms is that it relies on **subjective judgement** of a person's behaviour — it **can't** be **quantified** like it can with the statistical infrequency explanation. Whether a behaviour is socially deviant depends on the **context**:

1) **Cultural context** — **Rosenhan and Seligman's** criteria are based on a **Western** view of ideal mental health. For example, in the western world experiencing hallucinations is considered abnormal and can be seen as a symptom of schizophrenia. However, in some countries (e.g. Puerto Rico) hallucinations are often attributed to **external sources** (e.g. visitation by spirits) and aren't seen as abnormal.
2) **Reasonable explanation for the behaviour** — socially deviant behaviour can be **acceptable** if it has a **logical explanation** within a specific context, e.g. it's not 'normal' to climb through the window to get into your house, but it would be socially acceptable if you'd lost your keys.

There are also **ethical problems** with defining abnormality as deviation from social norms. This definition can be used to **justify** the **removal** of **'unwanted'** people from a society.

Practice Questions

Q1 Outline the statistical infrequency definition of abnormality.

Q2 Outline one strength and one weakness of the statistical infrequency definition of abnormality.

Q3 Outline two characteristics from Rosenhan and Seligman's list of seven features to define abnormal behaviour.

Q4 Why is it important to consider cultural context when defining abnormality?

Exam Question

Q1 a) Describe the definition of abnormality as deviation from social norms. [6 marks]

b) Evaluate the statistical definition of abnormality. [6 marks]

Abnormality — a very ordinary stomach...

You've probably been going through life quite happily thinking that abnormality was a pretty easy thing to define. But unfortunately it turns out that it's a bit more scientific than just pointing out weirdos in the street. In fact, some psychologists would actively advise against doing that. And probably many other people too. Bunch of spoilsports that they are...

Schizophrenia

These pages are for AQA, OCR and Edexcel. *A lot of people think that schizophrenia involves having multiple personalities, but it **really really doesn't**, so don't make this mistake in the exam else you'll look like a right plum duff.*

Schizophrenia Disrupts** the **Mind's Ability** to **Function

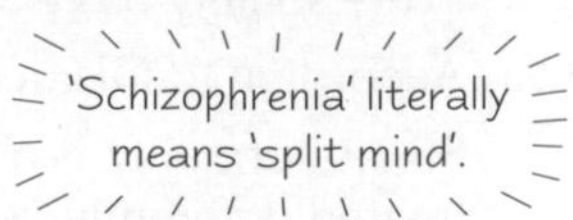
'Schizophrenia' literally means 'split mind'.

1) **Schizophrenia** is a **thought process disorder**. It's characterised by **disruption** to a person's **perceptions**, **emotions** and **beliefs**.
2) The onset of schizophrenia can be **acute** (a **sudden** onset, where behaviour changes within a few days), or **chronic** (a **gradual** deterioration in mental health that develops slowly over time).
3) **Males** and **females** are **equally** affected. In **males** schizophrenia usually develops in their **late teens** or **early 20s**, while **females** tend to develop it 4 or 5 years **later**. Overall, **0.5%** of the population is affected.
4) It's thought that schizophrenia **isn't** a **single disorder** but that there are various **subtypes** — however, there still **isn't** an agreed **definition**.

Schizophrenia** has Lots of Different **Clinical Characteristics

People with schizophrenia can experience a **range** of possible **symptoms**:

1 Perceptual symptoms

- **Auditory hallucinations** — **hearing** things that **aren't there**. People often hear **voices** saying **abusive** or **critical** things.
- Sometimes people **see**, **smell** or **taste** things that aren't there.

2 Social symptoms

- **Social withdrawal** — not **taking part** in or **enjoying** social situations.
- People might be **aloof** or **avoid eye contact.**

3 Cognitive symptoms

- **Delusions** — **believing** things that **aren't true**. People can have **delusions** of **grandeur** (where they believe they're more **important** than they are, e.g. that they're the king) or of **paranoia** and **persecution** (where they believe people are out to **get them**). Some schizophrenics also experience **delusions** of **control** — they believe that their **behaviour** is being **controlled** by **somebody else**.
- **Thought control** — believing that your **thoughts** are being **controlled**. For example, **thought insertion** is when people feel that someone's putting thoughts into their heads. **Withdrawal** is when they believe that someone is **removing** their thoughts. They might also believe that **people** can **read** their thoughts — this is **broadcasting**.
- **Language impairments** — **irrelevant** and **incoherent speech**. People often show signs of **cognitive distractibility**, where they **can't maintain** a **train** of **thought**. They might also **repeat sounds** (**echolalia**), **jumble** their **words** (**word salad**), make **nonsensical rhymes** (**clang associations**) and **invent words** (**neologisms**).

4 Affective / emotional symptoms

- **Depressive symptoms** — a **lack** of **energy** and **interest** in things, especially in **personal care** and **hygiene**.
- **Lack of emotion** — **not reacting** to typically emotional situations. This is also called **emotional blunting**.
- **Inappropriate emotions** — **reacting** in an **inappropriate** way, e.g. laughing at bad news.

5 Behavioural symptoms

- **Stereotyped behaviours** — continuously **repeating** actions, which are often **strange** and **don't** have a **purpose**.
- **Psychomotor disturbance** — **not** having **control** of your **muscles**. People may experience **catatonia**, where they sit in an **awkward position** for a **long time**. In this state people will sometimes **stay** in whatever position they're **put** in (so if you lift their arm over their head it'll stay like that **until** you move it **back**).
- **Catatonic stupor** — lying **rigidly** and **not moving** for **long** periods of **time**. People are **conscious** during these episodes and can **remember** what was going on **around** them, although they **don't** seem **aware** of it at the **time**.

Symptoms** Can be **Categorised** into **Two Types

The **symptoms** of schizophrenia are sometimes categorised as **Type 1** or **Type 2**:

1) **Type 1** symptoms are **positive** symptoms. This is where people **experience** something, feel that something is **happening** to them, or **display** certain **behaviours** — e.g. hallucinations, delusions, jumbled speech.
2) **Type 2** symptoms are **negative** symptoms. This is where people **don't** display 'normal' behaviours — e.g. they're withdrawn, unresponsive and show a lack of emotion.

Schizophrenia

The DSM-IV Classifies Mental Disorders

1) The **DSM-IV** is the fourth edition of the American Psychiatric Association's Diagnostic and Statistical Manual of Mental Disorders.
2) It contains a list of **mental health disorders**. Individuals are rated on **multiple axes** / **dimensions** and diagnostic **categories** are used, e.g. personality disorders and psychosocial problems.
3) It aims to give diagnosis of mental disorders **reliability** and **validity**:

For a person to be diagnosed as schizophrenic, the DSM-IV states that their symptoms must significantly impair reality testing — the ability to function in the real world. The symptoms have to have been present for at least six months.

Reliability

Reliability is how far the classification system produces the **same diagnosis** for a particular set of symptoms. In order for a classification system to be reliable the **same diagnosis** should be made **each time** it's used. This means that **different clinicians** should reach the **same diagnosis**.

Validity

Validity is whether the classification system is actually measuring what it **aims to measure**.

- **Descriptive validity** — how similar individuals diagnosed with the disorder are.
- **Aetiological validity** — how similar the cause of the disorder is for each sufferer.
- **Predictive validity** — how useful the diagnostic categories are for predicting the right treatment.

There can be *Problems* with the *Reliability* and *Validity* of *Diagnoses*

Problems with reliability

1) Schizophrenia diagnosis may be affected by **cultural bias**. For example, **Harrison et al (1984)** showed that there was an **over-diagnosis** of schizophrenia in **West Indian** psychiatric patients in Bristol.
2) No research has found any cause for this, so it suggests that the **symptoms** of **ethnic minority** patients are **misinterpreted**.
3) This questions the **reliability** of the diagnosis of schizophrenia — it suggests that patients can display the **same symptoms** but receive **different diagnoses** because of their ethnic background.

Problems with validity

1) **Rosenhan (1973)** conducted a study where people with no mental health problem got themselves admitted into a **psychiatric unit** by saying they heard voices — they became **pseudopatients** (see p.84 for full details).
2) Once they'd been admitted they behaved 'normally'. However, their behaviour was still seen as a **symptom** of their **disorder** by the staff in the unit. For example, one pseudopatient who wrote in a diary was recorded as displaying 'writing behaviour'.
3) This questions the **validity** of the **diagnosis** of mental disorders — once people are **labelled** as having a disorder, all of their behaviour can be **interpreted** as being **caused** by the **disorder**.

Practice Questions

Q1 What are the differences between positive and negative symptoms of schizophrenia?

Q2 What is the DSM-IV?

Q3 Outline one problem with the reliability of the diagnosis of schizophrenia.

Exam Question

Q1 Outline the clinical characteristics of schizophrenia. [6 marks]

Word salad — like crunchy alphabet spaghetti...

Like so many things in psychology, schizophrenia is incredibly hard to define. People can show a variety of symptoms, which can be classified in different ways. Learning this is a bit of a pain now, but at least it means you should have loads to say in the exam, and you can't really ask for more than that. Well, apart from a holiday in the Caribbean, private jet, yacht...

Explanations of Schizophrenia

AQA, OCR and Edexcel — jump on board. Different people have different ideas about what causes schizophrenia. This was mostly a sneaky little ploy dreamt up by psychologists and examiners to make your revision harder.

Schizophrenia Could be Caused by Biological Factors

Concordance rates are the chance that someone will develop a disorder if they're related to someone who has it.

1) Genetic Factors (Inherited Tendencies)

Being **genetically related** to someone with schizophrenia can significantly **increase** a person's **chances** of developing it. **Family** and **twin** studies have looked at **concordance rates:**

Gottesman (1991) reviewed about 40 twin studies and found that with **identical** (**MZ**) **twins** there was about a **48%** chance of **both** being schizophrenic. With **non-identical** (**DZ**) **twins** there was about a **17%** chance.

Evidence for...

1) **Shields (1962)** found that **MZ twins** raised in **different families** still showed around **50%** concordance.
2) **Adoption studies** have found that when children are **adopted** because one or both of their **biological parents** has schizophrenia, the **chance** of them developing it is still the **same**. This suggests that **genetics** are more significant than the **environment**.

Evidence against...

1) No study has found a **100%** concordance rate, so schizophrenia **can't** just be caused by **genes**. **Shared environment** may cause higher concordance rates in **family** studies because children **imitate** 'schizophrenic' **behaviours** from their relatives.
2) This means **other factors** need to be considered, e.g. biochemical or psychological factors.

2) Biochemical Factors

Post-mortems and **PET scans** have shown that schizophrenics have abnormally high levels of the neurotransmitter **dopamine**. These findings led to the development of the **dopamine hypothesis**, which states that **synapses** that use **dopamine** as a **neurotransmitter** are **overactive** in the brains of people with schizophrenia.

Evidence for...

1) **Antipsychotic** drugs **reduce** the **symptoms** of schizophrenia by **blocking** dopamine receptors. This suggests that it's the **overactive** dopamine receptors **causing** the symptoms.
2) Drugs like **amphetamines**, which **increase dopamine function**, can sometimes cause **schizophrenia-like** symptoms in people without schizophrenia.

Evidence against...

1) **Antipsychotic** drugs only work on the **positive symptoms** of schizophrenia, e.g. hallucinations. This means that increased dopamine function **doesn't** explain **negative symptoms** like social withdrawal.
2) The **link** with dopamine is **correlational**, so it doesn't show **cause and effect**. It may be that increased dopamine function is a **symptom** of schizophrenia, rather than a cause of it.

3) Neurological Factors

Abnormal brain structure, caused by **abnormal development**, could be the cause of schizophrenia.

Evidence for...

1) **Johnstone et al (1976)** compared the **size** of the **ventricles** (hollow areas) in schizophrenics' brains with non-schizophrenics' brains. They found that the people with schizophrenia had **enlarged ventricles**, which suggests that **schizophrenia** is **linked** to a **loss** of **brain tissue**.
2) **Buchsbaum (1990)** carried out **MRI scans** on schizophrenics' brains and found **abnormalities** in the **prefrontal cortex**.

Evidence against...

1) **Non-schizophrenics** can also have **enlarged ventricles**, which goes against **Johnstone's** evidence.
2) These findings are **correlational**, so they don't show **cause and effect**. It may be that abnormal brain structure is a **symptom** of schizophrenia, rather than a cause of it.

Explanations of Schizophrenia

Schizophrenia *Could be Caused by* ***Psychological Factors***

1 ***Behavioural*** *Factors*

Behaviourists argue that schizophrenia is **learnt** through **operant conditioning**. Someone may do something that gets a **positive reaction** or **reward** from others. This **encourages** the person to **repeat** the behaviour — it **reinforces** it.

Evidence for...	**Token economies**, which use **reinforcement** to encourage **'normal' behaviours**, can help **treat** schizophrenia (see next page). This suggests that some of the behaviour could be **learnt**.
Evidence against...	**Biological and psychological research** suggests that schizophrenia **isn't** just a **learnt behaviour**.

2 ***Psychodynamic*** *Theory*

Freud claimed that schizophrenia is caused by over-whelming **anxiety**. It's a **defence mechanism** involving **regression** into an **early stage** of **development**. **Hallucinations** are the **ego's** attempt to **restore contact** with **reality**.

Evidence for... **Laing (1967)** also argued that schizophrenics **lose contact** with **reality** as a way of **coping** with **social pressure**. He claimed that it was wrong to encourage schizophrenics to conform.

Evidence against... There **isn't** any **research evidence** to **support** Freud's theory. **Psychoanalysis isn't an effective treatment**, which suggests that psychodynamic theory **doesn't** explain what **causes** schizophrenia.

3 ***Socio-cultural*** *Factors*

The **social causation hypothesis** states that people with **low social status** are more likely to suffer from schizophrenia than people with higher social status. It's thought that factors like **poverty** and **discrimination** cause **high stress levels**, and that this can cause schizophrenia.

Evidence for...

Harrison et al (2001) found that people who were born in **deprived areas** were more likely to develop schizophrenia. This suggests that factors like **poverty**, **unemployment** and **crowding** have an **impact** on schizophrenia.

Evidence against...

These results are **correlational**, so they **don't** show **cause and effect**. The **social drift hypothesis** suggests that there are more people with schizophrenia in deprived areas because having schizophrenia gives them a **lower social status**, e.g. because they might be unemployed.

4 ***Cognitive*** *Factors*

Cognitive psychologists argue that schizophrenia is caused by **faulty information processing**. This leads to **delusions**, **thought interference**, **language impairment** and **memory problems**.

Evidence for...	**Neufeld (1978)** compared the cognitive processes of people with schizophrenia with a **control** group. The participants with schizophrenia took **longer** to **encode stimuli** and showed **short-term memory problems**. This suggests that their ability to process information was impaired.
Evidence against...	**Biochemical** research suggests that **cognitive** problems are **caused** by **increased dopamine function**, rather than faulty information processing.

Practice Questions

Q1 Outline the role that biochemical factors might have in causing schizophrenia.

Q2 Outline the socio-cultural factors that could explain schizophrenia.

Exam Question

Q1 Describe and evaluate explanations of schizophrenia [25 marks]

Explain schizophrenia — I can barely even spell it...

So there isn't just one definite idea about what causes schizophrenia — surprise surprise. At least these pages are quite useful though. When you're evaluating one explanation of schizophrenia, you can use all the other explanations as evidence against it — so you could use the evidence for social theory as evidence against genetic factors, or whatever. Not bad eh?

Treating Schizophrenia

This is for AQA, OCR and Edexcel. There are different treatments for schizophrenia, but most people benefit from a combination of a few of them. After all, why just have one when you can have them all — the more the merrier I say...

Schizophrenia Can be Treated Using Biological Therapy

Therapy using drugs is also called chemotherapy.

1) The **biological** approach to treating schizophrenia involves **drug therapy**.
2) Treatment is based on the **dopamine hypothesis** (p.68) — the theory that schizophrenia is linked to increased dopamine activity in the brain. **Antipsychotic drugs** (**neuroleptics**) work by **blocking dopamine receptors**.

Advantages

- Drug therapy is effective at reducing **positive symptoms**, e.g. hallucinations.
- It's **successful** for a large number of schizophrenia patients, meaning that more people can live in the **community** rather than being institutionalised.
- It's the most **widely-used** and **effective** form of treatment for schizophrenia. Almost all other treatments are used **alongside** drug therapy.

When you're evaluating a treatment for schizophrenia, you can use the advantages of another treatment as a disadvantage of the one you're evaluating.

Disadvantages

- Drug therapy **isn't** very effective for treating **negative symptoms** like social withdrawal.
- It treats the **symptoms** of schizophrenia but **not** the **cause**. Symptoms often **come back** if people stop taking antipsychotic drugs. This leads to the '**revolving door phenomenon**', where patients are constantly being discharged and re-admitted to hospital.
- There are **ethical issues** surrounding the use of drug therapy. Some people argue that drug treatment is a '**chemical straitjacket**' — it **doesn't** really **help** the patient, it just **controls** their **behaviour** to make it more socially acceptable and easier to manage.
- Most people will experience some **short-term side effects** when taking antipsychotic drugs, e.g. drowsiness, blurred vision, dry mouth, constipation and weight gain.
- **Long-term side effects** include increased risk of **diabetes** and **tardive dyskinesia** (involuntary repetitive movements that continue even after they've stopped taking the medication).
- **Clinical trials** have shown that as many as **two-thirds** of people stop taking antipsychotic drugs because of the side-effects. However, **newer** antipsychotic drugs seem to have **fewer long-term side effects** than the **older** ones.

Schizophrenia Can be Treated Using Psychological Therapies

1) Behavioural Therapy

1) **Behavioural** treatment for schizophrenia is based on **operant conditioning** — learning through **reinforcement**.
2) **Token economies** can help encourage people in **psychiatric institutions** to perform **socially desirable behaviours**, e.g. getting dressed and making their beds. Patients are given **tokens** which reinforce these behaviours — they can then **exchange** these for something they want, like sweets or cigarettes.

Advantages

- Token economy programmes can produce **significant improvements** in **self care** and **desirable behaviour**, even with **chronic institutionalised schizophrenics**.
- For example, **Ayllon and Azrin (1968)** set up a token economy with schizophrenic patients in a **psychiatric institution**. They found that the amount of socially desirable behaviour **increased** — patients went from performing an average of **5** chores a day to around **40**.

Disadvantages

- Token economies don't have high **ecological validity** — they don't **transfer** into the **real world**. Once people are away from institutions they often don't continue showing desirable behaviour, because there's **nothing** to **reinforce** it.
- The patients' behaviour might be **superficial** — they might only produce desirable behaviour if they're going to receive a token.
- There are **ethical issues** surrounding the use of **behavioural therapy**. It could be argued that it **doesn't** really **help** the patient, it just makes their behaviour more acceptable to other people.

Treating Schizophrenia

2 Cognitive Behavioural Therapy

1) Cognitive behavioural therapy (CBT) is based on the assumption that patients can be helped by **identifying** and **changing** their '**faulty cognitions**'.
2) Schizophrenic patients are encouraged to **reality-test** their **hallucinations** and **delusions**, e.g. to question and try to control the voices they hear.
3) They do **role-play exercises** and **homework** to test out their 'faulty thinking' and are helped to see the **consequences** of thinking differently. Through this they can gradually realise where the 'faults' in their thought patterns are, and can begin to change them.

Advantages

- **Sensky et al (2000)** found that CBT was **effective** in treating schizophrenic patients who **hadn't responded** to **drug treatment**. It was helpful with **positive** and **negative** symptoms, and patients **continued** to **improve** 9 months after treatment had ended.
- CBT puts patients **in charge** of their own treatment by teaching them **self-help strategies**. This means there are **fewer ethical issues** than with other therapies (e.g. drug therapy).

Disadvantages

- CBT only treats the **symptoms** of schizophrenia — it **doesn't address** the **cause** of the disorder.
- It's difficult to **measure** the effectiveness of CBT because it relies on **self-report** from the patient, and the **therapist's opinions**. This makes it **less objective**.
- Patients can become **dependent** on their therapist.

3 Psychotherapy

1) Psychotherapy aims to identify the **underlying cause** of the mental disorder.
2) This is done using different therapeutic techniques, e.g. **dream analysis** and **free association**.
3) When the **unconscious conflicts** that are causing the problems are made **conscious**, the therapist and patient can discuss and try to resolve them. This will hopefully lead to the disorder being cured.

Advantages

- It aims to treat the **cause** of the disorder, not just the **symptoms**.
- Patients have **more control** over their treatment than with other therapies, e.g. drug therapy.

Disadvantages

- **Other forms** of treatment (e.g. CBT) have been found to be more **effective**.
- It's **difficult to prove** the effectiveness of psychotherapy — it's based on **subjective data** and the **unconscious mind**. There's also a risk that patients will develop **false memories**, e.g. of childhood abuse.

Practice Questions

Q1 Outline some disadvantages of drug therapy in the treatment of schizophrenia.

Q2 How can token economies benefit schizophrenia patients?

Q3 Outline one advantage of CBT in the treatment of schizophrenia.

Exam Question

Q1 Describe and evaluate treatments of schizophrenia. [25 marks]

Chemical straitjackets — might be a bit itchy...

Well, at least after reading about all the things that can go wrong with your brain it's nice to know there are some treatments. Not as nice as walks in the rain or cuddles or pink wafers, no, but quite nice all the same. I'd love a cuddle right about now. If you're in a similar predicament then take a moment to hold this book close to you and have a little snuggle. Ahh...

Depression

AQA, OCR and Edexcel here. Everyone feels sad sometimes — it can be because a bad thing happens, or just be something that you can't quite put your finger on. It's only a problem when these feelings won't go away.

Depression is a Mood Disorder

Mood disorders are characterised by **strong emotions**, which can influence a person's ability to **function normally**. A mood disorder can affect a person's **perceptions**, **thinking** and **behaviour**. **Depression** is one of the most **common** mood disorders. There are many types, including:

1) **Major depression** (**unipolar disorder**) — an **episode** of depression that can occur **suddenly**.

- Major depression can be **reactive** — caused by **external factors**, e.g. the death of a loved one.
- Or, it can be **endogenous** — caused by **internal factors**, e.g. neurological factors.

2) **Manic depression** (**bipolar disorder**) — **alternation** between two **mood extremes** (**mania** and **depression**).

- The change in mood often occurs in regular **cycles** of days or weeks.
- Episodes of **mania** involve **over-activity**, **rapid speech** and feeling extremely **happy** or **agitated**.
- Episodes of **depression** involve the symptoms covered below.

Depression has Lots of Clinical Characteristics

People with depression can experience a **range** of possible **symptoms**:

Physical / behavioural symptoms
- **Sleep disturbances** — **insomnia** (being unable to sleep) or **hypersomnia** (sleeping a lot more than usual).
- Change in **appetite** — people may eat **more** or **less** than **usual**, and gain or lose **weight**.
- **Pain** — especially **headaches**, **joint ache** and **muscle ache**.

Affective / emotional symptoms
- Extreme feelings of **sadness**, **hopelessness** and **despair**.
- **Diurnal mood variation** — changes in mood throughout the day, e.g. feeling worse in the morning.
- **Anhedonia** — no longer **enjoying** activities or hobbies that **used** to be **pleasurable**.

Cognitive symptoms
- Experiencing persistent **negative beliefs** about **themselves** and their **abilities**.
- **Suicidal** thoughts.
- **Slower** thought processes — **difficulty concentrating** and **making decisions**.

Social / motivational symptoms
- Lack of **activity** — **social withdrawal** and loss of **sex drive**.

The DSM-IV Classifies Mental Disorders

The **DSM-IV** is the fourth edition of the American Psychiatric Association's Diagnostic and Statistical Manual of Mental Disorders. It contains a list of **mental health disorders**. Individuals are rated on **multiple axes / dimensions** and diagnostic **categories** are used, e.g. personality disorders and psychosocial problems. It aims to give diagnosis of mental disorders **reliability** and **validity**:

Reliability

Reliability is how far the classification system produces the **same diagnosis** for a particular set of symptoms. In order for a classification system to be reliable the **same diagnosis** should be made **each time** it's used. This means that **different clinicians** should reach the **same diagnosis**.

Validity

Validity is whether the classification system is actually measuring what it **aims to measure.**
- **Descriptive validity** — how similar individuals diagnosed with the disorder are.
- **Aetiological validity** — how similar the cause of the disorder is for each sufferer.
- **Predictive validity** — how useful the diagnostic categories are for predicting the right treatment.

Depression

There can be Problems with the Reliability of Diagnoses

1) For a person to be diagnosed with **major depression**, the DSM-IV states that at least **five symptoms** must have been present nearly every day for at least **two weeks**.
2) However, the diagnosis of depression isn't always **reliable** — people displaying the **same symptoms** don't always get the **same diagnosis**.
3) Also, women are **twice as likely** to be diagnosed with depression than men:

Both Dr. Jim and Dr. Bob would defend their diagnoses to the death.

- There don't seem to be any clear reasons for why **women** would be **more likely** to suffer from depression than **men**.
- Some researchers have claimed that it's to do with **hormonal differences** between men and women. Others have said it's because of **socio-cultural** factors — the different ways that males and females are **socialised** means they react differently to stressful life events.
- However, it could be that clinicians **expect** more women to suffer from depression than men, so are more likely to diagnose a **woman** with depression than a **man** who displays the **same symptoms**.

There Can be Problems With the Validity of Diagnoses

Rosenhan (1973) conducted a classic study that questioned the **validity** of the diagnosis of mental disorders (see p.84 for the full study). He believed that psychiatrists **couldn't tell the difference** between **sane** people and people with **mental disorders**.

1) People who didn't have any kind of mental health problem got themselves admitted into a **psychiatric unit** by claiming they heard voices — they became **pseudopatients**.
2) Once they'd been admitted they behaved 'normally'. However, their behaviour was still seen as a **symptom** of their **disorder** by the staff in the unit. For example, one pseudopatient who wrote in a diary was recorded as displaying 'writing behaviour'.
3) This questions the **validity** of the **diagnosis** of mental disorders — once people are **labelled** as having a disorder, all of their behaviour can be **interpreted** as being **caused** by the **disorder**.

Practice Questions

Q1 What's the difference between major depression and manic depression?

Q2 What is anhedonia?

Q3 Outline the cognitive symptoms of depression.

Q4 What is the DSM-IV?

Q5 What does validity mean in terms of the diagnosis of mental disorders?

Q6 Outline a study that demonstrates problems with the validity of diagnoses.

Exam Questions

Q1 Outline the clinical characteristics of depression. [10 marks]

Q2 Discuss issues surrounding the classification and diagnosis of disorders. [25 marks]

I've got reactive depression just from reading this...

Yes, these pages are a touch on the gloomy side, but depression affects a lot of people, so it's really worth knowing about. And it's also in the exam... Make sure you can describe the different types of depression, outline the major symptoms, say what the DSM-IV is and have a bit of a chat about reliability and validity. By then you'll have probably cheered right up...

Explanations of Depression

AQA, OCR and Edexcel. These pages cover the possible causes of depression. And no, having to spend all your time revising won't go down well with the examiners as a valid cause of depression. It'll get you neither marks nor sympathy.

Depression Could be Caused by Biological Factors

1) Genetic Factors (Inherited Tendencies)

Being **biologically related** to someone who has depression seems to **increase** a person's **chance** of developing it.

Evidence for...

1) **McGuffin et al (1996)** found that if one **identical (MZ) twin** has **major depressive disorder**, then in about **46%** of cases their **twin** is **also** diagnosed with it. For **non-identical (DZ) twins** the **concordance rate** is about **20%**.
2) **Wender et al (1986)** studied the **biological parents** of **adopted** children who had **major depressive disorder**. The **biological** parents were **8 times** more likely to have depression than the children's **adoptive** parents.

Evidence against...

1) The **concordance rates** found in **family** and **twin** studies **aren't 100%**, so **genetics** can't be the whole story. **Environmental factors** could also play a role.
2) Genetic factors only seem to explain **endogenous depression** (depression caused by internal factors) — **psychological** factors seem to have more **influence** in the development of **reactive depression**.

2) Biochemical Factors

Low levels of **serotonin** have been linked to depression. **Kety (1975)** developed the **permissive amine theory**, which states that **serotonin** controls the **levels** of the neurotransmitter **noradrenaline**. A **low level** of **serotonin** causes the level of **noradrenaline** to **fluctuate** — **low** levels of **noradrenaline** then cause **depression**, while **high** levels cause **mania**.

Evidence for...

1) **Anti-depressant** drugs work by **increasing** the **availability** of **serotonin** at the synapses by preventing its reuptake or breakdown. This suggests that it's the **low levels** of serotonin that **lead** to **depressive disorders**.
2) **Post-mortems** carried out on people who committed **suicide** have shown abnormally **low levels** of **serotonin**, suggesting that this may have **caused** their depression.

Evidence against...

1) Just because **anti-depressants** relieve the **symptoms**, it **doesn't** mean they treat the **cause**.
2) Low levels of serotonin could be a **result** of depression, not the cause.
3) **Psychological** research has found **alternative explanations** for the cause of depression.

Depression Could be Caused by Psychological Factors

1) Socio-cultural Factors

Social psychologists focus on how depression can be **triggered** by something **external**, e.g. a bereavement or divorce.

Evidence for...

Brown and Harris (1978) studied depression by **interviewing** housewives in London. They found that **61%** of the subjects **with depression** had recently experienced a **stressful life event**, compared with only **19%** of the **non-depressed** subjects. Of the subjects who had experienced a stressful event but had a **close friend**, only **10%** had depression. This can be compared with the **37%** of depressed subjects who **didn't** have a **close friend**. These results suggest that **depression** is **influenced** by **stressful life events** and a **lack** of **emotional support**.

Evidence against...

1) Brown and Harris's study just shows a **correlation**, so you can't prove **cause and effect**. It could actually be that depression makes some stressful life events **more likely** to happen, e.g. someone might be more likely to lose their job or get divorced as a result of their depression.
2) The effect of social factors **doesn't** explain why some people experience **endogenous depression** (sudden depression that occurs because of internal factors). Other approaches might have better explanations.

Explanations of Depression

2) **Behavioural** Factors

Behaviourists reckon that depression develops when **stressors** (e.g. death of a loved one or being made redundant) lead to a **lack** of **positive reinforcement**. The attention that depressive behaviour then draws (e.g. sympathy from others) can then provide **positive reinforcement**, meaning the person **learns** to continue being depressed. It may also be influenced by **learned helplessness**. This occurs when people **learn not to try** because they believe they'll **never succeed**.

Evidence for...

Seligman (1975) restrained dogs so that they **couldn't avoid** receiving **electric shocks**. Later when they **could** actually avoid the shocks they **didn't** even **try** — they displayed **learned helplessness**. This can be **generalised** to humans — when people **aren't** in **control** of **stressful events** they eventually **learn not to try** and improve them, causing them to become **depressed**.

See p.200 for more on Seligman's study.

Evidence against...

Behaviourist theory **ignores** the influence of **biological** factors. It also only explains **reactive depression** (depression caused by external events). It may be that biological factors are responsible for causing **endogenous depression.**

3) **Cognitive** Factors

Abramson et al (1978) developed **Seligman's (1975)** theory of **learned helplessness** into a **cognitive theory**.
They looked at people's **thought processes** in response to **failure** and stated that failure can be interpreted as:

1) **Internal** (the person's fault) or **external** (caused by something else).
2) **Global** (applies to all situations) or **specific** (just applies to this situation).
3) **Stable** (likely to continue) or **unstable** (could easily change).

Depressed people may see failure as **internal**, **global** and **stable** (it's their fault, happens in all situations and won't change).

This is just one example of a model of faulty cognitions — there are other models (see page 77).

Evidence for...

Beck et al (1979) found that depressed people had **negative** thought processes — they **exaggerated** their **weaknesses** and **played down** their **strengths.**

Evidence against...

This is just a **correlation** — it doesn't prove cause and effect. It may be that **negative thinking** is actually the **result** of depression, **not the cause** of it. Instead, **biological** or other **psychological** factors could be the cause.

4) **Psychodynamic** Theory

Freud claimed that if a child feels **unloved** by its **parents** it becomes **angry**. This creates **guilt**, so the anger is **redirected** towards the **self**. These feelings are **repressed**, but may later **return** following a **stressful life event**, causing **depression**.

Evidence for...

Brown and Harris (1978) found that the women they interviewed were **more likely** to have depression if they experienced **disrupted** childhood attachments, especially if their **mother** had **died.**

Evidence against...

There **isn't** any **research evidence** to **support** Freud's theory, so it's **unfalsifiable** (impossible to prove right or wrong). It also **ignores** the significance of **other factors** in causing depression, e.g. biological factors.

Practice Questions

Q1 Outline research evidence that supports the theory that genetic factors can cause depression.
Q2 Outline the role that serotonin might have in causing depression.
Q3 What evidence is there to suggest that depression is caused by stressful life events?

Exam Questions

Q1 Outline biological explanations for depression. [10 marks]

Q2 Describe and evaluate a psychological explanation for depression. [12 marks]

Genes can make you depressed — especially if the fly comes undone...

It's the usual drill here — learn an explanation of depression, then learn another one so you can use it to tear the first one apart. It's a wonder the psychologists who come up with these theories don't get more depressed themselves. You'd think having thousands of A-level students telling them they're wrong would upset them a bit. But no, they're as happy as Larry.

Treating Depression

This is for AQA, OCR and Edexcel. *Depression is horrible, so you'll be pleased to know that there are loads of treatments available for it. You may be less pleased to know that you have to learn them all, but try to keep your chin up.*

Depression Can be **Treated** Using **Biological Therapy**

Therapy using drugs is also called chemotherapy.

1) The **biological** approach to treating depression involves **drug therapy**.
2) Treatment is based on altering the levels of **serotonin** and **noradrenaline** in the brain. These **neurotransmitters** regulate things like emotions, sleep patterns, sex drive and reaction to stress.
3) There are **four** main types of antidepressant drugs:

- **Selective serotonin reuptake inhibitors (SSRIs)** increase the availability of **serotonin** by preventing its reuptake.
- **Tricyclic antidepressants (TCAs)** increase the availability of **serotonin** and **noradrenaline** by preventing their reuptake.
- **Monoamine oxidase inhibitors (MAOIs)** increase the availability of **serotonin** and **noradrenaline** by preventing their breakdown.
- **Serotonin and noradrenaline reuptake inhibitors** (**SNRIs**) prevent the reuptake of **serotonin** and **noradrenaline**, so increase their availability.

Ashley and George's sleep patterns were perfectly in sync.

Advantages

- Studies have shown that antidepressants are successful in **reducing** the **symptoms** of depression for **more than half** of patients.
- It's the most **widely-used** and **effective** form of treatment for depression. Psychological treatments are often used **alongside** drug therapy because antidepressants can remove some of the **symptoms**, allowing **other therapies** to focus on the **cause** of the depression.

Disadvantages

- Antidepressants only treat the **symptoms** of depression. **Other therapies** are needed to try and tackle the **cause** of it.
- There are **ethical issues** surrounding the use of drug therapy. Some people argue that drug treatment is a '**chemical straitjacket**' — it **doesn't** really **help** the patient, it just **controls** their **behaviour** to make it more socially acceptable and easier to manage.
- Antidepressants can have **side effects**, e.g. drowsiness, dry mouth, indigestion and nausea.

Depression Can be **Treated** using **Psychological Therapies**

1 Psychotherapy

1) Psychotherapy aims to identify the **underlying cause** of the mental disorder.
2) This is done using different therapeutic techniques, e.g. **dream analysis** and **free association**.
3) When the **unconscious conflicts** that are causing the problems are made **conscious**, the therapist and patient can discuss and try to resolve them. This will hopefully lead to the disorder being cured.

Advantages

- It aims to treat the **cause** of the disorder, not just the **symptoms**.
- Patients have **more control** over their treatment than with other therapies, e.g. drug therapy.

Disadvantages

- Psychotherapy can be **distressing** for people because they're encouraged to **recall traumatic events**. This can sometimes be more difficult to deal with than the original symptoms.
- It's **difficult to prove** the effectiveness of psychotherapy because it's based on **subjective data** and the **unconscious mind**. There's also a risk that patients will develop **false memories**.
- **Other forms** of treatment, e.g. cognitive behavioural therapies (see opposite page) and drug therapy have been found to be **more effective**.

Treating Depression

2 Cognitive Behavioural Therapies

There are several models that explain how **faulty cognitions** can lead to depression. For example:

Ellis (1962) — The **ABC model** claims that disorders begin with an **activating event (A)** (e.g. a failed exam), leading to a **belief (B)** about why this happened. This may be rational (e.g. 'I didn't prepare well enough'), or irrational (e.g. 'I'm too stupid to pass exams'). The belief leads to a **consequence (C)**. Rational beliefs produce adaptive (appropriate) consequences (e.g. more revision). Irrational beliefs produce maladaptive (bad and inappropriate) consequences (e.g. getting depressed).

Beck (1963) — Beck identified a **cognitive triad** of negative, automatic thoughts linked to **depression**: negative views about **themselves** (e.g. that they can't succeed at anything), about the **world** (e.g. that they must be successful to be a good person) and about the **future** (e.g. that nothing will change).

Cognitive behavioural therapy (CBT) aims to **identify** and **change** the patient's **faulty cognitions**.
This is generally what happens during CBT:

1) The therapist and client **identify** the client's **faulty cognitions**.
2) Therapists sometimes encourage their clients to keep a **diary** so they can record their thought patterns, feelings and actions.
3) The therapist tries to show that the cognitions **aren't true**, e.g. the client doesn't always fail at what they do.
4) Together, they set **goals** to think in more positive or adaptive ways, e.g. focusing on things the client has succeeded at and trying to build on them.
5) Although the client may occasionally need to look back to past experiences, the treatment mainly focuses on the **present situation**.

Advantages of CBT

- **Brandsma et al (1978)** found that **CBT** is particularly effective for people who put a lot of **pressure** on themselves and feel **guilty** about being **inadequate**.
- CBT **empowers** patients — it puts them in charge of their own treatment by teaching them **self-help strategies**. This means there are **fewer ethical issues** than with other therapies like drug therapy.

Disadvantages of CBT

- Faulty cognitions might be the **consequence** of a disorder rather than its cause. For example, depression may be caused by a chemical imbalance in the brain, which causes people to think very negatively.
- Cognitive therapies may take a long **time** and may be more effective when **combined** with other approaches, e.g. drug therapy.

Practice Questions

Q1 Outline the biological approach to the treatment of depression.
Q2 Give one advantage of drug therapy in the treatment of depression.
Q3 Outline what happens in cognitive behavioural therapy.

Exam Questions

Q1 Describe one approach to the treatment of depression. [10 marks]

Q2 Evaluate one approach to the treatment of depression. [12 marks]

This depression stuff is really getting me down...

...but not to worry, these are the last two pages on depression. And they are all about treatment — which is surely the least depressing aspect of depression. Anyway, best learn these pages pretty sharpish, before you sink into a murky mire of miserableness. Then you can move on to the much more cheerful topic of... anxiety disorders. Well, it's a bit more cheerful...

Anxiety Disorders — Phobias

Everyone's in again here. Anxiety isn't always a big problem — it can help get you motivated to make sure you perform your best. It's only when you start feeling anxious all the time, or about slightly odd things, that it becomes a disorder.

A Phobia is an Irrational Fear

A phobia is an **extreme**, **irrational fear** of a particular **object** or **situation**.
There are **three** types of phobia classified by the **DSM-IV**:

1 Specific phobias

This is a fear of specific **objects** or **situations**. There are **five** subtypes:

1) **Animal** type (also called **zoophobia**, e.g. fear of spiders)
2) **Environmental dangers** type (e.g. fear of water)
3) **Blood-injection-injury** type (e.g. fear of needles)
4) **Situational** type (e.g. fear of enclosed spaces or heights)
5) **'Other'** (any phobia that isn't covered in the categories above)

2 Social phobia

This is the fear of **being in social situations** (e.g. eating in public or talking in front of a group of people). It's usually down to the possibility of being **judged** or being **embarrassed**.

3 Agoraphobia

1) This is a fear of **open spaces**.
2) It's specifically linked to the **fear** of having a **panic attack** in a public place and **not** being able to **get away**.
3) It often develops as a **result** of **other phobias**, because the sufferer's afraid that they'll come across the **source** of their **fear** if they leave the house.

Phobias have Several Clinical Characteristics

The different types of phobia all have very **similar** clinical characteristics.

Cognitive symptoms	**Irrational beliefs** about the **stimulus** that causes fear. People often find it **hard** to **concentrate** because they're **preoccupied** by **anxious thoughts**.
Social symptoms	**Avoiding** social situations because they cause **anxiety**. This happens especially if someone has **social phobia** or **agoraphobia**.
Behavioural symptoms	Altering behaviour to **avoid** the feared object or situation, and trying to **escape** if it's encountered. People are often generally **restless** and **easily startled**.
Physical symptoms	Activation of the **fight or flight** response when the feared object or situation is encountered or thought about. This involves release of **adrenaline**, **increased heart rate** and **breathing**, and **muscle tension**.
Emotional symptoms	**Anxiety** and a feeling of **dread**.

There are Various Diagnostic Criteria for Phobias

The **DSM-IV** (see next page) classifies a fear as a phobia if you can put a tick next to these criteria:

1) There's **significant prolonged fear** of an object or situation.
2) People experience an **anxiety response** (e.g. increased heart rate) if they're exposed to the phobic stimulus.
3) Sufferers **realise** that their phobia is **irrational** and **out of proportion** to any actual danger. They may try to **hide** their phobia from other people, which can cause more anxiety.
4) Sufferers go out of their way to **avoid** the phobic stimulus.
5) The phobia **disrupts** their **lives**, e.g. they avoid social situations.

Sophie did everything she could to hide her parrotophobia.

Anxiety Disorders — Phobias

*The **DSM-IV** Classifies Mental Disorders*

Dr. Bale could pretend to read the DSM-IV all he liked — everyone knew he kept a comic inside it.

1) The **DSM-IV** is the fourth edition of the American Psychiatric Association's Diagnostic and Statistical Manual of Mental Disorders.
2) It contains a list of **mental health disorders**. Individuals are rated on **multiple axes / dimensions** and diagnostic **categories** are used, e.g. personality disorders and psychosocial problems.
3) It aims to give diagnosis of mental disorders **reliability** and **validity**:

Reliability

Reliability is how far the classification system produces the **same diagnosis** for a particular set of symptoms. In order for a classification system to be reliable the **same diagnosis** should be made **each time** it's used. This means that **different clinicians** should reach the **same diagnosis**.

Validity

Validity is whether the classification system is actually measuring what it **aims to measure**.
- **Descriptive validity** — how similar individuals diagnosed with the disorder are.
- **Aetiological validity** — how similar the cause of the disorder is for each sufferer.
- **Predictive validity** — how useful the diagnostic categories are for predicting the right treatment.

*There can be **Problems** with the **Validity** and **Reliability** of **Diagnoses***

Problems with validity

1) **Rosenhan (1973)** conducted a study where people who didn't have any kind of mental health problem got themselves admitted into a **psychiatric unit** — they became **pseudopatients** (see p.84 for the full details).
2) Once they'd been admitted they behaved 'normally'. However, their behaviour was still seen as a **symptom** of their **disorder** by the staff in the unit. For example, one pseudopatient who wrote in a diary was recorded as displaying 'writing behaviour'.
3) This questions the **validity** of the **diagnosis** of mental disorders — once people are **labelled** as having a disorder, all of their behaviour can be **interpreted** as being **caused** by the **disorder**.

Problems with reliability

1) Clinicians can show **bias** when they're diagnosing mental disorders.
2) For example, **Johnstone (1989)** found that patients from **lower social classes** tended to be given more **serious diagnoses** than patients from **higher social classes**.
3) This questions the **reliability** of the diagnosis of mental disorders — it suggests that patients can display the **same symptoms** but receive **different diagnoses** because of their social background.

Practice Questions

Q1 What are the five subtypes of specific phobias?

Q2 List some of the physical symptoms of phobias.

Q3 Outline a study that demonstrates problems with the validity of diagnoses.

Exam Question

Q1 Outline the clinical characteristics of phobias. [10 marks]

Keep calm keep calm keep calm keep calm keep calm keep calm...

These pages don't exactly make for relaxing bedtime reading do they — anyone else got a sweat on? On a lighter note, writing out 'keep calm' so many times has meant I've got that weird thing where the words have lost all their meaning and look really strange. It looks more like 'keep clam' now, which I suppose is actually quite sound advice...

Explanations of Phobias

AQA, OCR and Edexcel here. *There are lots of possible causes of phobias, and they won't learn themselves...*

Phobias *Could be Caused by* *Biological Factors...*

1 *Genetic Factors (Inherited Tendencies)*

1) Some phobias are much more **common** than others, and many of these are of things that can be **dangerous** to humans, e.g. snakes, spiders, heights.
2) This suggests that humans have **evolved** a **genetic predisposition** to fear these things because it has **survival value**. This is **preparedness theory**.
3) The assumption is that phobias have a **genetic** cause, so they should run in families, or be shared by identical twins who will have the same genes.

Mark's fear of heights was manageable, as long as Julie kept holding the bridge up.

Evidence for... Using a family interview method, **Reich and Yates (1988)** found a **higher** rate of social phobias amongst **relatives** than other disorders. **6.6%** of those with phobias had a relative with it too, compared to **0.4%** of those with panic disorders.

Evidence against... **Torgerson (1983)** found that identical (MZ) twins **don't** always share phobias. This suggests that **other factors** are also involved in causing phobias, e.g. psychological factors.

2 *Neurological Factors*

Biological theories explain why people can develop phobias without having had an associated bad experience.

Evidence for...

1) **Gray (1982)** identified the **behavioural inhibition system** — a circuit in the **limbic system** in the brain that's linked to **anxiety**. When something unexpected and possibly dangerous happens, signals are sent to this area from the **cortex**. This causes **anxiety** which may make the person 'freeze'. How **susceptible** someone is to anxiety and panic may depend on how **sensitive** this circuit is.
2) **Johnson et al (2000)** did a **longitudinal study** showing that adolescents who **smoked** were **15** times more likely to develop **anxiety disorders** later in life, especially if they were heavy smokers. This may be due to the effects of **nicotine**, which may make areas of the **brain** more **sensitive**.

Evidence against...

1) **Johnson et al's (2000)** research is **correlational** — it doesn't prove that smoking **caused** the anxiety.
2) This research **doesn't** take other factors into account. For example, **behavioural** research has shown that some phobias, especially specific phobias, can be **learnt**.

...or *Psychological Factors* *(surprise surprise)*

1 *Behavioural Factors*

Behaviourists believe that phobias are **learnt** through **classical** or **operant conditioning**.

Classical conditioning — This especially explains **specific phobias**. A previously **neutral** thing starts to trigger anxiety because it becomes **associated** with something **frightening**. **Watson and Rayner (1920)** conducted a study on an 11-month-old boy called **Little Albert**. A loud noise was made every time he played with a **white rat**. He then began to **associate** the **rat** with the **frightening noise**, and showed fear when he saw it (see p.194 for full details).

Operant conditioning — This especially explains **social phobia** and **agoraphobia**. A person's fear goes when they **get away** from the situation that causes **fear**. This is **negative reinforcement** — they **learn** to avoid the stimulus that causes anxiety because they feel **better** when they **escape** it.

Evidence for... Behavioural **therapies** are very **effective** at treating phobias by getting the person to **change** their **response** to the **stimulus** (see p.82). This suggests that they're treating the **cause** of the problem.

Evidence against... **Davey (1992)** found that only **7%** of spider phobics recalled having a **traumatic experience** with a spider. This suggests that there could be **other explanations**, e.g. biological factors. (But just because they couldn't remember the experience, this doesn't mean it didn't happen.)

Explanations of Phobias

2) Socio-cultural Factors

It's thought that **upbringing** could affect the development of **phobias**.

Evidence for...

1) **Arrindell et al (1989)** reported that people with **social phobia** claimed that their parents were **controlling, over-protective** and **didn't** show much **affection.** This suggests that **upbringing** can cause social phobia.
2) **Social learning theory** states that behaviour is influenced by your **environment** and the people you grow up with. Children may see that a parent or older sibling is afraid of something and **imitate** their **response**.

Evidence against...

1) The research on upbringing is **correlational**, and it relies on people's **memory**, which can be **inaccurate**.
2) **Other factors** may be responsible, e.g. some people may have a biological pre-disposition that makes them more likely to develop phobias.

3) Psychodynamic Theory

Freud argued that phobias **hide** an **unconscious fear**. The real fear creates so much **anxiety** that it's **displaced** onto something less frightening or embarrassing.

Evidence for...

Freud used the case study of **Little Hans** to support his theory. Little Hans had a **fear** of **horses**, which Freud thought was caused by **Oedipal conflict**. Freud claimed that Hans was **attracted** to his mother and frightened that his father would **punish** him for being his rival. This fear created so much **anxiety** and guilt that it was **displaced** onto horses, which were like Hans' father because they wore bridles (which looked like his beard) and had big penises. Right...

Evidence against...

1) Freud's theories are **unfalsifiable** — they're **unscientific** because they can't be proved wrong.
2) Hans had been very frightened by seeing a horse fall down in the street. It could be that this produced a phobia of horses through **classical conditioning**.

4) Cognitive Factors

Beck and Emery (1985) proposed that interactions between an anxious person's **cognitive processes** and their belief in their **vulnerability** makes them more likely to interpret stimuli as being threatening.

Evidence for...

Hope et al (1990) showed participants words written in different colours. Participants with social phobia took **longer** to name the colour of **social threat words** (e.g. 'failure'). This suggests that they **processed** them in a different way.

Evidence against...

- This **doesn't** show **cause and effect** — it could be that feeling vulnerable is a **symptom** of anxiety, not the **cause** of it.
- Phobias could be caused by other factors, e.g. **biological factors**.

Practice Questions

Q1 Outline evidence to support the genetic explanation of phobias.

Q2 How can phobias be explained by classical conditioning?

Q3 Outline evidence against the Oedipus conflict being the cause of Little Hans' phobia.

Exam Questions

Q1 Outline the biological explanations for one anxiety disorder. [10 marks]

Q2 Describe and evaluate psychological explanations for one anxiety disorder. [25 marks]

What was Little Hans' brother called? — Tiny Feet...

You've got to feel for Little Hans — somehow it's a bit more socially acceptable to be scared of horses than it is to be in love with your mum and scared of your dad's penis. In fact, these 'Little' chaps have had quite a raw deal overall — poor Little Albert's fear ended up being generalised to all white fluffy things, until he was afraid of Santa's white fluffy beard. Sob...

Treating Anxiety Disorders

***AQA, OCR and Edexcel**. If, like me, you've completely lost concentration and started chewing your fingers and staring at the wall, then these should be just the pages to pick you up and give you a good shake. Just what you wanted.*

Anxiety Disorders Can be Treated Using Biological Therapy

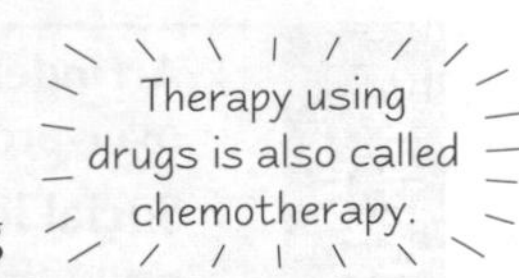
Therapy using
drugs is also called
chemotherapy.

1) The **biological** approach to treating anxiety disorders involves **drug therapy**.
2) **Anxiolytic drugs** (e.g. tranquillisers) such as benzodiazepines, **reduce anxiety** by increasing the activity of the neurotransmitter **GABA**. GABA produces a feeling of **calmness**.

Advantages

- **Benzodiazepines** take effect very **quickly**. This means that they're good for treating **anxiety** in the **short-term**, e.g. before stressful events like exams.
- **Davidson et al (1993)** compared the effects of **benzodiazepines** with a **placebo**, and found that benzodiazepines were **more effective** at reducing the symptoms of social phobia.

Disadvantages

- **Benzodiazepines** can cause side effects like **drowsiness**. They also cause physical and psychological **dependency**, so they **can't** be used **long-term**.
- The **symptoms** of anxiety often **return** when people come off medication.
- Drug therapy only treats the **symptoms** of the disorder. Other therapies are needed to try and tackle the **cause** of it, e.g. behavioural therapies.

Anxiety Disorders Can be Treated Using Psychological Therapies

1) Behavioural Therapies

Behavioural treatment for **specific phobias** is based on **classical conditioning** (learning through **association**). There are **two techniques** for treating specific phobias:

Systematic desensitisation — Wolpe (1958)

1) Systematic desensitisation works by using **counter-conditioning** so that the person learns to **associate** the **phobic stimulus** with **relaxation** rather than **fear**.
2) Patients **rank feared situations**, from the **least stressful** (e.g. saying the word *spider*) to the **most stressful** (e.g. holding a spider). They are then taught **relaxation techniques** like deep breathing.
3) The patient then **imagines** the anxiety-provoking situations, starting with the least stressful. They're encouraged to use the **relaxation techniques** and the process stops if they feel anxious.
4) Patients will gradually be able to work through the feared situations on the list without feeling **anxious**.

Exposure therapy

1) This involves exposing the patient to the phobic stimulus **straight away**, without any relaxation or gradual build-up. This can be done in **real life**, or the patient can be asked to **visualise** it. For example, someone who was afraid of heights might imagine standing on top of a skyscraper.
2) The patient is kept in this situation until the **anxiety** they feel at first has **warn off**. They realise that nothing bad has happened to them in this time, and their fear should be **extinguished**.

Advantages

- **Behavioural therapy** is very effective for treating **specific phobias**. **Zinbarg et al (1992)** found that **systematic desensitisation** was the **most effective** of the currently known methods for treating phobias.
- It works very **quickly**, e.g. **Ost et al (1991)** found that anxiety was reduced in **90%** of patients with a specific phobia after just **one session** of **therapy**.

Disadvantages

- There are **ethical issues** surrounding behavioural therapy — especially **exposure therapy**, as it causes patients a lot of anxiety. If patients **drop out** of the therapy **before** the fear has been extinguished, then it can end up causing **more anxiety** than before therapy started.
- **Behavioural therapy** only treats the **symptoms** of the disorder. **Other therapies** are needed to try and tackle the **cause** of it, e.g. cognitive behavioural therapy.

Treating Anxiety Disorders

2 Cognitive Behavioural Therapy

Cognitive behavioural therapy (CBT) helps patients by **identifying** and **changing** their **faulty cognitions**. For example, many people with **social phobia** assume that they'll **embarrass themselves** in social situations, so think it's best to avoid them. Here's what generally happens during CBT:

1) The therapist and client **identify** the client's **faulty cognitions**.
2) The therapist tries to show that the cognitions **aren't true**, e.g. the client doesn't always embarrass themselves.
3) Together, they set **goals** to think in more positive or adaptive ways, e.g. going to a party and talking to people they don't know. The aim is to prove to the client that their **negative thoughts** about what's going to happen are **wrong**, and so **reduce** their **anxiety**.

Advantages

- **CBT** is effective at treating phobias, e.g. **Thorpe and Salkovskis (1997)** found **reduced anxiety** in spider phobics after only **one session** of CBT.
- CBT **empowers** patients — it puts them in charge of their own treatment by teaching them **self-help strategies**. This means that it's a very **ethical** treatment.

Disadvantages

- Faulty cognitions might be the **consequence** of the disorder rather than its cause. For example, anxiety may be caused by a chemical imbalance in the brain which leads to faulty thought processes.
- Patients can become **dependent** on their therapist.

Stuart's faulty cognition had led to a disastrous footwear decision.

3 Psychotherapy

1) Psychotherapy aims to identify the **underlying cause** of the mental disorder.
2) This is done using different therapeutic techniques, e.g. **dream analysis** and **free association**.
3) When the **unconscious conflicts** that are causing the problems are made **conscious**, the therapist and patient can discuss and try to resolve them. This will hopefully lead to the disorder being cured.

Advantages

- It aims to treat the **cause** of the disorder, not just the **symptoms**.
- Patients have **more control** over their treatment than with other therapies, e.g. drug therapy.

Disadvantages

- Psychotherapy can be **distressing** for people because they're encouraged to **recall traumatic events**. This can sometimes be more difficult to deal with than the original symptoms.
- It's **difficult to prove** the effectiveness of psychotherapy — it's based on **subjective data** and the **unconscious mind**. There's also a risk that patients will develop **false memories**, e.g. of childhood abuse.

Practice Questions

Q1 What type of drugs can be used in the treatment of anxiety disorders?

Q2 What is meant by exposure therapy?

Q3 Outline what happens in cognitive behavioural therapy.

Exam Question

Q1 Describe and evaluate one or more treatment for an anxiety disorder of your choice. [25 marks]

I treat my anxiety disorder really well...

Yesterday I took it to the pictures, then I bought it a choc ice and let it go on the swings for half an hour. You've got to show you care sometimes. And it doesn't have to be anything fancy, just a little token of your affection is often enough. The most important thing is to spend some quality time together, make each other laugh, and just show a little bit more love...

Studies in Clinical Psychology

These pages are for Edexcel. *Just this one final push and then it's the end of the section. Soon you'll be able to forget about all the horrible things that can go wrong with your brain, and just concentrate on eating and sleeping and the telly.*

Rosenhan (1973) Studied Schizophrenia Diagnosis

Rosenhan's (1973) study highlighted the problems with the **diagnosis** of mental disorders.

Rosenhan (1973) — psychiatric classification can be inaccurate

Method 1: In a field study, eight 'normal' people tried to be admitted to 12 different psychiatric hospitals around the USA, with only one symptom — claiming they heard voices, saying 'empty', 'hollow' and 'thud'.

Results 1: Seven were diagnosed with **schizophrenia** and all eight were **admitted** to psychiatric hospital. On admission, they said they were sane and had faked symptoms to get admitted, but this was seen as a symptom itself. It took, on average, 19 days before they were released, usually with a diagnosis of 'schizophrenia in remission'. Other, real patients suspected that these people were not mentally ill.

Method 2: Rosenhan later told staff at a psychiatric hospital that one or more **pseudopatients** (normal people pretending to have schizophrenia) were trying to be admitted to the hospital.

Results 2: No pseudopatients appeared, but **41 genuine patients** were judged to be pseudopatients by staff.

Conclusion: Medical staff could not distinguish the sane from the insane (although many of the real patients could).

Evaluation: These results have important implications in terms of diagnosis. However, being a field study, it wouldn't have been possible to control all variables, and so the results lose some of their **reliability**. Staff would probably not **expect** 'normal' people to try to gain admission to a psychiatric hospital, and so this might explain why the participants were initially admitted. Also, they might have felt that it was better to admit somebody if there was a small chance that they could be a risk to themselves or others, than to turn them away. 'Schizophrenia in remission' is a diagnosis that is rarely used, which suggests the psychiatrists concerned may not have believed they were really suffering from schizophrenia. There are quite a lot of **ethical** considerations in this study — people had their freedom taken away, mentally healthy people may have received treatments, professionals were deceived, and the study risked genuine patients not being treated.

Remember — it's the medical staff here who are the sample being studied, not the pseudopatients.

Goldstein et al (1998) Studied Schizophrenia and Gender Differences

It's been suggested that schizophrenia patients show **gender differences** in social functioning.
Goldstein et al (1998) investigated whether this was related to neuropsychological performance.

Goldstein et al (1998) — gender and schizophrenia symptoms

Method: This was a **laboratory experiment** that aimed to find out whether there are differences in **neuropsychological performance** between male and female patients with schizophrenia. A sample of 31 patients with schizophrenia and a control group of 27 people who didn't have schizophrenia were used. The two groups were matched in terms of age, sex, ethnic and socioeconomic background and whether they were right or left handed. The level of functioning of both groups was rated using a series of neuropsychological tests.

Results: Male patients with schizophrenia performed significantly worse in **all** the tests compared with the males without schizophrenia. They also did worse in the tests of attention, verbal memory and executive functions than the female patients. The female patients were only significantly impaired in attention, executive functions, visual memory and motor functions compared with the females who didn't have schizophrenia.

Conclusion: Schizophrenic men show more cognitive impairment than schizophrenic women and are more likely to show impaired verbal processing.

Evaluation: This was a **laboratory experiment**, so there was strict **control** of **variables**. This means that the study has good **reliability** and it's possible to establish **cause and effect**. It has **real life applications** as it suggests that males with schizophrenia might need more care that focuses on verbal skills than women. It was an **ethical** study because the participants weren't harmed or deceived during the experiment. However, the sample size was quite small, so it's difficult to **generalise** the results to the rest of the population. The study lacks **ecological validity** because it was conducted in an **artificial setting** using tests that people don't normally have to do in real life.

Studies in Clinical Psychology

Swann et al (1992) Studied ***Depression***

Swann et al (1992) looked at whether people suffering from depression seek out **negative opinions** from others.

Swann et al (1992) — depression and negative feedback

Method: This study aimed to find out whether people with **depression** seek out **negative feedback**.

1) Participants were given the Beck Depression Inventory so that the researchers could diagnose whether they had **depression**. 28 participants were classed as nondepressed, 43 as dysphoric (having a low mood) and 13 were classed as depressed.
2) They were asked to complete a **personality test** and were told that their answers in the test would be **rated** by 3 '**evaluators**' who would form an opinion of the participant (this was **untrue**).
3) They were then shown the **fake feedback** from the three evaluators. This took the form of ratings on things like how interesting the participant seemed from their personality test. The feedback usually consisted of one positive rating, one neutral rating and one negative rating.
4) Lastly the participants were asked to decide which **evaluator** they'd like to **meet** the most, using a scale from 1 (wouldn't like to meet them at all) to 10 (would like to meet them a lot).

Results: **Nondepressed** participants were more likely to say that they wanted to meet the evaluator who had rated their personality **positively**. **Depressed** participants were more likely to choose to meet the person who gave them **negative feedback**.

Conclusion: People with depression seek out negative assessments of their personalities more than people who don't have depression.

Evaluation: These results have an **application to real life**, as they can help explain why people with depression might remain depressed. This was a **laboratory experiment**, so there was strict **control** of the **variables** which increases the reliability of the results. However, the results don't explain whether the tendency to seek out negative feedback **causes** depression, or whether it's one of the **symptoms** of depression. The study also **lacks ecological validity** — it didn't set up a situation that participants were likely to experience in real life, so it's **difficult** to **generalise** the results to the rest of society. The study was **ethical** — although the participants were **deceived**, they were fully **debriefed** afterwards. None of the participants regretted doing the experiment, or felt that they had been harmed by the procedure.

Practice Questions

Q1 What was the aim of Rosenhan's (1973) study?

Q2 Outline the method of Rosenhan's (1973) study.

Q3 Outline the results of Goldstein et al's (1998) study.

Q4 Explain one strength and one weakness of Goldstein et al's (1998) study.

Q5 Outline the method of Swann et al's (1992) study.

Q6 Was Swann et al's (1992) study ethical? Give a reason for your answer.

Exam Questions

Q1 a) Outline the method of one study into schizophrenia. [4 marks]

b) Evaluate the study you described in (a). [6 marks]

Q2 Describe and evaluate one study into depression. [12 marks]

Before you turn over — heed this warning...

...after you've been learning about mental disorders for a while, chances are you'll start to believe that you're suffering from all of them. It's what always happens. It's like when you read a medical encyclopedia and you convince yourself you've got rabies and meningitis and gout, and you end up making your dad wait with you for 6 hours in casualty. Just like that.

The Influence of Media on Social Behaviour

This section is for AQA only. *Violent television shows and video games get blamed for all kinds of problems these days — mostly for corrupting young people. Psychologists are interested in what effect they actually have on viewers...*

The **Media** May Influence Our **Behaviour**

1) **Social learning theory** suggests that we **model** our behaviour on behaviour that we **observe** — whether it's anti-social or pro-social behaviour.
2) There's much **debate** about whether the media influences our behaviour in this way. A central point to this debate is the effect of observing violence in TV programmes and video games — particularly on children's behaviour.
3) **Bandura's Bobo Doll experiments** (1961) showed that children who'd watched an adult behaving aggressively towards a doll were **more likely** to behave **aggressively** than those who hadn't seen the aggressive behaviour.
4) If the observed behaviour has a **positive outcome** we are **more likely** to copy it than if the outcome is negative.
5) Social learning theory also claims that if the model is **high status** or **admired** they are **more influential**.

Violent Media May be Used as a **Justification** for **Anti-social Behaviour**

1) Aggressive behaviour falls **outside the social norm** — it's considered to be **anti-social**.
2) Knowing this and still displaying aggressive behaviour can cause someone to feel **psychologically uncomfortable**.
3) **Justification theory** suggests violent media can be used to **reduce** this psychological discomfort.
4) If someone watches violent programmes or plays violent video games, they will become used to seeing aggressive behaviour — they may begin to think that it's **normal** and **acceptable**.
5) This helps them **justify** their own anti-social behaviour and feel **less guilty** about it.
6) This justification of their anti-social behaviour means that they're **more likely** to behave that way **again**.

There Have Been Many **Studies** Into the Effect of **Television** on **Behaviour**

Loads of studies have examined the **link** between **violence on TV** and **aggression**.

Huesmann et al (1984) conducted **longitudinal studies** which found a relationship between **exposure to TV violence** at a young age and the number of **criminal convictions** at the age of 30. They claimed it showed the development of anti-social behaviour and aggression.

Paik and **Comstock** (1991) conducted a **meta-analysis** that summarised the findings of over a thousand studies examining the link between **TV violence** and **aggressive behaviour**. The results suggested a **strong link** between exposure to violent programmes and aggressive behaviour.

The results of these studies show a **correlation** between exposure to violent TV programmes and aggressive behaviour, but they don't show **cause and effect**. This means we can't say for sure that watching violence on TV causes aggressive behaviour — it could be that **aggressive** children are **more likely** to **watch violent programmes**.

There have also been studies examining the effect that observing **pro-social behaviour** on TV has on **behaviour**.

Sprafkin et al (1975) showed 3 groups of children different TV programmes. Group 1 watched a programme where a boy **saves a puppy**. Group 2 watched a similar programme but with **no helping behaviour**. Group 3 watched a programme with **no interaction** between animals and humans. The children could hear the sounds of some distressed puppies and were placed in front of two buttons. They were told that each time they pressed one button they would be given **points** — the more points they got the bigger the prize they would be given. Pressing the other button wouldn't give them any points but it would alert someone to **help** the puppies. Group 1 children were the **most likely** to spend their time **calling for help** rather than collecting points.

Many studies **don't measure** whether pro-social behaviour is a **long-term** or **short-term effect** of exposure to such programmes. **Sagotsky et al** (1981) found that 6 and 8 year olds modelled cooperative behaviour **immediately after** they witnessed it. However, 7 **weeks** later, **only the older children** were still showing the behavioural effects.

The Influence of Media on Social Behaviour

Video Games and Computers May Also Affect Behaviour

1) The popularity of **video games** has stimulated new research into the influence that media has on behaviour.
2) Like other media (e.g. films), games receive **age ratings** depending on their content. Ratings are determined by things like violence, sexual themes, drug use, criminal behaviour or bad language.
3) It's thought that games may have **greater potential** to **influence behaviour** than other types of media due to their **interactive nature**.
4) Some people believe that violent video games can be held **directly responsible** for influencing some specific crimes.

   Example: The use of violent video games by the **Columbine High School shooters** has been cited by some people as a reason for the 1999 massacre that killed 13 people and injured 24 others. The families of some of the victims took **legal action** against the companies that produced them but were **unsuccessful**.

5) However, many people **don't believe** that video games can be blamed for crimes. They point out that most people who use the games don't go on to imitate the violent behaviour that they see in them.

A **meta-analysis** of early research by **Anderson and Bushman** (2001) suggests that playing violent video games does **increase aggression** and **decrease pro-social behaviour** in young people. This is **supported** by a **range of evidence** from both lab and field, and experimental and non-experimental studies. However, the effects have been **small in size** and there has as yet been **no longitudinal research**.

Studies have been carried out on the effect that violent video games have on the **emotions** of people playing them.

Anderson and Bushman (2002) — Video games and emotions

Method: This study was a **lab experiment** involving 224 participants in **two independent groups**. Participants played either a violent or non-violent video game and were then asked to 'finish off' three stories from a variety of 'story stems', e.g. one started with a minor car accident. Each participant was asked to describe what the main character would do, say and feel.

Results: Participants who had played the violent game described the main character as being **more aggressive** than those who'd played the non-violent game, e.g. shouting at, starting a fight with or stabbing the other driver.

Conclusion: Playing video games produces **aggressive thoughts** and **emotions** in players.

Evaluation: **Low ecological validity** may have led the participants to give responses which didn't reflect the way they would react in real life. Participants might have shown **demand characteristics** (see page 215) due to their recent exposure to violent scenarios. This was a lab study so there was good **control of variables** and the results are therefore **reliable**.

Practice Questions

Q1 Describe the role of violent media in justification theory.

Q2 What factors determine the age ratings of video games?

Q3 Describe Anderson and Bushman's (2002) study.

Exam Question

Q1 a) Describe and evaluate at least one explanation of media influences on behaviour. [10 marks]

b) "Violent video games have a more harmful effect than any other form of media." Discuss this statement. [15 marks]

You know what else is anti-social? Staying in to revise. Grrrrr.

Nothing to stress you out here — the media's always getting blamed for problems with today's society, so most of this stuff shouldn't come as a massive shock to you. You do need to learn all the different studies though — general waffling that the media can affect behaviour won't cut any mustard in the exam. Funny saying that, why would you want to cut mustard...

Persuasion and Attitude Change

These pages are just for AQA. Love, hate, approval, disapproval... attitudes we hold on countless different things. If attitudes predict behaviour it would be pretty nifty to know how to shape the attitudes of people around us.

Persuasion is the Art of Changing Someone's Attitude

Our **attitudes** are our feelings towards something — they can be **positive** or **negative** views.
Persuasion is **changing an attitude**, usually using **messages** about the object, person or concept in question.

1) The Hovland-Yale Model Identifies the Key Elements of Persuasion

1) **Carl Hovland** researched **effective persuasion techniques** at Yale University.
2) His team took an **experimental approach** to studying persuasion, systematically **changing one variable** at a time.
3) The results of his research became known as the **Hovland-Yale model** and identified **four important components** of persuasion:

- **The source of the message** — e.g. the **trustworthiness**, **expertise** and **attractiveness** of the persuader.
- **The message content** — e.g. the **number**, **strength**, **order** and **emotional appeal** of the arguments.
- **The recipient** — e.g. the **age**, **IQ** and **personality traits** of the person being persuaded.
- **The situation** — e.g. whether given **formally** or **informally**, and whether the message is **relevant**.

4) The Hovland-Yale model suggests the key factors involved in creating a change in attitude but **doesn't address why** these factors are important.

2) The Elaboration-Likelihood Model Identifies the Processing Routes of Persuasion

1) **Petty and Cacioppo** (**1986**) reckoned that a persuasion message can take effect through **two processing routes**:

- **The Peripheral Route** — low-level mechanisms such as **conditioning**, use of quick **decision making rules** (e.g. 'experts are always right') and **attractiveness** of the message determine our attitudes. The peripheral route **doesn't involve much analysis** of the merits of the message itself.
- **The Central Route** — high-level mechanisms, such as **evaluation of the source** and **content** of the message, determine our attitudes. Persuasion via the central route occurs when someone has the **time**, **motivation** and **ability** to **analyse** the message. When this happens, the likelihood that they'll elaborate on the information that they have increases.

2) The elaboration-likelihood model is comprehensive and can explain particular experimental findings, but it can't be used to predict them beforehand — it **lacks the predictive power** which a useful model should have.

There are Several Theories on the Links Between Attitude and Behaviour

1) Festinger (1957) Came up with the Theory of Cognitive Dissonance

1) The theory of **cognitive consistency** states that people like to hold attitudes that are in **agreement**.
2) If people hold **conflicting attitudes** it can lead to an uncomfortable psychological feeling known as **cognitive dissonance**. This can lead to **discrepancies** between someone's **attitude** and their **behaviour**.
3) When this happens a person might **change their attitude** to fit in with their behaviour in order to **justify** it.

	Festinger and Carlsmith (1959) — Creating cognitive dissonance
Method:	**Independent groups** of students were paid $1 or $20 to describe a series of dull tasks they had just performed as 'interesting' to a potential volunteer. Their post-experimental attitudes were measured.
Results:	The students who were paid $1 reported that they had **enjoyed the tasks more** than those paid $20.
Conclusion:	Without a worthwhile pay-off, the students paid $1 experienced **cognitive dissonance** and so **changed their attitude** towards the tasks to bring it in line with their **actions** (telling a volunteer they were interesting). The larger quantity of money received by the other students was sufficient incentive for them to **rationalise** and **justify** their lies (e.g. "I only said it for the money").
Evaluation:	This was a lab experiment so there was good control of variables, making the results **reliable**. However, the study lacked **ecological validity** as it wasn't a real-life situation.

Persuasion and Attitude Change

2 Bem (1965) Came up with Self-Perception Theory

1) Bem proposed that people **don't think** enough about their **attitudes** for any conflict between attitudes to cause cognitive dissonance.
2) His **theory of self-perception** suggests that people's attitudes are determined through **observing their own behaviour** — in the same way that we determine other people's attitudes through observation.
3) Bem used the results of **Festinger and Carlsmith's** (1959) study but interpreted them differently. He concluded that students paid $20 believed that the **money** was the reason that they had said the task was interesting. The students paid $1 actually believed that they found the task interesting — they had **no other justification** for their behaviour.

Martin didn't care how much they paid him — he knew that nothing could justify this behaviour.

Television is Widely Used for Persuasion

1) Television is used by **advertisers**, **political parties** and **health organisations** to persuade their audience.
2) TV is a really popular way of delivering a persuasion message because of the double whammy of **audio** and **visual information** which is delivered, and the potentially **huge audience**.
3) **Different techniques** are used to make TV persuasion as effective as possible:

- **Pleasant associations** — products being sold are often teamed with things the audience will automatically feel positive about, such as **humour**, **success** and **sex**. Through **classical conditioning**, the product may become associated with these things — the audience may be persuaded through the **peripheral route** that they need to buy it.
- **Making the message bizarre** — many TV adverts are 'off the wall' and totally **unconnected** to the product they're advertising. This encourages **deep processing** of the persuasion message and accesses the **central route** of persuasion.
- **Using familiar figures** — **celebrities** are often used to advertise products and they're usually **matched up** to the product they're selling, e.g. models advertising beauty products. People delivering the message don't actually need to be famous — just **recognisable figures**. A man in a white coat spouting long words will give an image of scientific credibility, for example. In this way, advertisers can tap into the **peripheral or central route** of persuasion by activating **mental associations** with the personalities used, or increasing motivation to **process** the message more deeply.

Practice Questions

Q1 List the four factors in persuasion identified by the Hovland-Yale model.

Q2 Explain the difference between the peripheral and central routes of persuasion.

Q3 Describe a technique used in TV for persuasion.

Exam Question

Q1 a) Describe and evaluate at least one model explaining how attitudes can be changed. [15 marks]

b) Discuss the effectiveness of television in persuasion. [10 marks]

The lots-of-revision model has one key element of persuasion — fear...

So there you have it — you should be able to persuade anyone of anything now. Just make sure that the source, content, recipient and situation of the model are correct, go at them via the peripheral and central routes, pay them enough money or confuse 'em until they don't know what they think anymore — and do it all through their telly. You can't go wrong.

The Psychology of 'Celebrity'

Once again, just AQA. *"When I grow up, I wanna be famous" trill countless starry-eyed children. As an outcome of the relatively new mass media, we've only just begun to look for ways to explain the phenomenon of 'celebrity'...*

Audiences Can Develop **Relationships** With **Celebrities**

1) The relationships that audiences develop with celebrities are very **different** from the relationships formed within **normal social networks**.
2) They are **one-sided**, with one person knowing lots and the other usually knowing nothing about the other party.
3) The term used to describe this type of relationship is **parasocial**.
4) The **study** of parasocial relationships between audiences and celebrities has become a branch of **social relationship research** in its own right.
5) As well as audiences developing relationships with celebrities, many people are **attracted** to the **concept of celebrity** and want to be one themselves.

Their relationship was distinctly one sided but that didn't discourage Molly.

The **Attraction** of Celebrity Can be Explained in an **Evolutionary Context**...

1) The **evolutionary explanation** for the attraction of celebrity is based on the idea that everyone has a basic selfish drive to ensure their **genes** have the best possible chance of being **passed on**.
2) Celebrity is seen as a way to achieve this and can be looked at from **two different perspectives**:
   - **Becoming a celebrity makes a person more desirable.** In evolutionary terms, it may result in gaining **economic advantage**, which may make a person **more attractive** to others. This then increases their chances of **passing on their genes**.
   - **Desirable people become celebrities.** Celebrities may be seen as individuals who are hugely popular due to their **personality traits**. So becoming famous acts as confirmation of having characteristics that others find attractive. **Hartup** (1992) researched the characteristics of people who became popular in their own social circles from an early age. The characteristics that were valued included **social dominance** and **athletic ability** in boys and **prettiness** in girls.

...or in a **Social Psychological Context**

1) Wann (1995) studied the **active role** that audiences play as **fans** — a **social psychological explanation** for the attraction of celebrity.
2) This has led to the creation of the term **fandom** — used to describe **a group of fans** of a particular celebrity. Fandom can provide individuals with:
   - **Enhanced self-esteem.**
   - **Escape**, **entertainment** and **excitement.**
   - **Enhanced family** and **group affiliation.**
3) The extent to which fandom provides these **varies** between individuals and contributes to how **likely** someone is to be a fan. For example, someone whose self-esteem is greatly increased and who finds high levels of entertainment and escape in fandom is likely to find the concept of celebrity more attractive than someone whose self-esteem is only slightly enhanced.
4) Several aspects of fandom are **very social in nature**, providing a group of people with a **shared focus of interest**. Some people believe that 'being a fan' of something can play an important role in adolescence — it might help young people make the **transition** from **parental** to **peer attachments** by providing a **common source** of gossip.

The Psychology of 'Celebrity'

There are *Three Stages* of *Fandom*

Explanations of fandom suggest that celebrity worship can be a result of **normal instincts** and **motivations**. However, sometimes fandom can take on a **more intense form** and becomes something which is **pathological**. **Three stages of fandom** have been identified:

1) **Entertainment-Social** — where the relationship with the celebrity exists as a source of fun, shared with others in a social group.
2) **Intense-Personal** — obsessive thoughts begin to arise in relation to the celebrity, (e.g. "Justin Timberlake is my soul mate").
3) **Borderline-Pathological** — obsessive thoughts begin to give rise to fully-fledged fantasies (e.g. "Justin Timberlake is my boyfriend") and behaviours (e.g. sending love letters to Justin Timberlake). It is at this stage that stalking may begin, which involves a level of pursuit that is intimidating.

Stalkers Don't Always Conform to the *Stereotypical Image*

The word '**stalker**' immediately conjures up images of an unattractive and obsessive loner-type, whose walls are decorated with news clippings and photographs of the star who has become the object of their fixation. This image is largely created by the media and contains several **misconceptions**, which **Spitzberg** is largely credited with de-bunking:

Myth: Stalking mainly affects celebrities

Stalking involving a well-known person is more likely to be reported in the media than stalking involving a member of the public — so it's clear why this would be assumed. However, it's estimated that around **21% of the population** will be pursued at some point.

Myth: Stalkers are strangers

In fact, in most cases stalkers have been involved in an **intimate relationship** with the person they're pursuing.

Myth: Stalking ends in violence

News reporting usually focuses on cases where there has been some dramatic ending, and films which portray a sensational account of stalking draw the most attention. However, stalking **doesn't usually involve violence.**

Practice Questions

Q1 What is meant by a parasocial relationship?

Q2 What are the three stages of fandom?

Q3 Give two misconceptions about stalking.

Exam Question

Q1 a) Discuss research into intense fandom. [10 marks]

b) Outline the social explanation of the attraction to celebrity. [15 marks]

Celeb worship is harmless. My fiancée Justin Timberlake totally agrees...

So in summary, it's normal to be interested in celebrities and what they do, unless you take it too far and become a stalker. But even if you do you'll still look normal, so no-one will know you're a stalker. Now just learn all the details and technical terms and you'll be all set for the exam. And whilst you do that I'll just nip out and grab my favourite glossy magazine...

Models of Addictive Behaviour

These pages are for AQA only. *Alcohol, smoking, gambling, chocolate, shopping... examples of things people claim to be addicted to. So what is it that makes them all so darn irresistible? Guess what... there's more than one theory.*

Addictive Behaviour Can be Explained by the *Biological Model* of Addiction...

The **biological approach** includes **neurological** and **genetic explanations** for addictions.

1) The *Neurological Approach*

Both the highs and lows of addiction can be explained at the level of **neurons**...

See page 132 for more on neurons.

1) The neurotransmitter **dopamine** is released at particular synapses in the brain and affects **motivation** and **pleasure** (amongst other things).
2) Some substances (e.g. food and addictive drugs), **increase the release** of dopamine or **prevent its reuptake** at synapses.
3) These both **increase dopamine levels** in the brain and so **dopamine receptors** on neurons are **stimulated** — this gives the person a feeling of pleasure or satisfaction.
4) Once the dopamine has been removed from the synapses (reuptake), this feeling **disappears**. In order to regain it, the person wants to take **more** of the substance.
5) If the substance is used **repeatedly**, the body becomes **used** to the **higher levels** of dopamine. The rate at which it's broken down increases and its **reuptake** also **increases**. This means that **more** of the substance is needed to produce the **same effect**. This is known as **tolerance**.
6) If the addict then **stops** taking the substance, they experience effects which are the **opposite** of the drug's effects. These are called **withdrawal symptoms** and can be removed by taking **more** of the substance.

2) The *Genetic Approach*

1) It's been suggested that some addictions are **inherited**.
2) A review of studies by Sayette and Hufford (1997) concluded that **identical (MZ) twins** showed a **higher rate of concordance** for **alcoholism** than **non-identical (DZ) twins**, suggesting that alcoholism is controlled to **some extent** by **genes**.
3) This can explain why, despite the fact that many people drink alcohol on a regular basis, only a **small proportion** develop an **addiction** to it.
4) However, there must be an **environmental aspect** to alcoholism as the MZ twins didn't show 100% concordance. It's also not clear whether the result is just **specific to alcoholism**, or can be generalised to addiction as a whole.

The true cost of his addiction only hit Andy when he was asked to settle his tab.

However, the biological model of addiction doesn't take **psychological** and **social influences** into account.

...by the *Cognitive Model* of Addiction...

The **cognitive approach** explains addiction by looking at the **thought processes** behind it. These could be shaped by a person's...

1) **attitude towards the behaviour** — e.g. 'alcohol helps me to feel confident and relaxed'.
2) **perception of others' opinions** — e.g. 'I need to drink to fit in'.
3) **perception of their ability to control their own behaviour** — e.g. 'I can't cope with social situations if I don't have a drink'.

The cognitive model can be used in therapy sessions to **reduce addictive behaviour**. Cognitive therapists help the addict to **identify** the **thoughts** that **trigger** their addictive behaviour. They're then taught **strategies** to **change** their behaviour, e.g. avoiding certain situations, and practicing new thought patterns. Cognitive therapy usually contains a **behavioural component** which teaches the addict **new skills**, e.g. alternative relaxation techniques.

Models of Addictive Behaviour

...and by the **Learning Model** of Addiction

The **learning approach** explains addiction by looking at the role the **environment** plays in the **maintenance** and **relapse** of **addictive behaviour**.

1) **Repeatedly** using a substance, e.g. heroin, in the **same environment** will lead to **associations** forming between the substance and the **stimuli** in the environment, e.g. needles, other addicts.
2) When these stimuli are present the body **expects** to receive the substance and will **compensate in advance** for certain **effects** of the drug. For example, heroin addicts feel anxious without the drug, because their body anticipates the increased relaxation that will follow its use.
3) This is known as **classical conditioning**, and is one of the factors that leads to the **initiation** of **addiction**, **tolerance** and **withdrawal effects**.
   - **Addiction** — The environmental stimuli lead to compensatory effects which are often the opposite of the drug effects. The user then wants the substance in order to remove these effects.
   - **Tolerance** — Compensatory effects oppose the effect that the substance has on the body, so larger quantities of the substance are needed to create the same effect.
   - **Withdrawal symptoms** — If the body experiences compensatory effects but doesn't receive the substance, the person will feel the opposite of how they would if they took the substance.

There is research evidence for this model of addiction.

Siegel et al (1982) — The effect of context on overdose likelihood

Method:	This was a **lab experiment** using **independent groups** of rats. Two groups of rats were given heroin until they developed a **tolerance** to it. After 30 days the heroin dose was **doubled**. For half of the rats, this dose was given in the **usual room**. For the other half, it was given in a **different room**.
Results:	32% of the rats that had the double dose in the usual room died, compared to 64% of the rats in the new room.
Conclusion:	**Tolerance** and **withdrawal symptoms** are a **conditioned response** to drug-related stimuli. When there's no familiar stimuli to allow anticipation of the drug, compensatory effects aren't triggered and the body is less prepared to deal with a larger quantity of the drug than usual. This increases the risk of death.
Evaluation:	This result can explain **unusual cases** of overdose where addicts have died after taking an amount of drugs which they had coped with in the past. Also, it can explain why many ex-addicts, having 'got clean', go back to taking drugs when they return home — there they are surrounded by stimuli that are **associated** with drugs. Studies like this have **real-life applications**. As a result of findings that drug-related stimuli can increase cravings, anti-drug campaigns no longer use posters which show drug paraphernalia, e.g. syringes and spoons.

Practice Questions

Q1 What is tolerance?

Q2 What are the three cognitive factors underlying addiction?

Q3 Describe the results of the study by Siegel et al (1982).

Exam Question

Q1 a) Outline and evaluate at least one biological explanation of addiction. [15 marks]

b) Discuss another explanation for the initiation, maintenance and relapse of addiction. [10 marks]

My tolerance for this topic is rapidly reducing...

There you have it — nice explanations for any sneaky little addictions you've got. I think the cognitive model explains my peanut butter on toast addiction pretty well — I can't get through the working day without it. But then again, it could be the dopamine hit that has me reaching for the toaster, or the sight of the toaster itself... which, now I think about it... mmm, toast.

Explaining Smoking and Gambling

No suprises here, just AQA again. *As the pastimes of gangsters and cowboys, you can understand why so many people think that smoking and gambling must be cool. But they'd be wrong — addictions are so last century.*

Many People Are **Addicted** to Smoking

The chemicals in cigarettes can cause diseases such as **cancer**, **emphysema** and **bronchitis**. Despite this, many people smoke and some continue to smoke after being diagnosed with one of these conditions — this is because smoking is **addictive**. Even though many smokers want to quit, the **success rate** of those who attempt it is **very low**.

Addiction to smoking can be explained in more than one way:

1 The **Biological Approach** Explains Smoking as an **Addiction to Nicotine**

1) There are many chemicals in cigarettes but it's the **nicotine** that causes **addiction**.
2) Nicotine stimulates the release of **dopamine**, increasing the level of dopamine in the brain and providing feelings of **pleasure** and **relaxation** (see page 92).
3) If nicotine's taken **regularly** the body **expects it** and **reduces** the amount of dopamine that's released naturally.
4) In order to maintain **normal dopamine levels** and the effect that they have on the body, nicotine needs to be taken regularly. This **reinforces smoking behaviour**, leading to more frequent smoking and **addiction**.
5) **Quitting** smoking is very difficult as the body becomes used to nicotine and **relies** on it to stimulate dopamine release. Quitting deprives the body of nicotine, leading to **low dopamine levels** until the body readjusts.
6) This causes unpleasant **withdrawal symptoms** such as anxiety, restlessness, sleep disturbance and weight gain.

2 The **Social Learning Approach** Explains Why People **Start** Smoking

1) **Social learning theory** states that new behaviour (in this case smoking), is learned through **observation**, or **modelling**. Whether the behaviour is imitated depends on the perceived **consequences**.
2) If smoking is **positively reinforced**, e.g. by **benefits** such as fitting in with peers, then it's likely to be **copied**. Seeing **role models** (e.g. parents or celebrities) smoking also encourages people to smoke.
3) Once someone has started smoking they will experience withdrawal symptoms if they stop. These encourage people to start smoking again (to remove the symptoms). This is known as **negative reinforcement**.
4) Often, smoking becomes **associated** with other activities and objects, e.g. alcohol — this is classical conditioning and it makes it difficult to not smoke in certain environments (see page 93).

	Akers and Lee (1996) — the effects of social learning over time
Method:	A five year **longitudinal study** of 454 secondary school students was conducted using **self-report questionnaire surveys**. These measured how frequently the students smoked and 'social learning variables'. These were things like whether friends smoked, how often friends smoked, and perceived attitudes of friends and parents towards smoking.
Results:	Significant **positive correlations** were found between the social learning variables and smoking.
Conclusion:	Social learning can partly account for whether smoking begins in adolescence.
Evaluation:	Methods relying on self report may be **unreliable**, and correlation doesn't prove that social learning causes smoking to begin. Also, the effect of social learning wasn't analysed to show the relative influence of different **variables**, e.g. gender or parental vs. peer influence.

There's Been **Debate** Over Whether Smoking is an **Addiction** or a **Habit**

For a long time cigarette companies claimed that people smoked for **psychological** reasons (smoking for pleasure, which becomes part of a routine), rather than **physiological** reasons (smoking to avoid the unpleasant withdrawal symptoms caused by changes in the brain). They argued that this meant smoking was a **habit** rather than an **addiction**. However, **both** the physiological and psychological aspects are important in smoking. The physiological impact of withdrawal symptoms are well documented but the effects of psychological dependence shouldn't be underestimated.

Explaining Smoking and Gambling

Gambling Doesn't Involve Any Substance Use But Can Still Be **Addictive**

Addiction to gambling can also be explained by many approaches:

1) The **Biological Approach** Explains Gambling as an **Addiction to Adrenaline**

1) The **stress** of awaiting the outcome of a bet triggers the release of the hormone **adrenaline.**
2) This induces an **adrenaline rush**, making the person more alert and experiencing a 'natural high'.
3) In order to regain this rush, gamblers will place **more bets** and a **physiological addiction** may develop.
4) **Repeated gambling** can cause the body to develop a **tolerance** to adrenaline. This can lead to more frequent gambling or bets involving more money in order to get the same rush.
5) **Other chemicals** triggered by stress could also be responsible for gambling addictions. There's some evidence that gambling releases **endorphins**, chemicals that block pain and negative effects of stress.

2) The **Psychodynamic Approach** Suggests Gambling is Driven By **Masochism**

1) **Bergler** (1958) proposed that gamblers gamble to **lose**, in order to **punish** themselves.
2) This **reduces** the **guilt** they feel from rebelling against their parents during childhood. He suggests that gamblers **identify** with the casino dealer or roulette wheel, etc. as **parental figures**.
3) Bergler presented **case studies** where treatment relevant to his theory was successful in curing some gamblers of their addiction but **scientific evidence** is still lacking at the moment.

3) The **Cognitive Approach** Suggests Gambling is Driven By **Faulty Reasoning Mechanisms**

1) **Decision making** can be based on **rational consideration** or **quick** (**sometimes faulty**) **rules**.
2) **Wagenaar** (1988) identified 16 rules that gamblers commonly use when making decisions. These include:

- **The illusion of control** — gamblers think of gambling as **skill-based**. This creates superficially high expectations when in reality the outcomes are often determined by chance alone.
- **Representative bias** — gamblers believe that **random events** should **look random**, e.g. 'tails' seems increasingly likely the longer a run of consecutive 'heads' lasts. Many gamblers believe that the longer a losing streak lasts the more likely a win will follow. This is known as the **gambler's fallacy**.
- **Illusory correlations** — gamblers have **superstitions** which they believe help them succeed, e.g. blowing the dice for a 6.
- **Fixation on the absolute frequency of successes** — gamblers can **recall many past wins**, just because they gamble so much. This creates a false image of how often they win.

Practice Questions

Q1 Describe the study by Akers and Lee (1996).

Q2 Define 'physiological' and 'psychological' dependence to smoking.

Q3 List the faulty reasoning mechanisms that can lead to gambling addiction.

Exam Question

Q1 a) Outline a biological explanation for addiction to smoking. [10 marks]

b) Outline an alternative approach to explaining this addiction. [10 marks]

c) Discuss the difference between smoking as a habit and as an addiction. [5 marks]

Exams = stress = adrenaline = addiction to exams. Something's not right...

There are a lot of people out there who think that smoking and gambling are evil addictions that ruin lives — and I'm one of them. If they didn't exist you wouldn't have to learn about them, the examiners couldn't ask you about them and we'd all be much happier. Unfortunately that's not the case, so you'd best get down to business and learn these pages. Enjoy.

Factors Affecting Addictive Behaviour

These pages are just for AQA. *Not everybody becomes an addict. Behaviours such as drinking and gambling remain controllable pastimes for many people, meaning that there must be individual differences at work...*

Low Self-Esteem Makes People *More Vulnerable* to *Addictive Behaviour*

Self-esteem is someone's judgement of their **own worth**. People with **low self-esteem** are **more likely** to show **addictive behaviour** than people with high self-esteem. Once an addiction has developed, low self-esteem can be a **barrier to recovery**.

Taylor et al (2006) — Low self-esteem as an early risk factor

Method: A **longitudinal study** of 872 boys from a wide range of ethnic backgrounds was carried out. They were assessed on measures of self-esteem at the beginning of the study and then 3 times over the next 9 years. A final assessment was done when they were between 19 and 21 years old.

Results: Eleven year-old boys with very low self-esteem were **1.6 times more likely** than others to become dependent upon drugs by the age of 20.

Conclusion: Low self-esteem in childhood predicts addictive behaviour in early adulthood.

Evaluation: The large, diverse sample suggests that the results can be **generalised** to the wider male population. It can't be generalised to the whole population as girls weren't involved in this study. Other studies have found that there's a stronger link between low self-esteem and depression and eating disorders in girls than between low self-esteem and addictive behaviour.

The *Attributions* of *Addicts* Can *Influence* Their *Behaviour*

Attributions are the **causes identified** by people as **explanations** for their and other people's behaviour. A person's view of what causes their behaviour often **differs** from the view of an **observer** — this is called **attributional bias**. Several studies have been carried out into the attributions of **addictive behaviour**:

Davies (1996) proposed that addicts' attributions **change** over the course of an addiction:

- **Pre-problem** — addicts attribute their behaviour to **free choice**, based on the pleasure they gain from it.
- **Problem recognition** — addicts attribute their behaviour to **external forces** that are out of their control. They refer to themselves as addicts.
- **Past substance use** — addicts attribute their behaviour to **controllable causes** and are able to recover. Or...
- **Down and out** — addicts see their addiction as **uncontrollable** so their behaviour continues.

McCormick and Taber (1988) found evidence to suggest that the attributions of addicts are:

- **Internal** — the cause is the **addict** themself.
- **Stable** — the cause will **always exist**.
- **Global** — the cause will exist in **all contexts**.

These types of attributions lead to a defeatist attitude known as **learned helplessness**, which reduces the chance of breaking an addiction.

Some *Social Contexts* Make People *More Vulnerable* to *Addictive Behaviour*

1) According to social learning theory, being **exposed** to other people's **addictive behaviour** may **increase the chance** of an **addiction forming** in the first place (see page 94).
2) Addictive behaviour often takes place in a **social forum**, e.g. 'crack-houses' and 'shooting galleries' for cocaine and heroin addicts. The **learning model of addiction** (see page 93) suggests that these **environments** become **associated** with addictive behaviour. Spending time in these places makes the addiction **more difficult to overcome**.
3) Studies have also shown links between the **attitudes** that young people are exposed to in social situations and their own attitudes towards **potentially addictive behaviour**.

Martino et al (2006) carried out a **longitudinal study** to look at the social factors that affect the **drinking habits** of adolescents. They concluded that the norms for drinking behaviour are learned through **social observations** and **interactions**. The **perceived approval** or **use** of alcohol by parents, other important adults and peers **increased the likelihood** of future decisions to **drink** and **get drunk**.

Factors Affecting Addictive Behaviour

The *Media* Can Influence *Addictive Behaviour*

The media may influence addictive behaviours by:

1 Causing an addiction to develop:

1) The growth of mass media has provided people with another **reference** for their own behaviour.
2) The **impact** that messages from the media have on individuals **varies**, depending on the number and strength of messages that they receive from other sources.
3) One way the media influences behaviour is through reporting the **behaviour of celebrities**. Research specifically focusing on the effect that celebrities have on behaviours is lacking, but Boon and Lomore (2001) found that 59% of young people have had their **attitudes** and **beliefs** influenced in some way by a celebrity.
4) The **media coverage** of **drug-using celebrities**, for example, may make drug use seem **glamorous** to some people. This can influence people's perceptions of the **consequences** of drug use, making them more likely to start using drugs.
5) More generally, the portrayal of some addictive behaviours in the media may influence people by **social learning mechanisms**. For example, if the media shows a drug user being **rewarded** in some way (their behaviour is **reinforced**), this acts as **reinforcement** for the **viewer** as well. This is known as **vicarious reinforcement** and makes it **more likely** that they would **consider drug use themselves.**

2 Preventing or breaking an addiction:

1) The **large audience** reached by mass media means that it can be used to promote positive messages, either to **prevent addictions forming** or to help people to **break their addictions.**
2) This may be done **intentionally**, with the **aim** being to **reduce addictive behaviour**. For example, **public health interventions** often make use of the media in campaigns aimed at reducing addictive behaviours such as **smoking**, **drinking** and **drug-use**.
3) Sometimes media coverage doesn't actively seek to reduce addictive behaviour but may do so **unintentionally**. For example, watching TV programmes and films that show the **negative effects** of drug use may **reduce** the **chances of people using drugs**.

Now that mass media had finally made it to Brenda's house she hoped she could break her addiction to frilly blouses.

Practice Questions

Q1 What is self-esteem?

Q2 Describe how addicts' attributions may change over the course of an addiction, according to Davies (1996).

Q3 What was concluded from Martino et al's (2006) study?

Exam Question

Q1 a) Describe and evaluate the roles of self-esteem and attributions in creating a vulnerability to addiction. [15 marks]

b) Briefly discuss the effect of social context on the development of addiction. [5 marks]

c) Outline two ways in which the media may influence addictive behaviour. [5 marks]

We can blame the media? That's a relief. I knew it wasn't my fault...

So the moral of this story is watch out for those plotting media types — if they can influence addictive behaviour who knows what else they can do. Before long they'll have you hatching evil plans to take over the world, introducing crazy laws like no work on Fridays and... Sorry, I was daydreaming there. Back to the revision — yeah, you need to learn this stuff.

Reducing Addictive Behaviour

These pages are just for AQA. *Prevention is better than cure. That's why health psychologists are trying to figure out how to stop addictive behaviour before it starts. And how to stop it once it has started, just in case.*

The **Theory of Reasoned Action** Explains How We **Decide How We'll Behave**

1) **Fishbein** and **Ajzen** (1975) developed the **theory of reasoned action** (**TRA**) model of behaviour.
2) It states that an individual's behaviour, e.g. whether they will give up alcohol, can be **predicted** by their **intention** to perform it. Intention is determined by two factors:

- The person's **attitude to the behaviour** — this is shaped by their **beliefs** about the **outcome** of the behaviour, e.g. 'I'll save money', and their **judgement** of whether the outcome is **positive or negative, likely or unlikely**.
- **Subjective norms** — this describes their **expectations** of the **social consequences** of the behaviour, e.g. 'My friends will think I'm boring', and their **motivation** to **follow these norms**, e.g. 'I want to be popular'.

3) Sheppard et al (1988) carried out a meta-analysis and found that the TRA had a **strong predictive use** — it was pretty good at predicting intentions and behaviour. It's also a useful model for knowing how to **alter** an individual's intentions and behaviour. However, it's been criticised for **neglecting factors** such as **habits** and **emotional aspects**, which are also important when intentions are being formed.

The **Theory of Planned Behaviour** is a **Modification** of the **TRA**

1) **Ajzen** (1991) added a third factor to the TRA — a person's **perceived behavioural control**, e.g. 'I don't have the will power to give up alcohol'. This factor **increases** the model's **predictive power**.
2) This theory is known as the **theory of planned behaviour** (**TPB**). It suggests behaviour is influenced in two ways:

- **Indirectly** — if a person believes that the behaviour is **too difficult** they don't form the initial intention to carry out the behaviour.
- **Directly** — if the **perception** of their own level of control is **accurate**, e.g. they don't have sufficient willpower, they won't succeed.

3) In contrast to the TRA, the TPB takes into account the fact that people **don't always have complete control** over their behaviour, as there may be obstacles that stand in their way.
4) Norman et al's (1998) study found that **perceived behavioural control** was a strong predictor of binge-drinking. The TPB could therefore be used to develop **intervention strategies** and **prevention programmes**.
5) Both models ignore the fact that there may be **discrepancies** between **attitude** and **behaviour** and that a person's behaviour is not always a reflection of their **intentions**. People's actions aren't always rational and based on deliberate decision making processes. This is especially true for **addictive behaviour**, which is often **irrational**.

The **Health Belief Model** Can be Used To **Predict Behaviour**

1) The factors that the **health belief model** uses as predictors of behaviour include someone's:

- **Perception of susceptibility and severity** — their belief of how **likely** and **serious** the threat to their own health is if they don't carry out the preventative health behaviour, e.g. the danger of developing lung cancer as a result of smoking.
- **Perception of cost-benefit** — they weigh the **benefits** of the behaviour (e.g. reduces cancer risk) against its **costs** (e.g. suffering withdrawal symptoms).

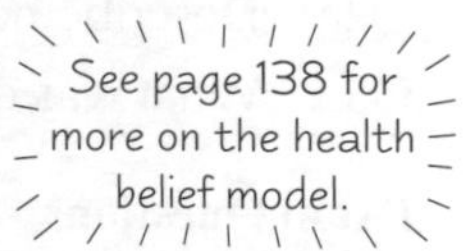
See page 138 for more on the health belief model.

2) The health belief model takes into account factors that **encourage** people to break their addictive behaviour. These factors are known as **cues to action** and include experiencing **symptoms** of health problems or exposure to **media campaigns**.
3) The model also considers the influence that **personal variables**, e.g. age, sex, social class and personality traits have on a person's perceptions.
4) The comprehensive nature of the model means that it's an ideal tool for designing **individual intervention strategies** and highlights the importance of **tailoring interventions** to an individual's personal profile.

Reducing Addictive Behaviour

A Range of Interventions Are Used to Reduce Addictive Behaviours

Biological Interventions

1) The biological approach to reducing drug and alcohol addictions involves a **gradual detox**, where the **quantity** of the substance used is **reduced over time**.
2) **Medication** may be prescribed to stop addictive behaviour, e.g. Antabuse® is prescribed to alcoholics. It causes nausea if it's combined with alcohol, discouraging alcoholics from drinking. The addict will form an **association** between drinking and nausea — this will continue even when they stop taking Antabuse®. This is known as **aversion therapy**.

Meyer and Chesser (1970) carried out a **repeated measures experiment**. A group of alcoholics who were prescribed Antabuse® were compared to a **control group**. Around **50%** of those taking Antabuse® stayed **teetotal** for at least a year — significantly more than in the control group. From this study they concluded that an **unpleasant response** can be **conditioned** to an **addictive behaviour**.

3) However, any medication prescribed has to be **carefully controlled** so it doesn't become an addiction itself.

Psychological Interventions

1) The psychological approach consists of a range of therapies that aim to change the way an addict **behaves** by changing their thought processes.
2) **Cognitive behavioural therapy** identifies the thoughts that cause the behaviour, e.g. 'I can't cope without cigarettes', and then changes this thought process. This is known as **cognitive restructuring**.
3) Cognitive behavioural therapy has had some **success**, e.g. it has enhanced the effectiveness of nicotine replacement treatment for quitting smoking.

Public Health Interventions and Legislation

1) Public health interventions address addictive behaviours on a **wide-scale** to **reduce** their **impact on society**.
2) For example, to reduce smoking the government **banned adverts** for cigarettes. They also ran **anti-smoking campaigns**, placed **warning messages** on cigarette packs and **increased prices**.
3) Many addictive behaviours are under **legislation**, e.g. smoking is illegal for under 18s and in public places.
4) Legislation creates **barriers** to the behaviour — this prevents many people from starting in the first place. One reason for this is that the **consequences** of the behaviour **increase** as it's illegal. Also, people are **less likely** to **observe** the behaviour and so are **less likely** to **copy** it (see social learning theory, page 94).
5) Legislation also increases the likelihood that people will **succeed** in attempts to **quit** their addictive behaviour. For example, as smoking in public is illegal, a smoker trying to quit will come across **fewer stimuli** that they associate with smoking (such as ash trays), making it easier for them to stop.

Practice Questions

Q1 According to the theory of reasoned action, what factors determine attitudes to addictive behaviour?
Q2 Describe the main findings of the study by Meyer and Chesser (1970).
Q3 Describe some commonly used public health interventions.

Exam Question

Q1 a) Outline the theory of planned behaviour. [5 marks]

b) Discuss some different interventions used to reduce addictive behaviours. [20 marks]

I need an intervention to sort out my TRA — tremendous revision anger...

Phew, that's a whopping amount of information on reducing addictive behaviour. You need to learn all the models of prevention and all the types of intervention that are so carefully described for you on these two pages. Lovely jubbly.

Studying Anomalous Experience

These pages are just for AQA. *It may make entertaining TV, but lots of people aren't convinced that paranormal abilities like telepathy really exist. And there's a very good reason for their doubt — a serious lack of evidence.*

Anomalous Experiences Can't Currently be Explained by *Science*

1) Something that **can't be explained by science** is called an **anomalous experience**. There are many different types:
   - **Out-of-body experience** — a sensation of **floating** around **outside** of your own body.
   - **Near-death experience** — sensations experienced when you're **close to death**, often interpreted as a glimpse into the 'afterlife'.
   - **Spontaneous psychic ability** (**psi**) — **extra-sensory perception**, e.g. telepathy, clairvoyance or psychokinesis (altering an object, e.g. moving, bending or softening it using the mind).
   - **Past-life experience** — remembering events from a **previous existence**.
   - **Anomalous healing** — healing through **unexplainable methods**, e.g. by a spiritual healer or through prayer.
2) Anomalous experiences **can't just be immediately rejected** — many things that were once considered mysterious, e.g. thunder and lightning, can now be explained scientifically.
3) So it's important that all anomalous experiences are **investigated thoroughly** — they may one day be explainable, either by what we **already know** about human behaviour, or accepted as something **completely new**.

Pseudoscience and *Fraud* Can be Mistaken For *Anomalous Experiences*

Pseudoscience

Explanations based on evidence that's been collected through **faulty scientific processes** are known as **pseudoscience**. The results of many demonstrations of so-called anomalous experiences turn out to be caused by methodological issues such as **cognitive bias** and **experimenter effects**.

Cognitive biases

Spontaneous events, such as having a dream come true, are the main reasons why people believe in anomalous experiences. People who believe in such things have been shown to be **more susceptible** to the **illusion of control** than people who don't. The illusion of control is a **cognitive bias** (a faulty judgement) which causes people to believe that they're able to **control** or **influence** the outcome of an event over which, in reality, they have no control.

Experimenter effects

The **outcome** of any psychological experiment can be affected by the **expectations of the experimenter** and how this manifests itself in their **behaviour**. Certain researchers consistently find significant results using the same methods whilst others consistently fail. This is known as **experimenter effects**. As a result of this, it's been suggested that only people who **don't believe** in that particular anomalous experience should be allowed to replicate the experiments. Experimenter effects exist in **both directions** though, and the expectations of sceptics could affect the experiment **just as strongly** in the **other direction**.

Fraud

Research has also been blighted by cases of **fraud**, where scientists have **deliberately deceived people**, invalidating observations and results. Researchers who believe in the anomalous experience are **more likely** to **miss the tricks** of fraudsters as they are biased towards results that are **consistent with their existing beliefs**.

People claiming to have **psychic abilities** usually demonstrate them **most successfully** when they have some **control** over how they show them and the way they are observed. In order to reduce the chances of pseudoscience and fraud being passed off as anomalous experiences, **Wiseman and Morris** (1995) developed a set of **methodological guidelines** for research into this area. They include advice on issues such as **randomisation of stimuli** and **preventing 'sensory leakage'** (soundproofing rooms, etc.).

Studying Anomalous Experience

Studies into Psi Often Provoke Controversy

1 Ganzfeld Studies Have Shown Mixed Results for ESP

Suddenly the idea of sensory deprivation seemed a lot more appealing...

1) **Ganzfeld studies** test participants for **extra-sensory perception** (**ESP**).
2) One participant, known as the **receiver**, is in a state of mild sensory deprivation. This is usually done by covering their eyes with halved ping pong balls, playing white noise through headphones and sitting them in a soundproof room lit with red light.
3) A participant in another room, the **sender**, then concentrates on a visual stimulus in an attempt to transfer it to the receiver.
4) The receiver is then shown **four stimuli** — one is the stimulus the sender attempted to transfer by ESP. If the receiver correctly identifies this stimulus it's called a **hit**.
5) The results and interpretation of Ganzfeld experiments vary:

A review of 28 Ganzfeld studies by **Honorton** (1985) showed a **38% hit rate**, significantly above the 25% rate of chance. He claimed that this provided **evidence for ESP**. **Hyman** (1985) disagreed, **criticising** the studies for a **lack of randomised stimuli**, **inconsistent judging procedures** and **selective reporting**. After consideration, Honorton and Hyman jointly agreed on suitable conditions to address these flaws and **autoganzfeld studies** were designed to take these into account. The results of autoganzfeld studies **still produced significant results.**

A **meta-analysis** by **Milton and Wiseman** (1999) of 30 autoganzfeld studies showed **no significant evidence for ESP**. This analysis was criticised for including studies which **deviated** from the conventional technique. When the ten studies closest to the original technique were analysed by **Bem et al** (2001), a **significant hit rate was found**.

2 Little Evidence Has Been Found for Psychokinetic Ability

1) Some people claim to have **psychokinetic ability**, which allows them to move objects using their mind alone.
2) Many people dispute these claims — they believe that **tricks** are used to make it appear that objects have been altered by psychokinesis. Several **magicians** have demonstrated how this can be done.
3) Belief in psychokinesis is often explained by cognitive biases such as the **illusion of control** (see opposite page).
4) To establish whether psychokinesis is possible researchers have searched for evidence in **laboratory conditions**:

One common method is to ask participants to **alter the outcome** of a computerised **random number generator**. This allows a lot of data to be collected in **controlled conditions**. **Holger et al** (2006) conducted a **meta-analysis** on the results of 380 such studies. They did find an effect but it was extremely small — it was probably only reported because of its **interesting** and **controversial nature**.

Practice Questions

Q1 What is pseudoscience?

Q2 Name two methodological issues which could explain so-called anomalous experiences.

Q3 Summarise the method used in Ganzfeld studies.

Exam Question

Q1 a) Explain the term anomalous experience, using examples. [5 marks]

b) Describe how pseudoscience can influence research into anomalous experiences. [10 marks]

c) Outline and evaluate the evidence for the existence of ESP. [10 marks]

I don't condone cheating — but telepathy would be a mighty useful skill...

This is all getting a bit odd now — what with past life and out-of-body experiences. If you're not too spooked out you need to learn about pseudoscience, fraud and the controversy around Ganzfeld studies. If you are too spooked out you need to learn about pseudoscience, fraud and the controversy around Ganzfeld studies as well. There's no getting away from it.

Factors Underlying Anomalous Experience

Again, these pages are only for AQA. *When it comes to the paranormal most people fall into two distinct groups — sceptics and believers. There's been loads of research into what makes people believe in the paranormal.*

Belief in Anomalous Experiences Varies Between Individuals

An individual's belief in anomalous experiences can be measured by the **paranormal belief scale** (**PBS**). Some studies using the PBS have found **moderate correlations** between paranormal belief and certain cognitive, personality and biological factors:

1) **Cognitive factors**. Paranormal belief has been found to correlate with low cognitive abilities, proneness to irrational beliefs and fantasy. Psychopathology (displaying behaviour indicating mental impairment) and dissociative experiences (disruption to mental processes, e.g. memory) also correlate with belief in the paranormal.
2) **Personality factors**. High levels of neuroticism and extraversion, as well as low levels of conscientiousness have been found to correlate with paranormal beliefs.
3) **Biological factors**. Women tend to show higher levels of paranormal belief than men.

Correlations don't necessarily show cause and effect — they just show that the variables are related.

Sometimes people use **paranormal explanations** to explain **normal experiences** that could be explained by science. This is known as **misattribution** and is more likely in people with a high level of belief in the paranormal.

Belief in the Paranormal Can Give a Feeling of Control

The development of paranormal belief has been linked with feeling a **lack of control in childhood**. This could be as a result of being a **younger sibling**, having **authoritarian parents**, experiencing **parental divorce** or **moving house regularly**. The belief in the paranormal is used as a way to **assert control** over the environment.

Lawrence et al (1995) — Childhood trauma and paranormal belief

Method: This was a **correlational study** using questionnaire methods on university students to measure the extent of the link between **childhood trauma** and **paranormal beliefs** and **experiences**.

Results: Reports of an abusive and traumatic childhood were **positively correlated** with paranormal beliefs.

Conclusion: Holding paranormal beliefs can act as a **coping mechanism** to reduce adulthood anxiety stemming from a perceived lack of control which developed in childhood.

Evaluation: The correlation found by the study was only **small** and self report data, particularly when it's retrospective, can be **unreliable**. Also, correlation doesn't show **causation**. Although some paranormal beliefs, e.g. psychokinesis, would suggest that we have control over the world, others suggest that we are at the mercy of higher forces, e.g. superstitious and religious beliefs. This study **doesn't distinguish** between the two.

Some Paranormal Beliefs Have Cultural Significance

In some cultures, certain paranormal beliefs are considered normal and are used to explain particular phenomena. For example:

1) In Taiwan, a state known as **Hsieh-Ping**, characterised by tremors and hallucinations, is explained as being possessed by an ancestral ghost that's attempting to communicate with the family.
2) In Mediterranean and Middle Eastern cultures, a run of bad luck is sometimes explained as being caused by the **Evil Eye**, cast on them by someone else.
3) In some sub-cultures in Southern USA **rootwork** is an explanation for illnesses believed to be related to hexes, witchcraft or the presence of evil people.
4) In Hinduism, it's believed that some gurus are able to **levitate**.

Lucy was thrilled to find herself in a culture where her levitation skills were accepted.

Factors Underlying Anomalous Experience

Many Factors Promote Belief in Anomalous Experiences

Deception and self-deception can promote belief in the paranormal

1) People who claim to have paranormal abilities are often accused of **deception**, particularly as a lot of the anomalous acts that they perform can be **simulated** by known tricks.
2) Some people, known as **believers**, are naturally inclined to believe in the paranormal and so are **easily convinced** by claims of paranormal abilities.
3) Believers may even rule out the possibility of **fraud** when witnessing a pseudo-psychic demonstration even if they're **told** that it's a trick.
4) This denial of rational evidence is known as **self-deception** and may be caused by **information processing biases** or the **emotional attachment** felt for such beliefs.

Superstitions are paranormal beliefs that allow people to feel in control

1) A **superstition** is a belief that an act or object will affect an event when there's **no logical reason** for it to do so.
2) They're the result of **cognitive biases** (errors of judgement caused by faulty thought processes) such as the **illusion of control** (see page 100). Superstitions give people a sense of **control** over uncontrollable events.
3) Superstitions can be **negative**, e.g. believing that breaking a mirror brings bad luck, or **positive**, e.g. believing that lucky charms bring good luck.
4) Positive superstitions may promote **optimism** and **self-efficacy** (belief in your ability to achieve something). This increased belief may increase the chances of the individual influencing the situation themselves. This is known as the **placebo effect**, and it **reinforces** the initial superstition.

Coincidences can be mistaken for anomalous experiences

1) A **coincidence** is when events **appear to be linked** (e.g. dreaming about a car crash and then being involved in one) when in fact the two events are unconnected and occurred closely together purely by **chance**.
2) **Cognitive biases** can cause people to mistakenly see coincidences as **evidence of paranormal events**. There are different types of cognitive biases that could cause this:
   - **The Availability Bias** — people judge how likely a coincidence is by how easily they can **recall** previous examples of it. **Positive examples** (e.g. having a dream that came true) are **more memorable** than negative examples (e.g. having a dream that didn't come true).
   - **The Representative Bias** — people's ideas of how likely a particular coincidence is are based on their judgement of how common it is in everyday life. If their **range** of experience is **small** they're likely to **misjudge** how likely the coincidence is — extreme outcomes are more likely.

Practice Questions

Q1 List cognitive, personality and biological factors that underlie belief in anomalous experiences.

Q2 Give examples of paranormal beliefs from other cultures.

Q3 Define 'self-deception', 'coincidence' and 'superstition'.

Exam Question

Q1 a) Describe how superstitions and coincidences can be mistaken for evidence of anomalous experiences. [15 marks]

b) Discuss the potential benefits to the individual of belief in the paranormal. [10 marks]

Rootwork — an explanation for illness related to evil dentists...

If you're a sceptic you're probably scoffing at all this anomalous experience malarkey by now. But chances are you've indulged in some superstitious behaviour in your time — touching wood, not walking under ladders, crossing your fingers — they all fall under paranormal belief. We all lie somewhere on the PBS, whether truly sceptical or out there giving the evil eye.

Research into Anomalous Experiences

Still just for AQA people. *Whether you believe in anomalous experiences or not, the paranormal can't be dismissed as hokum unless it's been researched properly. The problem is that a lot of the time it's quite hard to study...*

There's Been **Research** Into **Psychic Healing...**

Psychic healers claim they can treat illness and injury **without any physical intervention**. Instead, the healer moves their hands over the patient's body without making contact. The aim is to transfer a force and restore **balance** in the patient. Some studies have been done to try to determine whether psychic healing actually works.

Attevelt (1988) — Evidence for the psychic healing of asthma

Method:	In an **independent groups design**, 96 asthma patients were allocated to one of 3 groups — an **optimal group**, a **distance group** and a **control group**. Patients in the optimal group received treatment from a psychic healer in the usual way. The distance group patients were also treated by a healer, but this time from behind a screen. The control group didn't receive any treatment but the screen was present. Distance group and control group patients didn't know which group they belonged to as their physical experiences were the same. **Physical** and **subjective** measures of asthma symptoms were taken.
Results:	The **physical symptoms** of asthma (measured by peak flow) improved significantly in **all patients**. The **optimal group** improved significantly more than the other groups on **subjective measures** of well-being (i.e. they 'felt' an improvement).
Conclusion:	The lack of difference between **physical symptoms** of patients in the different groups shows that improvement was **not down to paranormal effects**. The **subjective improvement** in the optimal group patients but not distance group patients shows the influence of **psychological** rather than paranormal factors.
Evaluation:	Participants were **randomly allocated** to groups after being stratified (see page 214) according to the severity of their asthma. This prevented **bias** in the groups. The people who took the patients' peak flow measurements didn't know which group each patient belonged to. This also prevented **bias**. The use of a **control group** distinguished the psychological effects of visiting a healer from the physiological effects.

...Out-of-Body Experiences...

An **out-of-body experience** (**OBE**) is a sensation of floating **outside the body**, seeing the world from a different perspective. They're **spontaneous** and **rare** events so researching them is difficult. Most evidence is based on **case studies**.

Many people remain sceptical about OBEs and much of the research into them has been heavily criticised.

Tart (1968) — The Case of Miss Z

Method:	This **case study** was based on a young woman (Miss Z) who reported experiencing OBEs in her sleep since childhood. Tart brought her into a sleep lab for 4 nights to **compare** her reports of OBEs with **physiological data** collected from an EEG that monitored her brain activity. Also, numbers were written down and placed where they couldn't be seen from the bed (e.g. lying on top of high shelves). Miss Z was asked to find these target numbers during her OBE, whilst she was physically still in bed.
Results:	Miss Z's OBEs **correlated** with a particular pattern of non-dreaming, non-awake brain waves. On one occasion, she also correctly identified a 5 digit target number.
Conclusion:	OBEs have a **physiological** basis.
Evaluation:	The study had to rely on Miss Z's own reports of when and for how long she had left her body. These reports were **retrospective** and **subjective**. Tart couldn't be sure that Miss Z hadn't found out the target number conventionally, e.g. from seeing its reflection in the nearby clock face. This study isn't accepted as reliable psychological research by the wider scientific community.

Some recent studies have **induced** states similar to OBEs through brain stimulation of participants. This suggests that OBEs could be explained by **physiological mechanisms** causing a kind of 'waking dream'.

Research into Anomalous Experiences

...Near-Death-Experiences...

Like OBEs, NDEs are hard to prove and many psychologists question whether they actually occur or not.

There are obviously **ethical issues** involved in creating states of near death for the purposes of studying **near-death-experiences (NDEs)**. So, like OBEs, most research has to be taken from **case studies**. From an accumulation of 102 case studies, Kenneth Ring (1980) determined that:

1) Individuals reporting NDEs **don't fit** a particular **gender**, **age**, or **religious profile**.
2) There also appears to be **no link** between the reporting of a **NDE** and a person's **attitude** towards the paranormal.
3) Individuals who came close to death or were clinically dead for a period of time report experiences such as moving through a tunnel towards a **light**, **OBEs**, **reuniting** with **dead loved ones** and feeling total **contentment**. These experiences were found even when the moments leading up to near-death were particularly nasty.
4) **Medication** at the time of death **did not predict** the experience of NDE.
5) Reports of NDEs are more **coherent** than reports of hallucinations.
6) Individuals who report experiencing a NDE also report **life-changing shifts of attitudes**, often developing a newly found appreciation of life and loved ones.

...And *Psychic Mediumship*

Psychic mediumship is the ability to **communicate with spirits** and transmit messages from the dead to the living. There are a range of methods with which mediums claim they can communicate with the dead, including **telepathy** and being **possessed by spirits** that then talk through them. Studies of psychic mediumship are usually based on **séances** — intentional attempts to communicate with spirits. One of the most famous studies into psychic mediumship is the **Scole Experiment**.

The **Scole Experiment** took place in Norfolk between **1993** and **1998**. Researchers including Fontana, Ellison and Keen witnessed 37 séances in rooms that were thoroughly **searched** beforehand to try to **prevent any trickery**. A professional magician was also present to identify any attempts at **fraud**. During the séances a number of paranormal occurrences were reported. These included the **materialisation** of objects, **levitation**, patterns of **light**, **voices** and the appearance of **whole people** or **body parts**.

Some people believe that the Scole Experiment provides **evidence** of life after death and mediumship. No fraud was identified at any time during the experiment and the professional magician present confirmed that **no currently known trickery** could have produced the effects that were observed. However, the experiment has been **heavily criticised** and isn't widely accepted as evidence for mediumship. The **experimental conditions** were unreliable — to some extent they were controlled by the mediums. For example, the researchers wanted to use infra-red imaging (as most of the séances took place in darkness) but this was rejected by the mediums as they claimed it would distract them. Also, all the experimenters believed in the paranormal so may have shown **experimenter effects** (see p.100).

Practice Questions

Q1 Describe the findings of the study by Attevelt (1988).

Q2 Describe the case study of Miss Z.

Q3 Outline some typical features of a near-death-experience.

Exam Question

Q1 a) Outline the difficulties of studying paranormal experiences scientifically. [10 marks]

b) Discuss the effectiveness of psychic healing. [15 marks]

Revision — definitely a near death experience...

And that's the end of the section — yay. Once you've learnt these two pages that is. Then you'd best go back through the whole section to check you still remember all the fascinating stuff you've learnt on the way. Yep, back through the spooky bits, the addictions and the celeb worship, all the way to attitudes and persuasion. What a strange journey you've been on.

Explanations of Criminal Behaviour

You can skip these pages if you're doing AQA. *In fact, if you're doing AQA you can skip merrily all the way to Section 16. And as for the rest of you, currently wondering 'Why didn't I get to do AQA?', don't worry — this section is actually quite interesting. All the AQA people have to look forward to is research methods...*

Criminological Psychology Examines Why People Commit Crimes

Criminological psychology is all about the **drives** and **behaviour** of criminals. Criminological psychologists examine what makes someone cross the line and commit a crime. They also examine the aftermath of a crime — they look at the **criminal's reaction** to what they've done, as well as the psychological aspects of **court cases** and **punishment**.

Eysenck Explained Criminal Behaviour in Terms of Personality Types

Hans Eysenck was one of the first psychologists to examine human **personality**. He initially identified **two** main **personality dimensions** (scales) and suggested that everyone fits in somewhere along these dimensions:

1) **Neuroticism-stability** — individuals towards the neurotic end of this dimension show traits such as anxiousness and restlessness. Traits at the other end of the scale include reliability and calmness.
2) **Extroversion-introversion** — individuals towards the extrovert end of this dimension tend to be sociable, restless and assertive. Those at the other end tend to be quiet, passive and reserved.

In later research during the 1970s Eysenck added a **third personality dimension**:

3) **Psychoticism** — this scale shows how disposed an individual is to psychotic breakdown. Those who score highly tend to be aggressive, hostile and uncaring.

Eysenck's research suggested that individuals have a **genetic predisposition** to a particular personality type — this can lead to particular behaviours, including **criminal behaviours**. Eysenck believed that **psychoticism** was a good **predictor** of criminal behaviour. He also thought **extraversion** was a good indicator of criminal behaviour for **young** people, but **neuroticism** a better indicator for criminal behaviour in **older** people.

Raine Investigated the Link Between Brain Dysfunction and Criminality

Raine believed that there was an identifiable **biological disposition** for criminal behaviour. He suggested that a **biological dysfunction** within the brain could cause an individual to commit acts of violence.

Raine et al (1997) — Brain dysfunction and criminality

Method: Raine used **PET scans** to create 3-D images of the functional processes happening in the brains of 41 murderers (pleading not guilty by reason of insanity) and 41 control participants.

Results: The murderers showed **reduced glucose metabolism** in the prefrontal cortex, superior parietal gyrus and the corpus callosum, and **asymmetrical activity** in the two hemispheres. In other words some of their brain processes were **dysfunctional**.

Conclusion: The evidence **supported** a link between brain dysfunction and predisposition to violent acts.

Evaluation: The researchers used a **control group** who were matched on variables such as age and sex. However, researchers could not **randomly allocate** participants to the 'control' or 'killer' groups, so needed to be cautious when drawing conclusions about **causal relationships**.

Brunner (1991) Showed a Link Between Genes and Aggression

Studies in genetics have helped provide a link between **genes** and levels of **aggression**. For example, it's been found that mice lacking a gene for an enzyme that regulates brain **serotonin** levels displayed higher levels of impulsive aggression than those with normal serotonin levels. However, this can't necessarily be generalised to humans.

Human studies have been carried out though. **Adoption studies** in Denmark showed higher concordance rates of criminal activity between adopted children and their biological parents than with their adoptive parents.

Explanations of Criminal Behaviour

Daly and Wilson Gave an *Evolutionary Explanation* of Criminal Behaviour

Men are far more likely than women to engage in **criminal behaviour**. **Daly and Wilson (1988)** attempted to explain this in **evolutionary terms**:

1) They identified **fitness variance** between males and females. This is the idea that in a breeding system with many choices and variables, some males **monopolise** access to females.
2) So, while **women** are generally **successful** in their need to reproduce, some **men** don't actually get to reproduce at all. This **inequality** of fitness variance makes men highly **competitive** in the mating game, leading to a high level of **aggression**.
3) This raised aggression leads to a larger number of **homicides** being committed by men than by women. These acts of violence can often begin over a trivial matter but end in **serious violence** because the men involved are unwilling to back down due to male '**pride**' and the desire to **impress** their prospective mate.

The Learning Approach States Criminal Behaviour is *Learned* Not Inherited

The general principle behind this theory is that people can learn certain behaviours (including violent or criminal behaviour) by observing the behaviours of others and the outcomes of those behaviours.

	Bandura (1961) — The Bobo Doll Experiments
Method:	36 boys and 36 girls (average age 4 years) were put into two groups. **Group 1** watched an adult playing aggressively with an inflatable 'Bobo Doll'. **Group 2** witnessed only **non-violent** play in the adult model. Children were then given a **choice** of violent and non-violent toys to play with, including the Bobo Doll, and were **observed** by an unseen researcher.
Results:	The children who witnessed the **aggressive** behaviour were found to be **more** likely to behave aggressively in their own play than children who were exposed to a non-violent adult model. **Boys** were also found to be **more aggressive** than girls.
Conclusion:	Children learn aggressive behaviour through imitation of others.
Evaluation:	The study doesn't show whether the effects are **long-term**, and it also lacks **ecological validity** as it's not a real-life situation. There are also **ethical issues** surrounding the study as it encouraged violence.

There is also a concern that people might mimic violent acts that they see in the **media** (e.g. in films or computer games), as well as in real-life situations.

Practice Questions

Q1 What is criminological psychology?

Q2 Name the three personality dimensions outlined by Eysenck.

Q3 What did Bandura (1961) conclude from the Bobo Doll experiments?

Exam Questions

Q1 Describe how the learning approach can be used to explain antisocial behaviour. [4 marks]

Q2 a) Outline one explanation of why a person might turn to crime. [10 marks]

b) Evaluate explanations of why a person might turn to crime. [15 marks]

So men commit violent crimes because women all fancy Johnny Depp...?

So, two approaches covered here. The biological approach suggests that criminal behaviour's caused by our genes and the learning approach reckons that violent behaviour's learned by observing the behaviour of others. That should be enough theories for one topic. But hold on a jiffy — the next two pages seem to have more explanations of criminal behaviour...

Explanations of Criminal Behaviour

Just OCR people here. *The last two pages were about inherited and learned causes of criminal behaviour. Here are some other explanations for why some people commit crime – their **upbringing** and their **cognition (patterns of thinking)**.*

Farrington Tested Whether Disrupted Family Life Causes Delinquency

Farrington et al have tested several **hypotheses** since the '60s. They have looked to find out:

- If delinquency is more common among boys from **permanently disrupted families** than boys from intact families.
- How the boy's **age** at the time of the family disruption affects his risk of delinquency.

Farrington (2006) — The Cambridge Study of Delinquent Development

Method:	This was a **longitudinal study** of the development of antisocial behaviour in 411 male participants. The **sample** was taken from boys aged 8–9 who lived in a working class area of inner-city London. The study involved participants being tested at several ages using **questionnaires**, **participant interviews** and **parent interviews**, which were then compared as the study progressed.
Results:	**41%** of the males in the sample received **criminal convictions** aged 10–50. Those who turned to crime earliest tended to commit the most offences. Most importantly, the **main childhood risk factors** at age 8–10 for later offending were: • family criminality • risk-taking • low school attainment • poverty • poor parenting
Conclusion:	Aspects of **upbringing** can contribute to delinquent behaviour in later life.
Evaluation:	**Very detailed data** about the participants was collected, including changes over **time**. This allowed the development of the boys to be studied from a number of **different perspectives**. Over 90% of the participants were working class and white so the results can't be **generalised** to the whole population.

Sutherland Reckoned That Deviant Behaviour is Learnt From Peers

Edwin Sutherland (1939) formulated a **differential association hypothesis** which stated that people become deviant or show more deviant behaviours when they associate with **other deviant people**.

1) Sutherland believed that criminal behaviour could be **learned** in interactions with other deviant individuals.
2) People not only learn the **techniques** and **methods** involved in certain crimes, but they also pick up the **motives** and **attitudes** behind the crimes.
3) This theory explains why individuals imprisoned for a minor offence often **reoffend** when they're released. Spending time with **other criminals** in the institution (who may have committed more serious crimes) makes them likely to learn further criminal behaviours, which they may use when released.

Loeber Studied How Delinquency Develops in Young Males

Loeber found that various factors affect the risk of delinquency in young boys, including **socio-economic factors**, **family situation** and **personal attributes** such as IQ and level of impulsiveness.

Loeber (2002) — The Pittsburgh Youth Study

Method:	This was a **longitudinal study** of the development of antisocial behaviour, substance misuse and delinquency in young males. It began in 1987 and assessments were carried out **every six months**, then **once a year**. These involved the boys, their parents and teachers as **participant informers**. A large variety of tests (**interviews**, **observations**, **questionnaires**, etc.) were used to study behaviour development over time.
Results:	The higher the number of **'risk' elements** (e.g. **low socio-economic status**, **broken family**, **poor parental supervision**), the higher the chances of the development of serious delinquent behaviour. Approximately **2%** of the boys were later convicted of **homicide**. In most cases a **delinquent attitude** arose **before** delinquent behaviour was displayed. This attitude seemed to increase with age.
Conclusion:	The way a child is **brought up** plays an important role in their behaviour in later life.
Evaluation:	This was a **natural experiment** with **high ecological validity**. However, **uncontrolled variables** could affect the **reliability** of the results.

Explanations of Criminal Behaviour

Yochelson Found That Criminals Share a Pattern of Thinking

Samuel Yochelson believed that criminals actually **choose** a life of crime because they **enjoy** it.

Yochelson and Samenow (1976) — Criminal thinking patterns

Method:	**255 criminals** from **various backgrounds** were evaluated. Half of these had been found not guilty by reason of **insanity**. Four years of **psychodynamic testing** and **therapy** took place. The goal was to locate the **cause** of criminal behaviour, so that behaviour could be **changed**.
Results:	Patients **manipulated** sessions to provide the behaviour that the researchers were looking for. The patients used psychological theories to provide **excuses** for their criminal ways and to **demonstrate improvement** in behaviour in the hope of an earlier release. Some patients **appeared** to improve but **continued to commit crimes**, such as violating hospital rules.
Conclusion:	Yochelson believed the patients were **not actually mentally ill** — the only common factor they shared was a **specific pattern of thinking**. Yochelson and Samenow named these patterns of thinking **'Thinking Errors'** and believed it was these errors that led them to see their criminal behaviour as acceptable.
Evaluation:	The data used by Yochelson and Samenow was mostly **qualitative**, based on the researchers' own impressions during interviews with patients. It's possible for this type of data to be affected by **researcher bias**.

Kohlberg Thought Criminals Have a Different Moral Outlook

Kohlberg was interested in **moral development**. He believed it occurred over **six progressive stages**.

1) An action is morally wrong if the person who commits it is **punished** as a result (common in children).
2) The right behaviour is the one that is in **your own best interest**.
3) The right behaviour is the one that makes **other people** think positively about you.
4) It is important to **obey laws** and follow **social conventions** because they help **society** to function properly.
5) The right course of action is the one that promotes the **greatest good** for the **greatest number of people**.
6) Actions are driven by **abstract, universal principles** of right and wrong, which **don't** depend on the situation.

Serious offenders have a **moral outlook** that **differs** from that of the law-abiding majority — they **don't** follow these normal stages of moral development.

Gudjonsson Found That Violent Criminals Tended to Blame Others

1) Studies by **Gudjonsson** into how criminals **explained** their behaviour found that those who had committed the most **serious** types of crime, i.e. violent offenders, were also the most likely to **blame external causes**.
2) Criminals who blamed factors beyond their own control were also **less likely to feel remorse** for their crimes.
3) In addition, Gudjonsson found that criminals who blamed external factors for their actions tended to have **high psychoticism scores** in personality tests, which has itself been linked with criminal behaviour (see page 106).

Practice Questions

Q1 What was Sutherland's differential association hypothesis?

Q2 Suggest one possible criticism of the methods used by Yochelson and Samenow (1976).

Exam Question

Q1 a) Outline one or more theories for why someone might turn to crime. [10 marks]

b) Evaluate explanations of why some people turn to crime. [15 marks]

So many causes — I'm amazed there are any law-abiding citizens left...

There can't possibly be just one theory that explains why people turn to crime. Which is why you have so many to learn.

Eyewitness Testimony

Edexcel and OCR only. *Eyewitness testimonies often provide vital information — as long as they're accurate. This can be assessed using laboratory experiments, field experiments and natural experiments (see page 215).*

*Eyewitness Testimony Can Be Affected by **Misleading Information***

Using a **laboratory experiment**, **Loftus and Palmer (1974)** investigated how eyewitness testimony (EWT) can be **distorted**. They used **leading questions**, where a certain answer is subtly implied in the question:

	Loftus and Palmer (1974) studied EWT in a lab experiment
Method:	**Experiment 1:** Participants were shown a film of a multiple car crash. They were then asked a series of questions including 'How fast do you think the cars were going when they **hit**?' In different conditions, the word 'hit' was replaced with '**smashed**', '**collided**', '**bumped**' or '**contacted**'.
Results:	Participants given the word '**smashed**' estimated the **highest speed** (an average of 41 mph). Those given the word '**contacted**' gave the **lowest** estimate (an average of 32 mph).
Method:	**Experiment 2:** The participants were split into three groups. One group was given the verb 'smashed', another 'hit', and a control group weren't given any indication of the vehicles' speed. A week later, the participants were asked '**Did you see any broken glass?**'.
Results:	Although there was no broken glass in the film, participants were more likely to say that they'd seen broken glass in the '**smashed**' condition (32%) than any other (14% for 'hit' and 12% for 'contacted').
Conclusion:	**Leading questions** can affect the **accuracy** of an individual's memory of an event.
Evaluation:	This has implications for **police interviews**. However, this was an artificial experiment — watching a video isn't as **emotionally arousing** as a real-life event, which could affect recall. In fact, a later **field study** found that participants who thought they'd witnessed a **real** robbery gave a **more accurate** description of the robber. The experimental design might also lead to **demand characteristics**, where the results are skewed because of the participants' expectations about the purposes of the experiment. This would reduce its **validity** and **reliability**.

Anxiety** can Affect **Focus

Small increases in anxiety and arousal tend to **increase the accuracy** of memory, but **high levels** can have a **negative effect**. In **violent crimes** (where anxiety is likely to be high), the witness may focus on **central details** (e.g. a weapon) and neglect others.

Well, there were three of them, all huge with big sharp teeth...

	Loftus (1979) studied weapon focus in EWT
Method:	In a study with an **independent groups** design, participants heard a discussion in a nearby room. In one condition, a man came out of the room with a pen and grease on his hands. In the second condition, the man came out carrying a knife covered in blood. Participants were asked to identify the man from 50 photographs.
Results:	Participants in condition 1 were 49% accurate. Only 33% of the participants in condition 2 were correct.
Conclusion:	When anxious and aroused, witnesses focus on a weapon at the expense of other details.
Evaluation:	The study has **high ecological validity**, as it was a field experiment and the participants weren't aware that the study was staged. However, this means that there are also **ethical** considerations, as participants could have been very stressed at the sight of the man with the knife.

*Misleading Questions and Anxiety **Don't Always** Affect EWT*

A **field study** by **Yuille and Cutshall (1986)** showed that witnesses of a **real** incident (a gun shooting) had **remarkably accurate memories** of the event. A thief was shot and killed by police and witnesses were interviewed. Thirteen of them were invited to be **re-interviewed five months later**. Recall was found to be **highly accurate**, even after this time period. The researchers had included two **misleading questions** in the study but these were found to have **no effect** on the subjects' answers. This study had **high ecological validity** as it was based on a real-life event. However, the witnesses who experienced the **highest levels of stress** were also **closest** to the event — it's difficult to determine whether **proximity** or **stress** contributed to the accuracy of their recall.

Eyewitness Testimony

The **Cognitive Interview** was Developed to **Increase Accuracy**

Research has shown that the accuracy of eyewitness testimony is affected by many factors. Cognitive psychologists have played a big part in helping to **increase the accuracy** of eyewitness testimony. The **cognitive interview technique** was developed by **Geiselman et al (1985)** to try to increase the accuracy of witnesses' recall of events during police questioning. Here's basically what happens in cognitive interviews:

1) The interviewer tries to make the witness **relax** and tailors his/her **language** to suit the witness.
2) The witness recreates the environmental and internal (e.g. mood) **context** of the crime scene.
3) The witness reports absolutely **everything** that they can remember about the crime.
4) The witness is asked to recall details of the crime in **different orders**.
5) The witness is asked to recall the event from various **different perspectives**, e.g. from the point of view of other witnesses.
6) The witness avoids any **judgemental** and **personal comments**.

Another **Geiselman study (1986)**, involving a staged theft, showed that the cognitive interview technique did **enhance** memory recall and also **reduced** the effect of leading questions.

E-fits Can Be Used to **Recreate Faces** From **Witness Descriptions**

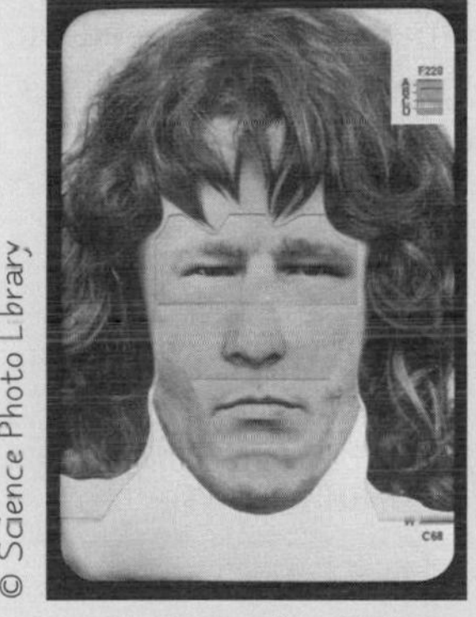
© Science Photo Library

Example of an E-fit.

1) **E-fits** (or **facial composites**) are pictures of suspects that are produced by **witnesses** (or in some cases victims) with the help of **computer software**.
2) Some studies suggest that we find it difficult to recognise **individual features** outside the context of a whole face. So, an important part of the E-fit creation process is that witnesses are **never** allowed to see the **individual features** that make up the E-fit **by themselves**.
3) Instead, the operator interviews the witness using a **cognitive interview** as described above and then uses their description of the suspect to create an **initial image**.
4) The witness is then allowed to view the image and make suggestions about how it can be **modified** to make it more accurate. The software allows the operator to **resize** and **redraw** the different features as necessary.
5) The E-fit can then be **published** in the hope that the suspect will be identified by people who know them.

Practice Questions

Q1 What was the main conclusion of the research by Loftus and Palmer (1974)?

Q2 How were the findings of Yuille and Cutshall (1986) different to those of Loftus (1979)?

Q3 What is an E-fit?

Exam Questions

Q1 Outline a laboratory study into eyewitness testimony. [4 marks]

Q2 a) Outline the use of the cognitive interview in eyewitness testimony. [10 marks]

b) Discuss the factors that can influence accurate identification. [15 marks]

A tall, thin man, quite short with black, fair hair — great fat bloke she was...

Well, thanks to this page I now haven't got a clue about what I've really experienced in my life. Did that man I saw shoplifting really have stubble, scars, piercings and a ripped leather jacket... Or was he actually a 12-year-old girl...

Interviewing Suspects

These lovely pages are for OCR peeps only. *And before you ask, OCR peeps, no, you can't just skip these pages and watch 'The Bill' instead. Or 'NYPD Blue'. Or any other police-based TV drama for that matter. Sorry about that.*

Vrij Examined How You Can Tell When Someone is **Lying**

When interviewing a suspect it's important for police to be able to tell whether or not they're telling the **truth**. **Aldert Vrij** has carried out extensive research into how a person's **behaviour** can be used to **detect deceit**.

Vrij et al (2000) used behavioural signals to detect deceit

Method:	73 nursing students were interviewed about a film that they had just been shown. Students either had to tell the truth or lie in response to the interviewer's questions. The researchers compared the **non-verbal behaviour** of the liars and the truth-tellers, as well as **what they said**. **Criteria-based Content Analysis** (CBCA) and **Reality Monitoring** (RM) techniques were used in the analysis of the verbal element.
Results:	There were several **verbal** and **non-verbal indicators** that showed participants were lying. Analysis of the non-verbal behaviour alone allowed the researchers to correctly identify lies and truths most of the time. Also using CBCA and RM further **increased** this percentage.
Conclusion:	Liars try to **compensate** in some way for their deceptive behaviour — they display behaviours that can be used to pinpoint lying through **body language**.
Evaluation:	The participants were **aware** that they were taking part in a truth study and may have unconsciously **changed** their behaviour accordingly. This was also an **artificial** situation, so the results lack **ecological validity**.

Vrij also examined the impact of two **personality traits** on deceptive behaviour: **public self-consciousness** and the **ability to control behaviour**. He discovered that people who were high in public self-consciousness **decreased** the hand gestures that they used during acts of deception. Also, people who were very able to control their behaviour **ceased** hand gestures completely during deception. People who were both low in public self-consciousness and inept at controlling behaviour **increased** their hand gestures while lying.

Vrij concluded that:

1) Deception causes **stress**.
2) This stress can be a direct result of **guilt** or could be caused by **fear** of being caught.
3) Deceivers will display **nervousness**.
4) Observers **expect** deceivers to show nervous behaviour and will **look** for it.

So, a liar must **suppress** or **cease** nervous behaviours to escape detection.

Inbau Wrote the ***First Interrogation Manual*** for the Police

The police use various different **interrogation methods**. **Fred Inbau** was a pioneer in the field — over many years he and his colleagues developed an interrogation technique that became widely used. It involved a period of **standard questioning** which, if this failed, was supported by a **second** line of questioning. Here, the blame of the crime was **shifted** or it was implied that the crime was **accidental** to make it easier for the suspect to confess.

The technique involved the use of **Reid's** (a colleague of Inbau's) **nine steps** of interrogation:

1) Direct **confrontation**.
2) Develop a **scenario** which offers an **excuse** for the crime.
3) Don't allow the suspect to **deny** that they're guilty.
4) Use **reasons** for the crime (e.g. accident, misunderstanding etc.) to move towards a confession.
5) The suspect may now be **confused** — maintain their **attention**.
6) Offer **alternatives** to the suspect or infer guilt.
7) Pose an alternative explanation — a scenario more **socially acceptable** but still implying guilt.
8) Make the suspect **talk through** the offence again.
9) Make the suspect sign a **confession**.

This technique has come under fire as it can be a **threatening** procedure for the suspects involved. If the questioner is dominant and forceful the **fear** that the questioning creates can result in a **false confession** (see next page). Vulnerable people can be at risk as **coerced internalised confession** can take place, where a suspect with no memory of a time can be convinced they are guilty even if they're not.

Interviewing Suspects

Some People Are More Likely to Give **False Confessions**

Some people are more likely than others to be coerced into giving **false information**, or even false confessions, during interrogation. **Gudjonsson (1992)** came up with the **Gudjonsson Suggestibility Scale** (**GSS**) in order to measure how **susceptible** a person is to **coercive interrogation**.

Gudjonsson Suggestibility Scale — Testing

A passage is read out loud to the participant. They then report all they can remember about what they have heard. Later they are asked a series of **questions** about the passage, some of which are **leading** (see page 110). They are then told in an **authoritative** manner that they have made several mistakes and must answer the questions again. This is known as negative feedback. The participant's answers to the two sets of questions are analysed and used to give them a **GSS score**.

Coercive interrogation is the use of harsh tactics (e.g. threats, intimidation) to force the subject into revealing the desired information.

Gudjonsson identified two different aspects of **interrogative susceptibility**:

1) **Yield** — this refers to the person's tendency to give in to **leading questions**.
2) **Shift** — this refers to the person's tendency to **change** their responses when put under **interpersonal pressure** (measured in the second part of the test).

Results from various studies indicate that the GSS has reasonable **internal reliability** (see p.216). Also, significant **test-retest stability** (see p.216) has been found, providing evidence for the **predictive validity** of the GSS.

The GSS (and associated research) have highlighted **issues** when interviewing suspects in police investigations. For example:

1) Some people are **more** susceptible to being coerced into specific answers than others.
2) Suggestible suspects could end up being **led** by the interviewer and merely agreeing with their line of questioning, rather than describing something that really took place.
3) If an individual is particularly susceptible to suggestibility they can be **coerced** into confessing something **untrue**.

For some reason suspects were far more susceptible to coercion when questioned by Rex...

...than by Ned.

Practice Questions

Q1 Name the two personality traits that Vrij identified in connection with deception.

Q2 Give one criticism of Reid's interrogation technique.

Q3 What are the two aspects of interrogative susceptibility identified by Gudjonsson?

Exam Question

Q1 a) Outline relevant research into detecting the lies of suspects. [10 marks]

b) Discuss the problems associated with the methods used to interview suspects. [15 marks]

I confess — I don't know what it was, but whatever it was I did it...

I don't understand — interviewing suspects is easy, isn't it... You just keep turning up in a dirty mac when they're least expecting it and follow them around smoking cigars at them until they finally crack and admit the whole thing. Or else try being Belgian, distract them with your unusually shaped moustache, catch them off guard and extract a confession. Simple.

Offender Profiling

This bit's just for OCR. *Finding the person who committed a crime is often tricky. Offender profiling can help with this.*

The Police Use **Offender Profiling** to Help Them **Identify** Suspects

The aim of profiling is to create an idea of the offender's **likely characteristics**. This helps the police to focus their resources on more likely suspects, and can create new leads within an investigation.

There are different styles of approach in offender profiling.

The American 'top-down' approach

The **FBI** began by **interviewing** 36 convicted serial killers and sex murderers to gain an insight into their thinking and behaviour. They were classified into two groups, **organised** and **disorganised**. Organised offenders were intelligent, socially and sexually competent, lived with somebody and planned their attacks. Disorganised offenders were less intelligent, socially and sexually incompetent, were loners and were more likely to behave impulsively and not plan the attacks in advance. These groups are used to compare information from **new crime scenes** to make judgements based on past experience.

The British 'bottom-up' approach

This approach was developed by **David Canter** and uses **psychological principles** more than the FBI approach. Canter saw the **crime scene** as a source of information — the behaviour of the offender at the crime scene would reveal information about their everyday life and characteristics (see below). Although Canter also analysed behaviour of convicted offenders, this is a much more **bottom-up approach**, as the focus is on the unique circumstances of an individual offender.

Several Factors Are Considered When **Developing a Profile**

Douglas et al (1986) reported that the **FBI** use **four** main stages when building a profile:

1) Assimilating **data** — collecting all the information available about the crime scene and victim.
2) **Classifying** the crime — identifying the **type** of crime committed.
3) **Reconstructing** the crime — this includes the behaviour of both the **offender** and the **victim**.
4) Creating a **profile** — making judgements about possible physical and lifestyle **characteristics** of the offender.

Canter (1994) identified **five** main characteristics that should be included in a profile:

1) **Personal** characteristics — e.g. personality traits.
2) **Criminal** history — types of offences they may have committed in the past.
3) Residential **location** — e.g. if a circle is drawn around an offender's crime scenes on a map, the offender is often found to live in the middle. This is known as **circle theory**.
4) **Domestic** and **social** characteristics — e.g. if the person is likely to live alone or have a family.
5) **Occupational** and **educational** history — likely type of employment and level of qualifications.

Using the crime scene to predict these pieces of information is known as geographical profiling.

There Are a Number of **Biases** and **Pitfalls** in Offender Profiling

1) Profiles can only be used for a **limited** range of crimes such as murders or rapes. They've been used to identify stalkers and arsonists but aren't suitable for use in crimes motivated by **material gain** such as robbery and theft.
2) **Douglas et al (1986)** suggest that the aim of offender profiling has been **misrepresented**. Profiling is not intended to identify a specific person, but instead aims to focus the investigation on a particular **type** of person.
3) Research into the effectiveness of offender profiling shows that it is **limited**. **Holmes (1989)** reported that in **192** cases where offender profiling had been used, arrests had been made in **88** cases. However, the profile only contributed to **17%** of these arrests.
4) **Copson (1995)** found that only **14%** of senior police officers felt that profiling had helped them to solve a case.

Offender Profiling

The **Rachel Nickell** Murder Case Was a **Misuse** of Offender Profiling

Rachel was a young woman murdered in front of her two-year-old son during a walk in the park in 1992. An offender profiler called **Paul Britton** developed a profile which was broadcast on TV, and four callers all identified the same person. The man **fitted the profile** although there wasn't any forensic evidence to link him to the crime.

An **undercover** female police officer befriended the suspect (Colin Stagg) and attempted to get him to confess to the crime during their 'relationship'. The suspect **never** admitted to her that he was the killer and denied involvement, but was still arrested and charged. When the case went to court he was **acquitted** and the misuse of the profile and the police tactics were strongly **criticised** by the judge. In 2008, another man, Robert Napper, **pleaded guilty** to Rachel's manslaughter on the grounds of diminished responsibility.

The Case Study of **John Duffy** is a More **Successful Example**

John Duffy is known as the **Railway Rapist** — between 1982 and 1986 he was responsible for 24 sexual assaults and three murders. **Canter** was asked by the police to analyse the details of the crimes to generate a profile, as forensic evidence suggested they were committed by one person (although sometimes with an accomplice).

The profile made Duffy seem a much more **likely suspect** than had previously been thought. The details of the profile Canter had created were very similar to Duffy's actual circumstances and characteristics. Canter suggested that the offender would:

1) **Live close** to the first three crimes — Duffy lived in Kilburn as suggested.
2) Be **aged** in his mid to late 20s — Duffy was in his late 20s.
3) Work in a semi-skilled or skilled **occupation** — Duffy was a carpenter.
4) Be knowledgeable about **railways** — Duffy worked for British Rail.
5) Have a **criminal record** that included violence — Duffy had been interviewed by the police for raping his wife at knifepoint.
6) Be small and feel **physically unattractive** — Duffy was 5′ 4″ and suffered from acne.
7) **Fantasise** about sex and violence — Duffy had hard-core pornography videos.
8) Be interested in **martial arts** — Duffy was in a martial arts club.

Canter believed that behaviour is generally **consistent**, so analysis of Duffy's behaviour during the crime gave information about his life and general behaviour. Once Duffy was arrested for the crimes it was discovered that he had started to murder his victims because he was once nearly recognised. Canter also discovered that Duffy burned the bodies of his victims to destroy the **forensic evidence** — he had learned about the procedures used by police for collecting evidence when he was arrested for raping his wife.

Practice Questions

Q1 Who developed the bottom-up approach to offender profiling?

Q2 Outline two aspects included in Canter's profiles.

Q3 Describe one problem with offender profiling.

Exam Question

Q1 a) Describe two different approaches to offender profiling. [10 marks]

b) Discuss the use of offender profiling in criminal investigations, using a case study to illustrate your answer. [15 marks]

The offender is likely to be a sweet old lady who likes kittens and scones...

Offender profiling has long been a popular choice for TV dramas, from 'Cracker' to 'The Wire in the Blood'. Great shows, but even before I read these pages I did have a suspicion that perhaps it wasn't realistic for a profiler to conclude from a couple of bloodstains and a shoelace that the killer is a car salesman aged 43 who collects stamps and wears loud ties...

Persuading the Jury

Only for you OCR lot. *If everything you've learned about on the last few pages is done properly (taking eyewitness statements, interviewing suspects, creating offender profiles) then you may well end up with a suspect going to court.*

*The **Jury** Decides if a Defendant is **Innocent** or **Guilty***

1) A **jury** in the UK is made up from a list of citizens who live within the jurisdiction of the relevant court.
2) Individuals are chosen from the **electoral roll**.
3) Technically, jury service is **compulsory**. However, individuals can **defer** their jury duty if they have a good reason for doing so, e.g. child-care needs.
4) If a juror appears to be **biased** about the case they can be asked to stand down.

The main problem with selecting a jury in this way is that people are not chosen on the basis of their **character**. Jurors could be **prejudiced** or **discriminate** against the defendant and this would therefore not lead to a fair trial.

*The Way **Testimony is Ordered** Can Affect the Jury's Decision*

1) One of the most standard models used by traditional legal systems is the **Bayesian model** of evidence.
2) The Bayesian model is based on a **scientific** model — it involves **collecting evidence** about a case that is either **consistent** or **inconsistent** with a **hypothesis** (e.g. that the defendant is guilty).
3) As evidence accumulates, the **degree of belief** in the hypothesis begins to change — to either **high** or **low** belief.

Pennington and Hastie put forward an alternative view — that jurors create a story of what they think happened. They then base their verdict on this story. These stories are made up of **three types of knowledge**:

1) Information learned about the case **during the trial.**
2) Knowledge of **similar crimes**.
3) Knowledge that people's **actions** are **motivated by goals** — i.e. there's a complete story.

Pennington and Hastie (1988) studied narrative stories in trials

Method: Participants were given **detailed evidence** taken from a trial. The **prosecution's** evidence was presented in different ways — either in a **structured** order that made it easy to construct a story, or in a **'chaotic'** order.

Results: In order to make sense of the events and situations, the participants created a **story** about what had happened. When evidence was given in an order that made the story easy to construct, subjects were more likely to develop a story **similar** to the events described. In these cases **78%** of participants found the defendant **guilty**. If, on the other hand, the evidence was given in a 'chaotic' order that made story construction difficult, then only **31%** decided upon the guilty verdict.

Conclusion: Participants could be led to a verdict by the **order** of the testimony. It was the ability to 'fill in the gaps' and construct a **realistic story** rather than actually examining and measuring the evidence that influenced their verdict.

Evaluation: The participants were **aware** that they were taking part in a study and this may have affected their behaviour. People may weigh evidence in a more scientific way in a **real** trial with a potentially serious outcome.

***Expert Witnesses** May Give Evidence in a Trial*

Some witnesses have nothing to do with the crime itself, but are **experts** who examine the evidence and report their findings. There are several types of witness who could be referred to as 'expert' in a criminal investigation:

- **Doctor/medical expert** — e.g. gives evidence about **injuries** in cases of assault, rape or murder.
- **Forensic scientist** — e.g. gives evidence about **fingerprints** and **physical evidence** left at a crime scene.
- **Forensic engineer** — e.g. gives evidence about the operational function of **machinery** or **material components** that could be involved in a crime investigation.

Evidence from an expert witness can have a significant effect on the conclusions drawn by a jury in a criminal investigation.

Persuading the Jury

Expert Witnesses Are More Likely to Persuade a Jury

Male jurors found Vicki a very persuasive expert witness.

1) **Krauss and Sales (2001)** discovered that jurors were **more** influenced by **clinical expert** testimony than by **actuarial** testimony (which analyses the probabilities of certain events).
2) Mock jurors watched videotaped examinations of the future danger of an offender. These were either made by **clinical experts** or by **lawyers**.
3) The examinations were made using **clinical techniques** or through actuarial methods of **risk assessment**.
4) Mock jurors then had to **rate** the dangerousness of the offender based on what they'd seen.

Krauss and Sales found that the jurors were more influenced by the clinical expert testimony, and that this preference for clinical opinion **remained** even after the presentation of **opposing** procedures designed to reduce the effects. A bias in favour of the clinical expert testimony was **confirmed** by a **rating scale** comparing the two types of testimony. The clinical expert testimony was rated higher on **credibility** and **level of science** as well as **influence** over the actuarial testimony.

Evidence Being Ruled Inadmissible Can Increase Its Effect

Sometimes in a court case, evidence is presented to a jury that is then ruled to be **inadmissible** (e.g. evidence based on hearsay). The jury is then told to **disregard** what they have heard. However, there's evidence that, far from disregarding such evidence, juries actually tend to take **more** notice of it.

Broeder (1959) — effect of evidence being ruled inadmissible

Method:	A **mock jury** was presented with evidence which was designed to favour a guilty verdict. Some jurors were then told that the evidence was inadmissible and that they must completely **disregard** it.
Results:	Participants who were given instructions to **ignore** the evidence gave **more guilty verdicts** that those participants who were allowed to use the information.
Conclusion:	Evidence ruled as inadmissible **increases** a jury's use of it. This is known as the '**backfire effect**'.
Evaluation:	This has **implications** for trials — legal teams can take advantage of the backfire effect by introducing unreliable evidence to the jury regardless of whether it is legally admissible. This could **compromise** the fairness of a trial. However, **demand characteristics** are likely to be a factor in a study like this — participants form an idea of what is expected from them in a study and deliberately do the opposite. The study also has low **ecological validity** as it occurs in an artificial setting.

Practice Questions

Q1 How is a jury selected in the UK?

Q2 How is Pennington and Hastie's view of how juries reach a decision different from the Bayesian model?

Q3 Name three different types of expert witness.

Q4 What is the 'backfire effect'?

Exam Question

Q1 a) Describe how a jury evaluates evidence in a criminal trial. [10 marks]

b) Discuss the problems of conducting research into the behaviour of juries. [15 marks]

Once upon a time, in a far-away land, there lived an armed bank robber...

So juries are persuaded by stories that make sense, believe experts over lawyers, and are unable to wipe inadmissible evidence from their minds. To be honest, I'm fairly sure I could have just told you all that without the trouble and expense of putting together fake juries and bothering them with evidence. Still, it's important to do these things properly.

Witness Appeal

Just for OCR again. *It's said that impressions of people are based 70% on how they look, 20% on how they sound, and only 10% on what they say. This may not be true, but jurors* ***can*** *be influenced by the looks and confidence of witnesses.*

The **Appearance** of the Witness Can Affect the Verdict

Castellow et al (1990) carried out experiments to assess whether a person's **appearance** influences a jury's verdict.

Castellow et al (1990) — the effect of appearance on juries

Method: 145 participants were presented with an **overview** of a fictional trial based on **real** sexual harassment trials. The scenario was taken from a '**her word against his**' perspective — i.e. there were no witnesses. Participants were split into four groups and given **photographs** of the plaintiff and defendant. The first group saw pictures of an **attractive plaintiff** and an **unattractive defendant**. The second group saw pictures of an **unattractive plaintiff** and an **attractive defendant**. The third group were given pictures where both the plaintiff and the defendant were **unattractive**. The fourth group were given pictures where both the plaintiff and the defendant were **attractive**. Subjects then had to indicate whether they believed that the defendant was **guilty**. Both defendant and plaintiff were also assessed using the **bipolar adjective scale**. This is a list of adjectives describing personal traits designed to measure personality types.

Results: The **attractive plaintiff/unattractive defendant** combination gave the **highest** percentage of guilty verdicts, and the **attractive defendant/unattractive plaintiff** gave the **lowest**. The '**beauty is good**' stereotype also arose — photographs of attractive defendants were rated more favourably on the bipolar adjective scale.

Conclusion: Physical attractiveness influences verdicts — verdicts rely on **appearance** as well as **evidence**.

Evaluation: Participants were aware that they were taking part in a study so **demand characteristics** could have become a factor. They were psychology students and may have been more likely to guess the aim of the experiment. This was also an **artificial** situation — participants didn't actually get to see the witnesses giving their evidence, so all they had to go on when forming an **opinion** of them (other than the written overview of the trial) was their photographs. This wouldn't be the case in a real trial, so physical attractiveness may have **less** influence than this study showed.

Brian wasn't worried — this face had never let him down before.

Witness Confidence Also Has an Effect

Witness **confidence** appears to have a significant impact on responses in court.

Penrod and Cutler (1988) — Effect of witness confidence

Method: Participants watched a **video** of the trial of a defendant accused of armed robbery. A number of variables were **manipulated**, e.g. witness confidence and retention interval. In the trial, the main evidence was that the victim of the robbery and a police officer both **positively identified** the defendant as the criminal. Participants had to judge whether the defendant was guilty.

Results: The only variable that affected the verdict given by the participants was **witness confidence**. **54%** of participants believed the defendant to be guilty when the eyewitness was **100% confident** compared to **39%** if the witness was only **80% confident**.

Conclusion: The **confidence** shown by a witness affects a juror's **belief** in their statement.

Evaluation: This has **implications** for the fairness of trials — witness confidence may actually relate more to the person's **personality** than to the accuracy or truthfulness of their statements. Using a video reduced the **ecological validity** of the study, and participants could also have shown **demand characteristics** and changed their behaviour.

Witness Appeal

Sometimes Children May Need to Give Evidence in Court

1) **Children** are likely to feel **scared** or **intimidated** when they have to give evidence in court.
2) They're classed as **vulnerable witnesses** within the UK legal system.
3) **Special measures** can therefore be taken to help them feel **safe** and so improve the quality of their evidence:

- The child gives evidence outside the courtroom, which is then fed via **live link** to the court.
- The child's evidence is **videotaped** and then played to the court.
- **Wigs** and **gowns** are removed to create an atmosphere that's less formal and intimidating.
- The child's evidence is given **in private** — members of the public are not allowed in court.
- **Screens** are used around the witness box to prevent the child witness from having to see the defendant.
- **Communication aids** such as alphabet boards can be used to help the child get their message across.

Steps Taken to Protect Children Might Affect the Trial Outcome

Research has been done into whether the measures used to **protect** child witnesses can affect the **outcome** of a trial.

Ross et al (1994) — the use of shields and videotape

Method: **150 participants** watched a **videotape simulation** of a sexual abuse trial. The key witness was a ten-year-old child who was shown testifying in **three different courtroom situations**:

- **Directly in front** of the defendant.
- In court behind a protective **'shield'**.
- **Outside the courtroom** with their evidence being shown to the jury via a video monitor.

The study used an **independent groups design**, so each participant saw only **one** of the three situations. The **guilt** of the defendant was judged after the mock jurors had watched and assessed the whole trial.

Results: The situation in which the child testified had **no impact** on whether participants convicted the defendant or not.

Conclusion: Measures taken to protect child witnesses have **no impact** on the outcome of a trial

Evaluation: A second experiment was carried out where the videotape simulation of the trial was **stopped** straight after the child had testified. In this experiment participants assessing the situation where the child testified **in front of the defendant** were **more likely** to convict the defendant. This suggests that protective measures **may** influence jurors but don't have a long-term effect. Both experiments had an **independent groups design**, meaning that **participant variables** could have affected the outcome of the experiment. Also, the quality of the **acting** could have varied between the three situations.

Practice Questions

Q1 What effect can appearance have on a jury?

Q2 Outline the results of Castellow et al's (1990) experiment.

Q3 What conclusion did Penrod and Cutler (1988) draw from their experiment into witness confidence?

Exam Question

Q1 a) Describe relevant research into the effect of shields and videotape on children giving evidence. [10 marks]

b) Evaluate the methodology used to investigate witness appeal in criminal trials. [15 marks]

So it helps if your star witness looks like Angelina Jolie...

Juries are only human — if someone looks nice, seems confident and shows genuine emotion on the witness stand then it's bound to make them seem more believable. The problem is, if you look like Quasimodo and stand there going red and mumbling, a jury might not believe what you're saying. Which seems tremendously unfair. But as we all know, life isn't fair.

Reaching a Verdict

Still just team OCR here. *We all know about this bit. This is the tense part you see at the end of courtroom dramas.*

Decision-making Within a Jury is a Complex Process

A **court hearing** consists of the following **stages**:

1) Prosecution's opening statement
2) Defence's opening statement
3) Witness evidence
4) Defence's closing argument
5) Prosecution's closing argument
6) Judge's instructions on proceedings
7) Jury deliberation
8) Judge's instructions on verdicts

Steve pulled out all the stops to distract the jury during the prosecution's closing argument

There are **key points** during a trial where the jury can be **heavily influenced** — particularly during **witness statements**, prosecution and defence **closing arguments** and **judge's instructions** (determination of facts, witness credibility, etc.).

Once the **discussion of facts** (among the jury) begins, jury decisions are influenced by **three** groups of factors:

- **Jury composition** — e.g. jurors' characteristics and attitudes, influence of individuals within jury.
- **Decision-making process** — e.g. majority influence, conformity, group 'polarisation', group-think, emergence of a leader.
- **Characteristics of defendant and witnesses** — e.g. stereotyping, physical attractiveness, race, accent.

According to **Hastie et al (1983)**, the decision-making process of a jury passes through **three stages**:

1) **Orientation process** — the jury decides on an agenda and discusses the evidence presented in court.
2) **Open conflict** — there's dispute between members of the jury and emotions can take over from common sense.
3) **Reconciliation** — conflicts are settled and a verdict is reached.

The Power of the Majority is a Strong Force in Jury Decisions

Studies have shown that a **majority** opinion tends to overcome even strongly held opposing views within a group.

Asch (1956) — Majority influence

Method:	Participants were shown displays containing three parallel lines and asked to state which one matched a target line. There was a degree of **uncertainty** as the lines were similar in length. Each experimental group contained only **one real participant** — the other members were confederates whose aim was to try and influence the real participant. Sometimes the confederates would select a line that clearly didn't match the target line to see what effect this had on which line the real participant chose. A **control** group contained no confederates — participants judged the line lengths in isolation.
Results:	Participants in experimental groups chose the **wrong** line **75%** of the time, compared to only **1%** for those in the control group.
Conclusion:	The majority has a **massive influence** on decision making.
Evaluation:	Participants were influenced by the majority into agreeing with them even **against** their better judgement. This is an example of **normative influence** — an influence that encourages individuals to **conform** with the expectations of others. Non-conformity leads to **alienation**, and so people tend to follow the majority out of a fear of standing apart. This has implications for **real-life** decision making situations in court — a majority in a jury is a powerful force, and other members might be convinced even if their own opinion is very different.

Reaching a Verdict

Minority Influence Can Also be Important in Jury Decisions

Moscovici was one of the first psychologists to consider the importance of **minority influence**. He pointed out that much of the **social change** in the real world was started by **small groups** of people who were able to **persuade** the majority to accept their point of view. His original experiment into minority influence is described below.

Moscovici (1969) — Minority influence

Method: Two experimental groups were made up of **four participants** and **two confederates**. They were shown slides that were different shades of blue and asked to state in turn what colour they were. In one group the two confederates consistently answered 'green' rather than 'blue' for the slides. In the other group the confederates answered 'green' 24 out of 36 times. There was also a **control group** which contained no confederates.

Results: In the **control group, 0.25%** of answers given by the participants were wrong. In the group with the confederates that answered green **most of the time, 1.25%** of participants answered wrongly. In the group where the confederates **consistently** answered green, **8.42%** of the answers given by the participants were wrong.

Conclusion: Minorities **can** exert an influence over majorities, though the effect is **not as powerful** as majority influence. **Consistency** is a key factor if a minority is to persuade a majority — if the confederates were inconsistent in their response then the effect decreased sharply.

Evaluation: The participants were **unaware** that the confederates were not part of the group like themselves. Also, they weren't told exactly what was being tested. These things should have helped to **avoid** the results being affected by **demand characteristics**. However, as it was a laboratory experiment the results lack **ecological validity**.

The experiment was repeated in 1980 with a slightly **different design**. This time the test was slightly more **ambiguous** — the **chromatic after-image** was tested rather than the colour of a slide. The chromatic after-image is the colour you see if you look at a single colour for a period of time and then at a white space. You should see the opposite colour to the one you have been focusing on, but obviously this is more open to **individual interpretation**. A **minority influence** was again found to encourage the majority to **change** their opinion.

These Experiments Have Real-life Implications for Juries

1) A **jury** coming to a decision is a **real-life example** of a group of people who will be subject to the influences of other people. Juries are groups of strangers with a wide variety of opinions and personality types who have to reach an agreement based on the evidence they have seen during a trial.
2) **Asch's** research shows that people often agree with the **majority**. So, if a majority of the jury agree on a verdict they will usually be able to persuade any members of the group who may have a different interpretation of events.
3) However, **Moscovici** showed that a minority **can** have an influence on a majority in certain circumstances. A **persuasive**, **consistent** minority in a jury may be able to convince the rest to reassess their opinion and even their underlying beliefs.

Practice Questions

Q1 Name the three stages in jury decision-making outlined by Hastie (1983).

Q2 What do the results of Asch's (1956) study show?

Exam Question

Q1 a) Describe the stages involved in a jury reaching a verdict and the main influences on this process. [10 marks]

b) Discuss the effect of majority and minority influence on decision-making in juries using relevant research. [15 marks]

Juries go through stages in decision-making and mustn't be too Hastie...

I think we've all experienced the majority influence at one time or another. You know perfectly well who the only player is to score in the finals of the UEFA Cup, Champions League, FA Cup and League Cup, but you allow your team to persuade you that it was Didier Drogba. And miss out on your chance to win that lifetime supply of dog food. It still hurts.***

* *It was Steven Gerrard.* ** *Lucky I haven't actually got a dog.*

Imprisonment

Yes, you've guessed it — these two pages are only for OCR. So, the jury's reached a verdict — they've decided the defendant is guilty and needs a spell in prison. But there's debate about whether or not this will change the criminal.

Lots of Criminals Continue to Commit Crimes After Being in Prison

Recidivism is just a fancy word that means **repeating** an undesirable behaviour after you've been punished for it. In the case of criminals and prison there are many factors which influence this:

1) Length of **time** spent in prison.
2) **Supervision** after release.
3) **Disciplinary** reports.
4) **Education** level.
5) **Seriousness** of crime committed.
6) Prisoner **ethnicity**.
7) Individual **experiences** in prison.

Conditional release is where a person is released early from prison under specified conditions, e.g. they may be monitored or supervised.

Studies have shown a link between **employment** after imprisonment and likelihood of reoffending. For example, **Gillis et al (2001)** found that offenders who found employment within six months of being released had fewer convictions than offenders who didn't take up employment during this time. **However**, this link doesn't necessarily show **cause and effect**.

Imprisonment Can Have a Big Effect on a Prisoner's Mental State

It's thought that prisoners may be more susceptible to problems with **depression** and more likely to attempt **suicide** than other people. **Enda Dooley** studied suicides in prisons in England and Wales.

Dooley (1990) — Depression and suicide risk in prison

Method: The **case notes** of **295** of the 300 suicides that happened in prison between 1972 and 1987 were studied.

Results: Prisoners serving **life sentences** and those convicted of **violent** or **sexual** offences were most at risk. There was an association between suicide and **guilt** over the offence. There was a history of **psychiatric problems** in about a third of cases and **self-harm** was common.

Conclusion: **Depressive illness** is likely to be a contributing factor to suicides in prison. Dooley thought that better **communication** between staff and prisoners is needed to reduce suicide rates.

Evaluation: Prisoners **don't** form a **random sample** of the general population — as a group they differ in terms of ethnicity, age, psychiatric history, socio-economic status, and marital and employment status. This makes it hard to measure exactly how much **more susceptible** to depression and suicide prisoners really are.

The Stanford Prison Experiment Had Shocking Results

Zimbardo et al (1971) carried out a controversial study of the psychological effects of being a **prisoner** or **guard**.

Zimbardo et al (1971) — The Stanford Prison Experiment

Method: Zimbardo set up a mock jail in the basement of the Psychology Building at Stanford University. Male undergraduate students answered a **newspaper ad** to volunteer for the study and were **tested** to make sure they were healthy and had no psychological issues. The 24 chosen students were then **randomly assigned** to take the role of **prisoner** or **guard**. The prisoners were given uniforms and numbers and the guards were given uniforms and mirrored sunglasses. The guards were given instructions, e.g. about filling in reports and details of shifts. They weren't allowed to use physical punishment. The prison was left to run its course.

Results: The experiment got out of hand. Some of the 'guards' began to behave in a **sadistic** way and by the end of the experiment many 'prisoners' were showing signs of **emotional distress**. The experiment had to be **abandoned** after only six days — it was originally planned to last two weeks.

Conclusion: The behaviour shown was due to the **situation** rather than **individual personality traits**. The participants conformed to what they perceived to be the role of prisoner or guard.

Evaluation: This study was widely **criticised**, as described on the next page.

Imprisonment

The Stanford Prison Experiment Was Widely Criticised

The Stanford Prison Experiment was criticised for being **unethical** but there were also problems with the **methodology**:

1) This was a **field experiment** and there was little **scientific control** of variables.
2) Zimbardo was **not** merely a neutral observer but took an **active role** as the 'prison superintendent' — he shaped and directed the course of the experiment.
3) **Demand characteristics** were a significant problem. The participants quickly took on and conformed to **stereotypical behaviours** and some critics claimed that what followed was little more than **role-playing**. However, self-reports from prisoners showed that they felt it was **real**.
4) **Selection bias** was another problem as participants were volunteers. It's been suggested that people keen to participate in a study of prison life might have **pre-existing tendencies** towards the type of behaviour observed.
5) Finally, the study was criticised for its lack of **ecological validity**. For example, 'prisoners' wore a chain on their right ankle (designed to remind them of the **oppressiveness** of the prison environment, according to Zimbardo) and were dressed in smocks with no underwear (to make them feel **humiliated** and **emasculated**). Neither of these things would be done in a real prison.

US Prison Policy Ignores the Findings of Psychological Studies

Twenty-five years after the original Stanford Prison Experiment, **Haney and Zimbardo (1998)** produced an article entitled 'The Past and Future of US Prison Policy: Twenty-five years after the Stanford Prison Experiment'. Several important points were made about **US prison policies**:

1) Prison in the US tends to be used primarily as a **punishment** and a way of **removing** criminals from society and **preventing** them committing further crimes. **Rehabilitation** of prisoners is **not** a major consideration.
2) **More** people are being imprisoned and for **longer periods**, leading to overcrowding and poor conditions.
3) There is increasingly **less** access to training, education and counselling for prisoners.

These policies **ignore** the results of the Stanford Prison Experiment and other relevant psychological studies. According to Haney and Zimbardo:

1) Prison environments are potentially **psychologically damaging** and so should be used **carefully**.
2) People can be **transformed** by a prison situation and begin to behave differently according to prison '**roles**'. It follows that they will also be affected by the **change** in **situation** after they are **released**.
3) Programmes are needed to **prepare** prisoners for their new situation and role outside prison. This is much more likely to lower rates of **recidivism** than harsher conditions and longer sentences.

Practice Questions

Q1 Give two factors that influence recidivism.

Q2 What did Dooley (1990) think should be done to reduce the suicide rate amongst prisoners?

Q3 What did Haney and Zimbardo (1998) recommend should change about US prison policy?

Exam Question

Q1 a) Describe relevant research which informs us about the effect of imprisonment on prison inmates. [10 marks]

b) Evaluate the methodology used to investigate the impact of imprisonment. [15 marks]

My cat displays recidivism by weeing on the sofa...

The Stanford Prison Experiment may have been a bit dodgy as a scientific study but there's no doubting the fact that the mock prison situation had a massive effect on the behaviour of previously perfectly normal and well-balanced young men. People sometimes behave in extreme ways when they feel an extreme situation makes their actions legitimate.

Alternatives to Imprisonment

You're going it alone again, OCR. Are you getting lonely yet? Prison isn't the only option if someone is convicted of a crime. Probation, a restorative justice approach or even the death penalty are other options that are used.

Probation is the Suspension of a Jail Sentence

Probation is used for less serious crimes as an alternative to imprisonment, and sometimes after imprisoned criminals have been released. Instead of serving a sentence in jail, the convicted criminal is returned to the **community**. They have to abide by the **probation conditions** (rules), which are imposed by the court. These can include:

1) **Supervision** by a probation officer.
2) Abiding by a **curfew**.
3) Living in agreed **accommodation** and staying within the same **area**.
4) **Drug rehabilitation** to reduce or eradicate drug use.
5) Wearing an **electronic tag**.

Pete rather didn't expect that his agreed accommodation would involve a parachute jump each morning.

This is a form of **community sentence** where criminals, although still mixing with society, **aren't** entirely free. They are expected to behave in a certain way in order to **pay** for their crime and **limit** their ability to commit further crimes. If criminals break the conditions, or commit further crimes, they're sent to **prison**.

The aim is partly to **punish** and **control**, but each offender is dealt with according to their **individual needs** — an attempt is made to help the offender to **change**. A comprehensive **treatment programme** is put into place that is designed to help the offender get over their problems and not reoffend.

The **Prison Reform Trust** believe that offenders should only be imprisoned if they've committed crimes so serious that they can't serve their sentence in the community. In 2003, the Prison Reform Trust report on sentencing was released.

Findings of the Prison Reform Trust Report on Sentencing (2003)

1) The UK prison population is **growing** because courts are tending to impose **more** and **longer** prison sentences rather than using **community penalties** like probation.
2) This is **not** due to a **lack** of community **options** — most sentencers are **happy** with the options available through the Probation Service, although there is concern that it's **underfunded**.
3) The report calls for sentencers to use imprisonment **less often**. It wants them to be **better informed** about the community penalties available and their effectiveness in preventing reoffending.

Restorative Justice is About Criminals Making Amends

Traditional justice is all about being **punished** for committing crimes. **Restorative justice**, on the other hand, focuses on criminals **making amends** directly to the people they've harmed with their behaviour. This helps the criminal to **take responsibility** for their actions, and makes them aware of the **real damage** they've caused.

1) It can be used for various offences from antisocial behaviour (e.g. **vandalism**) to serious offences like **assault**.
2) The victim must **volunteer** to use the approach and the offender must have **admitted responsibility**.
3) The process may involve the victim and offender **meeting** face-to-face or communicating by **letter**.
4) It can also involve offenders working to **undo** the damage they have caused, e.g. by removing graffiti.

A study by the Smith Institute (**Smith Report 2007**) found that restorative justice has many advantages:

1) It **reduced post-traumatic stress** in the victims, and they were **less likely** to want **violent revenge**.
2) Both criminals and victims were **more satisfied** with this approach than with traditional justice solutions.
3) It decreased the **costs** involved.

The main **problem** with restorative justice at the moment is that people are **reluctant** to use it.
Meirs (2006) found that it's hard to recruit victims and offenders to take part in the process.

Alternatives to Imprisonment

*Some Countries Use the **Death Penalty** for the **Most Serious Crimes***

The UK abolished capital punishment in 1969 but many other countries, such as the USA, China and India, still use the **death penalty** to punish the most serious crimes. In the USA it's only used in **murder** cases.

Supporters of the death penalty in the USA claim that it has the following advantages:

1) It acts as a **deterrent** to prevent people committing murder.
2) It's a punishment that **matches** the crime they've committed.
3) **Families** of murder victims have the right to see the murderer suffer the same fate.

There are also plenty of arguments **against** the practice:

1) DNA evidence has been used to **prove** that people have been executed for crimes they **didn't commit**.
2) There's evidence that the lethal injection causes **unnecessary suffering**.
3) It's more **expensive** to execute a criminal than to keep them imprisoned for life.
4) Research has shown that the death penalty isn't applied fairly and **discriminates** against minorities and the poor.

Eberhardt et al (2006) — Looking death worthy

Method: A **database** of over **600** 'death-eligible' defendants was used. Participants **rated** the faces of the defendants according to how stereotypically 'black' they appeared. These ratings were then compared with which defendants had actually been sentenced to death.

Results: When **black defendants** were accused of killing **white victims** the jury seemed to use the degree to which the defendant **appeared 'black'** as a gauge for the degree of punishment administered. **58%** of defendants rated as having stereotypically 'black' features (e.g. broad nose, thick lips, dark skin and hair) were sentenced to death, compared with only **24%** of those rated less 'black'. This effect **vanished** if both defendant and victim were black.

Conclusion: Black defendants accused of killing white victims are **much more likely** to be sentenced to death than those accused of killing other black people. This may be because juries view black-on-white crime as **interracial** conflict and black-on-black crime as **interpersonal** conflict. Jurors are influenced not simply by the knowledge that the defendant is black but also by **how stereotypically** black they appear. They see this as an indication of how **deserving** they are of the death penalty.

Evaluation: This study **supports earlier research** showing that black defendants are more likely to receive the death penalty, particularly if their victim was white. It also **supports lab-based evidence** showing that people associate black physical traits with **criminality**. It has **huge implications** for the use of the death penalty in the USA — it's unjust to discriminate based on race and appearance. This is a very serious concern for any punishment system, but particularly so where the penalty is death.

Practice Questions

Q1 What is probation?

Q2 Give three advantages of restorative justice over imprisonment.

Q3 What did Eberhardt et al (2006) conclude about the US death penalty?

Exam Question

Q1 a) Describe the restorative justice approach to managing the impact of crime. [10 marks]

b) Discuss the alternatives to imprisonment in controlling crime, using relevant research. [15 marks]

Kev woz ere — restorative justice sucks...

The murder rate in the USA is significantly higher than in other countries with a similar level of development. This seems pretty compelling evidence against the main argument in favour of the death penalty — that it discourages crime... Still, don't get too caught up in the rights and wrongs of the death penalty, because that's not what they'll ask you about.

Treating Criminal Behaviour

OCR and Edexcel only. *Lots of studies have shown that just sending a criminal to prison may not do anything to change their behaviour. These pages outline some of the methods that are used to actually try and treat criminal behaviour.*

*The **Token Economy Programme** is a **Behaviourist** Treatment*

1) The **token economy programme** has been used with various groups, including prison inmates.
2) It's a form of **behaviour modification** based on the behaviourist idea of **operant conditioning**.
3) Operant conditioning deals with the modification of behaviour through **consequences** — rewards which reinforce behaviour, and punishments which discourage the behaviour from happening again.
4) The token economy programme reinforces good behaviour by rewarding subjects with '**tokens**' for meeting their behavioural '**goals**'.
5) Tokens are saved up and can be **spent** to gain 'treats' or 'rewards'.

Token economy programmes must be **adhered to** in order for them to work. No other rewards can be given to the inmates or the token system will become pointless. Also, several things need to be established in order for the system to be set up:

1) The behaviour that is desired from the inmates must be clearly **defined**.
2) A **variety** of rewards must be given to encourage participation.
3) The **reasons** for token allocation must be clear.
4) What a token is **worth** must be clearly established, e.g. how many tokens equal a chocolate bar, etc.
5) The **rate** of earning tokens must also be established, i.e. how many a particular behaviour will earn.

6) Some people **don't** respond to this form of behaviour conditioning, but for others it can be a valuable incentive to achieve desired behaviour.

***Anger Management** is a **Therapeutic** Programme*

1) **Anger management** is a **therapeutic programme** often used with convicted violent criminals.
2) This approach assumes that violent behaviour is caused by **anger** and **frustration** — it's hoped that if individuals can learn to **control** this anger then their violent behaviour patterns will decrease.
3) Anger management is based on **cognitive behavioural techniques** and a specific programme has been designed for use in penal institutions.
4) The main aims of this treatment are to **reduce** the amount of **violence** within the prison and to improve individuals' **self-awareness** and **control**. It's hoped that it will still make a difference **after** release.
5) Courses usually involve a **two-hour session** each week for **eight weeks**. Participants are encouraged to **monitor** their own behaviour patterns and emotions so that they become increasingly aware of their own emotional changes. It's thought that this will help them to control their own emotions.

Ireland (2000) — the effectiveness of anger management

Method: Aggression levels of **50 inmates** in a young offenders' institution were measured two weeks **before** an anger management treatment programme was started. A **record** of each prisoner's aggressive **behaviour** over one week was kept, and they each completed a **questionnaire** and had a **cognitive-style interview**. A treatment programme of twelve one hour sessions over three days was started, and eight weeks later the measurements were **repeated**.

Results: There was an **improvement** in **92%** of participants. **8%** of prisoners were **worse** after the treatment.

Conclusion: The anger management programme was **useful** for treating aggressive behaviour in the short term.

Evaluation: It will have been difficult to **control other variables** that may have had an effect on inmates' anger, such as news from friends and family, interaction between inmates and relationships with staff. Also, all the participants in this study were young offenders in an institution, so the results can't be **generalised** to other groups, e.g. offenders in prison, released offenders, etc.

Treating Criminal Behaviour

Cognitive Skills Programmes Have Been Shown to Reduce Reoffending

Cognitive skills programmes are designed to teach offenders ways of reducing criminal behaviour. They aim to help offenders **monitor** their **thoughts** and **behaviours** and alter those that are **unhelpful**.

Friendship et al (2002) — Cognitive skills programmes

Method: **670** adult male offenders sentenced to serve two years or more were treated using **cognitive skills programmes**. The cognitive programmes used were **Reasoning and Rehabilitation** (72 hours of treatment) and **Enhanced Thinking Skills** (40 hours of treatment). Treatment **targets** aimed to improve participants' critical reasoning skills and cognitive style, and to help them understand the values that govern their behaviour, self-control, interpersonal problem-solving skills, and social perspective-taking. A **control group** of 1801 adult male offenders serving two or more years didn't participate in the cognitive skills programmes.

Results: A **significant difference** was found between reoffending rates in the treatment and control groups. Prisoners felt to be at a medium-low risk of reoffending showed a **14% reduction** in the treatment group compared to the control group. Those at a medium-high risk of reoffending showed an **11% reduction**. The low and high risk groups also showed a reduction but it wasn't large enough to be considered statistically significant.

Conclusion: Cognitive skills programmes help to treat criminals — **reoffending** and **reconviction** are **reduced**. This supports evidence from other studies.

Evaluation: This study used a **retrospective design** — variables were controlled for **after** the treatment. The control group were selected after the treatment group. A **randomised controlled trial**, where prisoners are randomly selected to receive treatment or not, would give better results. However, this wouldn't be ethical — withholding treatment could affect prisoners' chances of parole. The results of this study haven't been replicated in other studies. For example, in a later study looking at reconviction rates after two years, Falshaw et al (2003) found no difference between control and treatment groups.

Acupuncture Has Been Shown to Help With Drug Rehabilitation

A large proportion of UK prisoners have problems with **substance misuse**. Successfully treating this can help prevent them reoffending. **Wheatley (2005)** found that **ear acupuncture** helped in treating substance misuse.

Wheatley (2005) — Drug rehabilitation using ear acupuncture

Method: Patients were split into two groups. The **treatment group** received twice weekly ear acupuncture treatments and standard care for a four-week period. The **control group** received standard care only. Several **test scales** were used — muscle tension, drug cravings, stress levels, psychological well-being, etc.

Results: The control group's symptoms improved by **25%** while the treatment group's symptoms improved by **43%**.

Conclusion: Ear acupuncture can help rehabilitation of substance abusers.

Evaluation: This **supports earlier research** showing acupuncture to be helpful in treating drug misuse and alcoholism.

Practice Questions

Q1 What is a token economy programme?

Q2 What did Ireland (2000) conclude about anger management?

Exam Questions

Q1 Describe and evaluate one treatment or therapy used to treat criminal behaviour. [12 marks]

Q2 Discuss the problems of conducting research into treatments for criminal behaviour. [15 marks]

My anger is FINE, I'll manage YOUR anger for you in a minute, you little...

Prisoners in Wheatley's acupuncture study were also found to feel less stressed and more relaxed after acupuncture treatment. Amazing — you'd think someone jabbing a needle into your ear would have the absolute opposite effect.

Health Psychology

These pages are just for Edexcel. *Health psychology can be quite vague — it's basically just using psychological theories and research to improve people's physical and mental health. Which, unfortunately for you, covers quite a lot of stuff.*

Health Psychology Has Some Key Assumptions

I bet you thought you'd seen the last of key assumptions. Nope, I'm afraid there are a few more to learn...

1 **Biological** factors influence health. For example:
- **Drugs** can affect **hormone levels** and the functioning of the **nervous system.**
- **Drugs** can increase the activity of some **neurotransmitters** and decrease the activity of others.

2 **Cognitive** and **social** factors influence health. For example:
- People might feel that they have to drink alcohol in social situations in order to feel relaxed — **cognitive motivation**.
- **Social learning theory** might explain why people take drugs — they watch others doing it and then imitate them.

It had been a particularly stressful week and Angie felt the need for lots of relaxation.

3 **Health psychology** is about **promoting good health**. For example:
- Leaflets in doctors' surgeries **encouraging** healthy behaviour (e.g. using condoms).
- TV advertising campaigns **discouraging** unhealthy behaviour (e.g. binge drinking).

Health Psychologists Study the Effects of Drugs on Humans

An area of interest in health psychology is the **effect** of **drugs**. There are different **methods** to investigate this:

1) Experiments can **compare** a group of participants who have used a specific drug, with a control group who haven't used it. Any **differences** found between the two groups can be attributed to the **effects** of the drug.
    - **Wareing et al** (**2000**) compared a group of current and previous users of **MDMA** (**ecstasy**), with a **control** group who **hadn't** used MDMA.
    - They found that compared to non-users, the **functioning** in the **central executive** within **working memory** was **poorer** in both the current and previous users. Users also demonstrated **less accurate information processing** and had **higher** levels of **anxiety**.
    - This suggests that taking ecstasy has **negative** effects on **cognition** and **emotion**.
2) An **EEG** (electroencephalogram) can be used to record **brain activity** before, during and after the use of a specific drug. The results can be used to measure the **effect** of **drug treatments** on the **nervous system**. This can lead to the development of **drug treatments** for disorders like **depression**.

There are Problems With Using Human Participants

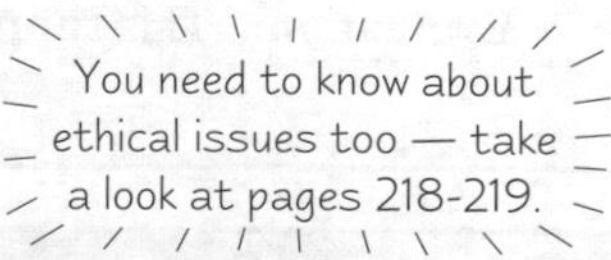

You need to know about ethical issues too — take a look at pages 218-219.

Humans are a real pain to do research on — there are often **validity** and **reliability** issues.
Validity is how far a study really tests what it **aims to test**. For example:

1) **Wareing et al's** (**2000**) study suggests that ecstasy use has negative effects on cognition and anxiety levels.
2) However, it's possible that people with **poorer cognitive skills** or **higher levels** of **anxiety** are **more likely** to experiment with **illegal drugs**.
3) This **lowers** the **validity** because the experiment might actually be testing what **causes** people to take ecstasy in the first place, rather than what **effect** it has.
4) In other words, the results are only **correlational** — you can't establish **cause and effect**.

Reliability is how **consistent** the results are (i.e. whether you'd get the same results if you did the test again).

1) **EEGs** have good reliability because the measurements aren't influenced by things like **experimenter bias**.
2) However, using human participants can still affect the reliability of EEGs — the results could be influenced by **other substances** they have used, rather than the drug being studied.

Health Psychology

Health Psychology Often Involves *Animal Research*

Health psychologists use **animals** in their research so they can study things that they **couldn't** study with **humans**. This is because the ethical guidelines are different for animal research (see page 220).
There are also other **advantages** to using animals:

1) Animals **reproduce** more **quickly** than humans. This makes it possible to study things like the effect of taking a substance while pregnant much more quickly than you could with humans.
2) In **laboratory studies** the animals' **environment** can be completely **controlled**. This allows researchers to control all of the **variables**, e.g. living conditions and food intake can be identical between different groups. It means that experiments are easy to **replicate**, so the results should be more **reliable**.
3) Strict **control** of the **variables** means that the results are less likely to have been caused by **extraneous variables** so it should be possible to establish **cause and effect**. This gives a study **experimental validity**.
4) **Koprich et al (2003)** found that giving **ecstasy** to **pregnant rats** resulted in **altered brain functioning** and **abnormal behaviour** in the offspring. It could be assumed from **Koprich et al's (2003)** study that if **humans** use ecstasy when they're pregnant, it could harm the unborn child. These results can then be used to **promote healthy behaviour** — women could be **warned** against using **ecstasy** when they're **pregnant** because it could **damage** the **foetus**.

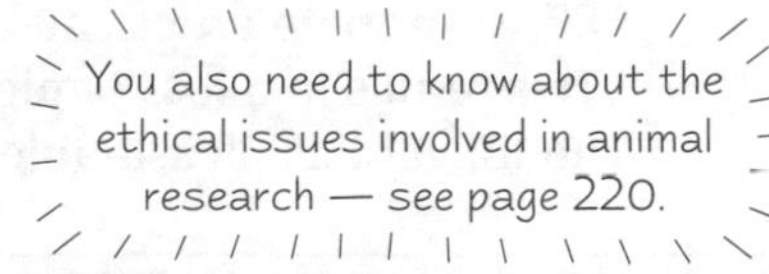

You also need to know about the ethical issues involved in animal research — see page 220.

There Are *Problems* With Using *Animals in Research*

As with all research, animal studies **aren't perfect**.

1) Using a **laboratory** setting in an experiment **lowers** its **ecological validity** — the animals might behave **differently** than they would in a **real life setting**. As well as this, some animals have been **bred** in **laboratories** for **generations**, so they may **never** show completely **natural behaviour**.
2) **Isolating** one **variable** to study also **reduces validity** — in the animal's **natural environment** there would be **several** variables operating at the **same time**, and each of them could **affect** its **behaviour**.
3) It may be **inappropriate** to **generalise** from **animals** to **humans**. Although there are similarities, there are also lots of **differences** between animals and humans in terms of **physiology** and **behaviour**. For example, the drug **morphine** has a **calming** effect on **humans** and **rats**, but it can produce **manic behaviour** in **cats**.

Practice Questions

Q1 Give an example of a biological factor that can influence health.
Q2 Give an example of a campaign to promote healthy living.
Q3 Outline the findings of Wareing et al's (2000) study.
Q4 What is meant by the validity of a study?
Q5 Outline one advantage of using animals to study health psychology.
Q6 Outline the problem of generalising from animals to humans.

Exam Questions

Q1 Describe one research method that uses humans to study the effect of drugs on behaviour. [4 marks]

Q2 Describe and evaluate the use of animals in laboratory studies when studying the effect of drugs. [12 marks]

Don't know about you, but I'm a bit worried by this section...

...after all, how much do you really want to know about your physical and mental health? It might turn out that I'm an utter raving loon, stressed out, depressed and dysfunctional with a major substance abuse problem to boot. Not sure that I'm up for those kinds of revelations. Oh well, can't be helped I suppose. So take a deep breath and step into the unknown...

Explanations for Substance Misuse

Edexcel only here. *Substance misuse means taking drugs in a way that can damage your health. As usual, different psychological approaches have different explanations for why people do it. Guess you couldn't expect anything less.*

There Are Biological Explanations for Substance Misuse

Why people use substances like drugs and alcohol could be down to **biochemical factors**.

1) Many drugs (e.g. heroin) cause the **release** of the **neurotransmitter dopamine**, which has a **pleasurable** effect.
2) This acts as a reward and makes the person want to **continue** using the drug.

- **Olds and Milner** (**1954**) tested this explanation by connecting an **electrode** to the **hypothalamus** in **rats' brains**. When the rats pressed a **lever**, the electrode **stimulated** the **hypothalamus**, leading to the release of **dopamine**.
- It was found that the rats **chose** to press the lever, which suggests that the feeling was **rewarding**.
- In another experiment, **Olds and Milner** (**1954**) found that rats would even walk over an area with a **painful electric current** running through it in order to get to the lever.
- This shows that the **release** of **dopamine** was **rewarding**, and the stimulus that caused it was **addictive**.

3) The effects of increased levels of dopamine can be gained from **natural sources**, such as **sex**, **food** and **exercise**, but using **drugs** can result in much more **intense** and **addictive** feelings.
4) However, **misuse** of a drug can affect the body's **natural** levels of **dopamine** within the **central nervous system**.
5) Because some drugs cause a **flood** of **dopamine** in the brain, the brain **reduces** its **own dopamine production**. This results in a **loss** of **pleasure** gained from other activities. Users develop an **addiction** when the drug itself **no longer** has **pleasurable** effects, but they need to keep taking it in order to **avoid** the **withdrawal symptoms**.

Biochemical Explanations Have Strengths and Weaknesses

Strengths

- Studies into **biochemical factors** involve **laboratory experiments** where the **variables** are strictly **controlled**. This means that it should be possible to establish **cause and effect**, because it's less likely that the results were caused by an **extraneous variable**.
- The effects of chemicals on the brain can be tested on **animals** and then **generalised** to **humans** (see page 129).

Weaknesses

- Explaining substance misuse in terms of neurotransmitter levels is **reductionist** (see page 245) because it **ignores psychological factors**.
- The **biochemical** approach also ignores the impact of **genetics** — it could be that **inherited tendencies** influence substance misuse. For example, **Doweiko** (**2002**) looked at **adoption records** for over 3000 people and found that **children** of **alcoholics** were much **more likely** to grow up to be alcoholics themselves. Being raised by **adoptive** parents who **weren't alcoholics** seemed to have **little effect**. This suggests that there's a **genetic influence** for **alcohol abuse**.
- There are problems with **generalising** results from **animal** research to **humans** (see page 129).

Theories From the Learning Approach Can Explain Substance Misuse

The **learning approach** offers a **psychological explanation** for substance misuse.

Operant conditioning explains substance misuse through **positive** and **negative reinforcement**:

1) The person is **positively reinforced** by the **pleasurable rewards** they get from using a substance. This could be the **physical** feeling of pleasure from a drug like **heroin**, or it could be the **social approval** and **acceptance** people feel from **smoking** or **drinking alcohol**.
2) **Negative reinforcement** is when people **keep taking** a substance to **avoid negative consequences** like **withdrawal symptoms**. The user learns that **continuing** to use the substance **prevents** the **unpleasant** withdrawal symptoms. Drug users may also want to **avoid** feelings of stress or boredom, or negative **social** factors like being the 'odd one out'.

Bandura's (**1973**) **social learning theory** suggests that people learn to misuse substances by **watching** and **imitating** others — e.g. friends, family or celebrities. It's especially likely to happen if the **role model** has a **high status** or if they get **rewarded** for the behaviour, e.g. with a **physical high** or with **social approval**.

Explanations for Substance Misuse

*There's **Research** to **Support** Explanations From the **Learning Approach***

- **Moolchan et al (2000)** found that **75%** of **teenage smokers** have at least one **parent** who **smokes**. They also feel that smoking helps them to **fit in** with their **peers**.
- These findings support **social learning theory**, as the subjects were **imitating** their parents.
- They also support the **operant conditioning** explanation — the **social approval** that subjects got from their friends for smoking acted as **positive reinforcement**.

- **Adesso (1985)** thought that children develop **expectancies** about the **effects** of **alcohol** through **observing** friends, family and role models. This supports **social learning theory** — it suggests that people learn how to behave when they're **drunk** by imitating others.
- **Christiansen et al (1982)** found that these expectancies are **modified** as an individual's **personal experience** with alcohol **progresses** — their **generalised** expectancies become more **specific**.

- **Baer et al (1987)** found that adolescents were **more likely** to use **alcohol** if they experienced **family conflict** or **stressful life events**. This suggests that they were using alcohol as a way of **avoiding negative things — negative reinforcement**. Learning this behaviour at a **young age** means it's likely to **continue** into **adulthood**.
- However, because this was a **correlational study** it's difficult to establish **cause and effect**. It could be that people are **more likely** to experience **family conflict** because they **drink alcohol**.

Learning Explanations** Have **Strengths** and **Weaknesses

Strengths

- Studies like **Adesso (1985)** (see above) use **human participants**, so they **avoid** the problems of generalising from **animal** experiments encountered in much biochemical research (see page 129).
- The learning approach helps to explain **psychological addiction** to substances that **don't** cause unpleasant physical withdrawal symptoms, e.g. cannabis.

Weaknesses

- The learning approach is **reductionist** because it assumes that everyone can become **addicted** in the **same way**. It **ignores individual differences** because it **doesn't explain** why some people who try drugs become addicted and others don't. This could be down to **biochemical** or **genetic** factors.
- It may not be possible to **generalise** findings that explain misuse of one drug to **other drugs**. For example, **Baer et al (1987)** explained **alcohol** abuse in terms of **negative reinforcement**, but this **doesn't** mean that abuse of **other substances** can be explained in this way.

It's likely that a **combination** of **biological** and **psychological** factors contribute to substance misuse. For example, some people might be **genetically predisposed** to drug abuse, but **environmental variables** (e.g. exposure to role models or stressful experiences) make it **more likely**.

Practice Questions

Q1 Outline research that suggests the release of dopamine is rewarding and addictive.

Q2 Describe drug misuse in terms of negative reinforcement.

Q3 Describe the findings of Moolchan et al's (2000) study on teenage smoking.

Q4 Identify the factors associated with drinking alcohol in the Baer et al (1987) study.

Exam Question

Q1 Describe and evaluate two explanations of substance misuse. [12 marks]

If only revision and exams caused a dopamine flood...

...life would be much nicer. Just imagine it — you're sitting here, learning all about substance misuse, and dopamine is making you feel that you're having a brilliant time. Think how much better everyone would do in their exams if revision was addictive. Now hold on to that thought and quickly learn these pages before you remember it's actually one big bore.

The Effects of Drugs

These pages are for Edexcel. *There are loads of chemicals out there that affect the way we think, act and feel. Some of them don't have a huge effect, like the ones in a nice cup of tea. Others are much more serious, like heroin and alcohol.*

Drugs** Have **Short-term** and **Long-term Effects

Addictive substances have **physical** and **psychological** effects, which have **short-term** and **long-term effects**.

1) The **short-term** effects of most drugs are a **change** in **mood**, **awareness** and **perception**:

- **Depressants** (e.g. alcohol) have a **sedative effect** — they make the user feel **relaxed**.
- **Stimulants** (e.g. cocaine, caffeine) make people feel more **alert**.
- **Hallucinogens** (e.g. LSD) cause **altered perception**.

2) **Tolerance** to a substance develops when a person uses it **regularly**, and then needs to use **larger quantities** to get the same effect from it.
3) **Physical dependence** means that a person will experience **physical withdrawal symptoms** if they **stop** taking it, e.g. vomiting, cramps, hallucinations. **Psychological dependence** leads to **psychological withdrawal symptoms**, e.g. irritability, insomnia and compulsive behaviour.

Heroin** Has **Short-term Effects** on the **Nervous System

First, here's a quick recap of the **nervous system** from AS:

1) **Neurons** are the cells that **transmit electrical signals** around the nervous system.
2) The **dendrites** receive the signals which then pass along the axon to the **synaptic knobs**.
3) There's a small **gap** between each neuron called a **synapse**.
4) **Neurotransmitters** are **chemicals** released from the synaptic knob that **pass across** the **synapse** — they pass on the **signals** to the dendrites of the next neuron.
5) Signals are transmitted around the nervous system and can lead to certain **feelings** or **behaviours**.
6) Some drugs **increase** the effects of a neurotransmitter — **agonists**. Other drugs **reduce** its effects — **antagonists**.

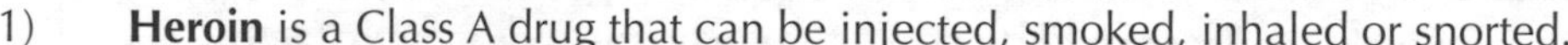

1) **Heroin** is a Class A drug that can be injected, smoked, inhaled or snorted.
2) Heroin stimulates **opiate receptors** in the brain. This has an **analgesic** effect — it **numbs pain**.
3) Heroin is also an **agonist** because it **increases** the effect of the neurotransmitter **dopamine**. This results in **over-stimulation** of **dopamine receptors**, leading to increased **pleasure**.
4) It's this combination which leads to the powerful **rush** and euphoria experienced when using heroin — it **dulls pain** and increases feelings of **well-being**. People usually experience this after a **few minutes**, depending on how they've taken the drug. After the initial rush, people feel **relaxed**, **drowsy** and **detached** from their surroundings. **First-time** users often **vomit** or feel **nauseous**.

Heroin Misuse** Causes **Psychological** and **Physical Dependency

1) Heroin users develop a craving for the drug and can develop **physical** and **psychological dependence** on it within a **few days** or **weeks** of first using it.
2) People can develop a **psychological addiction** to heroin because they want to experience the **first intense high** again. The habits and routine involved with addiction (e.g. buying the drug, meeting with the same people, etc.) can also be difficult to break.
3) Heroin is also highly **physically addictive**. Regular use quickly leads to increased **tolerance**, so **larger quantities** are needed to get the same feelings from it. After extended use heroin users **no longer** experience the rush but **continue** to take the drug to **avoid** the **unpleasant withdrawal symptoms**.
4) **Withdrawal symptoms** appear **quickly** in addicts who have developed **high levels** of **tolerance** to heroin — usually within **6-24 hours** after last taking it. This means that addicts need to take the drug very **regularly** to **avoid** these symptoms. **Withdrawal symptoms** include intense **craving** for the drug, **vomiting, diarrhoea, restlessness, compulsive scratching, insomnia, panic, cold sweats** and **cramps**.

The Effects of Drugs

Alcohol Has *Short-term Effects* on the *Nervous System*

Alcohol affects the **activity** of several **neurotransmitters** at the **synapse**:

- **Small amounts** of alcohol lead to **increased dopamine function**, so drinking it is **pleasurable**.
- The neurotransmitter **GABA** (gamma-aminobutyric acid) **inhibits activation** in the **central nervous system**. Alcohol **increases** the **inhibitory action** of **GABA**, so it acts as a **depressant**.

1) The short-term effects of alcohol are **influenced** by **gender** (women get drunk more quickly than men), **weight** (light people get drunk more quickly than heavy people), **food** eaten that day (alcohol is absorbed more quickly by an empty stomach) and use of **other substances**.
2) As intake **increases**, alcohol makes people feel **more confident** and **less inhibited**. They also become **lightheaded**, **talkative**, **less coordinated** and their **judgement** is affected.
3) **Larger** amounts of alcohol can have a **sedative effect** on some people (they become very relaxed or fall asleep). In others it can lead to **aggression**, **slurred speech**, **blurred vision**, **nausea**, **vomiting**, and **disturbed sleep**.
4) Moderate to large amounts of alcohol will lead to **withdrawal symptoms** the next day — a **hangover**. This usually involves **nausea**, **headaches**, **sweating** and **cramps**. Very heavy drinkers can experience **delirium tremens**, where they experience symptoms such as **hallucinations** and **delusions**.
5) People can **lose consciousness** if their **blood alcohol** level reaches **0.3%**. Levels of **0.5%** can cause **death**.

Alcoholism is *Psychological* and *Physical Dependency* on Alcohol

1) Steady heavy drinkers develop a **tolerance** to alcohol, meaning they need **increased amounts** to get the **same effects** from it. This is known as a physical dependency.
2) **Chesher and Greeley (1992)** found that **chronic heavy drinkers** could continue to **function** and appear relatively **normal** even with **blood alcohol levels** that could be **fatal** in people with **low tolerance**.
3) The **nervous system** becomes used to **constant high levels** of alcohol. As well as physical withdrawal symptoms (see above), **stopping drinking** leads to **psychological withdrawal symptoms**. These include **anxiety**, **mood swings**, **depression** and **confusion**. Many people drink in **social situations** and link the **environment** with **alcohol**, so it can be difficult to break this **psychological association**.
4) Long-term alcohol abuse can lead to **cirrhosis** of the **liver** (**loss of liver function** because of **scarring**) and **Korsakoff's syndrome** (long-term **memory loss**).

Practice Questions

Q1 What's meant by the term 'tolerance'?

Q2 What is the role of neurotransmitters in the nervous system?

Q3 Outline two heroin withdrawal symptoms.

Q4 Outline three short-term effects of alcohol.

Q5 What results did Chesher and Greeley (1992) find in relation to alcohol tolerance?

Exam Questions

Q1 Outline the short-term effects of heroin. [3 marks]

Q2 With reference to two specific drugs, discuss physical and psychological dependence. [12 marks]

Beauty is in the eye of the beer-holder...

These pages should be a doddle really — the stuff on the nervous system can be a bit complicated, but at least it's not all new and scary things that you've never done before. Just make sure that you can explain the short-term effects of heroin and alcohol, what tolerance and dependence are, and what withdrawal symptoms people get. Easy peasy lemon squeezy...

Treating Substance Misuse

***Just Edexcel again here**. This stuff on substance misuse can get quite depressing, so make sure you keep your spirits up (using completely legal methods of course). Onto treatment now anyway, which is at least a tiny bit more jolly...*

Drug Treatments Can Help with Heroin Dependence

The **biological approach** suggests using **methadone** as a **substitute** drug to treat heroin addiction.

1) **Methadone** works as a heroin substitute because it produces the same **physiological effects**. It's normally prescribed to heroin addicts by their **GP** to help them **avoid cravings** and **withdrawal symptoms** when they come off heroin.
2) People usually take methadone orally **once a day** in **liquid form**. They have to go a **pharmacy** and be **supervised** while they take it.
3) Because it's a **prescribed** drug, methadone is much **safer** than **heroin** because it **won't** have been **mixed** with any other chemicals. Taking it **orally** means that people **avoid** the **risks** associated with **injection**, e.g. infectious diseases like HIV and hepatitis, which can be caught by sharing needles.
4) Taking methadone **orally** also means that it works much more **slowly** than heroin, and **doesn't** produce the same intense **rush** or **euphoric feeling**.
5) This means it's **effective** for a much **longer** time than heroin and so needs to be taken **less often** to **avoid withdrawal symptoms**. If **heroin** is also taken, then methadone **blocks** the **pleasant effects** of it.
6) The aim is to gradually **decrease** the dose of methadone, until the user overcomes their **dependency**. However, this is a very **gradual** process and many people keep using methadone for **months** or **years** — they take a **maintenance dose** that helps them to **stay off** more **dangerous** street drugs.

There are Problems with Methadone Treatment

1) Methadone treatment works **differently** for **different people**. For example, **Swan** (**1994**) showed that a **6-month** programme worked **well** for **some people**, but **wasn't long enough** for **others**.
2) **Strain et al** (**1999**) found that addicts need to be given the **correct sized dose** for their individual needs to **prevent relapse**.
3) This shows how it's important to take **individual differences** into account, as the same treatment **won't work** for **everyone**.

1) Treating heroin addiction by just using methadone is **reductionist** — it only considers the **biological explanation** for drug misuse, and **ignores other factors**.
2) Methadone treatment often needs to be supported by **residential** or **out-patient rehabilitation**. **Self-help groups** like **Narcotics Anonymous** provide **social support** and encourage users to **identify** with a **non-using social group**.
3) People are **more likely** to **relapse** if they only take methadone and **don't** have any **other support**. This suggests that there are **other causes** for drug misuse, not just biological ones.

Self-help Organisations Can Help Alcohol Dependence

Alcoholics Anonymous (**AA**) is a worldwide **self-help group** to support people who have a problem with **alcohol**.

1) **AA** sees **alcoholism** as a **disease** without a cure. **Abstinence** (not drinking) can keep the disease under control.
2) Group members **meet** regularly to give each other **social support**. They're expected to treat information about other members as being **confidential**.
3) The content of meetings varies, but it often includes members **talking** about their **experiences** with **alcohol**.
4) AA involves a **twelve step programme** — a set of guidelines people should follow to help their recovery. The steps include members admitting that their drinking is **out of control**, acknowledging **past mistakes** involving alcohol and **making amends** for these mistakes.
5) Members are allocated a **sponsor** to **support** them through the twelve steps. The sponsor is a more **experienced** AA member who's been sober for a period of time.

Treating Substance Misuse

*AA Has a **Mixed Success Rate***

The Alcoholics Anonymous approach works better for some people than for others.

1) **Moos and Moos** (**2006**) compared alcoholics who'd attended AA for **more than 6 months** with alcoholics who'd **never attended AA**. When they followed them up after **16 years**, they found that the people who'd been to AA were **more likely** to have stayed sober. This shows the **long-term success** of AA.
2) The approach takes **individual differences** into account because it allows members to proceed through the steps at their **own pace**, and seek **more help** if they **need** it.
3) However, **Trice and Roman** (**1970**) found that certain **psychological traits** were **associated** with **success** in AA. Members were **more likely** to **stay off alcohol** if they felt **guilty** and had **affiliative needs** (wanted to form relationships with people and be part of a group). This suggests that AA **won't work** for **everyone**.

Prevention Campaigns** Aim to **Discourage Substance Abuse

You need to know about **one** drug prevention campaign, e.g. the **National Youth Anti-Drug Media Campaign**:

The **National Youth Anti-Drug Media Campaign** started in the **USA** in **1998**. It aims to **discourage teenagers** from using **recreational drugs**. The main focus has been on **preventing marijuana use**. **Billions** of dollars have been spent on the campaign, especially on **TV adverts**.

The campaign has had mixed results:

Positive Effects

1) **Palmgreen et al** (**2007**) studied teenagers who had **only** been **exposed** to the **National Youth Anti-Drug Media Campaign's** adverts, and **not** to any **other drug prevention programmes** (e.g. at school). They found that marijuana use had **decreased** since 2001, suggesting that the adverts had a **positive impact**.
2) **Longshore et al** (**2005**) found that teenagers who saw the adverts and had **drug prevention programmes** at **school** were **less likely** to smoke marijuana than those who **only** experienced **in-school programmes**.

Negative Effects

Hornik (**2008**) found that the **National Youth Anti-Drug Media Campaign** adverts either had **no effect** on **marijuana use**, or they actually led to an **increase** in marijuana use. There are **two** possible reasons for this:

1) The adverts emphasised marijuana use as a **big problem** among teenagers. This may have made teenagers think that marijuana use was **widespread** among their peers. So, the adverts may have **influenced** their **perception** of **social norms** in relation to marijuana use — they believed that many of their **peer group** were using the drug, so were **encouraged** to do the same in order to fit in.
2) The adverts may have increased marijuana use by **unintentionally highlighting** some of its **positive effects**.

Practice Questions

Q1 What is methadone used for?

Q2 What is meant by a maintenance dose?

Q3 What is the aim of Alcoholics Anonymous?

Q4 Outline one study that suggests AA is successful.

Q5 How did the National Youth Anti-Drug Media Campaign spread its message to teenagers?

Exam Questions

Q1 Describe one way of treating substance misuse in relation to a specific drug. [4 marks]

Q2 Outline and evaluate a campaign encouraging people not to use recreational drugs. [6 marks]

The AA didn't help my alcoholism at all — they just towed my car away...

I've spent pretty much the last 15 years waiting for an opportunity to use that joke — chuckling away to myself occasionally and feeling rather smug that I managed to think it up. So you can imagine my excitement when I realised my little beauty could finally be bestowed upon its adoring public. And to be honest, after all that it's actually a bit of an anticlimax...

Studies into Drug Use

This is just for Edexcel. *When I first saw what these pages are called I thought some cheeky psychologists had thought up a way of getting drunk all day and saying they were just 'doing research'. Actually, it's all far less scandalous...*

Stacy et al (1991) Studied **Cognition** and **Drink Problems**

Stacy et al (1991) — cognition and drink problems

Method: This was a **longitudinal study** where students completed a questionnaire about their attitude to alcohol **twice** over a **nine** year period. The **average age** was **18** at the start of the study and **27** at the end. The aim was to investigate whether certain **cognitive** and **personality traits** in **adolescence** would **predict drinking problems** in **adulthood**. Several variables were measured:

1) Participants' **alcohol consumption**.
2) **Cognitive motivations** — the **anticipated outcomes** of drinking alcohol, e.g. feeling more confident and relaxed, or feeling bad if they didn't drink alcohol.
3) **Sensation seeking** — how much participants looked for **new life experiences** and **thrills**, and how **susceptible** they were to **boredom**.
4) **Drinking problems** — this was measured by asking participants about **social** problems, **work-related** problems and **physical** problems that were **caused** by **alcohol**. They were also asked whether they'd ever **driven** under the influence of alcohol.

Results: Alcohol use in **adolescence** significantly predicted **alcohol use** and **drink driving** behaviour in **adulthood**. Adolescents who anticipated **positive outcomes** from drinking alcohol were **more likely** to have **drink problems** as **adults** — the **cognitive motivation** factor significantly **predicted problem drinking**. Adolescents who scored highly in the **sensation seeking** questions were **more likely** to drink alcohol in **adulthood**.

Conclusion: **Attitudes** towards alcohol and **alcohol-related behaviour** in **adolescence** can predict **alcohol-related behaviour** and **problems** in **adulthood**. People who have **positive expectations** about drinking alcohol as adolescents are **more likely** to develop **drink problems** as adults.

Stacy et al's (1991) Study has **Strengths** and **Weaknesses**

You need to be able to **evaluate** this study in terms of its **good** and **bad** points:

Strengths

1) **Experimental validity**: The **longitudinal design** of the study means there was good control over **participant variables** — the **same group** of **participants** took both questionnaires. The researchers **controlled** for people **dropping out** of the study by **comparing** the **original data** of participants who dropped out with those who continued. They found **no significant differences** between them in relation to **alcohol use**, which suggests that the people who dropped out **didn't** share any **common factors**.
2) **Application to real life**: This study suggests that it's important to look at factors like people's **attitude** towards alcohol (cognitive motivations), rather than just their current alcohol intake, to predict whether they're **at risk** of potential drink problems. This means that **prevention programmes** can be aimed at those who may be more **vulnerable** and therefore be **more effective**.
3) **Supporting evidence**: This study is supported by **Critchlow's (1987)** findings that **heavy drinkers** had more **positive expectations** about **alcohol use** than **non-heavy drinkers**.

Weaknesses

1) **Experimental validity**: It's impossible to know whether people's answers were **honest**, so this could affect the **validity** of the results. Participants may lie about things like drink-driving because of **social desirability bias** (wanting to portray themselves in the best way).
2) **Ecological validity**: It's difficult to **apply** the results of this study to **real life**, because the participants were in an **artificial setting**. Filling in a questionnaire about attitudes towards alcohol isn't a similar situation to the one people are usually in when they choose whether or not to drink alcohol. This could affect the **validity** of their answers.
3) **Methodology**: The results are **correlational**, so they **don't** necessarily show **cause and effect**. It could be that **other variables** that weren't studied cause drink problems in adulthood, and the **relationships** shown in this study are just **coincidental**.

Studies into Drug Use

Blättler et al (2002) Studied Heroin Addiction

Blättler et al (2002) — heroin treatment and cocaine use

Method: This was a **longitudinal** study carried out in Switzerland over an **18-month** period. It studied **heroin addicts** who **also** used **cocaine**, and aimed to find out whether **treatment** for **heroin addiction** could also **reduce cocaine use**. The study looked at **266** participants who were receiving **maintenance treatment** for their heroin addiction (**prescribed** doses of heroin). All of the participants had been **heroin addicts** for at least **2 years**, and had had at least **2 unsuccessful** attempts at **treatment**. **30%** of them also took **cocaine** on a **daily** basis, **54%** of them took it **occasionally**, and **16%** of them **never** took it. They also received **counselling** or **therapy** alongside their maintenance dose. The participants' **drug use** was measured using **self-report** every **6 months** and **urine tests** every **2 months** to see if they were still using illegal drugs during the treatment. They were also asked about **criminal activity**, **prostitution** and **involvement** with **other drug users**.

Results: After **18 months** of **maintenance treatment** and **counselling** for **heroin addiction**, the number of participants using **cocaine** fell from **84%** to **48%**. There was also a significant **drop** in involvement in **criminal behaviour**, e.g. the number of participants with an **illegal income** fell from **63%** to **10%**.

Conclusion: Treatment for **heroin** addiction can also reduce **cocaine** use and involvement in **criminal activity**.

Blättler et al's (2002) Study has Strengths and Weaknesses

You guessed it — you need to be able to **evaluate** this study in terms of its **good** and **bad** points:

Strengths

1) **Reliability**: The results are **reliable** because two **different techniques** were used to gather data — self-report and urine tests. This also means that the type of **data** is **broad** — **self-report** gathers **qualitative** data, and **urine tests** gather **quantitative data**.
2) **Ecological validity**: The study has good **ecological validity** because it was carried out in a **natural setting**, so the situation didn't affect the participants' behaviour. This means it should be possible to **apply** the findings to **other heroin addicts** in the same situation.
3) **Ethics**: The participants gave **informed consent** to take part in the study, they **weren't deceived** and they were able to **withdraw** if they chose to (see pages 218-219 for more on ethics in research).

Weaknesses

1) **Reliability**: Participants could be **dishonest** about their **drug intake** and **criminal activity** in **self-report** situations like interviews and questionnaires. This means that the results **aren't 100% reliable**.
2) **Generalisation**: The results of this study **can't** be **generalised** to all heroin addicts because the study focused **specifically** on heroin addicts in Switzerland for whom previous treatment had failed.
3) **Application to real life**: The study supports the use of **maintenance treatment** to help heroin addicts who also use cocaine. However, this type of treatment is very **expensive** so it's not always readily available.

Practice Questions

Q1 How long did Stacy et al's (1991) study last?

Q2 What did Stacy et al (1991) mean by cognitive motivation?

Q3 What was the aim of Blättler et al's (2002) study?

Q4 What percentage of Blättler et al's participants still used cocaine after 18 months of treatment?

Exam Questions

Q1 Outline the method of a study into alcohol misuse. [4 marks]

Q2 Describe and evaluate a study investigating the misuse of an illegal substance. [12 marks]

Heroine treatment — when Catwoman's in hospital...

Anyway, these pages look quite meaty, but they're pretty manageable once you get stuck in. Just don't fill up on bread first. If you're a vegetarian then I'm sorry to say that you haven't been catered for on this occasion — you'll just have to ignore this bit and pretend that you're revising from a meat substitute. Enough of this talk of food — on with the revision.

Theories of Health Belief

Just OCR this time. OCR people, you also need to know about disorders as part of your health and clinical psychology unit — see section 9 for this. *Right, on with some theories about how health is affected by beliefs about health...*

*Rosenstock (1966) Came Up With the **Health Belief Model***

The **Health Belief Model (HBM)** outlines how likely a person is to take **responsibility** for their **health**. It considers several **variables** to determine whether someone will **follow** recommended health **advice**, e.g. giving up **smoking**:

1) **Perceived susceptibility** — how much the person feels at **risk**, e.g. of lung cancer.
2) **Perceived severity** — how **serious** the person thinks the **consequences** will be if they **don't** follow advice, e.g. a smoker's attitude towards the symptoms of lung cancer will influence whether they try to give up.
3) **Cost-benefit** — a person will only follow health advice if they **believe** the **benefits** will **outweigh** the **costs**, e.g. a smoker might believe the benefits of quitting smoking (e.g. improved health, saving money) outweigh the costs (e.g. withdrawal symptoms).
4) **Cues to action** — cues that **encourage** a person to follow the health advice. They can be **internal cues** (e.g. physical symptoms like a smoker's cough), or **external cues** (e.g. a TV advert warning people about the dangers of smoking).
5) **Other variables** — **age**, **gender**, **socio-economic status**, **education** and **personality** can also influence whether someone follows health advice. For example, people with low socio-economic status and less education are more likely to smoke than people with a higher status and more education.

Studies have found evidence to **support** the **HBM**, for example:

1) **Janz and Becker** (**1984**) reviewed **46** studies that investigated the **HBM**. They found that a person's **perceived susceptibility** influenced whether they took **preventive health measures** like doing exercise.
2) **Becker et al** (**1978**) investigated **mothers'** use of **asthma medication** for their **children**. The **costs** included difficulty in getting to the chemist, following a schedule of treatment and disruption of planned activities. Mothers were **more likely** to follow the schedule if they were **married** and had a **higher level** of **education**.

Perceived Control** is an **Important Factor** of **Health Belief

Health belief is **affected** by whether people feel they're in **control** of their **health**.

Rotter (**1966**) developed the theory of a **locus of control**:

1) Rotter came up with a **scale** to measure the amount of **control** that people **feel** they have over their **behaviour** and what **happens** to them.
2) At one end of the scale is an **internal locus of control**. In terms of health, people with an internal locus of control feel that they're able to **control** their health, for example by exercising regularly, eating well and maintaining a healthy lifestyle.
3) At the other end of the scale, people with an **external locus of control** believe that **other factors** such as **fate** or **luck** control their health, so their behaviour doesn't have any impact.
4) People with an **external locus of control** are **more likely** to show unhealthy behaviour like **smoking**, because they don't believe their actions will have a major influence on their health.

Wallston et al (**1978**) identified **three** different **dimensions** of **locus of control** in relation to **health**:

1) **Internal** — people feel they have **control** over their health through their **behaviour**.
2) **Chance** — people feel that their health and their behaviour **aren't linked**, so they're **less likely** to show healthy behaviour like exercising.
3) **Powerful others** — people have a **strong belief** in **medical professionals**. This could lead them to **follow medical advice** carefully, which should mean they lead a **healthy lifestyle**. Or, it could mean they **don't** follow a **healthy lifestyle** because they believe any **problems** they develop can be **treated**.

Steptoe et al (**1994**) found a **negative relationship** between the **chance dimension** and **healthy behaviours**. This provides support for Wallston et al's theory. **Weiss and Larson (1990)** found a **positive relationship** between the **internal dimension** and **healthy behaviours**. This supports the theories of both Rotter and Wallston et al.

Theories of Health Belief

Self-efficacy** is the **Belief** that You'll **Succeed

1) **Bandura (1977)** stated that **self-efficacy** is about how much a person **believes** they can **achieve something**.
2) In terms of **health**, this could explain why some people **succeed** at **quitting smoking** or **losing weight**, and some **don't**. The theory suggests that some people **don't believe** they'll be able to **achieve** their **goals**.
3) A person's **self-efficacy** is affected by certain **factors**:

See page 166 for more on self-efficacy.

- **Previous experience** in the **same situation** — whether they've succeeded or failed before in the same situation can affect self-efficacy.
- **Modelling** — seeing **other people** succeed in the same situation can increase self-efficacy because the person can **model** themselves on those who have already succeeded.
- **Psychological factors** — feelings like **anxiety** spur some people on and **increase** self-efficacy. Others interpret it as a **sign** that they're going to **fail**, which **reduces** self-efficacy.
- **Social persuasion** — **encouragement** from other people can **increase** self-efficacy, **discouragement** can **decrease** it.

"Failure? I'm afraid that's not a word in my vocabulary."

1) **Conner and Norman (1995)** showed that people with **high self-efficacy** were more likely to perform **healthy behaviours**.
2) It was linked to **success** in **weight loss**, practising **safe sex**, **overcoming addiction** and **exercising**.
3) **Low self-efficacy** was linked to **depression** and **anxiety**.

*There are **Problems** With These **Theories***

A **strength** of these three theories is that they're **supported** by **research evidence**.
However, it's important to consider **other perspectives**.

1) **Rosenstock** and **Rotter's** theories are from the **cognitive approach**. They assume that behaviour is influenced by thought processes. This is **reductionist** (see p. 245) because it doesn't consider other explanations, e.g. that **health belief** can be influenced by those around you.
2) **Bandura's** theory is more from the **behaviourist approach**. Things like success in quitting smoking are influenced by **conditioning** — whether the healthy behaviour is **reinforced**, e.g. by encouragement from other people.
3) The **biological approach** would take a different view, and state that success in quitting smoking depends on **internal factors** such as the severity of the withdrawal symptoms, and the individual's willpower.

Practice Questions

Q1 What is meant by 'perceived susceptibility' in Rosenstock's (1966) Health Belief Model?

Q2 Give an example of an internal cue and external cue that could stop smoking.

Q3 Name the three dimensions of locus of control identified by Wallston et al (1978).

Q4 What is self-efficacy?

Q5 Identify a healthy behaviour associated with high self-efficacy.

Exam Question

Q1 a) Describe how Rosenstock's Health Belief Model can be used to explain healthy behaviour. [10 marks]

b) Compare and contrast two theories of health belief. [15 marks]

Beware the terrifying locust of control...

He's 30 feet high and he's coming to get you. His hobbies include playing the violin, setting ants on fire with his giant magnifying glass, and ten-pin bowling. Never agree to go down the megabowl with him though — he's a terrible loser. He's skinned people alive just for getting a half-strike. Oh, and please, please, please don't write locust in your exam...

Promoting Healthy Living

***Only OCR need to know about promoting healthy living. Everyone else can have another bag of crisps.** OCR people shouldn't feel too glum though — these pages are mostly about chip pans and TV campaigns, so they're not too bad.*

Media Campaigns** Aim to **Promote Healthy Behaviour

Media campaigns like TV adverts or posters can **promote** a **specific health behaviour**, e.g. the **safe** use of **chip pans**.

Cowpe (1989) studied the effect of chip pan fire campaigns

Method: This was a **natural experiment** measuring the effects of **TV adverts** that demonstrated how to prevent and put out **chip pan fires**. **Questionnaires** sent out before the campaign showed that more people **believed** they knew how to use chip pans safely than was reflected in **statistics** about the number of fires. The TV adverts were shown in **10** British television regions. Their **effectiveness** was measured by asking viewers in the regions to complete **questionnaires** about safe use of chip pans. **Fire service statistics** were studied to see whether the number of chip pan fires **reduced**.

Results: The questionnaires showed that **awareness** of **preventing** and **putting out** chip pan fires **increased** from **62%** to **96%** after the campaign. All regions showed an average **12% decrease** in the number of **chip pan fires**. Areas where television regions **overlapped** showed the **smallest reduction** in fires, suggesting that seeing the adverts too much **reduced** their **effectiveness**. The number of chip pan fires was lowest **during** the campaign, but figures **after** the campaign were still **lower** than they had been **before**.

Conclusion: **Media campaigns** can be successful in **increasing awareness** about chip pan safety, and **reducing** the number of chip pan fires. The biggest effect is seen **during** the campaign. Campaigns are **less successful** if people are **over-exposed** to them.

Evaluation: These results support **Bandura's (1977) self-efficacy** theory (see p.139). Viewers were made **more confident** about using chip pans safely, which made them **more likely** to **succeed** in doing so. The study had **good ecological validity** — the participants were in a **natural setting**, so the environment won't have influenced their behaviour. However, it's not possible to **control** all the variables in **natural experiments**. This **reduces experimental validity**, because the results could have been caused by an **extraneous variable**. The results are **correlational**, so they **don't** prove **cause and effect** — it could be that another unknown variable actually led to the reduction in chip pan fires.

Fear Appeals** Aim to **Scare People** into Being **Healthy

1) **Fear appeals** work by telling people that something **bad** will happen if they behave in a certain way, e.g. they'll **increase** their **risk** of **lung cancer** if they **smoke**, or get **STIs** through **unprotected sex**.
2) The aim is to **increase fear arousal levels** so that people are **motivated** to **change** their **behaviour** — this will then **reduce** their **fear**.
3) It's used a lot in **TV** and **poster campaigns**, e.g. anti-smoking posters show pictures of blackened lungs and TV campaigns show interviews with bereaved families whose relatives died of lung cancer.

Fear Arousal Doesn't** Always Lead to **Healthy Behaviour

1) **Janis and Feshbach** (**1953**) studied whether the **amount of fear** a campaign caused affected whether people would **change** their **behaviour**. They looked at people's behaviour after they'd seen different **dental hygiene campaigns** — one that created **minimal fear**, one that created **moderate fear** and one that created **strong fear**.
2) Participants reported **more anxiety** after the **strong fear** campaign, but this **didn't result** in **changed behaviour**.
3) They found that **36%** of people changed their dental hygiene behaviour if there was a **minimal** amount of fear, **22%** if there was a **moderate** amount of fear and only **8%** if there was a **strong** amount of fear.
4) It seems that the **strong warning** of what might happen if the participants didn't take care of their teeth actually **put them off** looking after them.

Shock tactics might not work because attention is focused on the **source** of the fear, rather than the **message** of the campaign. It's possible that the fear causes people to go into **denial** — they don't believe that something so bad could happen to them, so they don't take measures to prevent it. **Leventhal** (**1970**) suggested that campaigns are more **effective** if they tell people what they **should** do, rather than what they **shouldn't** do.

Promoting Healthy Living

Legislation Can **Force** People to **Adopt Healthy Behaviours**

Some healthy behaviours are considered so important that the **law** (**legislation**) is changed to make sure that people stick to them, e.g. wearing a seatbelt. Studies have looked into how effective this is.

Dannenberg et al (1993) — bicycle helmet laws and campaigns

Method: This was a **natural experiment** involving **7217** American **school children** aged **9-14** from three different areas of the USA (Howard County, Montgomery County and Baltimore County). A **stratified sampling** technique was used (one that's **representative** of the **target population**). 3494 responded and completed **surveys** about their use of **bicycle helmets**. The **law** in **Howard County** then changed to make bicycle helmet use **compulsory** for children, and an **educational campaign** also took place to encourage them to wear helmets. In **Montgomery County** there was an **educational campaign** but **no change** in **legislation**. In **Baltimore County** there was **minimal education** about bicycle helmets and **no change** in **legislation**. The children were **surveyed again** after these changes had taken place.

Results: According to the 'before' and 'after' surveys, bicycle helmet use **increased** from **11%** to **37%** in **Howard County**, from **8%** to **13%** in **Montgomery County**, and from **7%** to **11%** in **Baltimore County**.

Conclusion: **Educational campaigns** encouraging children to wear bicycle helmets are most effective if they're **supported** by changes in **legislation**.

Evaluation: The study has **high ecological validity** because the participants were in their **natural environment**, so their surroundings won't have affected their behaviour. It has a direct **application to real life** — areas that want to encourage children to wear bicycle helmets should combine educational campaigns with legislation. The **problem** with **Dannenberg's** study was that it relied on **self-report**. The children might have **lied** about wearing a bicycle helmet because they knew that they **should** wear one — the results could have been affected by **social desirability bias**. Because this was a **natural experiment** the researcher **couldn't control** all the **variables**. This means that it's difficult to establish **cause and effect** because the results could have been caused by an **extraneous variable**.

Research in other areas **supports** the claim that legislation increases healthy behaviours. E.g. **Ellingsen et al** (**2006**) found **decreased nicotine levels** in bar and restaurant workers after the introduction of a Norwegian **smoking ban** for staff and customers. By testing nicotine levels Ellingsen ensured that participants **couldn't lie** about whether they were smoking.

Practice Questions

Q1 What research method was used in Cowpe's (1989) study?

Q2 What percentage of participants were aware of how to deal with chip pan fires before and after the campaign?

Q3 What do fear appeals aim to do?

Q4 Outline Janis and Feshbach's (1953) findings.

Q5 Outline the three different conditions in Dannenberg et al's (1993) study.

Q6 Outline the conclusion of Dannenberg et al's study.

Q7 Why might Dannenberg et al's results have been affected by social desirability bias?

Exam Question

Q1 a) Outline how media campaigns can be used to promote healthy living. [10 marks]

b) Describe and evaluate one other method of promoting healthy living. [15 marks]

Fear appeals to me — but that's because I'm a ghost...

Don't get freaked out, I'm not really a ghost. And if I was I'd be like Casper. Anyway, I reckon that if someone showed me a really scary picture about what might happen to my teeth, I'd do something about it pretty sharpish. I don't know what those participants were thinking of. They're probably the sort who ignore the fact that they've got exams coming up too...

Adherence to Medical Advice

***OCR only**. Doctors and psychologists seem very interested in making sure everyone's as healthy as possible. It's pretty nice of them to bother I guess. The trouble is, sometimes people just don't do what they're told — naughty naughty...*

*Patients May Have **Specific Reasons** For **Non-Adherence** to **Medical Advice***

1) Patients sometimes choose not to **adhere** to (follow) medical advice.
2) If their reasons for this are **rational** they're said to show **cognitive rational non-adherence**.
3) There are several reasons why people may ignore medical advice:

- They feel that the **costs** of the **side effects** outweigh the **benefits** of the **treatment**. For example, Bulpitt and Fletcher (1988) studied the side effects of drugs prescribed to treat hypertension. They found that many patients suffered from physical side effects such as tiredness, erectile dysfunction and dizziness. They also showed psychological side effects such as impaired cognitive functioning. The **severity** of these side effects could lead some patients to stop taking their medication.
- The treatment might be too **expensive**. Studies, e.g. Safran et al (2005), suggest that over a quarter of older patients in the USA take less medication than they're prescribed to save money.
- The patient stops treatment to **test** whether it's **worked** or not. For example, Conrad (1985) found that many patients with epilepsy sometimes stopped taking their medication to check the effect it was having and to see whether they still had epilepsy or not.

4) In general, **adherence** to medical advice **decreases** the more **complicated** the treatment is, the **longer** it lasts for and the more **expensive** it is.
5) **Individual differences** may also have an affect on adherence. For example, Brown (2004) found that age, mental health, problem solving skills and self esteem were all important factors in non-adherence.

Adherence** to Medical Advice Can be **Measured Physiologically

Physiological factors can indicate whether medical advice has been adhered to. For example:

Samples of **blood** or **urine** can be tested for the **presence** of a **prescribed drug**. This shows whether the medication has been taken **recently** but doesn't test for **long-term adherence** — the patient may have taken their medication before visiting the doctor but not for some time previously.

Samples of **blood** or **urine** can be tested for the **effect** of a **prescribed drug**. The effects that the medication has can be seen as evidence that medical advice has been adhered to. For example, **Lustman et al (2000)** carried out glycohaemoglobin tests on diabetic patients. These measure the average blood glucose concentration over the previous four months, showing whether insulin treatment has been adhered to in the **long-term**.

The **doctor's own judgement** of the patient and their condition can be used as evidence of whether the patient has adhered to advice or not. For example, an overweight patient might be given advice to eat healthily and exercise more. If they lose significant amounts of weight it can reasonably be **assumed** that they've followed this advice.

The presence of **adverse effects** can indicate that advice hasn't been adhered to. **Butler et al (2004)** found that patients who didn't adhere to advice to take immunosuppressants after kidney transplants were likely to suffer from organ rejection. **De Geest et al (1998)** found that heart transplant patients who'd failed to take immunosupressants the majority of the time had a high chance of experiencing rejection.

Other methods that can be used to assess adherence include:

- **Patient self-report** — the patient keeps their **own record** of when they took their medication. A problem with this approach is that patients may **lie** about their adherence.
- **Pill counts** — patients bring their medication to appointments and the **number of pills left** are **counted**. However, doctors can only see **how many** pills have been removed from the bottle, not the number actually **taken**. Also, this approach doesn't provide any information on whether the pills were taken at the **correct time**.
- **Electronic pill container** — these record **when** the container's been **opened**, allowing doctors to see **exactly** when pills have been removed. However, they still don't show whether the patient **took** the medication or not.

Adherence to Medical Advice

There Are Ways to Improve Adherence to Medical Advice

There are several ways that adherence to medical advice can be **improved**:

1) **Improving communication** between doctor and patient so that the patient is clear on **what** to take, **when** to take it and the **reason** behind it.
2) Making adherence as **easy as possible**, e.g. making sure medication is **easy to take**, **convenient to transport** and **affordable** for the patient.
3) Providing **techniques** to help patients adhere to medical advice, e.g. advice on how to build medication into **daily routines**, and providing **electronic pill containers** that signal when medication should be taken.
4) Providing **positive reinforcement** for adhering to medical advice. For example, **asthma treatment** involves taking **medication** through an **inhaler**, which children often **don't enjoy** using. The **Funhaler** is a children's inhaler fitted with a **whistle** and a **spinner** which operate when it's used. This is a behavioural approach and provides **positive reinforcement** for taking the medication. Watt et al (2003) studied the effect of the Funhaler on adherence to medical advice:

Sasha knew she'd never miss a tablet again now that she had her shiny new portable pill box.

Watt et al (2003) — adherence to asthma medication in children

Method: This study involved **32 asthmatics** who used **traditional inhalers** regularly. They were aged between **18 months** and **6 years** and came from different socio-economic areas of Australia. They used the **Funhaler** for **2 weeks**. **Parents** were asked to complete a **questionnaire** about adherence to medication and attitudes towards it.

Results: **73%** of parents reported that they were **always successful** at getting their child to use the **Funhaler**, compared with just **10%** when they used the **traditional inhaler**. They reported that children were much **happier** to use the Funhaler. Parents were more likely to adhere to advice about **how often** to administer the medication when they were using the **Funhaler**.

Conclusion: The **Funhaler** improves **adherence rates** in asthma medication.

Evaluation: The study took place in a **natural setting** so has **ecological validity** and **applications to real life**. However, the experiment used a very **small sample** of participants, so there are problems with **generalising** the results to the rest of the population. As well as this, the **self-report** method means that there was no way of knowing whether parents were telling the truth, which reduces **experimental validity**. Also, the parents knew the aim of the study so might have shown **demand characteristics**, providing the answers that they thought the researchers wanted.

Practice Questions

Q1 What is meant by cognitive rational non-adherence?

Q2 Name two fluids that could be tested to measure adherence to medical advice.

Q3 How did Lustman et al's (2000) study measure adherence to medical advice?

Q4 Give a problem of using patient self-report as a measure of adherence.

Q5 What did Watt et al (2003) conclude about the use of Funhalers in treating asthma?

Exam Question

Q1 a) Outline reasons why people choose not to adhere to medical advice. [10 marks]

b) Discuss how adherence to medical advice can be measured physiologically. [15 marks]

Lustman — the superhero with special powers in... lets not go there.

So there you have it — why people don't follow medical advice, how to check if they're following advice and how to get them to follow advice. Learn those three dinky little topics and you can move on. Unless you're pining after one of those Funhaler thingymawotsits. And I wouldn't blame you. An inhaler with a whistle — what could be more fun than that...

Measuring Stress

This is just for OCR. *Stress isn't very pleasant, but it does have its place when it's spurring you on to do something. It's when people feel stressed all the time that it's a problem — it can have psychological and physiological effects.*

Stress** Can be **Measured** Using **Self-report

1) **Major life events**, like the death of a close relative or moving house, can be a big **psychological** source of stress.
2) **Holmes and Rahe** (**1967**) ranked the level of stress these life events cause on the **Social Readjustment Rating Scale (SRRS)**.
3) They made a list of **43** common life events and asked people to give each one a **score** to say how **stressful** it was. They called the numbers that made up each score the **Life Change Units (LCU)**. The higher this number of LCUs, the more stressful the event was.
4) Then they **ranked** the events from most to least stressful, for example:

The SRRS is also known as the Holmes Rahe Stress Scale.

Life event	Rank	LCU
Death of a spouse	1	100
Retirement	10	45
Christmas	42	12

Strengths

- The **SRRS** gives life events a **numeric value**, which means that the **amount** of **stress** can be **quantified**. Quantitative data is **more objective** and **easier** to **analyse** than qualitative data.
- The idea that some life events are more stressful than others is **supported** by research evidence. **Holmes and Rahe** (**1967**) studied hospital patients' records and noted any **major life events** that occurred **before** the person became ill. They found a **positive correlation** between the likelihood of **illness** and the **score** on the **SRRS** — the more stress a person experienced, the more likely they were to suffer illness.

Weaknesses

- The **SRRS** doesn't separate **positive** and **negative life events**. Stress and illness might be more linked to **negative life changes**. For example, a wedding might be stressful, but positive overall, while the death of a spouse might have a very negative stressful effect.
- It's **ethnocentric** (based on one culture) so it **can't** be **generalised** to everybody. For example, people who don't celebrate Christmas won't find it stressful.
- It doesn't consider the effect of **long-term** but **minor** sources of stress, such as **everyday hassles** at work (see page 146).

***Physiological Measures** of **Stress** can be Taken*

Stress affects the **body** in different ways. **Stress levels** can be measured using **physiological tests**.

1) **Heart rate** — A **chest strap** containing a **transmitter** measures **electrical activity** and indicates heart rate. **Increased** heart rate is a sign of **stress**.
2) **Blood pressure** — This is measured by putting an inflatable cuff on the arm which restricts blood flow. As it deflates, the pulse rate in the arm indicates blood pressure levels. **Stress** is associated with **high blood pressure**.
3) **Hormone levels** — **Blood** and **urine** can be tested for stress-related hormones. For example, **increased** levels of **adrenaline** and **cortisol** indicate **higher** levels of **stress**.
4) **Galvanic skin response** (GSR) — This measures the **electrical resistance** of the skin, which is affected by **moisture level** (sweat). **Increased** GSR is associated with **stress**.

There are **strengths** and **weaknesses** of using **physiological measures** of stress.

Strengths

- Physiological tests are **objective** — it's not possible to lie and the results **won't** be **influenced** by the participant or the researcher.
- The test results can indicate appropriate **treatments** for the stress — e.g. if someone has an **increased heart rate**, they can be put on drugs called **betablockers** to slow their heart down.

Weaknesses

- The tests might not be measuring stress. Other behaviours such as **poor diet**, **poor sleeping patterns** and **alcohol consumption** can also cause changes in these measurements. Each of these behaviours can be used as **coping mechanisms** when people are **stressed**. So it could be that **physiological changes** are caused by one of these **stress-related behaviours**.
- Technology isn't always 100% accurate.

Measuring Stress

A Combined Approach Can Increase Validity

A **combined approach** involves measuring the psychological and physiological effects of stress. **Johansson et al (1978)** used a **combined approach** when they were looking at the amount of stress experienced by workers at a sawmill. Here's a quick outline of the study so you can see the method they used.

Johansson et al (1978) — stress levels in sawmill workers

Method: The participants were **24** workers in a Swedish sawmill. They were an **opportunity sample** in a **natural experiment** with an **independent measures** design. The control group were **10 cleaners** who had a varied job where they could control the pace of work. The experimental group was **14 'finishers'** whose job role was more isolated, required more skill and was very repetitive. Their productivity levels set the wages for themselves and other workers in the factory, so they had lots of responsibility. Data was collected using a **combined approach**. Self-report was used to measure **psychological** effects like **mood**, **absenteeism** and **stress-related illness**. **Urine samples** were taken to measure **physiological** effects by looking at levels of **stress-related hormones**.

Results:
1) **Finishers** had had **more absences** and **stress-related illnesses** (e.g. headaches) compared to the cleaners.
2) **Finishers** reported **more negative moods** than the cleaners.
3) **Finishers** had **higher** levels of the stress hormones **adrenaline** and **noradrenaline** than the cleaners.

Conclusion: The high **responsibility**, **repetitive** nature of the work and **isolation** from others meant that the finishers showed more **psychological** and **physiological** signs of stress than the cleaners. This led to more health problems.

A combined approach can **increase experimental validity**...

Using more than one type of measurement means that researchers can gather **more data**. Getting **qualitative** and **quantitative** data means that the **disadvantages** of one method are **overcome** by the **advantages** of the other. For example, self-report is vulnerable to **social desirability bias**, while **physiological** techniques are more **objective**. However, **physiological techniques** only provide information on **physical changes** in the body, while **self-report** can give information on **cognitive** and **emotional changes**.

...but it has a **downside**...

Using more than one technique in a study can be **complicated**, **expensive** and **time-consuming**. This means that **sample sizes** have to be **smaller** to reduce the **cost** and amount of **time** the study takes. A smaller sample size **reduces** the **reliability** of the experiment, because you might get very different results from each participant. It also limits how far the results can be **generalised** to other people.

Practice Questions

Q1 What is the Social Readjustment Rating Scale (SRRS)?
Q2 Outline two disadvantages of the SRRS.
Q3 Name two different physiological measurements of stress.
Q4 What's meant by a combined approach to measuring stress?
Q5 Outline one disadvantage of self-report.

Exam Question

Q1 a) Outline the self-report method of measuring stress. [10 marks]

b) Describe and evaluate a combined approach to measuring stress, using relevant research. [15 marks]

If you think exams are stressful, try working at a sawmill...

Well I'll tell you this for free, I've never been more glad not to be a Swedish sawmill worker from the 1970s in my life. What a lucky escape that was. As well as all the problems they had with bad moods and hormone-filled urine, they had to deal with the daily strife of trying not to get their big seventies beards caught in the machinery. Not an easy task I can tell you.

Causes of Stress

***Just OCR again**. Studies, studies and more studies. It wasn't always like this you know. In Freud's day, psychology was just lying on a couch and talking about your mother until you felt better. I don't know when it all got so complicated...*

Daily Hassles are Stressful Everyday Events

Kanner et al (1981) suggested that stress is related to **minor** things, rather than the major life events put forward by **Holmes and Rahe (1967)** (see page 144). Examples of these **daily hassles**, which they named **irritants**, include having too many things to do, misplacing objects, and getting stuck in traffic.

Kanner et al (1981) — stress and daily hassles

Method:	**100** adults completed a **questionnaire** each month which asked them to choose which **hassles** they had experienced that month from a list of 117. They then had to **rate** each hassle to show how **severe** it had been for them. This was repeated for 9 months.
Results:	Certain hassles occurred more **frequently** than others, such as worrying about weight, family health and the rising cost of living. They found that people who gave **high scores** were more likely to have **physical** and **psychological** health problems. They also found that scores on an **uplifts scale** (containing events that make you feel good, e.g. finishing a task or getting on well with a partner) were **negatively** related to ill health — these events may **reduce** stress or protect us from it.
Conclusion:	Daily hassles are linked to stress and health.
Evaluation:	The weaknesses of **correlational methods** are relevant here — it isn't possible to establish a cause and effect relationship between the variables. The questionnaires resulted in **quantitative data**, which is useful for making comparisons, but they don't allow participants to explain why certain experiences are stressful to them, so potentially useful data is missed. Questionnaires rely on **honesty** in order for the results to be valid — participants may not be completely truthful about admitting that they find mundane daily events stressful. They also rely on the participants' **recall** being accurate.

Frankenhaeuser (1976) Found that Job Type Influenced Stress Levels

Weirdly, just like **Johansson et al (1978)** on page 145, **Frankenhaeuser (1976)** also studied Swedish sawmill workers.

Frankenhaeuser (1976) — stress levels in sawmill workers

Method:	Frankenhaeuser studied 2 groups of workers at a sawmill. One group had the **repetitive** task of feeding logs into a machine all day. The job was very **noisy** and the workers were **socially isolated**. They didn't have much **control** over their work as the machine dictated how quickly they could feed the logs in. The other group had a different task which gave them more control and more social contact. **Stress levels** were measured by testing **urine samples** and **blood pressure** (physiological measures).
Results:	The workers who had minimal control and low social contact had **higher** levels of **stress hormones** (**adrenaline** and **noradrenaline**) in their urine. They were also more likely to suffer from **high blood pressure** and **stomach ulcers**.
Conclusion:	A lack of control and social contact at work can lead to stress and health problems.
Evaluation:	The study was carried out in a **natural setting**, so it has **good ecological validity** because the results won't have been affected by an artificial environment. It was **ethical** because the participants **weren't deceived** or asked to do anything **distressing** that they weren't already doing as part of their job. It has a direct **application** to **real life** because it suggests that stress can be avoided in the workplace if people are given a variety of roles, more control over their work, and aren't isolated. However, the results are **correlational**, so they don't prove cause and effect. It could be that people with higher stress levels are more attracted to stressful jobs, and so **individual differences** would be a factor. The **sample** was very **small** and the study was only carried out in one Swedish sawmill. This means that the results can't be **generalised** to other occupations or nationalities.

You can also use the Johansson et al (1978) study (see page 145) as an example of work being a cause of stress.

Causes of Stress

Geer and Maisel (1972) Linked Stress to Lack of Control

Geer and Maisel (1972) studied the **physiological** effects of a **lack of control** over your environment.

	Geer and Maisel (1972) — stress and lack of control
Method:	Participants were shown **photographs** of **dead car-crash victims**. Their stress levels were measured using **galvanic skin response** (see page 144). The study was an **independent groups design** with 3 different groups. **Group 1** was given a button to press to make the pictures **disappear**, and a **noise** was sounded before each photograph was displayed. **Group 2** didn't have a button but were told that every 60 seconds a noise would indicate that a photograph would be displayed 10 seconds later. **Group 3** didn't have a button and were told that noises and photographs would be presented, but weren't given any information about timing.
Results:	**Group 1** experienced the **least** amount of stress, followed by **group 2**. **Group 3** had the **highest** stress levels.
Conclusion:	**Stress levels** are affected by the amount of **control** people have over their environment. **Group 1** had the lowest stress levels because they were able to control how long they looked at the photograph. **Group 3** had the **highest** stress levels because they didn't know when the distressing photograph was coming and were unable to make it disappear.
Evaluation:	This was a **laboratory experiment** with **strictly controlled** variables, so it's possible to establish **cause and effect** — not having control caused more stress. It's supported by Marmot et al's (1997) study (below), which found that a lack of control in the workplace led to more stress-related illness. However, the study wasn't very **ethical** because it caused **distress** to the participants. It was conducted in an **artificial environment**, so it lacks ecological validity and it's not possible to **generalise** the results to **real life**.

Marmot et al (1997) Linked Stress to Lack of Control in the Workplace

	Marmot et al (1997) — lack of control and illness in the workplace
Method:	Over **7000** civil service employees working in London were **surveyed**. Information was obtained about their grade of employment, how much control they felt they had, how much support they felt they had, etc.
Results:	Their medical histories were looked at 5 years later. Those on **lower** employment grades who had **less control** over their work were **more likely** to have **cardiovascular disorders**. People on the lowest grade of employment were **four times** more likely to die of a **heart attack** than those on the highest grade.
Conclusion:	Believing that you have **little control** over your work influences work stress and the development of illness.
Evaluation:	The study only looked at people with **office jobs**, so the results may not apply to other jobs. The findings are **correlational**, so it isn't possible to establish cause and effect. For example, **smoking** was found to be common in those who developed illnesses. Perhaps those who felt less control at work were more likely to smoke and the smoking caused the heart problems rather than stress. Data was obtained using **questionnaires**. This may have encouraged participants to be more **truthful** than they would have been if interviewed. However, some people might not have admitted to experiencing stress at work in case it harmed their job prospects.

Practice Questions

Q1 Outline the results of Kanner et al's (1981) experiment.

Q2 What method did Geer and Maisel (1973) use to measure stress levels?

Q3 Outline one weakness of Marmot et al's (1997) study.

Exam Question

Q1 a) Outline research into the effect of daily hassles on stress levels. [10 marks]

b) Discuss lack of control as a cause of stress, using relevant research. [15 marks]

Working down t'pit — a minor cause of stress...

As if it wasn't bad enough being a 1970s Swedish sawmill worker — people then go and come up with a whole load of other things you can get stressed out about too. What if those poor guys lost their keys, got stuck in traffic on the way to work, or accidentally sawed their kipper tie off? It's only now that I realise just how much I've neglected their plight.

Managing Stress

Still just for you OCR lovelies. *Learning about the causes of stress is all very well, but I can't help but think it would also be useful to know how to manage stress in case it does hit you. And it would seem that those examiners agree with me...*

Cognitive Techniques Can be Used to *Manage Stress...*

1) **Cognitive techniques** aim to manage stress by identifying and **altering** the **thought processes** that cause stress.
2) **Meichenbaum** (**1985**) developed a cognitive approach to stress management called the **Stress Inoculation Technique** (**SIT**).
3) The SIT introduces **minor** levels of stress to individuals, which allows them to **psychologically adjust** and **prepare** for stressful situations.
4) There are **three phases** to the SIT:
   - **Conceptualisation phase** — the person discusses their experiences of stress. They identify the cause of their stress, the impact it has on their life, their existing coping strategies and the effect these strategies have.
   - **Skills acquisition and consolidation phase** — they develop and practice coping skills (e.g. relaxation, communication or social skills) in a safe environment.
   - **Application and follow-through phase** — they apply their coping skills to a range of increasingly stressful situations. As they start to experience success the person becomes more confident about their ability to deal with stress.
5) This technique supplies people with a **wide range** of **strategies** that can be used in **daily situations**. Several studies have shown it to be effective, particularly if used alongside other techniques.

Alfie's mum made him practice the SIT every day.

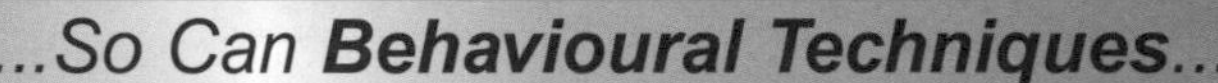

...So Can Behavioural Techniques*...*

1) **Behavioural techniques** aim to manage stress by **changing** the **behaviour** that causes it.
2) This is often done through **biofeedback**, where **physiological indicators** of stress (e.g. heart rate, blood pressure, etc.) are monitored in different situations and are 'fed back' to individuals. This allows them to identify which experiences, feelings and emotions **raise** and **lower** their stress levels.
3) Individuals can then use this information to **alter** their stress levels, e.g. using relaxation techniques like meditation or breathing control exercises.
4) This feeling of relaxation acts like a **reward** and encourages the person to repeat this as an involuntary activity.
5) The person learns to use these techniques in **real-life** situations.
6) **Budzynski et al** (**1973**) investigated the role of biofeedback in stress management:

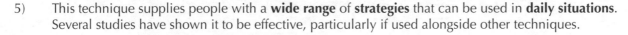

	Budzynski et al (1973) — biofeedback and tension headaches
Method:	The sample was **18 participants** who volunteered in response to a newspaper advert about headaches. The participants were screened to make sure they only suffered from tension headaches and were then divided into **three groups**. **Group 1** received **relaxation training** twice a week for 8 weeks. Their muscle tension was monitored by an EMG monitor which fed back information on muscle tension by making clicks. They were told that **more clicks** meant **more muscle tension** and **worse headaches**. They were encouraged to **relax** so that the clicks slowed down. **Group 2** received the **same relaxation training**, however they weren't told that the clicks reflected their level of muscle tension and a fake soundtrack of clicks was played to them. **Group 3** were the **control group**. They didn't have any relaxation training. Participants who'd had relaxation training were also told to **practise** the techniques at home.
Results:	At the end of the study and three months afterwards, **Group 1** had the **lowest muscle tension** and **fewer headaches**. They also showed **lower levels** of **hysteria**, **depression** and were **less preoccupied** with their **health** than they were before the study. Participants who'd **practised** the relaxation techniques at home showed **more improvement** than those who hadn't.
Conclusion:	Biofeedback can **reduce stress related illnesses** such as tension headaches.
Evaluation:	The presence of a **control group** and **Group 2** showed that it was the actual feedback was important, not just the presence of feedback. However the sample size is small, making **generalisation** difficult. Also, the results can't be generalised to other stress-related symptoms.

Managing Stress

...and Social Approaches

1) **Segerstrom and Miller (2004)** carried out a meta-analysis of 293 studies on the effect of stress on the **immune system**.
2) They concluded that **chronic** (long-lasting) stress **suppresses** the immune system.
3) This means that people suffering from stress are **more likely** to become **ill** and are **less able** to **fight illness** than they would otherwise be.
4) It's been suggested that **social support** (e.g. from families, friends, help groups) can **reduce stress**, and so reduce the impact on the **immune system**. If this is the case, we would expect people with **strong social support** to be **less likely** to become **ill** and **more likely** to **recover** from illness than those without a good social support system.
5) **Waxler-Morrison et al's (1991)** study can provide **evidence** for this:

Stress didn't feature highly in Poppy's merry little world.

Waxler-Morrison et al (1991) — social support for cancer patients

Method: This was a **natural experiment** investigating the effect of **social support** on **survival chances** of women with breast cancer. Data on social support (e.g. number of supportive friends, extent of contact with friends, size of social network, etc.) was collected from **133 women** with breast cancer using **questionnaires** and **interviews**. The women's **medical records** were followed over 4 years.

Results: They found that women with **better social support** had **better survival rates**. Types of support that were relevant included being married, having a job, having contact with friends and getting support from friends.

Conclusion: Social support increases chances of surviving breast cancer.

Evaluation: It's important not to **assume causality** — social support is associated with survival but doesn't necessarily cause it. Further investigation is needed to find the precise relationship between social support and cancer survival. The longitudinal design of the study reduces the influence of extraneous variables. However, the lack of a control group reduces the **reliability** of the conclusions that can be drawn from the results.

6) This study suggests that **social support** can be helpful in **reducing stress**, as the women with good social support networks were **more likely** to **survive** breast cancer. This could be because they were less stressed and so their immune system was working more efficiently than women without a good support system.

Practice Questions

Q1 How do cognitive techniques aim to manage stress?

Q2 What is the SIT?

Q3 What is biofeedback?

Q4 What effect does chronic stress have on the immune system?

Q5 Name one social factor that increases survival chances according to Waxler-Morrison et al (1991).

Exam Question

Q1 a) Outline a cognitive approach to managing stress. [10 marks]

b) Discuss how behavioural techniques can be used to manage stress. Include relevant research in your answer. [15 marks]

Worth keeping hold of your friends then — you might need 'em one day...

Ahhhh, so the old saying could be true — love really is the best medicine, and having lots of friends could help you survive cancer. That's good to know. Also good to know — cognitive and behavioural techniques for managing stress. Not quite as heart-warming, but just as necessary seeing as you've got an exam coming up in the not too distant future. So crack on.

Diagnosing Dysfunctional Behaviour

OCR only. Diagnosing dysfunctional behaviour is a tricky business. After all, you can't label someone 'dysfunctional' just because they're acting a bit weird. Nor can you use the word 'weird' in a medical diagnosis. People don't like it.

*It Can be **Difficult** to **Diagnose Dysfunctional Behaviour***

1) Diagnosing dysfunctional behaviour involves distinguishing between **normal** and **abnormal behaviour**.
2) However, sometimes it can be difficult to identify where the dividing line between the two is.
3) This is because the difference between normal and abnormal behaviour is **subjective** — behaviour that's considered **abnormal** by **one person** may be considered **normal** by **another**.
4) Also, it's **more difficult** to **measure** symptoms associated with **mental health** than symptoms associated with **physical health**. For example, a high temperature can be measured using a thermometer, whereas feelings of anxiety are much more difficult to determine and compare.

Rosenhan** and **Seligman (1989)** Identified **Features** of **Abnormal Behaviour

1) **Rosenhan and Seligman** (**1989**) identified **seven features** that can be used to **define** behaviour as abnormal:

- **Suffering** — for some disorders (e.g. anxiety) the individual reports experiences of suffering and distress.
- **Maladaptiveness** — behaviour that prevents the individual performing tasks and social roles. For example, a person with depression might want to stay at home rather than go to work.
- **Vividness and unconventionality** — behaviour that's different to what would be expected in a situation. For example, laughing at a funeral.
- **Unpredictability and loss of control** — behaviour that's uncontrolled, unpredictable, variable and inappropriate to the situation. For example, a student singing loudly during an exam.
- **Irrationality and incomprehensibility** — behaviour that doesn't have a rational reason behind it.
- **Observer discomfort** — behaviour that makes other people feel uncomfortable. For example, invading a stranger's personal space by sitting too close to them on the bus.
- **Violation of moral and ideal standards** — behaviour that doesn't fit in with the morals of society. For example, theft, violence, etc.

2) Some of these features are more common than others and some may even appear in **normal behaviour**. For example, many people will, on occasions, display **irrational behaviour**, fall short of **moral standards**, or experience **suffering** and **distress**. This **doesn't** mean that they have **dysfunctional behaviour**.
3) Also, some features are affected by **cultural factors**. For example, women displaying bare skin is considered normal in some cultures and a violation of moral standards in others.
4) So, it can still be **difficult** to define dysfunctional behaviour using Rosenham and Seligman's features.
5) However, in general, the **more features** of abnormal behaviour an individual displays and the **more frequently** they're displayed, the **more likely** they are to be **diagnosed** as showing **dysfunctional behaviour**.

*There are **Two Main Systems** For **Categorising Dysfunctional Behaviour***

Once an individual has been identified as showing dysfunctional behaviour, a diagnosis of what specific **condition** they have is made, based on the **symptoms** they show. There are two main systems for categorising dysfunctional behaviour:

Diagnostic and Statistical Manual of Mental Disorders (DSM)

- The **DSM** was first published in 1952 by the American Psychiatric Association (APA). It's now in its fourth edition.
- It contains information on the **symptoms** of 297 mental disorders grouped into **three axes** (levels). **Axis 1** contains **clinical disorders** (e.g. depression, schizophrenia), **axis 2** contains **personality conditions** (e.g. paranoid personality disorder) and **axis 3** contains **physical conditions** (e.g. brain injuries).
- The DSM contains two further axes — **axis 4** contains information on **environmental factors** that contribute to disorders and **axis 5** contains a **numeric scale** used to rate how well an individual is **coping** with their problems.
- The DSM is mainly used by health professionals for **diagnosis**.

Diagnosing Dysfunctional Behaviour

International Statistical Classification of Diseases, Injuries and Causes of Death (ICD)

- The **ICD** is published by the World Health Organisation (WHO) and has contained a section on mental disorders since its 1949 edition.
- It contains information on the **symptoms** and possible **causes** of disorders, as well as associated **social situations**.
- The ICD categorises **clinical disorders** (e.g. depression, schizophrenia) and **personality conditions** (e.g. paranoid personality disorder) on the **same axis**.
- The ICD is also used by health professionals for diagnosis.

Each recognised mental disorder has been given a numerical **code**. This code is the **same** in the **DSM** and the **ICD** to give continuity to health professionals using both classification systems. Both systems have a **western bias**, so aren't always suitable for use in **other cultures**.

Biases Can Lead to *Incorrect Diagnoses*

1) **Biases** held by health professionals can affect the diagnoses that they make — sometimes leading to **misdiagnosis**.
2) **Garb (1997)** identified **three main biases** that occur — **gender bias**, **race bias** and **social class bias**.
3) **Ford and Widiger (1989)** investigated the role of **gender bias** in misdiagnosis:

Ford and Widiger (1989) — gender bias and misdiagnosis

Method: Clinical psychologists were asked to read fictional case studies and then diagnose the condition of the patient. One case study outlined the symptoms of **antisocial personality disorder (ASPD)**. These include recklessness, impulsiveness and failure to conform to social norms. A second case study outlined the symptoms of **histrionic personality disorder (HPD)**, such as a need for approval and attention, and emotional behaviour. A third case study described some symptoms of **ASPD** and some of **HPD**. The **gender** of the patients was **variably** given as **male**, **female** or **unspecified**.

Results: The case study outlining symptoms of **HPD** was usually **correctly diagnosed** when the patient was said to be **female**, as was the case study outlining symptoms of **ASPD** when the patient was said to be **male**. However, when the case study of **ASPD** was labelled with a **female** gender, the psychologists often judged them to be suffering from **HPD**. Also, the case study of **mixed symptoms** was much more likely to be diagnosed as a case of **HPD** than **ASPD** when it was presented as a study of a **female** patient.

Conclusion: The psychologists showed **gender bias** in their diagnoses — being **female** increased the chances of being diagnosed with **HPD**. This is likely to be because the symptoms of HPD are seen as **female characteristics**.

Evaluation: The study is based on an artificial situation so lacks **ecological validity**. This means the results can't be **generalised** to real-life. Also, the case studies were based on criteria in an older version of the DSM so the results might not be **valid** anymore.

Practice Questions

Q1 Why can it be difficult to distinguish between normal and abnormal behaviour?

Q2 Name the two main classification systems of dysfunctional behaviour.

Q3 Give three biases that can occur in diagnosis.

Exam Question

Q1 a) Outline how abnormal behaviour can be categorised. [10 marks]

b) Discuss, using relevant research, how biases can impact on diagnosis. [15 marks]

Staying in to revise all day — decidedly abnormal behaviour if you ask me...

...but sadly necessary. After all, you do have an exam coming up. So it's probably best if you learn these pages — then you'll be able to answer questions on dysfunctional behaviour with knowledge, fluidity and style, impressing teachers and friends alike when your marks come back. And you won't have to resort to singing in the exam. That would be weird.

Explaining Dysfunctional Behaviour

Still just you OCR people. *As usual, those pesky psychologists want to know 'why', so here's a lovely double page about the possible causes of dysfunctional behaviour. I say 'possible' because there's a few different theories bouncing around...*

Dysfunctional Behaviour Can be Explained Biologically

The **biological approach** suggests that dysfunctional behaviour can be explained by **genetics**:

1) **Gottesman and Shields (1991)** reviewed studies on the role of **genetics** in **schizophrenia**.
2) They looked at **twin studies** comparing concordance rates of schizophrenia in **identical** (**MZ**) twins and **non-identical** (**DZ**) twins.
3) Overall, the results of the review showed a concordance rate of **48%** for **MZ twins** — much higher than the **17%** concordance rate for **DZ twins**.
4) This suggests a **genetic explanation** for schizophrenia. However, other factors must play a role as the concordance rate for MZ twins **wasn't 100%** despite the fact they share 100% of their genetic material.
5) Gottesman and Shields also looked at **adoption studies** to investigate the role of genetics in schizophrenia.
6) Adoption studies are useful as the offspring and their **biological** parents have **similar genetic material** but will live in **different environments**. So, if a parent and the offspring both have the disorder it's likely to be due to **genetic factors** rather than environmental factors. Similarly, if a child and their **adoptive** parent both have schizophrenia it would suggest that **environmental factors** play a larger role than genetics, as they both share the **same environment** but have **different genetic material**.
7) Gottesman and Shields found that adopted children with **biological** relatives who had schizophrenia were **more likely** to develop schizophrenia than other adopted children.
8) Again, this provides support for a **genetic explanation** of schizophrenia.

A concordance rate shows how often both twins have the disorder.

Dysfunctional behaviour could also be down to **physiology**. For example, many studies show that **neurotransmitters** (e.g. serotonin) could be responsible for dysfunctional behaviours.

Behavioural Explanations For Dysfunctional Behaviour Involve Conditioning

1) The **behavioural approach** suggests that dysfunctional behaviour can be learned through **conditioning**.
2) **Watson and Rayner** (**1920**) investigated the role of **classical conditioning** in the development of phobias.

Watson and Rayner (1920) — classical conditioning and phobias

Method:	This study involved an 11 month old boy named Albert. He showed no fear reaction to white, furry objects, e.g. cotton wool, a rat, a rabbit and a santa mask with a beard. During the study the rat was **repeatedly** presented to Albert. Each time this was done, a metal bar was hit with a hammer, creating a noise Albert found **distressing**. Albert was then shown the rat without the noise. He was also shown the cotton wool, the rabbit and the mask again.
Results:	Albert began to show a **fear reaction** to the **rat** when it was presented **without** the loud noise. He also showed the fear response to the **cotton wool**, **rabbit** and **mask**.
Conclusion:	Albert was conditioned to have a **phobia** of rats and objects he associated with rats.
Evaluation:	There are serious **ethical issues** in causing distress and creating phobias in a child. This is a case study, only involving one child, so there are problems **generalising** to the whole population. Not everyone goes on to develop a fear or phobia after a negative situation, so this explanation can't be the full story.

3) **Lewinsohn** (**1974**) explains **depression** using the principles of **operant conditioning**.

- He suggests that a person becomes depressed when they **don't experience** much **positive reinforcement**.
- Without positive reinforcement, the person becomes **less likely** to engage in constructive activities and events, which results in even **less positive reinforcement**. This can lead to **depressive behaviour**.
- Family and friends are likely to react to this behaviour. This provides the individual with the attention that they're missing, **positively reinforcing** the depressive behaviour.
- Although this idea can help to explain depression it **doesn't** explain **other dysfunctional behaviours**.

Explaining Dysfunctional Behaviour

There Are Also Cognitive Explanations of Dysfunctional Behaviour

The **cognitive approach** suggests that an individual's behaviours and emotions are determined by their **thought processes**. The **disruption** of normal thought processes causes **faulty cognitions**, such as:

1) **Maladaptive thoughts** — focusing, to an unnecessary extent, on negative experiences and emotions.
2) **Overgeneralisation** — interpreting a small number of negative events as a long-term, unalterable pattern.
3) **Mental filter** — focusing on one negative event at the expense of positive events, e.g. taking notice of one piece of negative feedback and ignoring large amounts of positive feedback.
4) **Jumping to conclusions** — interpreting an event in a negative way even if the evidence doesn't back up the conclusion. For example, if a friend acted in an offhand manner, someone with faulty cognitions would immediately assume it's because of something they've done rather than considering external factors.
5) **All-or-nothing thinking** — categorising anything that isn't quite perfect as a failure.
6) **Personalisation** — when individuals interpret negative events as a reflection of themselves, or blame themselves for things beyond their control.
7) **Magnification** — interpreting negative results as having a larger effect than they actually do.
8) **Minimisation** — interpreting positive results as having a smaller effect than they actually do.

These faulty cognitions can lead to **dysfunctional behaviours**. For example:

- **Beck (1963)** identified a **cognitive triad** of maladaptive thoughts. This triad is made up of thoughts people have about **themselves** (e.g. "I'm useless at everything"), the **future** (e.g. "I'll never improve") and the **world** (e.g. "You need to be better than I am to succeed in life"). If people focus on these negative thoughts it will **interfere** with their ability to **engage normally** in daily living and so leads to dysfunctional behaviour.
- **DiNardo (1988)** suggests that worry is a **normal cognition**. However, maladaptive thoughts increase worry to an **unreasonable extent**, which can lead to **dysfunctional behaviours**. This can include **Social Anxiety Disorder (SAD)** — where individuals worry excessively about other people and being judged by them.

They were determined to diagnose Simon with SAD. He was starting to think they'd never get the message that he just didn't like people.

- **Seligman (1975)** suggests that **dysfunctional behaviours** such as depression can be caused by an individual's belief that they have **no control** over a situation.
- This is known as **learned helplessness** and can be explained by faulty cognitions such as **overgeneralisation**, **maladaptive thoughts** and **jumping to conclusions**.

Practice Questions

Q1 What types of studies did Gottesman and Shields (1991) use to study the role of genetics in schizophrenia?

Q2 What are maladaptive thoughts?

Q3 What is learned helplessness?

Exam Question

Q1 a) Outline a biological explanation for dysfunctional behaviour. [10 marks]

b) Discuss, using relevant research, behavioural explanations for dysfunctional behaviour. [15 marks]

Personalisation — not the same as doodling all over your exam paper...

...and you shouldn't be wasting time on that anyway, not when you've got so much stuff to write about. Or at least you will have once you've learnt these pages. Three explanations of dysfunctional behaviour — biological, behavioural and cognitive, few bits of jargon like maladaptive and concordance, bit of psychological name dropping and Beck's your uncle — top marks.

Treating Dysfunctional Behaviour

Still just you OCRers, but there is good news — it's the last two pages of the section. Yipdeedoo. *The title says it all here — these pages are about how to treat dysfunctional behaviour. And as usual, there's more than one approach...*

Dysfunctional Behaviour Can be **Treated** Using a **Biological Approach**...

The **biological approach** to treating dysfunctional behaviour often involves **prescribing drugs** to a patient. For example:

1) Many studies suggest that depression is caused by **low levels** of the hormone **serotonin**. So, to treat depression serotonin levels could be **increased**.
2) This can be done using drugs called **selective serotonin reuptake inhibitors** (**SSRIs**), which reduce the reuptake of serotonin into neurons. This increases serotonin levels in the synapses in the brain (p.132) so receptors continue to be **stimulated**.
3) **Karp and Frank** (**1995**) investigated the **effectiveness** of using **drugs** to treat depression compared to using a combination of **drugs and psychotherapy**.
4) They found that treatment using **drugs and psychotherapy** was **no more effective** in treating depression than using **drugs alone**.
5) However, drug treatments can have **disadvantages** such as unpleasant **side effects**. For example, SSRIs can cause **nausea** and **headaches**. If the patient finds these too severe they may **stop taking** the medication.
6) This **non-adherence** to medical advice means that the **success rate** of the drug is **reduced**, even though it may be effective.
7) Also, drug treatment for dysfunctional behaviour has been **criticised** for just addressing the **symptoms** of the disorder and not the **cause**.

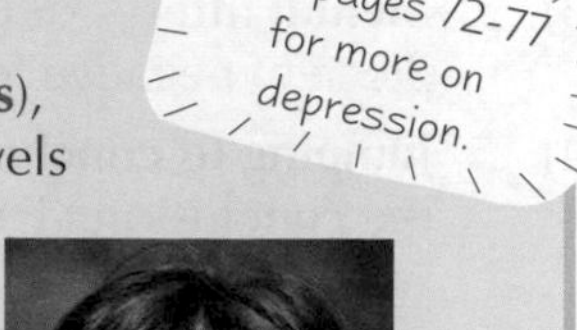

See pages 72-77 for more on depression.

Larry never suffered from low serotonin levels. In fact, he was feeling famously happy.

...a **Behavioural Approach**...

The **behavioural approach** to treating dysfunctional behaviour involves **conditioning**. For example:

1) **Wolpe** (**1958**) suggested **systematic desensitisation** could be used to treat **phobias**.
2) This involves introducing the feared stimulus to the person **gradually**, in a **relaxed environment**.
3) This can be done using a **fear hierarchy** — a list of items related to the feared stimulus, ranked in order of fear.
4) The least feared item is introduced to the phobic along with **relaxation training**. After a time the person will become conditioned to **associate** the stimulus with **positive feelings**, rather than fearful ones.
5) Once the person is no longer fearful of that item, they then move on to the **next item** on the hierarchy and repeat the relaxation techniques.
6) This technique has been shown to work in a number of studies. For example:

McGrath et al (1990) — successful treatment of a noise phobia

Method:	This was a **case study** of a nine year old girl with a **fear of loud noises** such as fireworks, party poppers, guns and balloons popping. With the help of a therapist she made a **fear hierarchy** of noises that frightened her and **rated** her fear levels for each object on a scale of 1 to 10. Over **ten sessions** she was exposed to noises on the hierarchy and taught **relaxation techniques** to use. The techniques included controlling breathing and thinking about playing with her toys at home (**positive thoughts**). At the end of the ten sessions she was asked to rate her fear of each object again.
Results:	By the end of the fifth session she was confident enough to pop a balloon herself. By the end of the tenth session her **fear level ratings** had **fallen** — from 7 to 3 for balloons popping, from 9 to 3 for party poppers and from 8 to 5 for a cap gun.
Conclusion:	**Systematic desensitisation** was an **effective treatment** for noise phobia for this child.
Evaluation:	The progress was still evident 3 months later, showing the positive effects **didn't reduce over time**. As this is a case study using one person there are problems with **generalising** to other people, and to other phobias.

Treating Dysfunctional Behaviour

...or a Cognitive Approach

The **cognitive approach** to treating dysfunctional behaviour addresses the **faulty cognitions** that cause the behaviour:

1) **Beck et al's (1976) cognitive restructuring therapy** focuses on identifying, testing and correcting faulty cognitions. It encourages the patient to **reassess** their thought processes and to develop more positive beliefs.
2) This is done by asking the patient to **monitor** and **record** their thoughts, feelings and behaviours.
3) These are then **examined** to see how logical and valid they are, and to establish **links** between cognitions and behaviours.
4) **Faulty cognitions** can then be **identified** — more rational thoughts can be substituted for them instead.
5) Over time the patient can learn to **correct** their **faulty cognitions**, becoming more able to deal with experiences and situations and **avoiding dysfunctional behaviour**.
6) One of the main **benefits** of the cognitive approach is that it addresses the **cause** of the dysfunctional behaviour rather than just treating the **symptoms**.

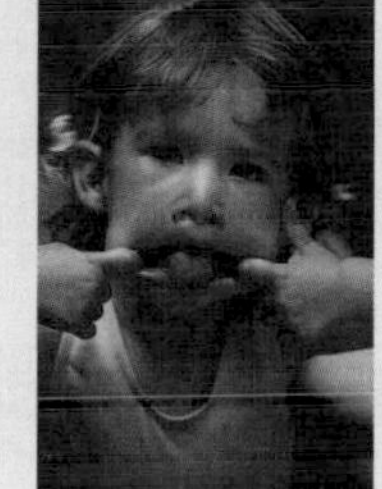

Amy couldn't write it down but she was still able to communicate how she'd been feeling.

Dobson (1989) carried out a **meta-analysis** on the **effectiveness** of cognitive therapy in treating depression:

- He looked at studies comparing patients who'd undergone **cognitive therapy** with a **control group** who hadn't received any treatment. He found that **cognitive therapy patients** had made better progress than **98%** of the control patients.
- Dobson also looked at the effectiveness of **cognitive therapy** compared to **behavioural therapies** and found that **cognitive therapy patients** made better progress than **67%** of patients receiving behavioural treatment.
- The effectiveness of **cognitive therapy** and **drug treatments** was also compared. **Cognitive therapy patients** had made better progress than **70%** of patients receiving drug treatments. This suggests cognitive therapy is **more effective** than treatment with drugs. However, drug treatment is a **broad category** covering many different types of drugs, some of which are more effective than others.

These results show how effective cognitive therapy is as an approach to treating depression. However, the results can't necessarily be **generalised** to other dysfunctional behaviours.

Practice Questions

Q1 What does SSRI stand for?

Q2 Give one disadvantage of using drugs to treat dysfunctional behaviour.

Q3 What is a fear hierarchy?

Q4 What was the conclusion from McGrath et al's (1990) study?

Q5 How does the cognitive approach aim to treat dysfunctional behaviour?

Q6 Outline one finding from Dobson's (1989) meta-analysis.

Exam Question

Q1 a) Outline the behavioural approach to treating dysfunctional behaviour. [10 marks]

b) Discuss cognitive treatments for dysfunctional behaviour. [15 marks]

I wonder which approach would be suitable to treat a revision phobia...

Pop the champagne and yell hurrah — you've reached the end of this extraordinarily long section. This stuff shouldn't blow your mind too much, it's just those old gems the biological, behavioural and cognitive approaches again. Oh, and a little tip — I'd learn the pages before you drink the champagne, it's generally easier that way round. Not that I'd know of course...

Sport Psychology

These pages are for Edexcel chaps only. *Oooh, Section 13 — unlucky for some. Hopefully not for you though.*

Sport Psychology *Focuses on* ***Three*** *Main Areas*

The three main areas in sport psychology are:

1) Understanding **why** people choose to take part in **particular sports**. E.g. **Kroll and Crenshaw (1970)** found that certain **personality types** were associated with interest in certain sports (see p.158).
2) Looking at the variables that influence whether somebody **does well** at sport. E.g. **Cotterell et al (1968)** found that the presence of an **involved audience** affects sporting performance (see p.170).
3) How to **improve** sporting performance. E.g. **Boyd and Munroe (2003)** investigated differences between climbers and athletes in their use of imagery as a **motivational technique** (see p.167).

Questionnaires *Are Used to Investigate Sport Psychology*

1) **Kroll and Crenshaw (1970)** used **Cattell's 16PF** (personality factors) test — a **multi-choice questionnaire** used to investigate 16 **personality traits**, such as openness to change, sensitivity and dominance.
2) They compared different sportspeople to see if particular traits were **similar** or **different** between sports.
3) They found that American footballers and wrestlers had similar traits, but that wrestlers and gymnasts differed significantly on social boldness, emotional stability, vigilance and self-reliance. There's more on this on p.158.

Questionnaires are **useful** because they can be used to collect a **lot** of **qualitative** and **quantitative** data (see next page) much more quickly than with a face-to-face interview. If kept **anonymous** they can also be used to collect data on topics that a sportsperson might not want to otherwise discuss, such as drug use or eating disorders.

But there are also potential **problems** with using questionnaires:

1) Their **validity** is reduced if leading questions (questions that suggest a particular answer) are used, as the answers don't then give a true reflection of the individual's responses.
2) They're vulnerable to **social desirability**, as most people want to show themselves in a positive way.
3) If the topic of the questionnaire is sensitive, e.g. drug use, then **ethics** can be a problem.
4) The **reliability** of questionnaires can be influenced by the way that sport psychologists interpret the results. It can be hard to clarify exactly what was meant by a particular answer, especially if **open-ended** questions have been used.

Correlations *Are Another Research Method Used in Sport Psychology*

Correlations are useful for showing the **relationship** between two variables, which can be positive or negative. They also show the **strength** of the relationship. However, they don't show **causality** (they don't prove one thing causes the other) — further research has to be carried out if a cause and effect relationship is suspected.

1) The **Yerkes-Dodson law** or **Inverted 'U' hypothesis** is the trend shown on a scattergraph (see p.233) when **performance** is plotted on the y-axis and **arousal** on the x-axis.
2) The relationship between these two variables shows that as arousal increases so does performance initially. But after an **optimum level** of arousal is reached then performance decreases with arousal.
3) This law is used in sport psychology to understand how to **maximise performance** in a wide range of sports.

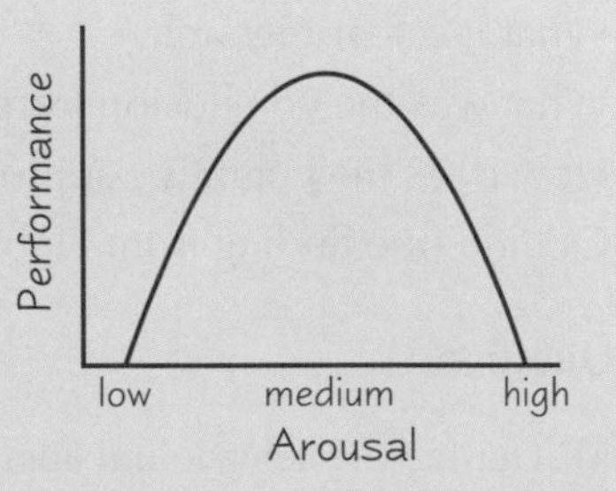

1) The **validity** of correlations is increased if a **significance test** (see p.224-225) is also used — it's possible to get a strong correlation just by chance, giving a misleading understanding of the relationship.
2) Using a correlation can be handy when a controlled experiment wouldn't be appropriate for **ethical** reasons. This is because correlations don't involve controlling any variables.
3) Correlations can test the **external reliability** (p.216) of a study — the test can be taken twice by the same people to see if the results correlate.

Sport Psychology

Some Studies Collect Qualitative Data

Qualitative data is **non-numerical** information and includes **descriptions**, **recordings** and **written notes**.

1) Qualitative data has **detail** and **depth** — it's rich and thorough information.
2) It's usually **collected** using open ended questions in interviews, surveys, case studies and questionnaires.
3) Or, a football coach could record a **video** of a match. This could be **analysed** by the coach to provide qualitative data which could be used to give players **feedback** on strengths and weaknesses. Improvements could then be made to their game.
4) Qualitative data can be **presented** in the form of a report and may include **quotes** from individuals.
5) It can also be changed into **quantitative** (numerical) data by using **content analysis**. This groups the data into categories which can then be **statistically analysed**. However, a possible disadvantage of this process is that the data can sometimes lose its meaning if taken **out of context**.
6) Qualitative data is useful because of the detail it provides. However, this detail can make it hard to get a **quick understanding** of the results of a piece of research.
7) It's also difficult to make **comparisons** between studies or individuals — there's wide scope for different researchers to **interpret** the data differently.

An Alternative is to Collect Quantitative Data

Quantitative data is **numerical** information. Numerical information can be **statistically analysed** and is usually collected using questionnaires, experiments and correlations.

Quantitative data can be **presented** in many ways including tables, bar charts, histograms and scattergraphs (see pages 232-233). **Statistical tests** can be used to show the strengths of relationships or make comparisons between groups. **Significance levels** can also be used to show how likely it is that results are **valid** and not due to **chance**.

The problems with qualitative data are overcome by using quantitative data, as comparisons and conclusions can be given **statistically**. However, quantitative data can **lack detail** and background information.

The test results showed that Fred and Velma's relationship was extremely strong.

Practice Questions

Q1 List the three main areas studied by sport psychologists.

Q2 Name the questionnaire used by Kroll and Crenshaw (1970).

Q3 What variable is plotted on the y-axis to give the Yerkes-Dodson law?

Q4 Give an example of how qualitative data can be used in sport psychology.

Q5 List three ways that quantitative data can be presented.

Exam Questions

Q1 a) Identify two research methods used in sports psychology. [2 marks]

b) Outline one of the research methods identified in (a). [3 marks]

Q2 Evaluate the use of qualitative and quantitative data in sport psychology. [12 marks]

The audience at my team's matches gets very involved — in booing us...

It really does increase our drive too — last week three of our players drove off home before half-time. This may not seem like a very thrilling introduction to sport psychology, but you have to know the basics about how the subject is studied before you can move on to the more interesting stuff. Don't expect any pages on 'The Psychology of Man United' though.

Explanations for Individual Differences

This page is for OCR and Edexcel people. *Obviously there are individual differences in sporting ability and participation — some people are Olympic gold medallists, some are enthusiastic (but rubbish) footballers in the park on a Monday night, and some much prefer to sit on the sofa and watch TV. But why... It may be due to their personality traits.*

Personality Can Be Measured Using **Psychometric Tests**

Psychometric tests measure psychological characteristics like intelligence or personality. They use **questionnaires** to collect data from individuals which is then analysed. The analysis helps psychologists to make judgements about the person and **compare** them to others — for example seeing whether they're **extraverted** or **introverted** (see below).

One example of a psychometric test used to measure **personality** is **Cattell's 16PF** questionnaire. This uses multi-choice questions to gather data about 16 key personality **traits**. These include emotional stability, vigilance, apprehension and perfectionism. Cattell believed everybody's personality could be summarised using these 16 traits.

The **advantage** of using this technique to measure personality is that data on a wide range of traits can be collected much more **quickly** than by conducting an interview. As the 16PF collects **quantitative** data (see p.157), making comparisons is easy, e.g. comparing the personality traits of different sportspeople. The **disadvantage** is that **validity** is reduced if people don't answer honestly. **Social desirability bias** may result in people giving answers that they think make them look good, rather than the true response.

Eysenck Used the **Biological Approach** to Explain Personality Traits

Eysenck (1978) used **Eysenck's Personality Questionnaire** (EPQ) to collect data on personality. He identified **three** main traits in personality:

The EPQ has the same pros and cons as the 16PF.

1) **Extraversion/introversion** — the extent to which someone's **outgoing** and looks for **excitement**, versus the extent to which they're **reserved** and prefer to keep to themselves.
2) **Neuroticism** (or emotionally stable/emotionally unstable) — the extent to which someone's **content** and less affected by **stress**, versus the extent to which they're anxious, worried and tense.
3) **Psychoticism** — the extent to which someone's vulnerable to **mental ill health** and **aggressive** behaviour.

1) Eysenck believed that these personality traits are **inherited** and that extraversion/introversion and neuroticism have different **biological causes**.
2) **Extraverts** have **low cortical arousal** and so seek out excitement to **raise** these levels. Introverts already have higher levels and so have less need to seek out arousal.
3) A **problem** with the **biological explanation** of personality traits is that it's **reductionist** (see p.245) and doesn't take into account other psychological explanations.

Kroll and Crenshaw Compared **Personality** in Four Types of **Sportsperson**

Kroll and Crenshaw (1970) — Personality in sportspeople

Method: American participants from **four sports** were used in an experiment using **independent measures**. The sports were American football, wrestling, karate and gymnastics. All participants were classed as high achievers in their sport as a **control measure**. Personality traits were measured using the **16PF** and the **Minnesota Multiphasic Personality Inventory** (MMPI), so that **reliability** could be tested.

Results: The **personality profiles** of wrestlers and American footballers were **similar**, while gymnasts and karate practitioners had **different** personality profiles to each other and to the footballers and wrestlers.

Conclusion: Different personality types are better suited to success in different sports. Success in sport isn't limited to one personality type.

Evaluation: The study used **control measures** (e.g. participants were all of a similar standard) and more than one personality measure was used, which increased the **validity** and **reliability**. The results can help **predict** which sports are best suited to particular personality types.

Explanations for Individual Differences

OCR people need to learn this whole page. For Edexcel just learn the bit on Social Learning Theory.

Freud Used Instincts to Explain Aggressive Behaviour

Freud (1923) believed that we're all born with **instincts**, two of which are the **eros** (drive for life) and the **thanatos** (drive for self-destruction). The thanatos drive tends to cause **aggression**. Sport can be a good way to **use** this natural aggression in a constructive way (**catharsis**), leading to more balance in other parts of life.

So, you might expect people involved in **aggressive sports** to be **less** aggressive in their everyday life than those who play less aggressive sports — their aggression is **expressed** in their sport. However, there's **no evidence** to support this. This may be because different people have **different** natural levels of aggression due to the unique balance between their different drives. Those with **higher** levels of aggression may choose **more** aggressive sports.

Social Theories Offer Alternative Explanations of Aggression and Sport

Berkowitz (1966) suggested that when people are **frustrated** they feel angry and this can lead to **aggression**. However, **environmental cues** need to be present to trigger the aggression. According to **cue theory** people learn to associate certain cues with letting out aggression — they act as triggers. Several studies support this theory:

Berkowitz and LePage (1967) gave participants **electric shocks** to make them feel angry. Afterwards levels of aggression were tested with either a **weapon**, **badminton racket** or **no objects** present. They found that people behaved **more aggressively** when the aggressive **cue** of the weapon was present than in the other two conditions.

This theory can be applied to **sports** where aggressive behaviour is expected, like boxing. Objects like the boxing rink or boxing gloves are **cues** that aggressive behaviour is appropriate.

Social Learning Theory Offers a Behavioural Approach to Sport

1) **Bandura (1963)** explained that aggression can be **learned** by observing and imitating aggressive role models. This is more likely to happen if the role model is **rewarded** for their behaviour or has status — in other words, if their behaviour is **reinforced**.
2) This theory can be applied to aggression in **sport** as people may see their favourite player behaving aggressively yet still earning a high salary and having a great lifestyle.
3) According to the theory, this would act as **vicarious reinforcement**, and the person is more likely to **replicate** the aggressive behaviour themselves when they play sport.
4) This situation could be improved by **educating** influential sportspeople so they are aware that their behaviour may be imitated, and by encouraging them to act as more **positive** role models instead.

Vicarious reinforcement is when behaviour is reinforced by seeing someone else rewarded for the behaviour.

Practice Questions

Q1 Identify two traits measured using the 16PF psychometric test.

Q2 Why did Kroll and Crenshaw (1970) use two different psychometric tests in their study?

Q3 What did Freud call the instinct for self-destruction?

Exam Questions

Q1 a) Describe a study that investigates the relationship between personality and sport performance. [10 marks]

b) Evaluate how personality can be measured, referring to relevant research. [15 marks]

Q2 Compare two explanations for individual differences in sport. [6 marks]

Your eros must be pretty stifled by now — not much life here...

Kroll and Crenshaw's finding that people with different personality types tend to prefer and do better in different sports has been backed up by a number of other studies. For example, Schurr et al (1977) discovered that people who competed in individual sports tended to be more sensitive and imaginative, while team players were more extravert and dependent.

Explanations for Individual Differences

This page is for OCR and Edexcel. Edexcel people — as well as knowing about Achievement Motivation Theory and Cognitive Evaluation Theory, you also need to know about Self-efficacy Theory. You'll find this on p.166.

McClelland et al's ***Achievement Motivation Theory*** *Has Three Parts*

According to **McClelland et al (1961)**, everybody has the following three **needs** in different amounts:

1) Need for **achievement** (N-Ach) — the need to achieve **challenging goals** or meet certain standards. People with **high** N-Ach will try **harder** tasks. Those with **low** N-Ach will either choose **easier** tasks to avoid failure or **very hard** ones to justify their failure.
2) Need for **power** (N-Pow) — the need to have **control** and **status**. People with **high** N-Pow may be more **motivated** to get **higher grade jobs** at work.
3) Need for **affiliation** (N-Affil) — the need for friendships and membership of **social groups**. People with **high** N-Affil may be more **motivated** to seek out **social interaction** than those with low N-Affil.

This idea can be applied to **sport**. For example, **N-Affil** may encourage people to take part in **team** activities. **N-Ach** may encourage people to set **goals** such as winning Wimbledon or running the London Marathon.

Sports-specific Achievement Motivation *was Studied by* ***Gill and Deeter***

Gill and Deeter's (1988) study had two aims — to develop a **questionnaire** that could be used to **measure motivation** in sport, and to investigate **specific aspects** of sport motivation. The **three aspects** investigated were:

1) **Competitiveness** — the desire to seek out and strive for **success**.
2) **Goal orientation** — the desire to reach **personal goals** in sport.
3) **Win orientation** — the desire to **win** in competitive sports against other people.

Participants who did **competitive** and **non-competitive** sports, as well as people who **didn't** do any sport, were given the final version of the questionnaire. This had **25 items** on it, and answers were given on a **5-point scale** ranging from 'strongly agree' to 'strongly disagree'. Examples of items included:

- 'The best test of my ability is competing against others' — tests **competitiveness**.
- 'The best way to determine my ability is to set a goal and try to reach it' — tests **goal orientation**.
- 'I try my hardest to win' — tests **win orientation**.

The results showed that **competitiveness** was the strongest predictor of who took part in sport, whether it was a competitive sport or not. Win and goal orientation had less of an influence and so it was concluded that competitiveness is the biggest motivation to take part in sport.

Ryan and Deci *Investigated Different Motivation* ***Techniques***

Ryan and Deci (2000) explain **two types** of motivation as part of their **Cognitive Evaluation Theory**:

- **Intrinsic** motivation — this is **inner** reward, such as telling yourself you've done well to swim 30 lengths or feeling like you've enjoyed yourself after a run.
- **Extrinsic** motivation — **external** rewards from others, such as praise for your swimming technique or a medal for taking part in a run. It can also be **negative**, such as being threatened with punishment.

1) Extrinsic motivation can make a person feel a **lack of control** over their circumstances — this can sometimes reduce intrinsic motivation.
2) Intrinsic motivation increases **self-determination**, meaning people are better able to **motivate themselves** and rely less on extrinsic factors which are outside their control.
3) Individual differences mean some people are more motivated to **avoid failure**, while others are more motivated to achieve a **specific goal**. These factors need to be considered when trying to **influence** motivation in sport.

Explanations for Individual Differences

This page is for Edexcel only.

The *Effect of Attribution* Can Also Explain Individual Differences

The **cognitive approach** to individual differences in sport involves **attribution** — this is the way we identify the **cause** of an event or behaviour. There are **two** types:

Internal/dispositional

This is when the cause is seen as something that comes **from within** us. For example, 'I won the race because I'm very good at sprinting.'

External/situational

This is when the cause is seen as coming from **outside ourselves**. For example, 'I won the race because my friends were cheering me on and supporting me.'

Biases can influence attribution:

1) **Self-serving bias** — if we **succeed** in a sport we're more likely to use **internal attribution**. For example, 'I won the tennis match because I practised so hard.' If we **don't** succeed we're more likely to use **external attribution**. For example, 'I lost the tennis match because the grass was slippery and ruined my performance.'
2) **Fundamental attribution error** — although we're more likely to use an **external attribution** for our **own failures**, others are more likely to use **internal attributions** for the same failures. So, in the tennis example, the player's coach is more likely to blame the player's lack of effort or concentration, rather than the grass.

Claire externally attributed her crushing defeat to Jorge's lack of clothing.

Dweck put these ideas into practice with his concept of **attribution retraining**:

Dweck (1975) proposed that if a coach uses **attribution retraining** with themselves and their players, they can influence **performance**.
1) For **coaches** this can include **avoiding** making negative comments about players, giving **positive feedback**, and reminding players about their **goals**.
2) For **players** this can include focusing on the aspects of their performance they can **change**, such as amount of practice and effort. Coaches can support players in this by helping them to change the **external factors** that they believe contribute to failure.

This is a good example of how psychological research is used in the **real world**.

Practice Questions

Q1 Name the three needs in McClelland et al's (1961) Achievement Motivation Theory.

Q2 What did Gill and Deeter (1988) mean by goal orientation?

Q3 Name Ryan and Deci's (2000) two types of motivation.

Q4 What is meant by external attribution?

Exam Questions

Q1 a) Outline theories of motivation in sport. [10 marks]

b) Evaluate theories of motivation in sport, including techniques to increase motivation. [15 marks]

Q2 Describe and discuss how research into motivation can help us to understand individual differences in sport. [12 marks]

I lost my lucky pants, and my toe hurts, and that pigeon put me off, and...

We all know that people involved in sport love to make excuses. Just listen to any Premiership football manager after their team suffers an unexpected defeat on a Saturday. But perhaps what they're actually trying to do is control external factors that might affect their team's performance, such as all the newspapers writing that they can't play for toffee.

Arousal

OCR peeps need to know everything on these pages. Team Edexcel just have to learn the inverted U hypothesis stuff.
Arousal isn't as exciting as it sounds I'm afraid — in this context it just means how ready for action or 'awake' you are.

Yerkes and Dodson Proposed the **Inverted U Hypothesis** of Arousal

Yerkes and Dodson's (1908) theory came from a study they did into **learning** in mice. The mice were able to avoid **electric shocks** (which increased arousal) by stepping into the brighter of two boxes. The study didn't achieve its original aim, but the **pattern** between amount of **stimulation** and amount of **learning** led them to develop the **inverted U hypothesis**. There's a diagram of the **inverted U scattergraph** on page 156.

As arousal increases so does performance, up to an **optimal level of performance**. At this point, if arousal continues to increase then performance will **decrease**. So, sportspeople need to find their **optimum level of arousal** to achieve their best performance. Too much or too little arousal will lead to **poorer performance**.

Three variables influence where someone's optimum level of arousal is:

1) **Personality** — performance is better for **introverts** at lower arousal levels and for **extraverts** at higher levels.
2) **Type of activity** — performance in sports that require very **careful movements**, such as snooker, tends to be better at lower levels of arousal.
3) **Skill** — performance is better for **skilled** players at higher levels of arousal. Less skilled players need less arousal to perform at their best.

This theory is very **general**, but later research has used the theory as a starting point and **refined** it further, e.g. Oxendine (1980) — see next page.

Lacey Challenged the Concept of **What is Meant By Arousal**

If heart rate, respiration, neural activity and skin conductance are all indicators of arousal, you'd expect them to be **closely correlated**. However, **Lacey (1967)** found no correlation between these physiological measures of arousal. So, Lacey suggested that different **types of arousal** need to be considered, rather than viewing it as a single concept. He suggested **three types**:

1) **Autonomic** — changes to do with the functioning of the **autonomic nervous system**.
2) **Behavioural** — changes to do with **observable behaviour**.
3) **Electrocortical** — changes to do with functioning within the **brain**.

According to Lacey, these types work **independently** of each other, and different types happen in response to **different stimuli**. He proposed **four elements** to support his theory about the types of arousal:

1) **Autonomic arousal** has an **inhibitory** effect on the **brain**, instead of an excitatory effect. This results in slower information transfer.
2) Specific **situations** result in specific patterns of autonomic response (**situational stereotypy**).
3) There is **dissociation** between autonomic and behavioural arousal, and between electrocortical and behavioural arousal.
4) There is dissociation between the **different physiological measures** used with arousal.

So, certain sporting situations might lead to specific responses in the autonomic nervous system. Knowing this will help when trying to **improve** performance or skills.

Thayer (1967) criticised Lacey's suggestions on the basis that it doesn't make sense to have the three types of arousal **dissociated** from each other. From an **evolutionary** point of view there's more survival value in having them **linked** together. His alternative understanding of arousal has more of a **psychological** than a physiological focus. He suggested **two types** of arousal:

1) **Energetic arousal** — when you feel full of energy, lively and vigorous.
2) **Tense arousal** — when you feel tense, worried and anxious.

Arousal

Several **Factors Affect** the **Optimum Level** of Arousal

Oxendine (1980) focused on the **optimum level of arousal** idea from Yerkes and Dodson's inverted U hypothesis. Several factors are thought to affect what the optimum level is:

1) **Skill level** — a sportsperson with a **low** level of skill will reach their optimum level of arousal **more quickly** than a more skilled sportsperson.
2) **The type of sport** — sports like bowling and archery require a **lower** level of arousal than sports like boxing and football. Sports like weight-lifting and rugby have the **highest** optimal arousal levels.
3) **Individual factors** — the same person may have a **different** optimum level of arousal on different days due to variables like tiredness and eating patterns. **Adrenaline** can overcome the effects of fatigue, so a person may be able to perform well even when they're tired if the event is emotionally charged.

Oxendine also suggested that the **types of skills** needed in a sport affect the optimum level of arousal.

Gross motor skills

These are movements that **don't** require fine precision movements.

Examples include throwing a **shot putt** or running **100 metres**. These skills need a **high level** of arousal as they involve **speed**, **strength** and may test **endurance**.

Fine motor skills

These are movements requiring **fine** and **precise** movements.

Examples include **snooker** or **darts**. These skills need a **low level** of arousal as they involve **focus**, closely **coordinated** movements and **concentration**. A high level of **control** over movements is required so arousal needs to be lower.

Manipulating a sportsperson's arousal levels so they're at the **optimum level** for their sport could help **improve performance**. Overall, Oxendine concluded that it's better to be **slightly higher** than the optimum level than slightly lower for **all types** of sport. **Wilkes and Summers (1984)** found that techniques used to increase arousal **could** be used with athletes to manipulate levels and improve performance.

Practice Questions

Q1 What name is given to Yerkes and Dodson's (1908) theory of arousal?

Q2 Name the three types of arousal identified by Lacey.

Q3 What is meant by energetic arousal?

Q4 What type of skills are associated with a low optimum level of arousal?

Exam Questions

Q1 a) Outline one theory of arousal. [10 marks]

b) Evaluate the suggestion that there are different types of arousal. [15 marks]

Q2 Describe and evaluate a theory of arousal in sport psychology. [6 marks]

Perhaps they should try that electric shock idea on the England team...

Just kidding, of course. Some interesting stuff here, especially for the sporty ones among you — you need to be very worked up and ready for action if you do rugby or shot putt but a bit more calm and chilled if you compete in snooker or archery. Yeah, I know, that's not rocket science and you probably already knew it, but you've still got the rest to learn.

Reducing Anxiety

These two pages are for OCR only. *Most of us have felt nervous before a big event. The problem for a sportsperson is that excessive anxiety before a big competition could actually end up ruining their performance. Not ideal...*

Spielberger Proposed Two Types of Anxiety

Spielberger's (1966) two types of anxiety are:

1) **Trait anxiety** — the type of anxiety that's part of an individual's **personality**. A person with high trait anxiety is a person who tends to worry about the future generally.

2) **State anxiety** — the type of anxiety that arises in response to a particular **situation**.

Spielberger reckoned that people with **higher trait anxiety** are more likely to be affected by **state anxiety** in stressful situations.

Martens (1977) Developed the SCAT to Measure Trait Anxiety in Athletes

1) The **Sport Competition Anxiety Test (SCAT)** consists of 15 items such as 'Before I compete, I worry about making mistakes' and 'Before I compete I feel calm'. Respondents reply with their choice of 'often', 'sometimes' and 'hardly ever'.
2) Five of the items are **irrelevant** to anxiety but are included to discourage **pattern response**.
3) Respondents get a score between 10 and 30 — a higher score indicates **higher levels** of trait anxiety.

Smith et al (1998) found that **test-retest reliability** (see p.216) of the SCAT was high at 0.77. They also found moderate levels of **validity** when the test was compared with other general anxiety inventories. However, the items tend to measure **somatic anxiety** (the physiological aspects like increased heart rate and blood flow). Smith et al suggested that **multidimensional** testing that includes **cognitive anxiety** would be more valid. Cognitive anxiety refers to the **psychological** aspects of anxiety such as thoughts and feelings.

The CSAI-2 Has a Multidimensional Approach

Martens et al (1990) developed the **Competitive State Anxiety Inventory 2 (CSAI-2)** to overcome the limitations of the SCAT. It measures three different aspects of **state anxiety** which are covered by 27 items on the questionnaire.

1) **Somatic anxiety** — an item example is 'My body feels tense'.
2) **Cognitive anxiety** — an item example is 'I feel nervous'.
3) **Self-confidence** — an item example is 'I'm confident I can meet the challenge'.

Brian had low self-confidence and was easily embarrassed.

Respondents either respond to the items with 'not at all', 'somewhat', 'moderately so' or 'very much so'.
Martens et al suggested that the three aspects have different relationships with **performance**:

1) **Somatic anxiety** and performance have an **inverted U relationship**, which relates to the **Yerkes-Dodson hypothesis** (see page 162). An increase in somatic arousal is associated with an increase in performance up to an **optimum**, after which it's associated with a decrease in performance.
2) **Cognitive anxiety** is **negatively correlated** with performance. As worry increases performance decreases.
3) **Self-confidence** is **positively correlated** with performance. As self-confidence increases performance also increases.

Knowledge of these relationships can be used by **coaches** to improve performance in their players. They'd want to:

- **optimise somatic anxiety**, avoiding too much or too little.
- **boost self-confidence**.
- **discourage cognitive anxiety** by minimising worry and encouraging positive feelings.

Reducing Anxiety

Cox et al (1998) Highlighted the **Practical Limitations** of the **CSAI-2**

The CSAI-2 has the **advantage** of being a **multidimensional** approach. However, the questionnaire takes about 5 minutes to answer and this is **too long** if it's being used to measure anxiety change during a game or match. For example, a tennis player only has short breaks between games and sets so it's **impractical** and players may **rush** to complete it. The other concern is that the questionnaire may be **intrusive** if used during breaks in play. For example, the nature of the items may result in a player **worrying about worry**. **Cox et al (1998)** investigated the usefulness of using a **shortened** version of the CSAI-2. The results were **mixed** and **validity** was reduced.

Other **Models of Anxiety** Investigate the Relationship with **Performance**

1) **Fazey and Hardy (1988)** developed Yerkes and Dodson's inverted U hypothesis by equating **arousal** with **anxiety**.
2) They felt that both **cognitive** and **physiological/somatic anxiety** have to be considered when looking at the relationship with performance.
3) They argue that the relationship suggested by Yerkes and Dodson is true when **cognitive anxiety** is **low**. If you **aren't** worried or feeling tense about an event your performance will **increase** as **physiological arousal/anxiety** increases. After the **optimum level** of arousal there will be a gradual **decrease** in performance.
4) If cognitive anxiety is **high** to begin with, as physiological arousal **increases** so does performance. However, after the **optimum** point is reached performance decreases very **suddenly** and **dramatically**.
5) This **catastrophic result** is because of the high level of cognitive anxiety, resulting in **cognitive overload**. The physiological and cognitive demands are **too much** for the individual to cope with and decline is rapid.

After **Catastrophe** it Takes Time to **Rebuild Confidence**

Hardy (1997) claims the key relationship in Fazey and Hardy's theory is the **balance** between levels of **cognitive** anxiety and **physiological** anxiety.

1) **High** physiological anxiety and **high** cognitive anxiety is associated with a **sudden collapse** in performance.
2) **High** physiological anxiety and **low** cognitive anxiety is associated with **good performance**.
3) **Low** physiological anxiety and **high** cognitive anxiety is associated with **poor performance**.

Although the theory is well respected within sport psychology it's difficult to **test empirically**. This is because of the problem of **measuring** and **controlling** the **three variables** of physiological anxiety, cognitive anxiety and performance all at once.

Practice Questions

Q1 What is the difference between trait anxiety and state anxiety?

Q2 Name the three aspects of state anxiety measured on the CSAI-2.

Q3 Why is Hardy's (1997) theory difficult to test empirically?

Exam Question

Q1 a) Outline the multidimensional approach to anxiety in sport. [10 marks]

b) Evaluate the multidimensional approach to anxiety, referring to other models. [15 marks]

You're playing at three — come out from under the bed...

Lots of sportspeople say that a few nerves before a big competition actually helps them to feel at their most alert and ready for action and improves their performance. But if their fear gets out of control then their concentration and judgement go, leading to catastrophe — as anyone knows who's watched a footballer hoof that vital penalty kick over the bar.

Self-Confidence and Improving Performance

Step back AQA people — these pages are just for Edexcel and OCR. One of the slightly annoying things about sport is that it's the cocky types who tend to do well. Of course, part of the reason they're cocky is that they're good at what they do, but the best sportspeople have a deeply ingrained self-confidence that even a bad performance can't shake.

Self-efficacy is a Specific Type of *Self-confidence*

Bandura (1977) described **self-efficacy** as belief in your ability to carry out a task **successfully**. If you have **low** self-efficacy you'll **give up** on the task more quickly, but if you have **high** self-efficacy you'll **try harder** and keep trying for longer.

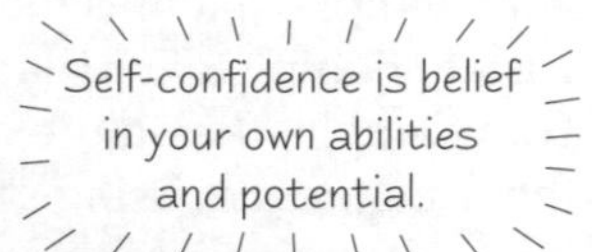

Self-confidence is belief
in your own abilities
and potential.

Bandura (1986) identified **four factors** that influence self-efficacy:

1) **Previous experience** — if a sportsperson has had success in the past this will increase their self-efficacy as they already know they can do it. Occasional failure can be managed by focusing on the successes.
2) **Vicarious experience** — seeing others with a similar skill level succeed gives a model that can be imitated.
3) **Verbal persuasion** — advice and encouragement can be given, e.g. by a coach, to increase self-efficacy.
4) **Emotional arousal** — arousal levels can decrease self-efficacy if they're overwhelming.

This theory can be used by coaches to manipulate self-efficacy. They can use **verbal persuasion**, teach techniques to manage **arousal levels**, and provide appropriate **role models**. It's well-respected in sport psychology and aspects of it are widely used in coaching and training.

Vealey Came Up With a Model of *Sport Confidence*

Vealey (1986) explained sport confidence as the amount of certainty an individual has about their ability to succeed in sport. His model identifies **three** key components:

1) **SC (self-confidence)-trait** — the level of confidence a person has generally in their sporting ability.
2) **SC-state** — the level of confidence they have in their sporting ability during a particular event.
3) **Competitive orientation** — how competitive they are.

1) He suggests that SC-trait and competitive orientation **work together** in a situation to give a level of **SC-state**.
2) The person then performs and this has an **outcome** in the form of a win or loss, or a personal result such as the time taken on a run.
3) This outcome then **influences** the SC-trait and competitive orientation, e.g. a win will increase general confidence and can influence desire to win in future events.
4) A poor result may lead to lower general confidence and may make the person more or less determined to compete in future events.

An **advantage** of this model is that it was designed specifically with **sport** in mind, unlike self-efficacy, which is a general theory that can be applied to sport. There's evidence to support Vealey's model, e.g. **Gould et al (1999)** found that self-confidence was **higher** in **more successful** players compared to less successful players.

Goal Setting is a Psychological Technique Used to *Improve Performance*

Goal setting means setting targets that encourage improvement in a sport.
Burton et al (2001) identified **three** types of goals:

1) **Process goals** — improving the actions involved in a sport, e.g. a diver trying to pull their legs in as far as possible during a tuck dive.
2) **Performance goals** — a result involving competing with yourself, e.g. getting a personal best time on a run.
3) **Outcome goals** — a result involving competition with others, e.g. winning a gold medal at the Olympics.

Goals need to be both **challenging** and **achievable**. If they're too easy or too hard people won't be motivated. Different types of goals may be more appropriate to particular sports. **Kingston and Hardy (1997)** found that **process goals** improved self-efficacy and confidence in golfers, as well as reducing their cognitive anxiety.

Self-Confidence and Improving Performance

Another Technique to Improve Performance is the Use of Imagery

Imagery is the use of **mental images** and pictures relating to a sporting situation, and involves:

1) **Mental practice** of aspects of the sport — the sportsperson can **practise** their skills by looking at their style. Skills can be performed mentally in slow motion so the person can think about them in detail and focus on how to improve.
2) **Relaxation** — imagery can involve techniques which influence **arousal levels**, such as controlled breathing.
3) **Increasing self-confidence** — **Bandura (1997)** believed that imagery can increase **self-efficacy** if a person visualises themselves performing a skill and succeeding. They're then more likely to believe they can succeed and be confident about future performance.

Boyd and Munroe (2003) Investigated the Use of Imagery

This study aimed to find out which **specific functions** of imagery are used by climbers, and to **compare** climbers' use of imagery with track and field athletes.

	Boyd and Munroe (2003) — Imagery in climbing
Method:	38 track and field athletes and 48 climbers completed two **questionnaires** (the Sport Imagery and the Climbing Imagery questionnaires) on their use of **imagery** in their sport. The questions were designed to test how much they used **cognitive** and **motivational functions** of imagery. Cognitive imagery involves performing skills and developing strategies, while motivational imagery involves controlling anxiety/ arousal and goal-orientated behaviours.
Results:	Both climbers and athletes used **both types** of imagery, but **athletes** were found to use the **motivational** functions of imagery **significantly more** than climbers did. The biggest difference was in the motivational imagery function relating to **achieving goals**. There was no difference in the results between advanced climbers and beginners.
Conclusion:	Climbers may have less need of the motivational imagery function related to achieving goals because they're less likely to be in **competition** with each other or aiming for an **extrinsic prize**. Instead the rewards are **intrinsic** — the pleasure of the climb itself is important.
Evaluation:	The use of a questionnaire allowed a lot of **detailed information** to be collected, but the results relied on participants being able to analyse their own use of imagery **accurately** and **honestly**. Also, a small sample size was used which reduces the **reliability** of the results. This study was useful in highlighting the fact that 'sport' actually covers a broad range of sport types — psychological concepts may need to be **applied differently** in different sports.

Practice Questions

Q1 What is meant by self-efficacy?

Q2 What are the three components of Vealey's (1986) model of sport confidence?

Q3 What is meant by imagery in sport psychology?

Exam Questions

Q1 Tony plays volleyball and wants to improve his performance.
Give suggestions to help him, referring to psychological evidence in your answer. [12 marks]

Q2 a) Outline a study related to the use of imagery in sport. [10 marks]

b) Discuss how self-efficacy and self-confidence apply to sport psychology. [15 marks]

I'd definitely need to control my anxiety if I was hanging off a cliff face...

With all this info on improving confidence and performance, chances are you'll end up as a professional sportsman and won't have to worry about silly little things like exams. But, just in case that doesn't pan out, you'd better learn it all. After all, I think I'm great at football and picture myself in the World Cup final every night, and I'm still always left on the bench.

Group Cohesion

OCR, these pages are for your eyes only. *Group cohesion is the factor that brings a number of people together. This may be because of a specific goal, e.g. to win the league or improve on last year.*

Carron Developed a Model for Understanding Aspects of Cohesion in Sport

Cohesion is just how well the members of a team are bonded. Carron identified two types of cohesion:

1) **Task cohesion** is the extent to which players work together towards the team goal, e.g. winning the league.
2) **Social cohesion** is the strength of the social relationships and commitment to each other within the team.

Carron (1982) identified four factors that influence task and social cohesion:

1) **Personal factors** — including satisfaction, motivation, similarity of experience and individual differences.
2) **Team factors** — including the importance of goals, the team's ability and communication.
3) **Leadership factors** — including the coach's leadership style and their effort to encourage cohesion.
4) **Environmental factors** — including size of the group and contractual responsibilities for professional players.

In turn, the amount of cohesion has two types of **outcome** in sport:

1) **Group outcomes** — including level of stability within the team and effectiveness of the team's performance.
2) **Individual outcomes** — including importance of individual goals and effectiveness of personal performance.

Knowledge of this model can be used by coaches to **manipulate** variables in order to increase levels of **cohesion** and the corresponding **performance** levels.

Tuckman Proposed a Theory of How Teams Develop

Tuckman (1965) reckoned that teams develop in **stages**. Tuckman's four stages were:

1 Forming

The group gets together and behaves quite **formally** as people get to know each other. The **goal** of the group is identified at this stage to ensure good **task cohesion** (see above). In sport, the coach would play an important role here — it would be their job to encourage **social cohesion** (again, see above) and remind players of the importance of the goal.

2 Storming

Members of the group try to establish their place in the group's **hierarchy**. Individuals may try to push their own preferences on the group, and may meet with **resistance**. In sport, the role of the coach at this stage would be to help players find their place in the team so **confrontation** is minimised.

3 Norming

At this stage the **norms** of the group are established and the group starts to work effectively together. The team works together towards a **shared goal**, and training patterns and team strategies are accepted by everybody. If any individuals don't accept the norms, the group may slip back to the **storming** stage.

4 Performing

The group works well together at this stage — players work as a team using their individual skills to the team's advantage. They're **focused** on their goals and **enjoy** working together. The team has its **best chance** of sporting success at this stage. The coach's role is to get the team to this stage as quickly as possible. If teams have a **high turnover** of players this will be more difficult as team membership will change regularly.

Group Cohesion

Social Loafing Has a Negative Effect on Group Cohesion

Social loafing is where people make **less effort** in a task when they perform it in a **team** compared to when they perform it **individually**. People think that their effort is less likely to be **noticed** in group situations and so don't work as hard. **Latane et al (1979)** tested social loafing under experimental conditions.

Latane et al (1979) studied social loafing

Method:	This was a **repeated measures** design where participants were asked to clap or shout as loudly as possible and the **noise levels** produced were measured. Participants were tested individually, in pairs, and in groups of four and six.
Results:	The average individual noise level **dropped** as group size increased.
Conclusion:	People make **less effort** in a task when they're part of a group.
Evaluation:	This was a very **artificial** situation so the experiment had low **ecological validity**. The results might not be replicated in a real sporting situation, as the teams of participants in the experiment had no meaningful common goal to work towards — making a loud noise isn't quite the same incentive as winning a match. Sportspeople might well increase their effort and **avoid** social loafing if the team goal meant a lot to them.

Latane et al (1979) Then Tested Social Loafing Using **Different Conditions**

1) The findings of the study above could have been produced by the individual noises not being **well synchronised**. This would lead to the group effort not registering as loudly as it should, even if each member **was** actually putting in the same effort as they had individually.
2) In a second experiment participants were **blindfolded** and wore **headphones** so they couldn't see or hear any other people. They were isolated in separate rooms and were **led to believe** that they were shouting in a group for the group conditions, even though they were actually still alone.
3) The **same** results were found — as the supposed group size **increased**, individual effort **decreased**. This **supports** the social loafing hypothesis and increases the validity of the first experiment.

Some types of sport such as **tug-of-war** may be **more** vulnerable to social loafing, as it's hard to identify an individual's lack of effort. In other sports, such as **netball**, it would be more difficult to get away with it, as everyone in the team has their **own role**. Coaches can try to **reduce** social loafing by **praising** and recording individual efforts so that players feel their contribution is important and is being noted.

Practice Questions

Q1 Name Tuckman's (1965) four stages of group development.

Q2 What effect will a high turnover of players have on team development?

Q3 Identify the four factors that influence cohesion in Carron's (1982) model.

Q4 What is meant by social loafing?

Exam Question

Q1 a) Describe Tuckman's (1965) theory of team development. [10 marks]

b) Discuss the concept of social loafing in sport, including relevant research in your answer. [15 marks]

Social loafing — done in the beer garden most Saturday afternoons...

The Latane et al (1979) study is a good example of clever research — they realised there was an alternative explanation for their results so they came up with a new experimental design to rule it out. I feel a bit sorry for their participants though, standing there blindfolded, yelling and clapping in a room by themselves. How embarrassing. Pretty funny to watch though.

The Effects of an Audience

Edexcel just need to learn the top half of this page, for OCR it's the whole thing. *An audience can affect performance in sport. For some people it spurs them on, for others the pressure's too much and they fall apart. Same as in exams...*

Evaluation-apprehension Theory Explains the Effect of an Audience

Cottrell's research developed previous work on **audience effects** — the idea that the presence of other people affects performance. His (**1968**) **evaluation-apprehension theory** suggests performance is affected when others observe and make **judgements**. The judgements can be negative or positive, for example praising or criticising a swimmer's technique. The theory suggests the audience needs to be **involved** in some way to have an effect.

	Cottrell et al (1968) — the influence of an audience
Method:	The aim was to compare the **influence** of an audience with the mere **presence** of an audience. In an experiment with an independent groups design, 45 participants were split evenly into three conditions and tested on their ability to recognise nonsense words they'd been instructed to learn. In the '**alone**' condition they were tested by themselves. In the '**audience**' condition two other people watched the test. In the '**mere presence**' condition there were two other people present but they were wearing blindfolds.
Results:	There was a significantly **higher** number of correct responses in the **audience** condition compared to the alone and mere presence conditions.
Conclusion:	The study **supports** the evaluation-apprehension theory. The audience condition had the highest result, suggesting that participants in this condition believed the people watching would be assessing their performance and so tried harder. In the mere presence condition the audience were present but **not observing**, suggesting that an audience has to be more **involved** for a change in performance to occur.
Evaluation:	The study was a laboratory experiment so there was a high level of **control** over extraneous variables. The disadvantage of this is that **ecological validity** is reduced, because in a real-life sporting situation other variables would affect performance in the event.

Zajonc Tested the Effect of an Audience Using Cockroaches

The aim of Zajonc's (1965) experiment was to investigate **audience effects** on tasks of different **complexity**.

	Zajonc (1965) investigated audience effects using cockroaches
Method:	Cockroaches were put in a run with a light at one end (cockroaches have a natural reaction to run from light). When the light was switched on the time taken to run to the other end was measured. This was conducted in **three different conditions**: • **Lone** condition — only one cockroach present at a time. • **Co-action audience** condition — two cockroaches tested together in the run. • **Non co-action audience** condition — one cockroach tested in front of an audience of cockroaches who were stationary and not able to use the run. Using the straight run was classed as a **simple** task for the cockroaches. The conditions were then **repeated** using a **maze** instead of a run — this was identified as a **complex** task for the cockroaches.
Results:	In the **simple** task the cockroaches were slowest in the lone condition and fastest in the co-action audience condition. In the **complex** task the cockroaches were fastest in the lone condition and slowest in the co-action audience condition.
Conclusion:	The presence of others increased **arousal** and improved the performance of a simple task, particularly if the 'audience' were performing the same task at the same time. The opposite effect was found on a complex task — the increased arousal from the presence of others had a negative effect on performance because of the difficulty of the task.
Evaluation:	If this principle was applied to **sportspeople** then it would mean that an audience or other competitors would **benefit** an athlete who had high skill levels and experience. The performance of athletes with less experience and poorer skills would **suffer** from the presence of others. However, the study was carried out on cockroaches and so the results can't really be **generalised** to humans. It's unlikely that a cockroach would react to an audience in the same way as a human would.

The Effects of an Audience

This page is just for OCR.

Home Advantage *is the Tendency to* **Win** *When Playing at* **Home**

Schwartz and Barsky (1977) looked at the results of various sports matches played at home and away in 1971 to measure levels of performance. They wanted to know if they showed evidence of a home advantage.

	Schwartz and Barsky (1977) — Home advantage
Method:	Data on results of matches played at home and away in baseball, professional American football, college American football and hockey was collected throughout 1971.
Results:	In all four sports **more than half** of home games resulted in a win.
Conclusion:	Playing at home gives teams an **advantage** resulting in better performances.
Evaluation:	This was a **natural experiment** using data from actual games so it had very high **ecological validity**. The results also agreed with what had been hypothesised. However, the study only used results from one year — this reduces the reliability of the findings and means they can't be generalised to all years. Also, the study only took place in the USA so the results can't be applied to other cultures.

This study gave rise to the following ideas:

Arousal levels are higher when playing at home because of the presence of **supporters**. This mostly benefits **strong** teams when they are playing weaker teams, as it increases the relative difference in ability. **Nevill and Cann (1998)** looked at crowd size in Scottish and English football leagues from 1985 to 1996. They found that home advantage was strongest when crowd size was **large**. Small crowd size reduced the home advantage.

Madrigal and James (1999) criticised the Schwartz and Barsky study — they reckoned that they didn't control well enough for the **quality** of the teams. They said quality could be measured by looking at the team's **history** of results. Although the study did control for quality of performance during the data collection period, Madrigal and James suggested that using a longer time period would give better and more reliable measurements.

Practice Questions

Q1 What is the main idea in Cottrell's (1968) evaluation-apprehension theory?

Q2 What were the conditions in the Cottrell et al (1968) study?

Q3 What took place in the non co-action audience condition in Zajonc's (1965) study?

Q4 Which group of cockroaches was fastest in the complex task in Zajonc's (1965) study?

Q5 Give a definition of home advantage.

Exam Questions

Q1 a) Describe research into the home advantage in sport psychology. [10 marks]

b) Discuss studies investigating the effects of an audience on performance. [15 marks]

Q2 Drawing on your knowledge of sport psychology, discuss the effects of an audience on performance. [12 marks]

And then the cockroach scored the winner with a lovely diving header...

Scientists often use animal models to help them in their research, but the way cockroaches behave in front of other cockroaches can't really tell you that much about human behaviour in front of an audience. We're just too different, which is a good thing. I don't want John Terry and Frank Lampard scampering under the fridge when I switch the light on.

Leadership and Coaching

These two are just for OCR. *Good coaches have to be successful leaders in order to inspire competitors to glory.*

Trait *and* ***Type Theories*** *Can Explain Leadership Potential*

No-one would describe Boris as an introvert.

1) **Eysenck (1963)** used two dimensions to identify common qualities in personality types — **introversion/extraversion** and **neuroticism/stability**.
2) People in the **extraversion/stable** category are described as having **sanguine** qualities. These include being easygoing, lively and having leadership skills.
3) Eysenck's theory suggests that successful leaders will have this type of personality — **emotionally stable** and **extraverted**. This is an example of a '**type**' theory.

Trait theories associate certain **characteristics** with leadership potential. For example:

1) **Cattell (1956)** identified **16 personality factors** or **traits** that could be used to describe individuals. People who have traits like **self-reliance** and **social boldness** would be expected to make better leaders.
2) **Allport (1965)** identified 4500 trait words and split them into three categories — **cardinal**, **central** and **secondary**. Leaders have traits that make them suitable for the role, such as assertiveness and intelligence.

The **'Great Man' theory** of leadership is another example of a **trait** theory. It assumes that individuals are **born** with qualities that will make them great leaders. When the need arises they'll then assume control and lead others to victory or social change. The theory is very **military-based** and uses examples from history as evidence, e.g. Winston Churchill. It's **gender biased**, as historically women wouldn't be in positions of political power. It's also **culturally biased** as it has Western assumptions of what progress and success should involve.

Contingency Theories *Provide an Alternative Explanation*

Contingency theories suggest that there isn't one best way of leadership. Instead, the approach that's most suitable will depend on the demands of the **situation**. **Fiedler (1967)** suggested **two** styles of leadership.

1) **Task-orientated** — leaders are most focused on the **task** and getting the job done. They're most effective in **very favourable** conditions or **very unfavourable** conditions.
2) **Person-orientated** — leaders are most focused on the **people** involved and their happiness levels and interpersonal relationships. They're most effective in **moderately favourable** conditions.

Chelladurai (1978) investigated **contingency theories** and developed the **multidimensional model** of leadership in sport. A number of factors have to be considered in this model in order to understand the effectiveness of a leader. First, three types of **characteristics** — known as the **antecedent conditions**, need to be assessed:

- **Situational characteristics** — variables like the nature of the task and the resources available to them.
- **Member characteristics** — variables like the players' ability and gender.
- **Leader characteristics** — variables like experience and coaching style.

Next, three types of **leader behaviour** are proposed:

1) **Required** leader behaviour — the **social norms** and **formal rules** of a sport will dictate that certain behaviours are required. For example, a coach has to attend all training sessions and arrive on time.
2) **Preferred** leader behaviour — members of the team will have **preferences** about the behaviour of their leader. These may be related to **personal variables** like experience, gender and age.
3) **Actual** leader behaviour — this is the **observable** behaviour that the leader shows in their role. For example, giving personalised support to an injured player who's rejoining the team.

Chelladurai suggests that the **antecedent conditions** will influence leader behaviours. If the three **leader behaviours** then **agree**, there will be **optimum performance** and **satisfaction**. If the required and actual leader behaviours are **different** to the preferred behaviour, there will be **good performance** but **poor satisfaction.** If the required leader behaviour is **different** to the preferred and actual behaviour, there will be **good satisfaction** but **poor performance**.

Leadership and Coaching

Coaches Play a Vital Role in Competitors' Performance and Enjoyment

Smith and Smoll designed **Coach Effectiveness Training** (**CET**) to instruct new coaches on things like team building and confidence building. CET uses **cognitive behavioural techniques**. **Smith et al** (**1979**) investigated CET to see how **effective** it is.

Smith et al (1979) — Coach effectiveness training

Method: **31 men** who were Little League Baseball coaches in the US were put into either a **control group**, who received no training, or an **experimental condition**. Coaches in the experimental condition had a two-hour training session that covered **cognitive-behavioural guidelines**. The guidelines had been developed to encourage better relationships between teammates and between players and coach. They also aimed to increase self-confidence and decrease concerns about losing. The coaches were also given **behavioural feedback** and taught **self-monitoring techniques** so they could assess how well they were adopting the guidelines. Coaches were then observed during the season and assessed using the **coaching behaviour assessment system** (CBAS). Players were assessed for self-esteem and attitudes towards the coach.

Results: Coaches from the experimental group demonstrated a **change** in their coaching behaviour after the training. The players viewed them more **positively** and **performance** was better. **Self-esteem** in players from the trained group increased, with the biggest differences in players with **lower** initial levels of self-esteem.

Conclusion: Coach effectiveness training is **worthwhile** as it has a beneficial effect on both the coaches and players.

Evaluation: The study only had a **small sample size**, making it difficult to generalise the results. It also only covers baseball, so CET could work differently in other sports. However, the findings have been **supported** by later research. Additional research has also developed this study by trying to identify which **specific aspects** of the cognitive-behavioural techniques are most important. Players with **low self-esteem** are very influenced by their coach's behaviour, so this knowledge can be used to support and develop individual players who most need attention.

Coach Roberts knew that until those outfits were changed the team's self-esteem would remain low.

Practice Questions

Q1 Name the three categories of trait identified by Allport.

Q2 Give a trait that would be associated with strong leadership according to Cattell's (1956) trait theory.

Q3 Outline the basic assumption of the 'Great Man' theory.

Q4 Name the two styles of leadership suggested by Fiedler (1967).

Q5 Which sport was used in the Smith et al (1979) study?

Q6 What were the results of Smith et al's (1979) study?

Exam Question

Q1 a) Describe theories of leadership in sport. [10 marks]

b) Discuss the efficacy of coach effectiveness training. [15 marks]

So we know what makes a good coach. Shouldn't we win a bit more then...

Coaches obviously need expertise in the sport they coach, but as you've seen on these pages they need other qualities too. Their personality is important, although as it's been found, there isn't just one set of characteristics that makes a good leader. What works also depends on the team's particular situation, the personalities within it and the coaching techniques used.

Exercise and Pathology

These two pages are for OCR only. *You probably already know that exercising has benefits for your health — you can't turn on the TV or walk down the street without spotting another campaign to remind you of that fact. There's loads of research to back this up, which should help to convince any couch potatoes amongst you.*

Bernstein et al Investigated the Link Between Exercise and Cancer Risk

1) Previous research has found that the more exposure a woman has to **ovarian hormones** (oestrogens), the greater her risk of breast cancer.
2) The more **menstrual periods** a woman has, the greater her exposure to ovarian hormones.
3) Regular exercise can **reduce** exposure to ovarian hormones — physically active girls tend to start their periods **later** and are **less likely** to have **regular** periods to begin with.

This relationship was studied further by Bernstein et al (1994).

Bernstein et al (1994) — Exercise and cancer risk in women

Method: 545 women recently diagnosed with breast cancer and 545 women without breast cancer were **interviewed**. They were asked which types of exercise they'd done since their periods started, how many hours per week they did, and how old they were when they started and finished participating. The **case group** and **control group** were **matched** on the variables of age, race, number of pregnancies and neighbourhood they lived in. They were all 40 years old or younger at diagnosis.

Results: Women who did an average of **5 hours or more** of exercise a week were 50% less likely to develop breast cancer compared to less active or inactive women.

Conclusion: Participation in regular activity **reduces** women's vulnerability to breast cancer.

Evaluation: The study was designed with a high level of **control** which increases the **validity** of the findings. However, it relied on participants being able to **accurately recall** their exercise behaviour, which could be affected by memory failure or distortion. The study shows that although susceptibility to breast cancer due to family history can't be changed, exercise can help to **reduce the risk**.

Lox et al Investigated the Effects of Exercise on HIV Patients

Lox et al (1995) designed a study which aimed to measure changes in the **perception of well-being** in HIV patients. Patients were put on various 12 week exercise programmes and their well-being before and after was compared.

Lox et al (1995) — Exercise and well-being in HIV patients

Method: 33 participants with HIV-1 were allocated to an **aerobic exercise** group, a **weight-training** group or a **stretch and flexibility** group. They took part in their activity for 45 minutes, three times a week. **Questionnaires** on physical self-efficacy, mood state and life satisfaction were completed before and after the 12-week exercise programmes.

Results: Those in the **aerobic** and **weight-training** groups had **significantly improved** levels of physical self-efficacy, mood state and life satisfaction compared to before the programme. These groups had **significantly better** results than the stretch and flexibility group.

Conclusion: HIV patients can benefit **psychologically** from participation in regular physical exercise.

Evaluation: The study included **controls** such as requesting participants not to take part in other forms of exercise, which increased the **validity** of the results. However, the sample was only small which makes it more difficult to **generalise** the findings to other HIV patients. The findings might not apply to **other illnesses** either. The symptoms of some illnesses would **prevent** people taking part in aerobic or weight-training exercise, e.g. later stages of multiple sclerosis. Also, there was no control group.

These studies demonstrate the **physical** and **psychological** benefits of exercise. This type of research supports the use of **funding** for advertising campaigns to encourage healthy lifestyles and regular exercise. These studies are also useful examples of how psychology has a role in the **real world**. Applying their findings can reduce the incidence of illness or improve the experiences of people who are already ill.

Exercise and Pathology

Hausenblas and Carron Investigated Eating Disorders in Athletes

The aim of this study was to compare rates of **eating disorders** between athletes and non-athletes, and in sub-categories of athletes.

There's more about eating disorders on p.32–37.

Hausenblas and Carron (1999) — Eating disorders in athletes

Method: The study was a **meta-analysis** of 92 studies investigating eating disorders. Levels of anorexia, bulimia and drive for thinness were examined in male and female non-athletes and athletes from different sports.

Results: The study produced the following main findings:

1) Male athletes were **significantly more likely** to experience anorexia, bulimia and drive for thinness than male non-athletes.
2) Female athletes were **significantly more likely** to experience anorexia and bulimia than female non-athletes. However, there was no significant difference in drive for thinness.
3) **Bulimia** was more prevalent in sports requiring endurance, those judged on aesthetic qualities or those that are weight-dependent.

Conclusion: Athletes are **more likely to have eating disorders** than non-athletes. Fitness will be more of a concern to athletes so they'll tend to monitor food intake more than non-athletes.

Evaluation: This was a meta-analysis so it included a very large amount of data from many different studies, improving the **validity** of the results. The findings have a number of **real-life implications** for sport psychology, as discussed below.

The Results of the Meta-analysis Have Implications in Sport Psychology

1) If athletes are known to be **more vulnerable** to eating disorders then coaches and families can be more aware of the potential for problems. This may help **prevent** problems escalating and becoming more serious.
2) The **direction** of the relationship between eating disorders and exercise needs to be considered carefully. It may be that the pressures and demands of the sport **encourage** eating disorders, e.g. being slim would help a gymnast and weight is a large factor in boxing. On the other hand, it could be that people vulnerable to eating disorders are **more attracted** to sport. **Thompson and Sherman (1993)** suggested that involvement in sport can be used to **justify** strict control over food intake and close attention to weight.
3) Some studies have only found **small differences** in eating behaviour between athletes and non-athletes, while other studies have found that eating disorders were **significantly higher** in **elite** athletes. Differences between the results of different studies are likely to be due to differences in variables like the **level** and **type** of sport analysed.

Practice Questions

Q1 Outline the results of Bernstein et al's (1994) study.

Q2 Give a positive evaluation point for Lox et al's (1995) study.

Q3 What was the aim of Hausenblas and Carron's (1999) meta-analysis?

Exam Question

Q1 a) Describe, using relevant research, the relationship between cancer and exercise. [10 marks]

b) Discuss the problem of eating disorders in athletes. [15 marks]

Hoping these pages would say that exercise was bad for you? Bad luck...

The evidence in favour of exercise being good for you is compelling — there's really no questioning it. Regular exercise helps prevent all kinds of illnesses and has psychological benefits too. Which makes it surprising that elite athletes are more likely to suffer from eating disorders than us mere sporting mortals. Another example of how complicated psychology can be...

Exercise and Mental Health

***Just OCR again here.** Oh great, another two pages about how wonderful exercise is for you. Just what I need. Especially when I've cancelled my gym membership and it's raining outside. Everything's working against me. Grrrr.*

Exercise Leads to the Release of Chemicals Called Endorphins

1) **Steinberg and Sykes (1985)** first proposed the **endorphin hypothesis**, which states that exercise releases chemicals in the body called **endorphins**.
2) **Endorphins** have a similar effect to opiates — they have a **pain-killing** effect and create a feeling of **well-being** by binding to **opioid receptor sites** in the nervous system.
3) Many sports are thought to result in endorphin release, including **swimming**, **running** and **cycling**.
4) According to the hypothesis, the **euphoria** that people sometimes experience after exercise ('runner's high') is due to endorphin release. However, it's hard to test this as endorphin levels **can't** be directly measured. Blood plasma levels are used but only give an **indirect measurement**.
5) Another effect of endorphins is that they can reduce **negative mood states** like depression, so people who take part in exercise feel happier afterwards. **Daniel et al (1992)** found that men and women who took part in aerobics classes felt calmer and more relaxed. They were less likely to experience feelings of depression, anger and confusion.

Tom's secretary appreciated he wanted to keep his spirits up but this was a step too far.

Although the endorphin hypothesis is widely accepted, there's actually **little firm evidence** to support it. It's also **reductionist** (see p.245) as it only involves a biological explanation. Alternative theories of exercise and mental health include Ransford's (1982) **social interaction hypothesis** (which views exercise as an opportunity to spend time with other people) and Bahrke and Morgan's (1978) **distraction hypothesis** (which suggests exercise focuses attention away from problems).

Exercise May Improve Mental Health

Leith and Taylor (1990) reviewed 81 studies into the benefits of exercise for **mental health**. They looked at research conducted over a ten-year period and put the studies into three groups according to the experimental design — **pre-experimental** (no true control group), **quasi-experimental** (no random assignment) and **experimental**. The **samples** in the studies varied widely and many different **variables** were included over the 81 studies.

1) The **pre-experimental** group consisted of nine studies, **seven** of which showed **significant improvements** in mental health. For example, **Renfrow and Bolton (1979)** compared adult males who went running or jogging with inactive adult males using the **16PF questionnaire**. This was in the pre-experimental group because differences before and after starting running weren't considered, meaning there was no true control. They found a significant difference between the two groups on several **personality traits**. The group who exercised were more forthright, self-sufficient, independent and liberal.

2) The **quasi-experimental** group consisted of 46 studies, **36** of which showed **significant improvements** in mental health. For example, **Tucker (1983)** compared 113 male college students who began weight-training twice a week for 16 weeks with 127 students who didn't weight-train. **Self-concept** was measured using a questionnaire, and the weight-training group showed a significant improvement compared to the control group. This improvement was **greatest** in participants who had lower levels of self-concept at the start of the study.

Self-concept is the opinion a person has about themselves.

3) The **experimental** group consisted of 26 studies — half showed significant improvements in mental health. For example, **Marsh and Peart (1988)** investigated the effect of a 6 week physical training programme on girls aged 13 to 14 years. There were benefits for **physical fitness** but their **self-concept** didn't change significantly.

This research review highlighted the **methodological problems** involved in studying this area. It's difficult to have a high level of **control over other variables** whilst also ensuring that studies are **realistic** and **ecologically valid**. Leith and Taylor also commented that studies needed to gather **greater detail**, e.g. on duration and type of exercise.

Exercise and Mental Health

Morgan Investigated the **Mood States** of Athletes

1) **Morgan (1979)** used a **Profile of Mood States** (POMS) questionnaire to collect information on the **personality traits** of different athletes.
2) Using this data he developed a **mental health model** which proposed that **successful athletes** are more likely to have **positive mental health** than unsuccessful athletes.
3) **Negative** mental health is associated with below average levels of energy, but above average levels of anger, fatigue, confusion, depression and neuroticism.
4) **Positive** mental health is associated with above average levels of energy, but below average levels of anger, fatigue, confusion, depression and neuroticism.
5) Morgan presented findings from several studies to support his model. In one study he used the POMS questionnaire to **successfully predict** 10 out of 16 finalists in the 1974 US heavyweight rowing team.

The **Usefulness** of Morgan's Model May Be **Limited**

1) If the model and questionnaire were used for **team selection** then an outcome of **negative** mental health would work **against** an individual. However, Morgan found it **wasn't a perfect predictor** of performance and he himself said it **shouldn't** be used for selection purposes.
2) Athletes could **manipulate** their answers to the POMS questionnaire to give results indicating positive mental health, which may not reflect their actual mood state. This is another reason **not** to use the model and POMS for selection purposes.
3) **Rowley et al (1995)** conducted a **meta-analysis** of the research testing the model. They suggested that the differences between more and less successful athletes weren't as great as originally thought, which **weakens** the usefulness of the model.
4) Also, mood states are unlikely to be **consistent** over time. For example, a person's levels of fatigue, anger and vigour are all likely to change regularly. Therefore, it'd be inappropriate to compare an individual to **group averages**. Instead, an individual's results **over time** could be analysed for changes and to see if there is any potential relationship with their sporting progress.

Practice Questions

Q1 What are endorphins?

Q2 Identify one effect of endorphin release.

Q3 How many studies did Leith and Taylor (1990) include in their review?

Q4 What proportion of the experimental studies Leith and Taylor (1990) examined showed a significant improvement in mental health?

Q5 What do the initials POMS stand for?

Q6 Which mood states are positive mental health associated with according to Morgan's mental health model?

Exam Question

Q1 a) Outline one theory of the relationship between mental health and exercise. [10 marks]

b) Evaluate research into the benefits of exercise on mental health. [15 marks]

Running gets you high — so why is exercise still so unpopular...

What are we all still doing sitting at home watching telly and eating biscuits... Why aren't we out on the streets, jogging... It's free, improves your mental health, reduces the risk of cancer, and now I find out it also gets you high in a legal and in fact praiseworthy fashion. I'm off right now. Just as soon as I've finished this biscuit that is. And maybe that slice of cake...

Issues in Exercise and Sport

This bit's just for OCR. *The finishing line is in sight. Keep that brain stumbling along for a little while longer and then you can do the mental equivalent of collapsing on the floor and pouring a bottle of water on your head (i.e. watch Hollyoaks).*

Costill et al (1991) Investigated Burnout and Withdrawal in Sport

Costill et al (1991) investigated the effect of different amounts of **training** on swimmers.

	Costill et al (1991) — Effect of training intensity on performance
Method:	24 male college swimmers were put into two groups in an experiment using a **matched pairs** design. For the first four weeks the groups trained **together** once a day for a session lasting 1.5 hours. For the next six weeks the group in the **'long' condition** trained twice a day for 1.5 hours and those in the **'short' condition** trained with them just once a day. After this period the two groups trained **together** again for just one session lasting 1.5 hours for another 14 weeks. The swimmers had **blood tests**, **muscle samples** analysed and their **technique** assessed, in addition to taking part in **competitions** as usual.
Results:	Overall the swimmers **improved** their performance, endurance and swimming power but there weren't any **significant differences** between the two groups. The **short** condition had a **greater improvement** in sprinting performance in the earlier stages of the training.
Conclusion:	An increased amount of training **doesn't** provide an advantage on performance. Some of the physiological changes actually suggested a slight **negative influence** on the body. The researchers suggested that heavy training has a negative effect on arm power and strength in swimmers, possibly because of the effects on the **muscle fibres**. However, these effects disappear quickly if training volume is reduced.
Evaluation:	The study only used swimmers so the results can't be **generalised** to other sports. Also, the **limited sample** of 24 swimmers makes it difficult to generalise the findings to other groups. For example, younger swimmers may benefit more from increased amounts of training if they need more experience in the sport.

Huddy and Cash (1997) Investigated Body Image in Sport

A person's **body image** is how they perceive and feel about their body.
Huddy and Cash (1997) compared the body image of **marathon runners** with a control group.

	Huddy and Cash (1997) — Body image of marathon runners
Method:	139 male marathon runners were **matched** on age and weight with a **control group**. Their **attitudes** towards their physical health, fitness and appearance were measured, as well as their **body mass**.
Results:	There were several key findings: 1) The runners rated their appearance, fitness and health **more favourably** than the controls. 2) The runners were **more likely** to be interested in their **fitness** and **health** than the controls, but they were **less likely** to be interested in their **appearance** than the controls. 3) There was a **correlation** between **body mass** and **concern** about weight in the control group, but **not** in the runners' group. 4) There was **no relationship** between amount of running and body image in the runners' group. 5) People in the control group were more likely to be **dieting** than the runners. 6) Runners had a **lower body mass index** on average than people in the control group.
Conclusion:	People who participate in marathon running have a **better body image** than those who don't. It's likely that they're investing the time and effort in order to achieve the body type they prefer, reflected by a **lower body mass index** and an **interest in health and fitness**.
Evaluation:	The study had a higher level of **control over variables** than previous research, which increases the **validity**. However, the findings do not agree with research by **Ibrahim and Morrison (1976)**, who compared non-athletes with athletes from both **individual** and **team sports**. They found no difference in **self-esteem**, which is related to body image. This suggests that the findings of the Huddy and Cash (1997) study can be applied to individual sports such as marathon running but **not** to team sports.

Issues in Exercise and Sport

Drug Abuse is an Issue That Affects Many Different Types of Sport

1) Athletes might decide to use drugs for **medicinal** reasons, for **recreation** or to **enhance** their sporting performance.
2) Like everyone else, athletes aren't allowed to take illegal drugs. However, **legal** drugs that would improve their performance and so give them an **unfair advantage** when they compete are also **banned**.
3) These include **anabolic steroids** (which increase strength), and some **stimulants** (which increase alertness and heart rate, amongst other things).

Maganaris et al (2000) showed that **expectancy** about the effects of **anabolic steroids** affected sporting performance.

Maganaris et al (2000) — Expectancy and performance

Method: Eleven national-level **competitive power-lifters** aged 18 to 24 from the same training group gave their consent to take part in the research. In order to create **expectancy effects** of increased performance they were asked to take an oral drug which they were told was a new type of **anabolic steroid**. In fact, it was a **placebo** that would have no actual effect on performance. For one week the athletes were told when to take the tablets and their **performance** in different lifts was tested. After the first week **five** of the athletes were told that the tablet was only a placebo and became the **placebo group**. During the next week performance was **tested again** in both the experimental and placebo group.

Results: All athletes showed a **significant improvement** in performance in the first week, and the experimental group **continued** to improve in the second week. The placebo group **didn't** show a significant improvement in the second week, after they knew the truth about the tablets.

Conclusion: The findings suggest that expectancy effects **do improve performance**. The placebo group's improvement ceased once they knew the truth about the tablets, showing that expectancy about the drug's effect was **causing** the improvement in the first week. The experimental group showed an improvement over **both** weeks as they always believed they were taking anabolic steroids.

Evaluation: There are **ethical concerns** with allowing people to think they are taking an illegal drug, but the participants were fully **debriefed** after the two weeks. They'd also shown a **prior interest** in anabolic steroids, which further justified the procedure. The results were convincing but the **sample size** was very small and participants were from a single training group, so it might not be appropriate to **generalise** them. Participants in this type of sport could also be particularly **susceptible** to this kind of effect, so it might not be appropriate to **generalise** the findings to different sports.

Practice Questions

Q1 Describe the training patterns of the two groups in Costill et al's (1991) study.
Q2 Give an example of a measurement taken during Costill et al's (1991) study.
Q3 Which type of sport was used in Huddy and Cash's (1997) body image study?
Q4 Identify one finding from Huddy and Cash's (1997) study.
Q5 How many power-lifters took part in Maganaris et al's (2000) study?
Q6 Outline an ethical problem with Maganaris et al's (2000) study.

Exam Question

Q1 a) Describe a study investigating body image in sport. [10 marks]

b) Discuss some of the issues the coach of a swimmer training for a competition needs to consider. Refer to specific evidence in your answer. [15 marks]

Those athletes should try revising this — then they'd see what burnout is...

I love the placebo effect. Call me weird, but it's just so fascinatingly strange that your mind can have such a powerful effect on your body. Those power-lifters thought they were performing to the best of their ability before they took anything at all but they can't have been — just by taking a sugar pill they were able to improve their performance still further.

Attachment

This section is just for Edexcel. *An early attachment with a caregiver is arguably the most important relationship we form in our lives. Psychologists are interested in how and when our first attachments form and what influences them.*

An **Attachment** is a **Close Emotional Bond** Between Two People

1) The first attachment formed in a child's life is with its primary caregiver.
2) This bond is thought to be very important, forming a **template** for future attachments.
3) Because of this, the **development** and **nature** of early attachments have received much attention.
4) As usual, psychologists have come up with a variety of theories and it's thought that there's more than one type of attachment (see page 182).

Freud's Theory of Attachment is a **Psychodynamic Approach** to Attachment

Freud's theory of attachment suggests that an infant has an inbuilt need for **oral gratification** (through feeding), and **wants to be close** to the person who can fulfil this need, i.e. **the primary care giver** (usually the mother). In other words they form an **attachment** to this person to secure a food source — Freud called this **cupboard love theory**. Many people thought that the theory was too **simplistic** and further studies into factors determining attachment have been carried out:

Harlow (1959) — factors determining attachment

Method: The study tested infant monkeys' attachment to providers of **food** versus providers of **comfort**. In **laboratory experiments** rhesus monkeys were raised in isolation. They had two 'surrogate mothers'. One was made of metal and had food attached. The other was made of cloth, providing comfort but no food.

Results: Infant monkeys spent more time with the **comfort-providing** surrogate than the food-providing surrogate.

Conclusion: Infant monkeys **aren't driven** solely by their need for **food**.

Evaluation: This was a **laboratory experiment**, so there was strict control of the variables and it's unlikely that the results were affected by an unknown variable. It can be argued that you can't **generalise** the results of this study to humans, but support for the conclusion has been found in studies of human infants. There are **ethical issues** regarding how the monkeys were treated and the study also lacked **ecological validity** as the monkeys weren't in their natural environment.

Bowlby's (1951) Theory of Attachment **Rejects** the Cupboard Love Theory

John Bowlby rejected the psychodynamic theory for being **too narrowly focused**. He took forward the critical role of the mother into his own approach, but as more than just a provider of food. The key ideas of his theory are...

1) **Adaptiveness** — humans have **evolved** to behave in a way that makes them **more likely to survive**. Attachment to caregivers and wanting to be near them (particularly in dangerous situations) increases their chance of survival.
2) **Monotropy** — infants will form **one attachment** that is **much stronger** than any other (usually with their mother).
3) **Critical period** — infants that don't develop a strong attachment **by the age of three** are at risk of never doing so. Their **social** and **emotional development** could be **seriously damaged**.
4) **Internal working model** — the first attachment an infant makes will form the **template** for **future attachments**.
5) **Social interactions** — infants will form attachments with **long term caregivers** that are **responsive** to them.

Comments on Bowlby's theory of attachment:

1) Bowlby's theory is one of the most **influential** in the area of attachment theory. There is some **evidence** for his claims, e.g. Harlow's (1959) study supports the idea that we have evolved a need to form attachments.
2) Many people believe that Bowlby's emphasis on the role of mothers **undervalued** the importance of **fathers**.
3) The **critical period** is now thought of as a **sensitive period** where it's **desirable**, rather than essential, that attachments are formed. If attachments aren't formed it won't necessarily cause **long term damage**.
4) There's evidence that the idea of monotropy is incorrect — many children form **multiple attachments**.

Attachment

The **Biological Approach** to Attachment is Based on **Evolutionary Theory**

The **biological approach** to attachment is similar to Bowlby's idea of **adaptiveness**. It suggests that individuals who form attachments are more likely to pass on their **genes** — the protection that the relationship offers to an infant makes it **more likely to survive** to reproductive age. **Cross-species research** has been used to develop human attachment theory:

Lorenz (1935) — Attachment through imprinting

Method:	The attachment behaviour of two groups of geese were observed. One group of geese were raised normally, the other in an incubator (with no mother). The first **moving object** that the normally raised geese saw was their **mother**. For the geese in the incubator it was **Lorenz**.
Results:	The geese raised in an incubator treated Lorenz the **same way** the normally raised geese treated their mother — they followed him around.
Conclusion:	Infant geese will form an attachment to the **first nearby moving object** that they see. This is called imprinting.
Evaluation:	This study suggests that **proximity alone** can cause an attachment to be formed. However, it can be argued that you can't **generalise** the results of this study to humans — the results could be species specific. There are **ethical issues** regarding how the geese were treated and the study also lacked **ecological validity** as the geese in one group weren't in their natural environment. **Variables** could only be strictly controlled for the geese in the incubator, so the results for the group raised normally could have been affected by an unknown variable.

This **inbuilt mechanism** in geese for forming attachments is also seen in humans. Whilst they don't follow the first moving object that they see, babies and carers display behaviours that **encourage attachments to form**. For example:

Infants...

- Automatically **adjust their positions** in order to cuddle up to the parent.
- **Smile** when they see faces (or objects resembling faces).

Carers...

- Are **attracted** to the features of a baby's face.
- Experience **stress** when they hear a baby crying.

Comments on the evolutionary approach to attachment:

1) Much of the evidence supporting the biological approach to attachment is based on **ethology** (research into **animal behaviour**), so applying it to human behaviour involves big **generalisations**.
2) The evolutionary approach isn't as **comprehensive** as Bowlby's approach — it covers only one aspect of it.
3) Explanations are often based on sensible **speculation** instead of direct evidence.

Practice Questions

Q1 What is cupboard love theory?

Q2 Describe the main findings of Harlow's (1959) study.

Q3 What is meant by monotropy?

Exam Questions

Q1 a) Outline Bowlby's (1951) theory of attachment. [6 marks]
b) Evaluate Bowlby's (1951) theory of attachment. [6 marks]

Q2 Describe and evaluate the contribution of the psychodynamic approach to attachment theory. [12 marks]

Attachment to someone who gives you food — sounds reasonable to me...

So babies turn out to be pretty canny little creatures then — they set their sights on people who can give them food and comfort and who appear to be around all the time. They then lure them in with genetically programmed smiles and hang around for the next 18 years eating all the food, spending all the money and generally creating chaos. Absolute genius.

The Strange Situation

Just for Edexcel again. *Ainsworth's study placed babies in what she called a Strange Situation but it wasn't that strange — to go* ***really*** *strange you'd need something like Bill Clinton... wrestling... a parsnip.*

Ainsworth's **Research** Aimed to Understand **Attachment**

Ainsworth et al (1978) investigated attachment types.

1) They collected data on the **behaviour** of around 100 mothers and children (aged 12-18 months).
2) The research used a method of **controlled observation** designed by Ainsworth — called the '**Strange Situation**'.
3) The Strange Situation was **specifically designed** to see how children dealt with **stress** and **separation**.

The Strange Situation Involves a **Specific Sequence of Events**

The mother is told **how to behave** during each stage of the study.

Stage 1	The observer leaves the mother and child in a room containing toys.
Stage 2	The child may start to **play with the toys**. The mother sits on a chair and **doesn't get involved** with the play. If the child doesn't start to play after 2 minutes the mother will **encourage them**.
Stage 3	A stranger comes into the room, and for the first minute they sit on a chair and **remain silent**. For the second minute they **talk with the mother**, and then they approach the child. The mother then quietly **leaves the room** so the child won't notice.
Stage 4	The stranger and the baby are **alone** — the stranger can attempt to **comfort** the child if it's upset.
Stage 5	The mother comes back and encourages the child to **play**, and at the same time the **stranger leaves**. If the child is upset the **mother** will comfort him/her. The mother then leaves again but this time **she says goodbye** to the child.
Stage 6	The **baby is alone** — neither the stranger or the mother are present.
Stage 7	The **stranger comes back** and will attempt to **comfort** the child if he/she is upset.
Stage 8	The mother comes back, **says hello** to the child and picks him/her up. At the same time the stranger **leaves quietly** so the child won't notice.

Stuart was so annoyed at being left alone, he went postal.

- Stage 1 lasts for **30 seconds**. All the other stages in the experiment last for **3 minutes**.
- If the child becomes very **distressed** in stages 4, 6 or 7 the length of time is **reduced**.
- Stage 5 is **lengthened** if the child needs more time to start playing with the toys again.

Ainsworth's (1978) Study Found **Three Main Types of Attachment**

1) **Securely attached** – found in **70%** of the children — the child is **pleased** when the mother returns.
   - When the mother is present the child plays **happily** and **confidently** and doesn't need lots of attention and interaction. However, when the mother leaves the child is **upset**.
   - Children with this attachment type are upset by their **mother leaving**, rather than being alone.
   - The stranger can **pacify** the child a little but the mother is **preferred**.
2) **Anxious-avoidant** — found in **15%** of the children — the child **avoids** the mother when she returns.
   - When the mother is present the child seems **indifferent** to her and **isn't overtly upset** if she leaves.
   - Children with this attachment type are upset at being **left alone**, rather than the mother leaving.
   - The child will allow the stranger to comfort them **as much** as they will allow the mother.
3) **Anxious-resistant** — found in **15%** of the children — the child is **difficult to comfort** and appears **upset** and **angry**.
   - When the mother is present the child is **tearful** and **doesn't play easily**.
   - Although the child may seek comfort, they will **resist it** when given.
   - Children with this attachment type are the **most upset** when the mother leaves and are **resistant to the stranger**.

The Strange Situation

The Strange Situation has Been Used in **Different Countries**

Ainsworth et al's (1978) findings have been shown many times in the **USA**, but it wasn't then known whether they could be applied to other **cultures**. **Cross-cultural studies** have since taken place:

Van Ijzendoorn and Kroonenberg (1988) — cross-cultural studies

Method: Van Ijzendoorn and Kroonenberg carried out a **meta-analysis** of 32 studies of the Strange Situation in 8 different countries (e.g. Japan, Britain, Germany). They were analysed to find any overall patterns.

Results: The percentages of children classified as secure or insecure were fairly **similar** in the countries tested. Secure attachments were the **most common** type of attachment across the countries studied. Some differences were found in the distribution of **insecure attachments**. In Japan, **5%** of children showed the avoidant type, and **25%** the resistant type. In West Germany however, **35%** showed the avoidance type and only **8%** the resistant type.

Conclusion: There are **cross-cultural similarities** in raising children, producing common reactions to the Strange Situation.

Evaluation: Children are brought up in **different ways** in different cultures. In **Japan**, babies usually spend **all their first year** with their mother, so they have **no experience** of separation. This means they get **more upset** in the Strange Situation environment and are likely to be classified as having **anxious-resistant** attachments. **Grossman et al (1985)** suggested that **independence** could be seen as **highly desirable** by parents in **West Germany**. Therefore children were more likely to seem to have an **anxious-avoidant** attachment. The way that other cultures raise their children needs to be taken into account in the Strange Situation context, otherwise the research could become ethnocentric (see page 242).

Strange Situation Research is **Not Totally Reliable**

Ainsworth's sample was **large** — about **100 families**. Her results should therefore be **pretty reliable**. However...

1) One of the problems with the observation method is that it's difficult for observers to monitor **all aspects** of behaviour at the same time. Researchers overcame this by **videotaping the procedures** so that there was **maximum opportunity** for specific behaviours to be noticed.
2) Although the Strange Situation does represent **real-life situations** (parents do leave their children with **strangers**, e.g. babysitters), the behaviour in stages 2 and 3 is slightly **artificial**. Many parents would attend to their child in a new situation, and the initial silence of the stranger isn't **representative** of everyday situations — and so it isn't **ecologically valid**.
3) The studies don't collect a **range** of information. A detailed analysis of the **mother's behaviour** could have been useful — it may be the cause of the attachment type.
4) Although the durations of stages were reduced if the children were very upset, this research did involve putting very young children in a situation which is meant to be **strange and distressing**. The stress experienced by the children in the studies needs to be weighed up against the **usefulness** of the findings of the research.

Practice Questions

Q1 Outline the stages of the Strange Situation experiment.

Q2 Name the three types of attachment that Ainsworth (1978) found.

Q3 How do Japanese children differ in their attachment types compared to Ainsworth's (1978) results?

Q4 Outline one issue with Strange Situation research.

Exam Question

Q1 a) Outline the strengths and weaknesses of the Strange Situation research. [5 marks]

b) Discuss cultural differences that have been found in attachment types. [4 marks]

Get this stuff really securely attached — to your brain...

It's the classic childminding tale — mother has child, mother gives child over to psychological research, mother leaves child in roomful of toys for half an hour whilst she yo-yos back and forward, child experiences distress and crying and wonders why it then ends up growing old with an inexplicable aversion to wooden bricks and small bears. Doesn't sound very fair.

Separation and Deprivation

Edexcel people, keep ploughing on. *Being separated from a caregiver or deprived of them altogether can seriously affect a child's development. So how about some more theories and studies to look at? My thoughts exactly...*

*Attachment Can be Disrupted by **Separation** or **Deprivation***

Separation is where a child is away from a **caregiver** they're attached to (such as their mother). The term's used when it's a **relatively short** time, just hours or days — not a longer or permanent separation.

Deprivation describes the **loss** of something that is **wanted or needed**. So, 'maternal deprivation' is the loss of the mother (or other attachment figure). A more **long-term** or even **permanent** loss is implied.

*Separation Can Have **Major Effects***

Robertson and Bowlby (1952) suggest that children who have been separated may go through the following stages. The stages are referred to as the **'PDD model' — Protest, Despair, Detachment**:

1) **Protest** — During the first few hours, the child will **protest** a lot at being **separated** from its mother (or other attachment figure), by crying, panicking, calling for its mother, etc.

2) **Despair** — After a day or two, the child will start to lose interest in its surroundings, becoming more and more **withdrawn**, with occasional crying. They may also eat and sleep less.

3) **Detachment** — After a few days, the child will start to become more **alert** and interested again in its surroundings. It will cry less and may seem to have **'recovered'** from its bad reaction to the separation. However, its previous attachment with its carer may now be permanently **damaged** — the trust and security may be lost.

Robertson and Robertson (1968) — evidence for the PDD model

Method:	In a **naturalistic observation**, several children who were experiencing short separations from their carers were observed and filmed. For example, a boy called John (aged around 18 months) stayed in a residential nursery for nine days while his mother had another baby.
Results:	John showed the signs of passing through **'protest'** for the first day or two. Then he showed **despair** — he tried to get attention from the nurses but they were busy with other children so he gave up trying. Then he showed **detachment** — he became more active and content. However, when his mother came to collect him, he was reluctant to be affectionate.
Conclusion:	The short-term separation had very **bad effects** on John, including possible **permanent damage** to his attachment with his mother.
Evaluation:	John's reaction might not have been due to separation — it could have been down to his new environment or the fact that he was getting much less attention than he was used to. There will have been little control of **variables**, and it would be difficult to replicate each **individual situation** to test the reliability of the results. However, as the study took place in a natural setting, the results will have **ecological validity**.

Some comments on the PDD model include:

1) These findings suggest that **separating a child from its carers should be avoided** whenever possible. This has important implications for childcare practice, e.g. children should be allowed to visit or remain with their mothers during a stay in hospital. Sounds fair enough to me.

2) **Many factors** influence how a child reacts to a separation. These include age (older children will cope better), the quality of the care received during the separation, the individual temperament of the child and how often it has experienced separations. So, **separations do not necessarily produce the PDD effects**. They may even be good for the child (see pages 188-189).

3) Studies have shown that there's a difference between children placed in an **institutionalised setting** and those in **foster care**. It would seem that as long as children are still receiving **emotional support**, they manage to cope with the separation.

Separation and Deprivation

*John Bowlby (1951) Studied Long-Term Maternal **Deprivation***

Even if short-term separation may not necessarily be bad for a child, **John Bowlby** argued that long-term **deprivation** from an attachment figure could be harmful. He produced his **maternal deprivation hypothesis**:

1) Deprivation from the main carer during the **critical period** (the first 3 years), has harmful effects on a child's emotional, social, intellectual and even physical development. Not so good.
2) Long-term effects of deprivation may include **separation anxiety** (the fear of another separation from the carer). This may lead to problem behaviour, e.g. being very clingy, and avoiding going to school. Future relationships may be affected by this emotional insecurity. Bowlby's research showed evidence for this.

Bowlby (1944) — 44 Juvenile Thieves

Method:	**Case studies** were carried out on the backgrounds of 44 adolescents who had been referred to the clinic where Bowlby worked because they'd been stealing. A **control group** of 44 'emotionally disturbed' adolescents who didn't steal was used.
Results:	17 of the thieves had experienced frequent separations from their mothers before the age of two, compared with 2 in the control group. 14 of the thieves were diagnosed as 'affectionless psychopaths' (they didn't care about how their actions affected others). 12 of these 14 had experienced separation from their mothers.
Conclusion:	Deprivation of the child from its main carer early in life can have very **harmful long-term consequences**.
Evaluation:	The results indicate a link between deprivation and criminal behaviour. However, it can't be said that one **causes** the other. There may be **other factors** that caused the criminal behaviour. Although case studies provide a lot of **detailed information**, the study relied on **retrospective data**, which may be unreliable.

This study, and others on institutionalisation and hospitalisation, suggest that long-term effects of separation include:

1) **Affectionless psychopathology** (as seen in the 44 Juvenile Thieves study).
2) **Anaclitic depression** — involving appetite loss, sleeplessness, sadness and impaired development.
3) **Deprivation dwarfism** — infants are physically underdeveloped due to emotional deprivation.

Some comments on Bowlby's maternal deprivation hypothesis:

1) Other evidence supports Bowlby's claims. **Goldfarb (1943)** found that orphanage children who were socially and maternally deprived were later less intellectually and socially developed.
2) The evidence has **criticisms**: Bowlby linked the thieves' behaviour to maternal deprivation, but **other things were not considered**, e.g. whether the poverty they grew up in led them to steal. The children in Goldfarb's study may have been most harmed by the **social deprivation** in the orphanage rather than the maternal deprivation.

Even when deprivation has harmful effects, these may be reversed with appropriate, **quality care**. For example, **Skeels and Dye (1939)** found that children who had been socially deprived (in an orphanage) during their first two years of life quickly improved their IQ scores if they were transferred to a school where they got one-to-one care.

Practice Questions

Q1 What is the PDD model?

Q2 What does Bowlby's maternal deprivation hypothesis propose?

Exam Question

Q1 a) Outline one study into the effects of separation. [3 marks]

b) Evaluate Bowlby's (1944) study of 44 juvenile thieves. [6 marks]

The PDD model can also be applied as a reaction to excessive studying...

It's a bit scary when you think about it — who knows how many times your mum popped out to the shops when you were a kiddie and how it's affected you. That aside, I'm afraid you need to learn all the theories and studies on these pages so you can wow the examiners with your impressive knowledge and searching psychological insights. So you'd best crack on.

Privation

These pages are only for Edexcel. *Deprivation refers to the loss of an attachment, whilst privation means that attachments have never taken place. Cases of privation in young children are normally the result of child abuse.*

Privation** Means That Attachments Have **Never Been Formed

Psychologists have studied situations of privation to learn about the **effects** on children, and to find out if **quality care** can **reverse** the effects later in a child's life.

Curtiss (1977) looked at what had happened to a 13 year old girl known as **Genie**.

1) Until she was found, aged 13, Genie had been **tied to a chair** and **locked in a room**.
   - Contact with her family had been very **limited** and **abusive**.
   - She had **physical problems** (she couldn't really **walk**), had **poor social skills** and **no language skills**.
   - She had been **beaten** for making noises and so **made very little sound**.
2) After she had been discovered she spent a **year in hospital** and then **four years** living with a foster family:
   - During this time Genie was given **specialist treatment** and managed to develop **limited language skills** — she could only use **short, ungrammatical sentences**.
   - Over time her **social skills** improved and she formed **attachments** with the family and other caregivers.
3) Genie was then **returned to her mother**, but she was unable to cope with Genie's needs.
4) She was placed in various **foster and care homes** but was the victim of **further abuse** and **lost** some of the skills that she had acquired since being discovered.

This study suggests that privation has **negative effects** on development that can only be **partly overcome** by quality care.

Koluchova (1972) reported a different privation case study known as the **Czech twins**.

1) The twin brothers were abused by their stepmother and kept **locked in a cellar** from the age of 18 months to 7 years. During those 5½ years they were **beaten** and **not fed properly**.
   - Like Genie, they also had **physical problems**, e.g. **rickets** because of their poor diet.
   - They **didn't talk**, were **very small** and couldn't stand up or walk properly. They were **easily frightened** by other people and the dark.
   - Their **intelligence levels** appeared to be **very low** and their overall development similar to **3-year-olds**.
2) The twins were hospitalised and then went to a school for children with **extreme learning difficulties**.
3) Their development began to **improve** and at the age of 9 they were adopted by two sisters who were experienced in fostering children. The twins received **high quality care** as the women were very dedicated to helping them.
4) Follow-up research by Koluchova found that:
   - At 11 the twins' **language skills** had caught up and were **normal** for their age.
   - At 14 they were **behaving normally**, had no mental health problems and their IQ seemed normal.
   - At 20 they were described as having **good social skills** and loving relationships with their foster parents and extended family.
   - At 29 they continued to behave normally, enjoyed **positive relationships** with other people and had **responsible jobs** as a technical training instructor and a computer technician.

This study suggests that with **high quality**, **continuous care** the effects of privation can be reversed.

*The **Case Study Method** has **Advantages and Disadvantages***

See page 230 for more on case studies.

1) Case studies allow us to study situations that couldn't be reproduced in an **experimental situation** — deliberately stopping children from forming attachments is an **extreme form** of **child abuse**.
2) Case studies can provide a very **in-depth**, **detailed analysis** of a situation. In both of these examples the children were **studied for years** and many aspects of their development were **monitored over time**.
3) Ideally Curtiss and Koluchova should have remained **detached** and **objective** when studying the children. Realistically this would've been **difficult** to do and their judgements might have been quite **subjective**.
4) A major problem with case studies is that they can't be **generalised** to the **wider population** — these examples describe **unique situations**.

Privation

The Reversibility of Privation Differs According to the Situation

The case studies of Genie and the Czech twins show **very different outcomes** for their subjects. There are several possible reasons for this:

1) The Czech twins study saw a much more successful outcome than the Genie study. This may be because the twins **had each other** to form an attachment with:
   - Even though they were unable to look after each other, the **presence** of the other might have allowed them to make an **emotional bond**. This might also have helped them to make **subsequent attachments**.
   - Genie had very **limited contact** with her family. Although later in life her mother tried to take responsibility for her, they did not have an attachment during her **early years** of confinement.
2) It's very likely that Genie had **problems** which affected her development and meant that she would never be able to gain full language and social skills.
   - These could be **innate problems** that she was born with and may have been the reason her father locked her away in the first place. It's obviously not an excuse though...
   - Alternatively the problems could be the result of the **physical abuse** she received, or a mixture of both.
3) Genie had to leave the foster family she was living with because the **funding ran out** and they were finding it difficult to cope with her limited social skills. In comparison, the **continuity of care** was much better for the twins and probably helped with their **development of attachments**.

The Studies Have Methodological and Ethical Issues

1) The **validity** of Koluchova's research has been questioned because the twins had each other to bond with. They were able to form some kind of attachment so the study isn't a **true example of privation**.
2) It's very difficult to make **comparisons** between cases of privation. Privation is such an **unusual occurrence** that it's better to deal with each situation as it emerges. However, research into previous examples can be used to **inform** and **improve** the treatment given in subsequent situations.
3) The research into privation is **retrospective** — it looks back at events that have already happened. Therefore the findings **rely on memory** which is often **subjective** and details can be **forgotten**.
4) Examples of privation involve **child abuse**, so the people who have the most information may be **unwilling** to provide it. Genie's father, who was responsible for her being locked away and beaten, **killed himself** when he realised his abuse has been discovered.

Czech, not checked.

Practice Questions

Q1 What is privation?

Q2 What problems did Genie have when she was found?

Q3 Describe the development of the Czech twins from the age of 9 years onwards.

Q4 Suggest one reason for the different outcomes in the Genie and Czech twins case studies.

Q5 Why is the retrospective aspect of privation research a problem?

Exam Questions

Q1 Describe and evaluate research into privation. [12 marks]

Q2 Outline the issue of reversibility of privation. Refer to psychological evidence in your answer. [12 marks]

Gruelling? Yes. A bit unpleasant? Yes. Need-to-know stuff? Absolutely.

Obviously, no one really wants to sit around reading about cases of abuse all day. But case studies like Genie and the Czech twins are the only possible opportunities for psychologists to investigate the effects of privation on children. The more they can find out, the better the chances are of reversing the effects in future cases. Which would be good news all round, really.

Daycare

For Edexcel again. *'Daycare' refers to any* ***temporary care*** *for a child provided by someone other than the parents or guardians they live with. Lots of studies have been done to see whether daycare has an effect on development.*

Daycare has Advantages and Disadvantages

Studies into daycare have found that it can have both positive and negative effects on children. Here are some studies that explore the impact of daycare on attachment, peer relations and aggression. Lucky you...

Clarke-Stewart et al (1994) — positive effects of daycare

Method: This study was made up of a series of separate **observations**, to examine the effects of daycare. One experiment compared the **peer relationships** of 150 children aged 2-3 years, who were either cared for at home or in daycare. The children were from a range of social backgrounds. In another experiment, the **strength of attachment** of 18-month-old children was studied using the Strange Situation (see page 182). Children who had at least 30 hours of daycare per week were compared with children who had 'low intensity' daycare (less than 10 hours per week).

Results: The 2 to 3-year-olds who had experienced daycare were better at coping with social situations and had more experience of peer relationships than those cared for at home. In the Strange Situation experiment, the 18-month-olds who had high intensity daycare were just as distressed when separated from their mothers as those who had low intensity daycare.

Conclusion: Daycare can have a positive effect on the development of peer relationships. Attachment in 18-month-olds is not affected by temporary separation.

Evaluation: The observations were **controlled**, so the study could be replicated. However, the Strange Situation is artificial, so the study lacks **ecological validity** and the results can't be **generalised** to other children.

Shea (1981) — positive effects of daycare

Method: Children aged between 3 and 4 were videotaped in the playground during their first 10 weeks at nursery school. Their behaviour was assessed in terms of **rough-and-tumble play, aggression, frequency of peer interaction, distance from the teacher** and **distance from other children**.

Results: Over the 10 weeks the children's peer interaction increased and their distance from the teacher decreased. There was a decrease in aggression and an increase in rough-and-tumble play. The increase in sociability was more evident in children who had attended day care 5 days a week rather than 2 days a week.

Conclusion: Daycare causes children to become more sociable and less aggressive.

Evaluation: This was a **naturalistic observation**, meaning that the study has high **ecological validity** because none of the behaviour was manipulated. However, it means that the results could have been affected by **extraneous variables**. The behaviour was open to interpretation, so the findings could be biased — e.g. it could be difficult to differentiate between 'aggression' and 'rough-and-tumble play'.

Belsky and Rovine (1988) — negative effects of daycare

Method: Infants were placed in the **Strange Situation** to assess how secure their attachments with their mothers were. One group had experienced no daycare and one had experienced at least 20 hours of day care per week before their first birthday.

Results: The infants who had received daycare were more likely to have an **insecure** attachment type. They were either **'anxious-avoidant'** — ignored their mother and didn't mind if she left, or **'anxious-resistant'** — uneasy around their mother but upset if she left. Those who hadn't had daycare were more likely to be **securely attached**.

Conclusion: Daycare has a **negative** effect on an infant's development of attachments.

Evaluation: The Strange Situation is a **controlled observation**, so there was **good control** of the variables. However, this means that the study lacks **ecological validity**, because it creates an artificial situation. **DiLalla (1998)** also found negative effects on children's **peer relationships** — the more daycare children had, the **less prosocially** they behaved, i.e. the less they helped, shared, etc.

Daycare

Research into How Daycare Affects Development **Varies Widely**

It seems that nobody can really decide whether daycare is good or bad for children.
Here are some of the reasons why the findings vary so much:

1) The studies focus on slightly different things (e.g. quality of care, age of child), and use different **samples**.
2) There are **methodological problems** with the studies that might lead to inconsistent results. E.g. Clarke-Stewart has admitted that the **Strange Situation** isn't a good way of assessing attachment in infants who have daycare (despite using it in her study). They're used to temporary separation so might respond indifferently and be wrongly classed as '**insecure**'.
3) All of these studies rely on **correlations**, so it's not possible to establish **cause and effect**.
4) They also don't take **individual differences** like temperament into account, and there could be **cultural differences** that are ignored (see pages 242-243).

So, How Do I Make a **Great Daycare Centre...**

...I hear you cry. Well sit tight and all will be revealed.

An important variable that can affect the results of studies is the **quality** of daycare that the kiddies receive. **Scarr (1998)** identified several factors that make for good daycare:

1) Good **staff training**
2) Adequate **space**
3) Appropriate **toys** and **activities**
4) A good **ratio of staff to children**
5) **Minimising staff turnover** so that children can form **stable attachments** with carers

Arnold didn't like to complain, but the toys at his old daycare centre had been much better.

Vandell et al (1988) found that children who had **good quality** daycare were more likely to have **friendly interactions** with others compared to those receiving **lower quality** daycare.

This shows that **high quality daycare** can have a **positive effect** on a child's **social development**.

Practice Questions

Q1 Did Clarke-Stewart et al (1994) find that daycare had positive or negative effects?

Q2 Evaluate a study that shows that daycare has negative effects.

Q3 Why might the results from studies into the effects of daycare differ from each other?

Q4 So, how do you make a great daycare centre?

Exam Question

Q1 a) Outline research findings on the positive effects of daycare on development. [6 marks]

b) Evaluate research findings on the positive effects of daycare on development. [6 marks]

If this is all getting too difficult you can always blame it on your daycare...

So to round up, there are positive and negative effects of daycare and no one's worked out whether it's a good or bad thing yet. Excellent, glad that's sorted. Anyway, you need to be able to describe and evaluate studies on the effects of daycare and, given that we don't know whether it's helpful or harmful, you'd better learn both its advantages and its disadvantages.

Developmental Problems — Autism

Keep going, Edexcel people. Nearly there. *We can learn a lot about typical development by studying conditions where an individual's development has 'gone wrong' in some way. Autism is one widely recognised example.*

Autism Affects **Many Aspects** of an **Individual's Functioning**

1) It is typically diagnosed **before** the age of **30 months** and affects about **1** person in every **100** (mainly boys).
2) The profile and severity of an autistic individual's symptoms vary widely from person to person, but the condition is summarised by the **Triad of Impairments** model:

> **Triad of Impairments Model**
>
> 1) Impaired **social interactions** — e.g. lack of enjoyment gained from **sharing experiences** with others, **underdeveloped relationships** with peers.
> 2) Impaired **communication** — e.g. delayed **language** development, inappropriate **emotional** expression.
> 3) Impaired **social imagination** — e.g. an inability to **play imaginatively** with toys or other people.

3) These impairments are accompanied by **repetitive** or **stereotyped behaviour**, e.g. inflexibility with routines.

It's Been Proposed That **Autism is Inherited**

Abnormalities in brain structure (which may be either hereditary or a genetic birth defect) could explain autism.

Ritvo et al (1985) — a twin study that supports a genetic link

Method: The study was a concordance analysis with an independent group design. 23 pairs of identical (MZ) and 17 pairs of non-identical (DZ) twins were compared for the rate at which both twins of the pair were diagnosed as autistic.

Results: MZ twins showed a 96% concordance rate, compared to 24% concordance shown between DZ twins.

Conclusion: There is a genetic component to autism.

Evaluation: Ritvo et al's sample size is quite small (only 40 pairs of twins), so the results might not be as comprehensive or reliable as would have been liked. Similar studies on ordinary siblings (who will have the same genetic similarity as DZ twins) show concordance of around only 2%. This suggests that the environment, which twins are more likely to share, may also play a role in the development of autism.

Another Explanation Proposes a **Lack of Mental Capacity**

The psychological approach suggests that autistic children lack what **Cohen (1985)** called a **theory of mind**. They lack the mental capacity to imagine the world from the **perspective** of **another person**.

Baron-Cohen et al (1985) studied theory of mind in autistic children

Method: Three groups of children were studied — children with autism with an average age of 12 years, children with Down's Syndrome with an average age of 11 years, and 'normal' children with an average age of 4 years. The experimenter had two dolls, Sally and Anne. Sally had a basket, Anne a box. Children were asked to name the dolls (the **naming question**). Then Sally was seen to hide a marble in her basket and leave the room. Anne took the marble and put it in her box. Sally returned and the child was asked, 'Where will Sally look for her marble?' (**belief question**). The correct response is to point to the basket, where Sally believes the marble to be. They were also asked, 'Where is the marble really?' (**reality question**) and 'Where was the marble in the beginning?' (**memory question**). Each child was tested twice, with the marble in a different place the second time.

Results: **100%** of the children got the **naming**, **reality** and **memory** questions correct. In the **belief** question, the children with Down's Syndrome scored **86%**, the 'normal' children **85%**, but the children with autism scored **20%**.

Conclusion: The findings seem to suggest that autistic children have an **under-developed theory of mind**, sometimes called **mind-blindness**. They seem unable to predict or understand the beliefs of others.

Evaluation: Dolls were used throughout the study, causing it to lack **ecological validity**. Also, children with autism may in fact have a more highly developed theory of mind and understand that dolls don't have beliefs. Repeating the study by acting out the scenes with **humans** might show an increase in ability on the tasks. However, when **Leslie and Frith (1988)** did a similar study with real people and not dolls, the same pattern of results was obtained.

Developmental Problems — Autism

Autism Affects a Child's Development

Some psychologists have suggested that the main way that autism can be detrimental to a child's psychological development is preventing them from being able to develop a **theory of mind**:

- To have a social or emotional relationship with other people, it's important to understand and interpret different **emotional states** or **points of view** — for this you need to have a theory of mind.
- If autistic children don't develop a theory of mind, their development is affected and they find interaction difficult.

Language Development

1) Autistic children don't seem to understand that other people may have a different point of view to their own. Because of this they don't show **joint attention.**
2) Joint attention means being able to **share the experience** of seeing or watching something by **following another person's gaze** or pointing gestures — normally developing children can do this from the age of about 9 months.

You ain't seen us, right?

3) Autistic children won't **initiate** these episodes, and they also won't **respond** to attempts made by other people to **engage their attention** — such as **shifting gaze**, **pointing** or **making exclamations** towards objects of interest, e.g. "look at the skateboarding bunnies".

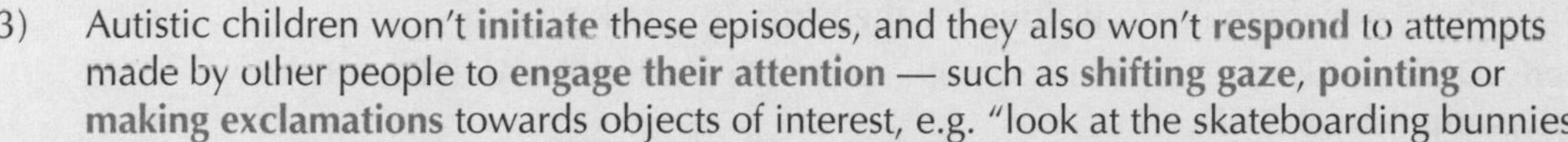

4) It's through these episodes that children initially **learn language** — it's only by turning to look at the skateboarding bunnies as the adult gives them that **label**, that a child will know what skateboarding bunnies are.
5) Not only will an autistic child fail to learn new labels, but they will learn the **wrong thing** if they associate the new word with whatever it is they are focused on **at the time.**
6) As well as having problems learning words, **speech development** is often **slower than average** in autistic children.

Social Development

Due to **mind blindness**, autistic children increasingly fail to meet **developmental landmarks** as they get older.

1) At **age four**, children usually begin to grasp the concept of **deception**. However, autistic children will not **doubt the truth** of what others say to them, or consider the possibility of **lying themselves.**
2) This is also seen in a lack of understanding of **humour**, and later **metaphor.**
3) At **age nine**, when children begin to master some of the more complex **social graces**, autistic children will continue to **make social mistakes** by being **honest** rather than **tactful.**
4) Right up to adulthood, autistic individuals will show impairment when it comes to **interpreting** another person's **emotional state** by reading their **tone of voice** and **facial expressions**. This may result in them appearing to be **insensitive.**

Practice Questions

Q1 Outline the Triad of Impairments associated with autism.

Q2 Describe the main findings of the study by Ritvo et al (1985).

Q3 Outline the method of Baron-Cohen et al's (1985) study.

Q4 What is meant by a 'theory of mind'?

Exam Questions

Q1 a) Describe a psychological explanation of autism. [6 marks]

b) Outline evidence supporting a biological explanation of autism. [6 marks]

Q2 Explain how a lack of a 'theory of mind' could impact on a child's development. [12 marks]

The skateboarding bunny approach — it's the new psychodynamics...

Crikey, all this child psychology's a bit hard to stomach sometimes, isn't it? Make sure you have a good understanding of theory of mind and you can talk about Baron-Cohen (I'm pretty sure it isn't the one that played Borat, before you ask) until the cows come home, the sun sets in the west, the fat lady sings, or you get lots of marks. Whichever happens to come first.

Developmental Problems — ADHD

Only for you lucky Edexcellers again. *The behaviour of kids with ADHD is now better understood than ever — it turns out that some 'naughty' children need more than Supernanny to sort them out...*

ADHD is One of the Most Common Behavioural Disorders to Affect Children

1) ADHD (attention deficit hyperactivity disorder) affects **3-5%** of school age children, most of whom are **boys**.
2) ADHD is usually diagnosed in **early childhood** and many children show symptoms into **adolescence** and **adulthood**.
3) ADHD behaviours can affect a child's everyday functioning.
4) There are **three subtypes** of ADHD, each of which has specific behavioural symptoms:

- **Inattentive ADHD** — children have **difficulty focusing** on tasks because of a **reduced attention span**. They also get **bored easily**.
- **Hyperactive-impulsive ADHD** — children are **restless**, **fidgety** and have trouble sitting still. They have difficulty in **waiting for their turn** to speak or act.
- **Combined ADHD** — children have the symptoms of both **inattentive ADHD** and **hyperactive-impulsive ADHD**.

There are Biological Explanations of ADHD

1) The Neurological Explanation

Neurological explanations suggest that ADHD is caused by differences in how the brain works.

Zametkin et al (1990) — Evidence of differences in ADHD brains

Method: This study was a **laboratory experiment** using an **independent groups design**. The brain activity of 25 adults with ADHD was compared to that of 50 adults without ADHD by scanning their brains (using PET) whilst they did tasks requiring them to focus on stimuli. A PET scan shows the rate at which particular parts of the brain metabolise glucose (use it for energy) — the higher the rate, the higher the activity in that area.

Results: Glucose metabolism in the brain was **8.1% lower in ADHD sufferers** than for adults without ADHD.

Conclusion: Lower use of glucose in the brain may cause ADHD symptoms. Low rates in the prefrontal cortex are particularly telling as this is an area involved in controlling attention, motor activity and planning ahead. These are directly linked to the inattentive, hyperactive and impulsive behaviours seen in ADHD.

Evaluation: The **methodology** of this study is flawed by the ADHD group having more men than the normal group. When there are equal numbers of men and women the difference between groups' brain activity is not significant. The findings of this study haven't been **replicated** in studies using children and adolescents.

2) The Genetic Explanation

Genetic explanations suggest that ADHD is inherited.

Levy et al (1997) — A twin study that supports a genetic link

Method: This study was a **concordance analysis** of **two independent groups**. 849 pairs of identical (MZ) and 1089 pairs of non-identical (DZ) twins aged under 16 were compared for the rate at which both twins of the pair were diagnosed with ADHD.

Results: MZ twins showed 82.7% concordance, compared to 37.9% concordance shown between DZ twins.

Conclusion: There is a **strong genetic component** to ADHD.

Evaluation: The large sample used in this study means that the results should closely match the whole population — this means they can be **generalised**. Similar concordance rates have been **replicated** in other studies. However, as concordance rates aren't 100% for MZ twins there must be some **environmental influence** that contributes to ADHD.

Developmental Problems — ADHD

ADHD Affects a *Child's Development*

ADHD affects the development of children in different ways. Two main areas affected by ADHD are:

Social Development

1) Children with ADHD are often **unpopular** with their peers and experience **rejection**. Different factors contribute to this:
    - **Poor concentration** — this makes it difficult to **interact** with a child with ADHD. Other children may find their inability to remember and follow the **rules** of games annoying.
    - Their **lack of attention** in conversations can be interpreted as **rudeness**.
    - **Erratic behaviour** — children with ADHD can often **disrupt lessons**. This may frustrate others if they feel that it's negatively affecting their own learning.
2) The more that children with ADHD become aware of their lack of social skills, the more likely it is that they will **withdraw from their peers**.
3) Poor social skills also limit their **job opportunities** in adulthood, as well as reducing the likelihood of them having a **'normal' family life**.

Her ADHD wasn't the issue, it was the scary wardrobe choices that hindered Lucy's social development.

Academic Performance

1) Children with ADHD may struggle academically:
    - The **symptoms** of the disorder can negatively affect their learning. For example, **lack of attention** may mean they don't listen fully to explanations, and **poor concentration** can prevent them from completing tasks to the best of their ability. Children with ADHD often show **erratic behaviour** — this may lead to them being removed from lessons, which also disrupts their learning.
    - Studies suggest that between 20 and 25% of children with ADHD have a specific **learning difficulty**. These affect specific aspects of a child's learning, e.g. a child with a **reading disorder** will have lower reading skills (e.g. speed, accuracy) than expected for their age and intelligence.
2) Many children with ADHD experience **failure at school**, with only a minority going on to higher education. This could be partially due to **negative experiences** at school (e.g. problems interacting with peers), leading to a **lack of motivation**.
3) Adults with ADHD often end up in **lower paid**, **temporary employment**.

Practice Questions

Q1 Describe the three subtypes of ADHD.

Q2 Outline Zametkin et al's (1990) study.

Q3 Describe how ADHD may affect a child's social development.

Q4 Suggest why only a minority of children with ADHD go on to higher education.

Exam Questions

Q1 Describe and evaluate an explanation of ADHD. [12 marks]

Q2 Describe and explain how ADHD can impact on a child's development. [12 marks]

Don't know about you but I've got a serious attention deficit right now...

And that's the end of the section — you're done. Well, as soon as you've learnt these two pages that is. You need to know the possible causes and effects of ADHD, as well as the characteristics of the disorder. That last one should be easy to remember — it's probably how you're feeling right now, restless, fidgety, trouble focusing on tasks and easily bored.

Theories of Learning

These two pages (and in fact the whole section) are just for OCR. *This section is all about the psychology of education, so basically you're going to be learning about learning. Those examiners have a warped sense of humour. Oh, and there are a few other theories of learning that you need to know about scattered around in the book — see pages 50-55 for stage theories and social construction theories and page 45 for the theory of multiple intelligences. Good times.*

The **Stimulus-Response Process** May Play a Part in **Learning**

1) Behavioural psychologists focus on **observable stimulus-response processes**.
2) They believe that learning's nothing more than developing new **behaviours** and skills through **conditioning**.
3) **Watson** was a behaviourist who claimed human behaviour is a result of specific **stimuli** triggering specific **responses**. He also believed that these responses could be **changed** quite easily as a result of **experience**.

Watson and Rayner (1920) — Little Albert

Method: A nine-month-old boy named **'Little Albert'** was given a white rat to play with. After an initial period of play, whenever he moved to touch it a metal bar was struck with a hammer behind his head.

Results: Before the **conditioning** took place, Little Albert showed **no fear** of the rat and would play with it happily. After conditioning with the loud noise behind his head, Little Albert began to show **phobic reactions** to the rat and would burst into tears when he saw it.

Conclusion: **Classical conditioning** had been successfully used to create a phobia — Little Albert had learned to **associate** the sight of the rat with a feeling of fear. Later it was found that his phobia also extended to other white furry objects including a rabbit, a dog and even a fur coat.

Evaluation: This study is a useful demonstration of Watson's theory that **stimulus-response** relationships can be **manipulated** relatively easily and even **created artificially**. However, it's highly **unethical**, especially as the conditioning of Little Albert was never **reversed** as the researchers had originally intended.

Rewards and **Punishment Affect Learning**

1) **Skinner** took Watson's stimulus-response idea a step further and declared that behaviour is also affected by its **consequences**, e.g. rewards and punishments. His theories are fundamental to our **education system**:
   - Students work for things that bring **positive** experiences (**reinforcers**), e.g. rewards and praise.
   - Students work to avoid things that bring **negative** experiences (**reinforcers**), e.g. failing exams.
   - Students also work to avoid **punishment**, e.g. detentions.
2) **Habitual** behaviours are developed from those that are **repeated and reinforced** regularly. This is why it's important that teachers develop a routine with classes.
3) A **lack** of reinforcement can also shape behaviour, as the behaviour will then be **changed** until it begins to get some kind of reinforcement. This is why teachers often **ignore** bad behaviour altogether — they hope that the lack of reinforcement will cause the student to change their behaviour in order to receive positive reinforcement.

Ausubel Came Up With the Idea of **Advanced Organisers (AOs)**

Ausubel developed the concept of **advanced organisers**. These take **prior learning** and **knowledge** into account.

1) AOs are **descriptions** of what is about to be learnt — often set out as '**learning objectives**' at the start of a lesson. Teachers may also provide a **list** of topics and sub-topics to describe the new content that's to be covered.
2) AOs can take several other forms, e.g. **narratives** (new information presented in the form of a story) or **graphic organisers** (images and charts used to present new information).
3) AOs are **cognitive strategies** that help learners **integrate** new information with existing knowledge.
4) They can also be used to help teachers monitor **progression** — students can be asked to point out similarities and differences between the old and new facts, make summaries or give critical appraisals.

Ausubel's work pleased **behaviourists** (even though it's a cognitive theory) because he emphasised that learning must be as **active** and **meaningful** as possible — students must show a response to stimuli and must receive reinforcement.

Theories of Learning

Curry Used an *Onion Model* to Categorise Learning Styles

We each have our own strategies and styles when it comes to **learning** — we all approach it in **different** ways. Some approaches are more effective than others, and you can use **more than one** strategy or style at a time. **Curry** (**1983**) reviewed research on many different learning strategies and devised **one model** which pulled **nine** of the main theories together. Curry's model organised learning as follows:

instructional preference
information processing style
personality style

1) **Instructional preference** (outermost layer)
This layer consists of the student's preferred type of **learning environment**.

2) **Information processing style** (middle layer)
This layer is concerned with the way a student **takes in** and **processes** information, e.g. whether they use their senses (sensory registering), make enhanced associations, use a coding system, etc.

3) **Cognitive personality style** (innermost layer)
This layer consists of **personality** dimensions, e.g. how the student's traits influence their approach to learning.

The closer a layer is to the **surface** of the 'onion', the more easily it is **influenced** or changed. The closer a layer is to the **centre** of the 'onion', the more **permanent** and unchangeable it is. This model can be used to **categorise** learning styles and **adjust** learning methods to make the process as **effective** as possible for students.

People Have *Different Cognitive Styles*

Riding and Raynor (1999) devised a four-part model of **cognitive styles**. The model classifies individuals by the way they perceive and remember information, and by their preferred approach to using information in problem-solving.

1A	**Wholist:** likes to see the **complete situation** first.
1B	**Analyst:** likes to see the **constituent parts** first.
2A	**Verbaliser:** prefers to learn through written/spoken **words**.
2B	**Imager:** prefers to learn through **diagrams** or **pictures**.

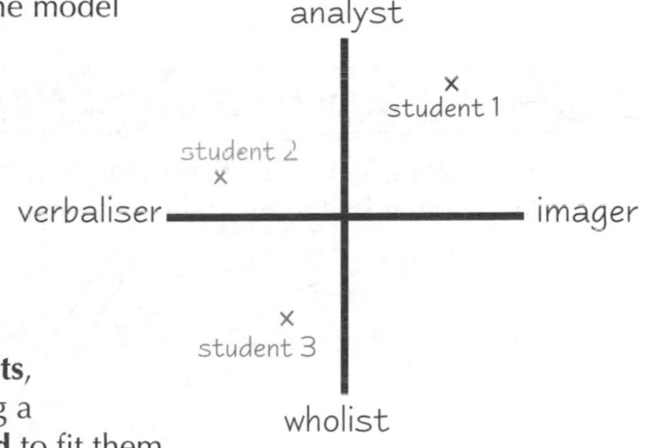

Different individuals will use the various cognitive styles to **different extents**, as shown in the diagram. E.g. student 1 is an analyst and imager. Knowing a student's learning preferences means that learning strategies can be **tailored** to fit them.

Practice Questions

Q1 Explain why Watson and Rayner's (1920) 'Little Albert' study was unethical.

Q2 How did Skinner develop Watson's stimulus-response ideas?

Q3 Explain what is meant by the information processing style in Curry's onion model (1983).

Q4 Name the four cognitive modes described by Riding and Raynor (1999).

Exam Question

Q1 a) Describe one behavioural explanation of knowledge acquisition. [10 marks]

b) Discuss theories that take variations in learning strategies into account. [15 marks]

So now they're comparing students to onions — it's enough to make you cry...

Should be easy enough to remember Curry's onion model. If only the other theories on this page were as delightfully named you'd have no probs. Salad's tomato theory perhaps, or maybe Sandwich's bread model. Sadly, they're not, and instead you need to learn about the rather dull sounding theories of Watson and Rayner, Skinner, Ausubel and Riding and Raynor. Sorry.

Motivating and Encouraging Students

__This is for OCR only.__ Motivation for doing things varies between people. Your motivation to read these pages is probably to find out more about the fascinating theories and delight in my dazzling wit. Or perhaps it's just to pass your exams.

Motivation Can Come From Internal or External Sources

Your **motivation** is basically the reasons you engage in certain behaviours.
It's often referred to as a 'drive' and can come from a variety of sources.

1) **Intrinsic motivation** comes from internal sources (within you), e.g. a sense of **enjoyment** or **achievement**.

2) **Extrinsic motivation** comes from external sources (outside you), e.g. a **monetary reward** or a **punishment**.

Claxton believes that students should develop **intrinsic motivation** rather than relying on rewards and punishments (external motivation). He suggests that this can be done by teachers acting as **'coaches'** — helping students to think about their **feelings** about learning and re-evaluate the **costs and benefits** they associate with it.

Motivation to Learn May Link to Your Drive to Stay Alive

Psychodynamic psychologists (e.g. **Freud**) argue that motivation is linked to two basic **drives** in the unconscious mind — the **'life'** and **'death'** drives, **Eros** and **Thanatos**. According to this theory, you're motivated to learn because it helps you satisfy your life drive (**Eros**). For example:

1) By gaining qualifications you increase your chance of earning a good **salary**.
2) This means you can afford a nicer lifestyle and will be more attractive to potential **reproductive partners**.
3) A nice home, food, healthcare and partner should result in healthy children who can pass your **genes** on.

Learning May Be a Basic Human Need

Maslow (1943) devised a **hierarchy** to show how human needs can be **categorised** and **prioritised**.
This is a **humanist theory** and is known as **Maslow's Hierarchy of Needs**:

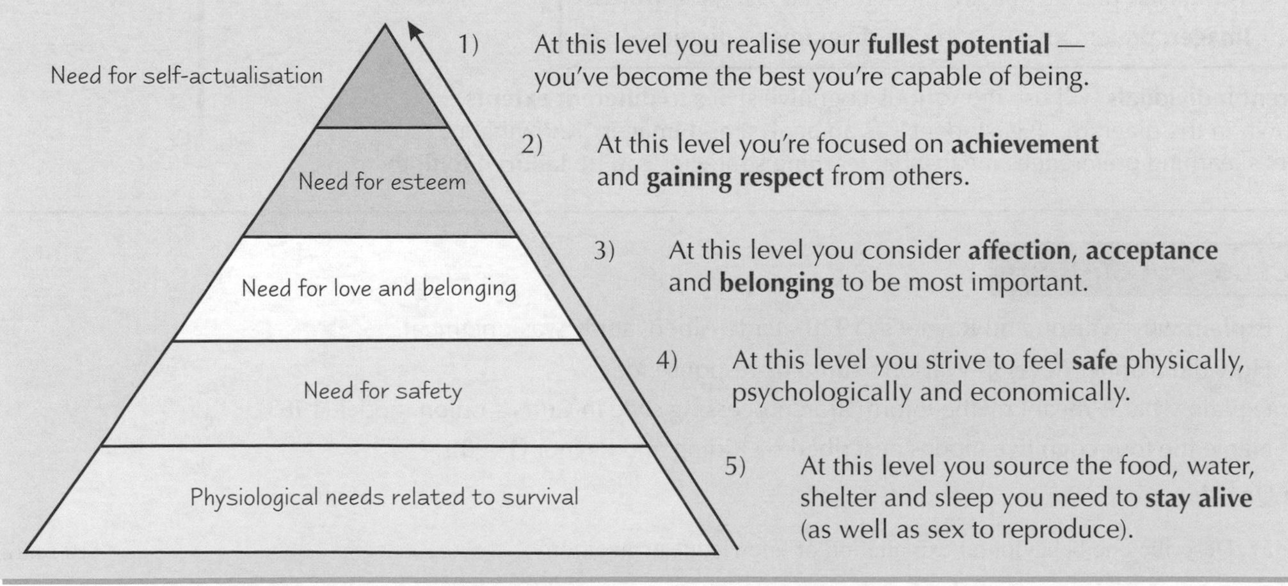

Need for self-actualisation
Need for esteem
Need for love and belonging
Need for safety
Physiological needs related to survival
1) At this level you realise your **fullest potential** — you've become the best you're capable of being.
2) At this level you're focused on **achievement** and **gaining respect** from others.
3) At this level you consider **affection**, **acceptance** and **belonging** to be most important.
4) At this level you strive to feel **safe** physically, psychologically and economically.
5) At this level you source the food, water, shelter and sleep you need to **stay alive** (as well as sex to reproduce).

Maslow believed that we spend our entire lives trying to reach the **top** of the hierarchy, but that **nobody** ever gets there. Sad. He also stated that until **lower level needs** are met, you **can't** attempt to satisfy higher level needs.

This seems to make sense if you apply it to **real life** — e.g. who'd be interested in reading a psychology book if they were extremely hungry or in immediate physical danger... This has obvious implications for **education** and explains why it's so important for teachers to consider the **backgrounds** of their students.

Motivating and Encouraging Students

Attribution Can Affect Motivation

Weiner suggests that the way you **perceive** events in your life can have a massive influence on your level of motivation. He proposed that people **attribute** (explain) their own and other people's behaviour in different ways — they either put it down to internal or external factors. Weiner suggests that forming an attribution is a **three-stage process**:

1) You **observe** a specific behaviour.
2) You determine that the behaviour was **intentional**.
3) You attribute the behaviour to **internal** or **external** causes.

Weiner reckoned that the most important factors when it comes to making attributions are **ability**, **effort**, **task difficulty** and **luck**. He also stated that there are three **fundamental dimensions** linked to these factors — individuals use these to **explain** and **justify** their own actions and the actions of people around them.

1) **Locus of control**: whether control over the action is located **internally** or **externally**.
2) **Stability**: whether the cause **changes** over time or not.
3) **Controllability**: whether the cause is something you can feasibly **control** or not.

Attribution theory suggests that, overall, people tend to make **self-serving attributions** — they take the credit if they've done well but blame external causes if they've failed. They're driven to do this by motivational and emotional factors.

Attributing behaviour to an **internal cause** means you've made a **dispositional attribution** — you've decided that factors within the person caused the behaviour.

1) In situations of **failure** you're far more likely to make dispositional attributions of **other people**. 'They failed the exam because they're stupid.'
2) In situations of **success** you're far more likely to make dispositional attributions of **yourself**. 'I passed the exam because I'm clever.'

Attributing behaviour to an **external cause** means you've made a **situational attribution** — you've decided that factors outside the person caused the behaviour.

1) In situations of **failure** you're far more likely to make situational attributions of **yourself**. 'I failed the exam because it was noisy outside.'
2) In situations of **success** you're far more likely to make situational attributions of **other people**. 'It was a really easy exam.'

Practice Questions

Q1 What is the difference between intrinsic motivation and extrinsic motivation?

Q2 Explain how the life drive 'Eros' might motivate someone to learn.

Q3 List the five levels in Maslow's hierarchy of needs.

Exam Question

Q1 a) Describe a humanist theory of motivation. [10 marks]

b) Discuss cognitive theories of motivation. [15 marks]

I fell over because it's very slippery, but he fell over because he's stupid...

Well, we never had all this motivational coaching lark in my day, I'll tell you that for ninepence. It was the old carrot and the stick when I was at school — eat this carrot, they said, or I'll hit you with this stick. And I've turned out alright. Still, if thinking over your feelings about learning and doing a cost-benefit analysis floats your boat, who am I to argue...

Motivating and Encouraging Students

OCR only. *People aren't robots. How much we enjoy our learning makes a huge difference to our level of success.*

Play Has an Important Role in Learning

1) **Play** is a behaviour that you find in animals with an advanced level of **cognitive complexity**.
2) Play actually requires a lot of **thinking** — it's self-directed and imaginative.
3) Play helps you **explore** your world and **develop skills** through your senses — it helps you **learn**.

Research has been carried out to see how play benefits learning.

	Weikart (1993) — The need for play
Method:	This was an **independent measures** design involving 123 African-American children aged 3 or 4 years old. The participants were split into **two groups**. One of the groups had **no preschooling**, the other group followed a **'High/Scope' preschool programme**, which is based around **child initiated activities** and **actively learning** by **doing**. Data was collected from **school records**, **IQ tests** and **interviews** with the participants, their parents and teachers. The study continued until the participants were 27.
Results:	At ages 5-7, participants who'd followed the High/Scope programme scored **significantly higher** in **IQ tests** than participants who had no preschooling. They also did better in **reading** and **maths** and showed **more commitment** to school. By age 19, a significantly higher proportion of participants who hadn't attended preschool had been **arrested** than those who attended High/Scope. By age 27, the High/Scope participants had a **higher rate of high school graduation, higher earnings** and **fewer arrests**.
Conclusion:	**Active learning programmes** that use **play** have long-lasting **benefits** including more pro-social behaviour and confidence in adolescence. They may help to develop social and cognitive skills, which lead to greater **school readiness**.
Evaluation:	There's a long gap between pre-school and adolescence and many **extraneous variables** are likely to have affected the participants during this time. The results only show a **correlation** — cause and effect can't be determined here.

*You Need **Emotional Intelligence** to Learn Successfully*

1) **Emotional intelligence** (EI) is the ability to **understand** and **manage** your own and other people's **emotions**.
2) So, if you have a **high EI**, you manage emotions and relationships **well**.
3) **Goleman (1995)** reckoned that you need a good understanding of your own and other people's emotions in order to be a **successful learner**.
4) Students who **underperform** at school or who have behavioural problems are often found to have **low EI**.

Jess had a high EI so knew she was feeling extremely irritated by the giant red man muscling in on her photo.

The **four domains** of emotional intelligence are:

Self-awareness

Do you know which **emotions** you're feeling and why?

Do you understand how your emotions affect your **behaviour**?

Are you aware of your **strengths** and **weaknesses**?

Self-management

Can you manage your **impulsive** and **negative** feelings effectively?

Do you stay **calm** and think clearly under pressure?

Are you **flexible** and can you cope with change?

Social awareness

Do you **listen** well to others?

Can you relate well to people from **different backgrounds**?

Are you **sensitive** to the emotions of other people?

Relationship management

Do you communicate **clear messages**?

Are you able to **inspire** and **guide** people?

Do you work well in a **team**?

Motivating and Encouraging Students

Ability Grouping Can Have **Positive** and **Negative** Effects

When people are placed in groups according to their level of ability it's called **ability grouping**.

Sukhnandan and Lee (1998) — Implications of ability grouping

Method:	This was a **literature review** of over 20 studies into the effects of **ability grouping** on students. It focused on comparing **streaming** (where students are assigned to one particular class based on overall ability and stay with that class for most/all subjects), **setting** (where students are assigned to a group for each subject based on ability in that particular subject) and **within-class grouping** (where a class is divided into smaller groups and each group is given different tasks/instructions) to **mixed ability teaching** (where the class is formed of students with a range of abilities and everyone receives the same tasks/instructions).
Results:	No significant difference was found between the different conditions. Streaming and setting both appeared to **reinforce social divisions** between students and had **no positive impact** on the achievement of students (it may even have a **negative impact** on 'bottom set' students).
Conclusion:	Streaming and setting should be **abandoned** in schools, as they do more **harm** than good.
Evaluation:	Studies like this have benefits — they have implications for **real-life situations**. However, many other studies have **challenged** these findings, e.g. **Argys et al (1996)** found a negative impact on the performance of **higher ability** students when lower ability students were moved into their class.

The positive effects of setting and streaming

1) Higher ability students don't have to **wait** for others to catch up, and lower ability students don't have to try and **rush** their work.
2) Teachers can deliver lessons with the **right level of detail** for the abilities of the students.
3) Students may work **harder** to try and stay in a 'good' set, or to move up into one.

The negative effects of setting and streaming

1) Students often feel **labelled** by their set. Those in lower sets may experience **low self-esteem** — this can cause them to stop trying altogether.
2) Students in lower sets/streams are often from **ethnic minorities** and **lower socio-economic** backgrounds — this suggests that the system may discriminate against these students.
3) Even within sets and streams there will be a **range** of abilities — no students are ever identical.

Practice Questions

Q1 How can play help children to learn?

Q2 What is involved in a 'High/Scope' learning programme?

Q3 What is meant by the term 'emotional intelligence'?

Q4 Name the four domains of emotional intelligence.

Q5 What was the main conclusion of Sukhnandan and Lee's (1998) study?

Exam Question

Q1 a) Outline how emotion can be a factor in learning. [10 marks]

b) Discuss the effects of grouping students according to ability, referring to relevant research. [15 marks]

Alright Year 13 — who wants to play in the wendy house...

It's not just humans who play — lots of other animals with complex behaviours and social bonds also play when they're young. It helps them learn and develop skills they'll need to survive in later life. Humans continue their play as adults, and again they're not alone — adult dolphins also play, and those of you with dogs and cats will know that they do too.

Beliefs and Expectations

This bit's just for OCR. *Success at school may have just as much to do with how you think about yourself as it does with doing your homework. That's not an excuse for putting this book down and going off for a daydream though...*

Conforming to the Role of 'Student' May Be the First Hurdle

When children first start school there's a strong expectation that they'll **conform** to the role of 'student' and show respect for their teachers in the form of **obedience**. Students who choose not to conform to this **stereotype** often underperform — it's thought that this is because they're less well-adjusted to school life and learning.

Riley (1995) — Adjustment to school

Method:	The **reading development** of children arriving at school was assessed as they progressed from basic literacy to early reading. This was compared to how positively or negatively they'd **adjusted** to their new school and role as students.
Results:	Children who had a **slow** or **negative** adjustment to school were **four times worse** at reading by the end of their first year compared to those who had a **quick** and **positive** adjustment to school.
Conclusion:	The **willingness to conform** to the role of being a student may have an impact on academic achievement.
Evaluation:	These findings are only **correlational**, so cause and effect can't be identified for certain. For example, students who failed to conform to their roles may have more difficult home circumstances — this could lead to behavioural difficulties and also mean they had less support with their reading at home.

A Perceived Lack of Control Can Cause You to Stop Trying

Seligman believed that humans and animals **learn** to act in a **helpless** way in certain situations as a result of their past **experiences**. Although his theory has useful applications for education, his studies were a bit on the **unethical** side...

Seligman and Maier (1967) — Dogs and electric shocks: Part 1

Method:	Dogs were allocated to three different conditions. **Group 1** dogs were put in harnesses, left for a time and then removed from the harnesses. **Group 2** and **Group 3** dogs were paired up and put in harnesses together and then given **painful electric shocks**. In **Group 2**, one dog of each pair had access to a **lever**, which when pressed would **stop** the electric shock. In **Group 3**, one dog in each pair also had access to a lever, but this did **nothing** when pressed. To make it even more complicated, the Group 3 dogs' shock would only stop when the Group 2 dog pressed its lever to stop its electric shock.
Results:	Group 3 dogs showed signs of **clinical depression** long after the Group 1 and Group 2 dogs had recovered.
Conclusion:	The Group 3 dogs had realised that they had no control over their electric shocks and so 'gave up' psychologically — they were demonstrating **learned helplessness**.

Seligman and Maier (1967) — Dogs and electric shocks: Part 2

Method:	The dogs were then placed in a box where they received further electric shocks. They were able to avoid the shocks if they **jumped** over a low partition into another part of the box.
Results:	The Group 1 and 2 dogs jumped the partition but the **Group 3** dogs **stayed** where they'd been placed — many just lay down and whined.
Conclusion:	The Group 3 dogs had previously learned that they couldn't control their situation, so they didn't believe they had any control in the new situation either — they had **generalised** their helplessness.

Although very cruel and **unethical** these experiments do provide convincing evidence. Although they used dogs, research with humans has found **similar effects** — people who experience a lack of control demonstrate learned helplessness and become more **passive** and less able to **improve** their situation as a result. This has implications for **learning** — those who struggle without success and feel helpless may be more likely to **give up** altogether. A lack of control in other areas of life could also affect learning if the feeling of helplessness is **generalised**. So, it's important for teachers to consider students' backgrounds.

Beliefs and Expectations

Self-esteem May Be an Important Part of Success in Education

1) It's a pretty common idea that if you have low self-esteem and think you're going to fail at something, then you probably won't actually do too well.
2) Maslow's Hierarchy of Needs (page 196) suggests that you need to feel that you're **accepted** by others and that you **belong** before you can focus on improving yourself **intellectually**.
3) **Carl Rogers** was a **humanistic** psychologist who agreed with this principle — he developed the concept of **student-centred learning** in order to help boost **self-esteem**.

In student-centred learning:

1) The needs of the **student** are put first.
2) Only topics that have **direct relevance** to the student and their future are covered.
3) Students are encouraged to take an **active role** in their education, rather than just passively receiving information.

This is the opposite to traditional education — where teachers were at the centre of learning.

Rogers believed that approaching education in this way would allow students to spend more time on **experiential learning**, as opposed to traditional **cognitive learning**. This goes back to the idea that we don't learn by being told — we learn by **doing**.

Boosting student self-esteem through student-centred learning has the following benefits:

1) Students will feel more **confident** and so will be more willing to try new experiences that stretch and **challenge** them.
2) Students will feel more **motivated** to succeed. This should make them better able to overcome any **obstacles** in their way.
3) Students will feel more **assertive** — they'll be more likely to **ask** for the help and resources that they need.

Mark liked the "learning by doing" approach but was starting to think some instructions on landing might have been helpful.

There's more on Rogers' theory on the next page.

Practice Questions

Q1 Which area of learning did Riley focus on in his 1995 study?

Q2 Why is it difficult to determine cause and effect in Riley's study?

Q3 What term was used to describe the 'giving up' behaviour of the Group 3 dogs in Seligman's experiments?

Q4 How is Maslow's Hierarchy of Needs relevant to Rogers' ideas about student-centred learning?

Q5 What happens in student-centred learning?

Exam Questions

Q1 a) Describe how conformity to social roles may affect academic success. [10 marks]

b) Discuss how the concept of learned helplessness could be applied to students. [15 marks]

Q2 a) Outline relevant research which informs us about how a lack of control can lead to learned helplessness. [10 marks]

b) Discuss, using relevant research, how low self-esteem and negative attitudes could affect learning. [15 marks]

You need to learn this stuff. Take my word for it, don't wait to find out...

Oooh that Seligman, I'd like to give him a taste of his own medicine. Let's put him in a harness and administer some electric shocks and see how he feels about it — I bet he'd be feeling pretty fed up after a couple of hours too. Nowadays things are more tightly controlled (see p.220) but in the past some pretty cruel things were done in the name of science.

Personal and Social Development

Just for OCR again. *Your time at school isn't just about the academic side of things. You'll also develop personally and socially during your adolescent years, and these changes in identity will also affect your education and learning.*

Erikson Said You Have to Work Through Crises Throughout Life

Erik Erikson (great name) believed that everyone experiences **crises** throughout their lives and that to develop a **healthy personality** you must work through several conflicts. He described **eight** of these typical **psychosocial stages**:

Age	Psychosocial conflict	Successful outcome
1st year	Trust vs. mistrust	Infants learn to trust their caregiver
2nd year	Autonomy vs. shame/doubt	Children develop independence in basic skills (failure leads to self-doubt)
3–6	Initiative vs. guilt	Children begin to exert control and power (but too much causes guilt)
6 to puberty	Industry vs. inferiority	This is in more detail below — lucky you
Adolescence	Identity vs. identity confusion	Teens develop a sense of self and personal identity
Early adulthood	Intimacy vs. isolation	Young adults form intimate relationships
Middle age	Generativity vs. stagnation	Adults create and build things that will outlast them and contribute to society, e.g. children, careers, homes
Old age	Integrity vs. despair	Older adults reflect on their life and feel fulfilled (or regretful)

The **industry/inferiority conflict** is particularly relevant to education and learning:

1) When we first start school it comes as a shock to the system. The things that are valued by the adults around us seem to **change**. We're no longer **rewarded** for just playing — we're expected to work.
2) Children quickly realise that to gain praise and rewards they must be **academically successful**. Some will therefore work hard and enjoy learning — they'll demonstrate '**industry**'.
3) On the other hand, some children **fail** to achieve and might start to feel '**inferior**', especially if they feel they're a **disappointment** to adults like their parents and teachers.

Acceptance and Approval Are Very Important

1) **Carl Rogers**, a humanistic psychologist, believed that all learners have a basic need to be **accepted** by others (see Maslow's Hierarchy of Needs, page 196). This has to be fulfilled **before** they can reach their academic potential.
2) He claimed that students actively seek out the **approval** of others and constantly look for ways to **impress** their teachers and fellow students (although this may be in the form of **disruptive attention-seeking**).
3) When the learner feels that they're accepted by others they become more confident that their '**real self**' (how they are) is congruent with their '**ideal self**' (how they'd like to be). They experience boosted **self-esteem** and make good learners — **independent**, **creative**, **assertive** and **flexible**.
4) When the learner feels that they're **not** accepted by others they become worried that their 'real self' is incongruent with their 'ideal self'. They experience feelings of **rejection**, **depression**, **alienation** and **hostility**. In this state they **won't** make good learners.
5) Rogers believed that students could be divided into **high**, **low** and **medium self-esteem** groups, and that level of self-esteem is **directly related** to academic success.

Personal and Social Development

Moral Development *May Be Linked to Understanding* ***Social Rules***

Developmental psychologists have many contrasting views on how the development of children's **morals** links to their understanding of **social rules**. Some claim that moral and social rules develop together as **one entity**, while others claim they're **completely different thought processes**. There's more on moral development on pages 56–57.

Piaget (**1932**) believed children learn morals and social rules by **actively engaging** with the world and with others:

1) Initially, children stick to rules because they have a strong **respect** for people in **authority roles** (i.e. adults). This is known as the **heteronomous** stage.
2) Gradually, children begin to realise that rules are **useful** in **social interactions**, e.g. rules for co-operation help relationships with peers to run smoothly. This is known as the **autonomous** stage.
3) To help moral and social understanding, children should be taught how to make decisions and solve problems **co-operatively** with others. They should be encouraged to develop rules based on **fairness**.

Kohlberg (**1981**) believed that children learn morals and social rules as a way to **avoid punishment**:

1) Children are **afraid** of **punishment** and the consequences of **disobedience** — it's **not** that they have an inherent respect for authority (as Piaget thought).
2) Children focus very much on the **consequences** of actions, so this is what they consider when making decisions about moral and social rules.
3) To help with moral and social understanding, children should be taught how to move up to the next level of **moral reasoning**. They'll then be able to consider and overcome **contradictions** of their fixed views, e.g. by taking into account **intentions** as well as consequences.

Turiel (**1983**) identified **two separate domains** — moral and social:

1) Children's **moral domain** consists of ideas and beliefs about **rights**, **fairness** and **harm**. These ideas are **rigid** and there'll be an immediate **black or white** response if others break these rules.
2) Children's **social conventional domain** consists of ideas and beliefs about the **function of rules**, e.g. in order to maintain an orderly classroom. These ideas are much more **flexible** and dependent upon context — there'll be **grey areas** in what children agree counts as a transgression.

Practice Questions

Q1 What did Erikson mean by the terms 'industry' and 'inferiority'?

Q2 Name three other psychosocial conflicts identified by Erikson.

Q3 Explain what Rogers meant by the terms 'real self' and 'ideal self'.

Q4 What does the heteronomous stage of Piaget's theory of development involve?

Q5 What were the two domains identified by Turiel (1983)?

Exam Question

Q1 a) Describe one theory of moral development in the context of social rules. [10 marks]

b) Discuss why acceptance and approval are important in learning. [15 marks]

No, I didn't do my homework — my self-esteem was a bit low last night...

Actually that would be a rubbish excuse. The feelings Carl Rogers is talking about don't work like that — you probably wouldn't even be aware of them. His ideas can explain why some people give up on school altogether and seek their approval elsewhere, which can sometimes lead them into trouble. So stick to 'the dog ate my homework' instead...

Interactions Between Students

These pages are just for OCR. *Interactions with your peers at school help you to develop social skills and abilities that you can't get from interacting just with adults. But not all peer interactions are pleasant experiences.*

*Development of **Empathy** and **Morals** is Affected by **Others***

Gilligan (1982) proposed the following stages for the development of **empathy** and **morals**:

1) Level one: **self-oriented** — your focus is on your **survival** and your own needs.
2) Level two: **other-oriented** — your own needs are devalued as you recognise the needs of **others** instead.
3) Level three: **universal oriented** — you're aware of universal obligations towards **both** yourself and others.

Gilligan also suggested that many theories about the development of empathy and morals are **incorrect** — they attempt to find **similarities** between males and females, often by taking an **androcentric** (male-centred) view. Instead, she proposed that, in general:

1) Girls develop their morality based on **caring** and **responsibility**.
2) They emphasise **connections** between people.
3) Their guiding rule is to **never turn away someone who's in need**.

1) Boys develop their morality based on **justice** and **rights**.
2) They emphasise **separations** between people.
3) Their guiding rule is to **always treat others fairly**.

Gilligan suggests that in order for both males and females to develop empathy and morals to the highest level, the education system must avoid looking for a narrow **'one size fits all'** set of human capacities. It should instead focus on helping both male and female students to **discover** their own strengths and **respect** the strengths of others.

Academic Success** is Affected by **Relationships With Peers

Hartup (1989) distinguished between **vertical** and **horizontal** relationships:

1) **Vertical relationships** occur between students and their **parents** and **teachers**.
They provide you with **protection** and **security** and help you gain knowledge and independence.
2) **Horizontal relationships** occur between students and their **peers**.
They help you to develop basic skills (e.g. cooperation), as you're exposed to many **complex interactions**.
3) Hartup believed that **both** types of relationship are needed for optimum development.

Horizontal relationships can affect **academic performance** in different ways, depending on their nature.

Academic success is helped by friendships

Students who make **friends** amongst their peers are likely to become **better learners** because:

1) They have enhanced **self-esteem**, which gives increased **motivation** and **positive risk-taking** (p.201).
2) They enjoy lessons more as they enjoy the **alliance** and **companionship** of other learners.
3) They feel able to **express** themselves in group work, and are willing to share **physical resources**.

Academic success is hindered by bullying

It's been suggested that students who experience **bullying** are likely to **suffer academically**, because:

1) **Self-confidence** diminishes — students are less likely to contribute to lessons for fear of **ridicule**.
2) **Behavioural problems** may develop as a reaction to feeling upset and **angry**, or as a means of **impressing** other students.
3) Students may fail to attend school at all, and **truant** to avoid the bullying.

Bullying can be **verbal**, **physical** or **mental** — and bullying via text and email is on the increase.

Interactions Between Students

A 'Whole School Approach' Can Help Tackle Bullying

Tatum and Herbert (1997) reckoned that in order to successfully **reduce bullying** a number of key factors must be considered — they came up with what's known as a '**whole school approach**'.

Home/school partnership — where **parents** and the **school** work together as a team:

1) Parents are involved in the initial drafting of the school's **anti-bullying policy**.
2) Parents are provided with a copy of school **rules** and may be asked to sign home/school **contracts**.
3) Parents are kept informed about new **anti-bullying initiatives** in school and are encouraged to get involved.
4) An '**open door**' policy is promoted, so parents feel comfortable in contacting the school about bullying.

Peer support — where **other students** are used to support victims of bullying, or potentially vulnerable students:

1) **Befriending schemes** involve vulnerable students being paired up with kind students who'll look after them.
2) **Peer mentoring schemes** involve introducing vulnerable students to older students who can give advice.
3) **Conflict resolution** or **circle time** — these methods encourage students to openly air their concerns and tackle the causes of anti-social behaviour. They're often used in primary schools.
4) **Co-operative group work** — teachers will often carefully select students for group work to avoid situations where there's a risk of bullying. This will also promote co-operative work.

Herbert (1989) believed that getting **peers** involved is very important in tackling bullying. He thought that the **social pressure** from other students to behave pro-socially is much more effective than the **condemnation** of individual bullies by someone in **authority** like a teacher or parent.

Assertiveness training — where 'at risk' students are given training to reduce their chances of being a victim. They're taught:

1) To realise that the bullies are the **weak** people, not those who are bullied.
2) How to use body language, eye contact and tone of voice to appear more **confident**.
3) Strategies for **responding verbally** to threats, manipulation, name calling, etc.
4) How to get **support** from others to help stop the bullying.

Although these sorts of programmes **vary** massively from school to school they've enjoyed **great success** — in some schools they've reduced bullying by up to **80%**.

Practice Questions

Q1 What was Gilligan's (1982) main criticism of theories of moral development?

Q2 What is meant by a vertical relationship?

Q3 Give two ways that friendships with peers can help academic performance.

Q4 Explain what is meant by a 'home/school partnership'.

Exam Question

Q1 a) Describe how friendships and bullying can affect academic success. [10 marks]

b) Discuss strategies for reducing bullying in schools. [15 marks]

I'm not talking in class — I'm developing my horizontal relationships...

Bullying is a horrible thing. Everybody knows that the bullies are the weak ones and are just doing it to hide their own insecurities and feel more powerful, but that doesn't really help when you're the one being tormented by them all the time. There's lots that can be done about it now though, so nobody should have to suffer in silence. Or, for that matter, suffer at all.

Interactions Between Students and Teachers

These two pages are reserved for OCR students. *Students are taught by teachers. And teachers are people (mostly). So, guess what... there are social psychological factors that come into play when they interact as well. Marvellous.*

The **FIA** Compares Teacher and Student **Communications**

The **Flanders Interaction Analysis** (FIA) is a system that focuses on **spoken** communication patterns in classrooms.

1) A repeated measures design is used to observe lessons.
2) In each lesson several **measures** of communication are taken, e.g. video recordings, notes using codes, etc.
3) **Ten categories** are used to classify the different forms of communication — **patterns** from the lessons emerge across these categories:

The FIA focuses on spoken communication, but remember that a lot of the communication between teacher and students is non-verbal (eye contact, tone of voice, gestures, etc.). This can also transmit their expectations to students (see below).

Teachers generally show more **initiating** behaviour — they lead the lesson and introduce new ideas. They may:

1) **Accept feelings** of students, and clarify or repeat their feelings so other students can hear.
2) **Praise or encourage** ideas or behaviour, or give positive non-verbal feedback (e.g. nodding).
3) **Accept or use ideas of students**, e.g. by building on an idea or suggestion.
4) **Ask questions** about the lesson content.
5) **Lecture**, giving facts or opinions with little input from the students.
6) **Give directions**, **commands or orders** which the students are expected to comply with.
7) **Criticise or justify authority**, where the teacher attempts to change unacceptable behaviour.

Students generally show more **responding** behaviour — they react to ideas.

8) **Student response to teacher** — where freedom to express their own ideas is limited.
9) **Student initiation** — where students are able to start a new line of thought and ask questions.

There's a tenth category that's used when teachers and students **aren't** showing a particular type of behaviour.

10) **Silence or confusion** — points in the lesson where the FIA observer can't draw any conclusions.

Teachers Have Certain **Expectations** of Students

1) When a teacher first meets a student they might make a **snap judgement** about what to expect from them, based on **age**, **gender**, **ethnicity**, **social class** and **physical appearance**.
2) Teachers may also base their judgements on **quantitative** details of a student's **prior attainment**, or on **qualitative** information that previous teachers have shared. Teachers may even make judgements if they've taught other members of the **same family**.
3) Depending on whether the teacher has high or low **expectations** of a student, they'll **behave differently** when they interact with them. This will affect the student's **reaction** to the teacher and their **future interactions**.
4) If a teacher has **high** expectations, students feel **valued** and **challenged**. They usually work hard to live up to the aspirations that their teacher has for them.
5) If a teacher has **low** expectations, students **aren't motivated** and may **behave badly** as they've less to strive for.
6) Both outcomes will further **reinforce** the teacher's expectations, and so the pattern continues. The teacher has **labelled** the student, and the label has become a **self-fulfilling prophecy**.

- **Brophy and Good (1974)** found that students seen as high achievers were given chances to answer questions **three to four times more often** than those seen as low achievers. Low achievers also received **less feedback** than their peers.
- **Kerman (1979)** found that teachers worried about **embarrassing** low ability students and so called on them less. However, this just encouraged these students to **'tune out'**.

Interactions Between Students and Teachers

*Moving From **Primary** to **Secondary** School Involves **Changes***

Galton and Morrison (**2000**) found that many primary school students experience a lot of **apprehension** about moving to secondary school, as they face many **changes** to their school routine. For example:

Primary

1) Students stay with **one** teacher for all subjects.
2) Students stay in **one** room on quite a **small** site.
3) Students stay with the **same** classmates all day.

Secondary

1) Students may see upwards of **15** teachers, one or more for each subject.
2) Students move to a **different** room for every lesson, on a much **bigger** school site.
3) Students may be split into **different** subject groups or sets for each lesson.

*Primary and Secondary **Teachers** Use **Different Approaches***

1) **Galton et al** (**1999**) conducted an analysis of the **teaching styles** of primary school teachers, and found that most of the time they were focused on **containing** and **supervising** student activity.
2) **Open questions** (where a variety of possible ideas and solutions are acceptable) were **rarely** used (only **5%** of the time).
3) **Closed questions** (where only one specific answer is acceptable) and **factual recital** questions were used relatively **frequently** (**18%** and **29%** of the time respectively).
4) **Most** frequently used were questions relating to **task supervision** (**32%**) and a significant amount of questioning (**15%**) was also devoted to **routine matters**.

It's much harder to determine patterns in the questioning used by secondary school teachers as each subject requires a different approach. However, in general, many more **open questions** are asked and students are expected to be a lot more **independent** in their learning (e.g. using note taking, research and revision).

Galton suggested **'bridging'** or **'transition' projects** would help to link primary and secondary learning:

1) Students **start** a project with their class teacher at the end of **Year 6**.
2) Students **complete** the project at the start of **Year 7** within one or more subjects.
3) Ideally, students also work on the project with their **parents** over the summer to strengthen the link.
4) Although such projects are growing in popularity there are obvious **practical problems** to overcome, as all schools in the area need to participate in the scheme in order for all children to be able to take part.

Practice Questions

Q1 Briefly describe the procedure used in the FIA system.

Q2 Describe the findings of Kerman's (1979) study into how teachers treat low ability students.

Q3 Describe three differences between primary and secondary school.

Exam Question

Q1 a) Outline differences between teacher and student communications. [10 marks]

b) Discuss the effect that teacher expectations may have on a student's attitude and attainment. [15 marks]

One minute you're colouring in, the next it's algebra and Bunsen burners...

It's a confusing time, and it can also be very intimidating. I remember the first few days of my time at 'big school' — the uniform was different, the kids were different, the teachers were different, and I spent most of my time wandering around the maze of corridors trying to find room 9B and wishing I was safe back in my cosy primary school classroom.

Dealing With Students' Needs

These pages are (surprise surprise) for OCR. *No two students are the same, so a big part of educational psychology looks at dealing with individual needs. This is especially important for those with special educational needs.*

Individual Support Can Help *Lower-Achieving Students*

1) **Bloom (1984)** found that students' results improve when they're taught on an **individual** (one-to-one) basis.
2) He also found the biggest improvement was with previously **low-achieving** students.
3) Bloom developed a model known as a **taxonomy** to show the hierarchy of different learning and thinking skills. He reckoned that **individual support** could help students to develop skills and **move up** the hierarchy.
4) **Anderson and Krathwohl** (**2001**) modified and updated Bloom's taxonomy. They suggested that students progress through the stages remembering, understanding, applying, analysing, evaluating and creating.

A) **Remembering** and **understanding** are basic **foundation skills** that are usually used in initial learning — whether it's learning to count or learning about rocket science.

B) **Applying** requires students to take the knowledge they already have and **generalise** it to new situations. Some students struggle with this — they need to be explicitly taught links as they can't see the **connections** themselves.

C) **Analysing** and **evaluating** requires students to think **critically** as well as comparing and contrasting ideas. These are higher level skills — they're usually only seen in higher achieving students.

D) **Creating** is the skill at the top of the hierarchy. Students must be completely comfortable with all the other skills — they need to be able to generate their own original **ideas**, **arguments** and **suggestions**.

Lucas was sure that his creativity placed him near the top of the hierarchy.

If a teacher was to give every student in a **mixed ability class** the same task they could, in theory, get several **different** types of response. This would depend on which level each student is working at. For example, if an essay question was set on ethics in psychology, students may:

A) simply **recall** ethics-related facts, perhaps listing the BPS guidelines (**remembering** and **understanding**).
B) talk about how ethics are **used** in research, as well as giving everyday **examples** (**applying**).
C) **critically discuss** ethical issues in research, e.g. weighing up pros and cons (**analysing** and **evaluating**).
D) express a personal **opinion** on the difficulty of designing a study without any ethical issues (**creating**).

1) If students working at the bottom of the hierarchy don't receive **focused**, **individualised support** they're unlikely to **spontaneously** move up to the next stage of thinking. Similarly, students at one of the middle stages are also likely to remain **stuck** where they are.
2) When students receive individual support (either via one-to-one teaching or from a teaching assistant) they can be **guided** towards the higher levels. For example, **frameworks** (structural outlines of the task) can be provided to prompt critical thinking.

Mixed Ability Groups and *Sets* Have *Advantages* and *Disadvantages*

Although there's some evidence to suggest that **higher ability** students **benefit** from being taught in sets rather than mixed ability groups, there's little evidence that **lower ability** students gain any benefits. In fact, placing lower ability students in sets could even have a **negative** effect on them, as their **self-esteem** may suffer, and they'll have fewer **role models**. There's more on the evidence for this, as well as the advantages and disadvantages of ability grouping, on page 199.

Dealing With Students' Needs

Remedial Support Can Be Used to Help Those Who Have Fallen Behind

Remedial just means providing a **remedy** or **repair**. Remedial support programmes like '**Reading Recovery**' are used in schools to help students who've fallen behind get back to where they should be for their age.

Reading Recovery (RR)

1) RR is an **early intervention** programme designed to reduce **literacy problems** in students who show poor progress in their reading and writing after the first year of school.
2) Students undergo **intensive** daily reading/writing sessions with a **specialist** teacher for around 15–20 weeks.
3) Sessions are completely **individualised** and are designed to meet the precise needs of each student.
4) The programme **ends** once the student reaches the **average** literacy level for their age.
5) Students are then **monitored** annually to make sure they don't fall behind again.

Teaching Can Be Tailored to Meet Students' Needs

Differentiation is a **proactive** approach to teaching — teachers **tailor** their approach to meet students' needs, rather than expecting students to modify themselves to fit the teaching. This approach means that the different learning styles of individual students are taken into account and the needs of each student should be met — even in a mixed ability class.

There are several different types of differentiation:

1) **By dialogue:** the complexity of **language** the teacher uses is **tailored** to individual students.
2) **By independence/responsibility: peer** and **self-assessment** is used more often with more able students.
3) **By outcome** or **response:** students answer at their own level so that very **different outcomes** result from the same task. However, there's debate over whether it actually counts as differentiation.
4) **By pace:** less able students move forward **gradually** while more able students are free to move forward as **quickly** as they need to.
5) **By resource or text:** some students can work with more **complex resources** than others — materials are selected based on difficulty (density, readability, actual content, etc.).
6) **By support:** some students need more **help** than others to complete the tasks set. Support can come from various resources, e.g. teaching assistants, other students, etc. — it's not necessarily from the teacher.
7) **By task:** a **variety of tasks** are provided that meet the abilities of individual learners, e.g. a fill-in-the-blanks worksheet (a **cloze exercise**) for less able students, and an **open-ended essay question** for more able students. Both would be on the same topic and done in the same lesson.

Practice Questions

Q1 According to Bloom (1984), which students show the greatest improvement as a result of individual teaching?

Q2 Give one disadvantage of mixed ability groups.

Q3 What is remedial support?

Exam Question

Q1 a) Outline how individual support can help students. [10 marks]

b) Discuss the methods of differentiation that could be used in a mixed ability class. [15 marks]

So everyone should be able to pass their exams — bloomin' marvellous...

Various things to get your head around here — individual support helps you do better at school (never would have guessed that), whilst ability grouping might not be so useful (see p.199 for more details). There's also bits and bobs on differentiation for you to learn. But that shouldn't be a problem. After all, remembering is at the bottom of the thinking skills hierarchy...

Minority Ethnic Groups

Just OCR again — doesn't anyone else do any work around here? *There's evidence that the ethnic group you belong to can have an influence on how well you end up doing at school. Which doesn't seem right to me...*

There Are Differences in the **Academic Success** of Different **Ethnic Groups**

Research carried out into the academic performance of **pre-school** and **primary school** children from different ethnic backgrounds has found **little difference** between ethnic groups. But, by the time pupils reach **secondary school** it's a different story — there are **clear differences** in achievement according to ethnic group.

There are various possible **explanations** for why these patterns occur:

1) **Family life/background** — on average, Chinese students do much better in secondary school than white British students. This could be because Chinese families may tend to be more **supportive** and **encouraging** of their children's schooling and may place a greater emphasis on **achievement** than the parents of white British students.
2) **Subcultures** — as students from ethnic backgrounds are in the minority in most UK schools they may form their own '**in groups**' or '**subcultures**' to gain a sense of **identity** and **belonging**. These groups will have their own group norms and views, which could either help or hinder learning.
3) **Racism** — students who are victims of **racist bullying** may underperform at school, or refuse to attend at all.
4) **Labelling/self-fulfilling prophecies** — if a student is **labelled** by a teacher and is treated in accordance with this label they may start to **internalise** and **accept** it (a self-fulfilling prophecy, see page 206).
5) **Language** — for some students **English isn't their first language**. This causes obvious difficulties if they're being taught in a classroom where English is the main language (see below).

The subculture at Bunington Boys School was very different to your average school.

Language Strategies Can Help Overcome **Language Effects**

1) For **over half** of students in inner London, English is **not** the language they hear at home.
2) More than **300 languages** are spoken by children in London's schools alone.
3) These include **Bengali**, **Turkish**, **Arabic**, **Portuguese**, **French** and **Vietnamese**.
4) Students who aren't taught in their first language are at a **disadvantage** — they may be prevented from achieving their full potential and being academically successful.
5) There are **several strategies** that can be used to help **overcome** language effects.
6) Which one is **most appropriate** depends on several things, e.g. student numbers, number of languages, teacher expertise, funding for resources, etc.

- Students are split into classes or groups where they can be instructed in their **first language** as well as learning English. However, this requires lots of students who speak the same language.

- Students are put in groups with students who speak other languages. The teacher then gives the information **in each language in turn**. However, in one class there could be dozens of languages.

- Students are put in a mainstream English class but have a **teaching assistant** who can **translate** the information for them. However, this can be quite costly.

- Students are put in a mainstream English class and receive **extra English lessons** with an **EAL specialist**. This is the most commonly used method in secondary schools, but there are negatives for the student — e.g. they may not understand all of the language in their mainstream lessons and so may underperform.

Minority Ethnic Groups

Different **Strategies** Can Be Used to **Overcome Prejudice**

Some of the educational difficulties experienced by ethnic minority students may be due to **prejudices** held by peers and teachers from other ethnic backgrounds, or even by students or teachers from the same ethnic group. **Allport's (1954) intergroup contact theory** suggests that these prejudices develop when individuals in a group haven't experienced **positive contact** with individuals of another group.

Strategies that can be used to **overcome** these **prejudices** are important in schools.

Aronson (1978) — The Jigsaw Classroom

1) In Aronson's jigsaw classroom, the class is split into ethnically diverse, equally sized **groups**. The concepts and facts that students need to learn in the lesson are then **split** between the group members, with each student being responsible for learning something different.
2) Once each group member has learnt their part, they have to **teach** their information to the rest of the **group** — so the students will only learn everything once the whole group has contributed.
3) Groups may also be asked to **share** their work with the rest of the class.
4) In this way, students from different ethnic backgrounds are mixed up, are asked to **work together** in **intergroup tasks** and have to **rely on each other** in order to learn.
5) The jigsaw classroom seems to work on an **individual** basis but some evidence suggests that new views aren't **generalised** beyond classmates — they're seen as **exceptions to the rule** and stereotypes still remain.

Klein (1996) — Positive Role Models

1) Klein suggested that many minority ethnic groups have high **aspirations**. However, their **expectations** about actually achieving these are much lower.
2) Students need to see **role models** like them (e.g. with successful careers) to believe that they can also succeed.
3) Students would also benefit from ongoing exposure to **non-traditional role models** and **mentors** — this would help them to break down stereotypes.

Mac An Ghaill (1988) — Positive Support

1) Many girls from ethnic minorities become **inconspicuous** — they don't excel in lessons but don't present behavioural problems either.
2) These girls can therefore end up being **ignored**. This means they might miss out on receiving any real **support** — so they might not reach their true potential.
3) Teachers just need to recognise that they could be encouraged to achieve their potential by being given **adequate** and **appropriate** positive support.

Practice Questions

Q1 Give one possible reason for ethnic differences in educational attainment.

Q2 Why are strategies to overcome prejudice important in schools?

Q3 Outline Aronson's (1978) jigsaw classroom.

Exam Question

Q1 a) Outline strategies that can be used to overcome language effects in schools. [10 marks]

b) Evaluate methods for overcoming prejudice based on ethnic background in education. [15 marks]

If only that Esperanto thing had worked out...

You may be too young to remember, but Esperanto was supposed to be a universal language. Only no-one bothered to learn it.

Gender Differences in Education

A final two pages just for OCR. *There's a 'gender gap' in the UK in terms of how well males and females do at school. Despite a lot of effort to solve this problem, the evidence suggests that the gap is actually getting wider.*

*There Are **Gender Differences** in Educational Achievement*

Females generally do better than males at school, for example:

1) **SATS (Key Stage 3):** each year more females than males achieved a **Level 5** in English, Maths and Science.
2) **GCSEs (Key Stage 4):** females gain more GCSEs at grades **A* to C** than males do.
3) **AS/A2 Levels (Key Stage 5):** females gain more A Level **passes** than males do.

Males tend to excel in subjects that involve **logical**, **spatial**, **sequential** or **physical** work. They often choose subjects such as:

1) Mathematics
2) Physics
3) ICT
4) Engineering
5) Business Studies
6) Physical Education

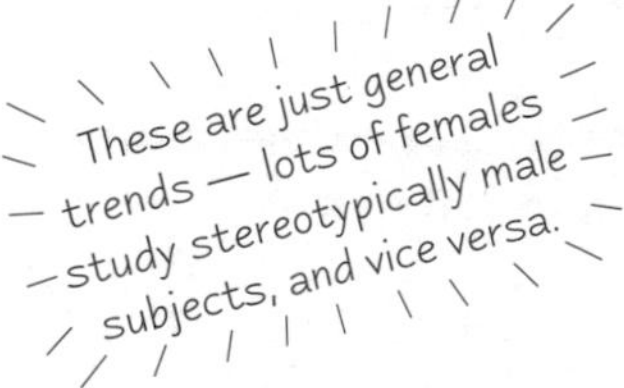

These are just general trends — lots of females study stereotypically male subjects, and vice versa.

Females tend to excel in subjects that involve **verbal**, **imaginative** or **empathetic** work. They often choose subjects such as:

1) Psychology
2) English Language/Literature
3) Art and Design
4) Sociology
5) Biology
6) Languages

*There Are **Biological Differences** Between the **Brains** of Males and Females*

It's been suggested that **biological differences** in male and female brains are the cause of differences in **cognitive abilities** between genders.

1) **Hormones**: many researchers believe the influence of male hormones (e.g. **testosterone**) and female hormones (e.g. **oestrogen**) on the brain **before birth** and during **puberty** may affect cognitive abilities.
2) **Brain weight**: on average, male brains weigh around **1400 grams** whereas female brains weigh around **1250 grams**. However, we need to take relative body mass into account.
3) **Types of tissue**: generally, males have more **grey matter** (responsible for information processing) whereas females have more **white matter** (which provides connections between processing centres).
4) **Lateralisation of function**: some theorists, e.g. **Bradshaw** (**1989**), suggest the **left hemisphere** of the brain is responsible for logical and analytical thought (traditionally thought of as a male trait) whereas the **right hemisphere** controls emotional and creative thought (thought of as a female trait). However, **language** is located in the left hemisphere and **numerical computation** is found in the right hemisphere, so the theory doesn't completely hold.

*An **Evolutionary Perspective** Can Help Explain the Difference*

If you think about it in evolutionary terms, some aspects of the gender gap may be explained:

1) **Males** would have been responsible for **hunting** across large territories, as well as developing and using **tools** — so, logical, spatial, sequential and physical skills would have been required.
2) **Females** would have been responsible for maintaining the **home environment** and for **raising children** — requiring verbal, imaginative and empathetic skills.

Jackie cursed her luck that she was born into a species where the girls had to do everything.

Gender Differences in Education

*Different **Strategles** Can Be Used to Help **Boys and Girls** Learn*

Gender is known to affect education in several ways:

1) **Preferred learning styles** — females are more likely to be **auditory** (talking/listening) learners and males are more likely to be **kinaesthetic** (movement-based) learners.
2) **Behavioural reactions to the school setting** — females are more likely to opt out of education in a **passive**, **non-aggressive** way, while males are more likely to opt out in an **active**, **aggressive** way.
3) **Peer group norms/levels of influence** — females are more likely to **encourage** hard work and **praise** each other for academic success, while males are more likely to **devalue** education and **deride** academic success.
4) **Response to task type** — generally, females perform better with coursework-based tasks, as they respond well to **deadlines** and **open-ended** tasks. Males tend to perform better in exams than coursework as they respond to **pressure** and take a **last-minute** approach.

So, **targeted strategies** are needed to engage and support **both** genders so that no-one is at a disadvantage.

'Boy-friendly' education

1) Include a **competitive** element by turning activities into contests where possible.
2) Set work in a series of short, structured chunks to help maintain **concentration**.
3) Build in opportunities for **kinaesthetic learning** and movement to combat fidgeting.
4) Use **analytic** rather than empathetic approaches, e.g. in English literature males may prefer to analyse the technique an author uses to convey feelings, rather than trying to empathise with the characters themselves.
5) Encourage males to develop their discussion skills by providing **scaffolding** (a framework to guide their discussion).
6) Encourage older male students or fathers to **mentor** students and give positive messages about education.

'Girl-friendly' education

1) Traditionally, more emphasis has been placed on engaging the **boys** in the class, because they're more likely to become disruptive, than on engaging the girls.
2) This often means that girls in mixed gender classes experience a very **androcentric** (male-centred) education — e.g. an English teacher is more likely to select a fiction book about football for a mixed gender group than they are to choose one about ballet.
3) However, there's a growing movement to make sure education is appropriate for the needs and interests of girls. More **'girl-friendly' activities** like group work and discussion tasks are included, and weaker areas are developed, e.g. skills of **précis** (concise communication) and confident group **leadership**.

Practice Questions

Q1 List three subjects typically preferred by males and three typically preferred by females.

Q2 Describe one difference in the type of tissue generally found in male and female brains.

Q3 Explain, from an evolutionary perspective, why males might have developed logical and spatial skills.

Q4 What is meant by a kinaesthetic learner?

Exam Question

Q1 a) Outline the differences in educational achievement in terms of gender. [10 marks]

b) Discuss strategies that can be used to enable the learning of boys and girls. [15 marks]

Come on — let's race to see who can finish their essay first...

Not going to work, is it... You'll see a lot of words like 'generally', 'usually' and 'tend to' on these pages. Nobody's trying to say that all boys like Physics and exams and all girls like English and coursework. Obviously everyone is different, but there are definite trends in what males and females do and achieve, and there's plenty of evidence to prove it too.

Designing Psychological Investigations

Everyone's on board for Research Methods. *If you want to study something, you need to have a clear idea about exactly what information you need to collect, and what the most appropriate method might be.*

Research Takes **Samples** From a **Target Population**

It's really important that the sample is **representative** of the population. It should include the **variety of characteristics** that are found in the group, e.g. the group **'student'** includes both **males** and **females**. If the sample is **biased** in any way, it's hard to **generalise** any findings to the whole population.

There are many different ways to select a sample:

1) **Random sample** Everyone in the target group has an **equal chance** of being selected. Although this is **fair** and will probably provide a **good variety** of people, it doesn't guarantee that the sample will be **representative** — some subgroups could be **missed**.
2) **Systematic sample** Taking every *n*th name from a **sampling frame** (a record of all the names in a population), e.g. every 3rd name from a register, or every 50th name from a phone book. This is useful if there is a sampling frame available, but it isn't **truly random** or **representative**, and subgroups may be missed.
3) **Opportunity sample** Studying **whoever is available** at the time, e.g. students. This is **quick**, **easy** and **cheap**, but it's very unlikely that the sample will be **representative**.
4) **Self-selected sample** Participants **volunteer**, e.g. by responding to a newspaper advertisement. This can **save time** and there may be many replies, producing a **large sample**. However, it's unlikely to be representative as only certain types of people are likely to volunteer.
5) **Stratified sample** All of the **important subgroups** in the population (e.g. different age or ethnic groups) are identified and a **proportionate number** are **randomly obtained**. This can produce a fairly representative sample, but it takes a lot of **time/money** to do and subgroups may be **missed**.

Here's a reminder of some of the different **research methods** used for psychological studies, and their advantages and drawbacks. Most of this should be familiar to you from AS, but you can never have too much information...

Questionnaires — Face-to-Face, on the Phone, or via the Internet

Questionnaires are a **self-report** method.
Self-report methods involve asking participants about their feelings, beliefs and attitudes, etc.

Advantages
Practical — can collect a large amount of information quickly and relatively cheaply.

Disadvantages
Bad questions — leading questions (questions that suggest a desired answer) or unclear questions can be a problem.
Biased samples — some people are more likely to respond to a questionnaire, which might make a sample unrepresentative.
Social desirability bias — people sometimes want to present themselves in a good light.
What they say and what they actually think could be different, making any results unreliable.
Ethics — confidentiality can be a problem, especially around sensitive issues which people might not want to discuss.

Other self-report methods include **interviews** and **case studies** (see page 230).
Self-report methods often provide **qualitative data**.

Correlational Research Looks for **Relationships** Between Variables

Correlation means that two variables appear to be **connected** — they rise and fall together, or one rises as the other falls.

BUT it **doesn't** always mean that one variable **causes** a change in the other, e.g. as age increases so might stress, but ageing doesn't necessarily **cause** stress.

Advantages
Causal relationships — these can be ruled out if no correlation exists.
Ethics — can study variables that would be unethical to manipulate, e.g. is there a relationship between the number of cigarettes smoked and incidences of ill health?

Disadvantages
Causal relationships — these cannot be assumed from a correlation, which may be caused by a third, unknown variable. Sometimes the media (and researchers) infer causality from a correlation.

Designing Psychological Investigations

Experiments can be done in a laboratory or in the natural environment.

Laboratory Experiments are Controlled and Scientific

1) The aim is to **control** all relevant variables except for **one key variable**, which is altered to see what its effect is. The variable that you alter is called the **independent variable** (see p.222).
2) Laboratory experiments are conducted in an **artificial setting**.

Advantages

Control — the effects of extraneous variables (those that have an effect in addition to the key variable, see p.222) are minimised.
Replication — you can run the study again to check the findings.
Causal relationships — it should be possible to establish whether one variable actually causes change in another.

Disadvantages

Ecological validity — experiments are artificial and might not measure real-life behaviour.
Demand characteristics — participants' behaviour changes when they know they're being studied. They may respond according to what they think is being investigated, which can bias the results.
Ethics — deception is often used, making informed consent (see p.218) difficult.

Field Experiments are Conducted Outside the Laboratory

In **field experiments**, behaviour is measured in a **natural environment** — like a school, the street or on a train. A **key variable** is still altered so that its effect can be measured.

Advantages

Causal relationships — you can still establish causal relationships by manipulating the key variable and measuring its effect. However it's very difficult to control all the variables in a field experiment.
Ecological validity — field experiments are less artificial than those done in a laboratory, so they reflect real life better.
Demand characteristics — these can be avoided if participants don't know they're in a study. They will behave as they usually do in real life.

Disadvantages

Less control — extraneous variables are often much more likely in a natural environment.
Ethics — often can't give informed consent and can't be debriefed. Observation must respect privacy.

Natural Experiments Measure but Don't Control Variables

A **natural experiment** is a study where the independent variables **aren't** directly manipulated by the experimenter. In other words, things are left as they naturally would be.

Advantages

Ethics — it's possible to study variables that it would be unethical to manipulate, e.g. you can compare a community that has TV with a community that doesn't to see which is more aggressive.

Disadvantages

Participant allocation — you can't randomly allocate participants to each condition, and so extraneous variables (e.g. what area the participants live in) may affect results. Let's face it — you've got no control over the variables so it's ridiculously hard to say what's caused by what.
Rare events — some groups of interest are hard to find, e.g. a community that doesn't have TV.
Ethics — deception is often used, making informed consent difficult. Also, confidentiality may be compromised if the community is identifiable.

Practice Questions

Q1 Why might you get an unrepresentative sample when carrying out questionnaire-based research?
Q2 Describe a disadvantage of correlational research.
Q3 What are the main advantages of laboratory experiments?

Exam Questions

Q1 Describe what a field experiment is and outline the main advantages and disadvantages. [4 marks]

Q2 Outline the main differences between laboratory experiments and natural experiments. [8 marks]

Designing Psychological Investigations

These pages are for AQA and OCR people only. *All research studies involve some sort of testing or measuring of participants. But, if you want the results to be meaningful, the tests need to be both reliable and valid.*

Reliable *Tests Give* ***Consistent Results***

Reliability refers to how **consistent** or **dependable** a test is. A reliable test carried out in the **same circumstances**, on the **same participants** should always give the **same results**. There are different types of reliability:

Internal reliability — **different parts** of the test should give **consistent results**. For example, if an IQ test contains sections of supposedly equal difficulty, participants should achieve similar scores on all sections.

The internal reliability of a test can be assessed using the **split-half method**. This splits the test into two halves, e.g. odd and even numbered questions, and the results from each half should produce a **high positive correlation**.

External reliability — the test should produce **consistent results** regardless of **when** it's used. For example, if you took the same IQ test on two different days you should achieve the same score.

The external reliability of a test can be assessed using the **test-retest method**. This involves **repeating** the test using the **same participants**. A reliable test should produce a **high positive correlation** between the two scores. A problem with this is that the participants may have changed in some way since the first test, e.g. they may have learnt more. To avoid this, external reliability can be checked using the **equivalent forms test**. This compares participants' scores on two different, but equivalent (equally hard), versions of the test.

Inter-rater reliability — the test should give **consistent results** regardless of **who** administers it. For example, if two researchers give the same person the same IQ test they should both record the same score.

This can be assessed by **correlating** the scores that **each researcher** produces for **each participant**. A **high positive correlation** should be found.

Valid *Tests Give* ***Accurate Results***

Validity refers to how well a test measures what it **claims to**. For example, an IQ test with only **maths questions** would not be a valid measure of **general intelligence**. There are different types of validity:

1) **Internal validity** — the extent to which the results of the test are caused by the variable being measured, rather than extraneous variables.
2) **External validity** — the extent to which the results of the test can be generalised, e.g. to a larger population.
3) **Ecological validity** — the extent to which the results of the test reflect real-life.

Validity can be **assessed** in different ways:

- A quick (but not very thorough) way of assessing validity is to simply **look** at the test and make a judgement on whether it **appears** to measure what it claims to. For example, an IQ test that just consisted of maths questions could be identified as having low validity by this method.
- **Comparing** the results of the test with the results of an **existing measure** (that's already accepted as valid) can help to determine the validity of the test.
- The results of the test can be used to **predict** results of **future tests**. If the **initial** results **correlate** with the **later** results it suggests that the test has some validity and can continue to be used.

Designing Psychological Investigations

Reliability and ***Validity*** Can Both be ***Improved***

There are several ways that the **reliability** and **validity** of tests can be **improved**:

Standardising research

Standardising research involves creating **specific procedures** which are followed every time the test is carried out. This ensures that all the researchers will test all the participants in **exactly the same way**, e.g. in the same sequence, at the same time of day, in the same environment, with all participants receiving exactly the same instructions. This reduces the possibility of extraneous variables affecting the research. Therefore it will help to improve **internal validity, external reliability** and **inter-rater reliability**.

Mark had spent all morning standardising the procedure and was feeling pretty smug about the end result.

Operationalising variables

1) **Operationalising variables** involves **clearly defining** all of the research **variables**.
2) For example, in a study of whether watching aggressive TV influences aggressive behaviour, the terms '**aggressive TV**' and '**aggressive behaviour**' need to be defined.
3) 'Aggressive TV' could include cartoons or human actors. One of these might influence human behaviour and the other might not — this needs to be taken into account when planning, carrying out and drawing conclusions from the investigation.
4) Similarly, 'aggressive behaviour' could refer to physical and verbal aggression, or just physical aggression.
5) Clarifying this from the start improves the **reliability** and **internal validity** of the test.

Pilot studies

Pilot studies are small scale **trial runs** of the test. They're used to check for any problems before the test is carried out for real. They also give researchers practice at following the procedures. Pilot studies allow the **validity** and **reliability** of the test to be **assessed in advance**, which then gives the opportunity for **improvements** to be made.

Practice Questions

Q1 Explain the difference between internal reliability and external reliability.

Q2 How does the split-half method test for internal reliability?

Q3 Why does standardisation help to improve the reliability and validity of research?

Q4 What is a pilot study?

Exam Questions

Q1 Describe how validity could be assessed in any two pieces of psychological research that you've studied. [8 marks]

Q2 Give one way of improving reliability in a study. [4 marks]

Reliable tests? Who cares. Reliable results are what you need right now.

So, it turns out that 'reliable' and 'valid' are more than just terms to bandy around and throw into answers with some sort of vague idea that they're good things for studies to be. They've got specific meanings and you need to know them. These examiner types are so demanding — it's like they've got nothing better to do than sit around thinking up stuff for you to learn.

Ethics

These two pages on ethics are for everyone. *Remember Milgram's obedience research from AS? The one that led participants to believe that they were giving potentially lethal electric shocks to others. It was a bit... "unfair", let's say.*

Ethics are an Important Issue in Psychology

1) Psychological research and practice should aim to improve our **self-understanding**, be **beneficial** to people and try to **improve the quality of life** for individuals.
2) As professionals, psychologists are expected to do their work in an **ethical manner**.
3) **Ethical guidelines** are **formal principles** for what is considered to be acceptable or unacceptable.
4) In the UK these are produced by the **British Psychological Society (BPS)**.
   However, questions are raised about whether the guidelines are **adequate** and **appropriately applied**.

Ethical Guidelines Must Be Followed During Research

Informed Consent

- BPS guidelines state that participants should always give **informed consent**.
- They should be told the aims and nature of the study before agreeing to it.
- They should also know that they have the **right to withdraw** at any time.

1) **BUT** if the participant is under 16 years of age they **can't give consent** (although a parent can).
2) In **naturalistic observation** studies, consent is not obtained. In this case the research is acceptable provided that it is done in a **public location** where people would expect to be observed by others.
3) Even when informed consent is supposedly obtained, issues may be raised. **Menges (1973)** reviewed about 1000 American studies and found that **97%** had not given people all the information about the research.

Deception

- If participants have been deceived then they cannot have given **informed consent**.
- However, sometimes researchers must **withhold information** about the study because the participants wouldn't behave **naturally** if they knew what the aim was.

1) The BPS guidelines state that deception is only acceptable if there is strong **scientific justification** for the research and there's **no alternative procedure** available to obtain the data.
2) Researchers can also ask **independent people** if they would object to the study. If they wouldn't, then the study may be done with naïve participants (although the naïve participants **may not agree** with others' opinions).
3) Participants could just be given **general** details — although if too little is said they may feel **deceived**, but if participants know too much then they may not behave naturally.
4) The **severity** of deception differs, e.g. research on memory may involve **unexpected** memory tests (that participants weren't informed about). This is **less objectionable** than the deception involved in Milgram's study.

Protection from harm

- The BPS guidelines say that the risk of harm to participants should be **no greater** than they would face in their normal lives. It's hard to **accurately assess** this.

1) Research procedures can involve physical and psychological discomfort, e.g. **Glass and Singer (1972)** exposed participants to noise to make them stressed, and participants in **Milgram's** research suffered extreme distress.
2) Some people face **risks** in their work (e.g. soldiers) but that doesn't mean they can be exposed to risks in research.
3) Researchers don't always **know in advance** what might be distressing for participants.

Debriefing

- Debriefing is supposed to return participants to the state they were in **before the research**.
- It's especially important if **deception** has been used.

1) Researchers must fully explain what the research involved and what the results might show.
2) Participants are given the **right to withdraw their data**.

Ethics

5 **Confidentiality**

- None of the participants in a psychological study should be **identifiable** from any reports that are produced.

1) Data collected during research must be **confidential** — researchers can't use people's **names** in reports.
2) Participants must be **warned** if their data is not going to be completely anonymous.
3) However, some groups or people might be **easily identifiable** from their **characteristics** — more so if the report says where and when the study was carried out, etc.

Some Research Raises **Sensitive Social Issues**

1) Findings from psychological research may highlight **social issues** and create negative effects or reactions in society.
2) Socially sensitive research can be defined as research that may have implications for the individuals in the research, or for groups in society — e.g. the participants' families, or particular cultural groups.

e.g. Research into **genetics** raises many issues:

1) Research into whether there are genetic influences on **criminal behaviour** raises important questions about **free will** (see p.244) and whether genetics can be used as a **defence** against being convicted for a crime.
2) Also, there's the possibility of **compulsory genetic testing** to identify people with a particular gene.
3) Such **screening** could also identify genes linked to psychological disorders such as **schizophrenia**.
4) Although this may potentially help people it could also lead to **anxiety** and **social stigma**, especially as people may have a **genetic vulnerability** for a disorder but not actually **develop it**.

e.g. Using a factor like **race** as an **independent variable** is a very sensitive issue:

1) Some studies using **IQ tests** have shown possible **racial differences** in **intelligence**.
2) The issue is whether this is an **appropriate topic** for research because of **social tensions** that the results and conclusions may produce.
3) Such research is often **discredited** because of **methodological problems** with the IQ tests that were used. For example, they may have been **biased** towards some social-cultural groups — this shows that we need to be careful about the **conclusions** that we draw from research methods.

Guidelines May Be Needed for **Socially Sensitive Research**

Obviously, psychologists don't **deliberately** set out to perform studies that are going to have a **negative impact** on people. But, sometimes the research can have **extensive implications** that researchers don't take into account when performing and reporting the study. The effect on members of the wider society can be damaging.

1) Some people think that socially sensitive topics should be **avoided**, particularly when there is the potential for the findings to be used as a basis for **discrimination** in education, employment, etc.
2) Alternatively it's argued that research can **remove ignorance** and **false beliefs** from society, and **Aronson (1999)** argues that psychologists have a **responsibility** to study these areas.
3) However, there is also a **responsibility** to consider how findings may **impact society**, how the data may be **used** by different groups, who **owns** the data, how it is **presented** to and by the media, etc.
4) The **BPS** currently has **no guidelines** for these issues, so this may need to be addressed.

Barry's research into flying penguins was abruptly halted when it was discovered exactly how he was getting them airborne.

Ethics in Animal Research

This page is only for people taking Edexcel. *An extra bit of ethics for you lot — all about being kind to our furry friends.*

There Are **Ethical Issues** When Using **Animals** in Psychological Research

1) Many psychological studies involve **animals** — either to learn about their behaviour or about human behaviour.
2) Some research has caused animals to **suffer**, e.g. **Harlow's** (**1959**) research on isolated monkeys (see p.180).
3) Animal research is **controversial**, with many people believing that it shouldn't be allowed, or that more stringent guidelines should be implemented. Recently there's been **increasing concern** for animal welfare.
4) Some people think that psychologists need to find ways to reduce the **number** of animals used in research and to reduce the **harm** that's caused to them.
5) Before determining whether a study should be carried out, the **costs** to the animals need to be weighed against the possible **benefits** of the research.
6) **Bateson** (**1986**) suggests that animal testing should only be allowed for **high quality research** that's likely to be **beneficial**, and that research that causes animals **extreme suffering** should **never** be allowed.

There Are **Laws** That **Regulate** Animal Research

In the UK, the **Animals** (**Scientific Procedures**) **Act** (**1986**) regulates animal research. It states that:

1) Animals should be studied in their **natural environment** whenever possible. Researchers should try not to disturb the animals or their environment, produce stress, or disturb nesting sites.
2) Studies should use **as few animals as possible**. This can be achieved by designing the research carefully and ensuring that appropriate measures provide enough data for statistical analysis.
3) When animals are kept in **captivity** the housing should be **appropriate** for the species, e.g. providing perches and dust baths for birds, with enough space for sufficient exercise. Also, **social species** should be kept **together** whenever possible.
4) No distress should be caused to animals unless:
   - The researcher has a **licence** — specifying the species, the number of animals and the exact procedures that will be used.
   - There is good scientific **justification** for the research.
   - **No other procedure** could be used to produce the required data.
5) Animals commonly used in research must be obtained from **government approved suppliers**, and less common species must be obtained from **reputable suppliers**.

Practice Questions

Q1 What are 'ethical guidelines' and why are they needed in psychology?

Q2 Why is it sometimes impossible to obtain informed consent from participants?

Q3 When is it permissible to deceive participants?

Q4 What act regulates animal research in the UK?

Exam Questions

Q1 Describe three BPS guidelines for psychological research with human participants. [6 marks]

Q2 Discuss why ethical guidelines are important in psychological research with humans. [12 marks]

It's the debriefing part that bothers me — I'd rather stay clothed, thanks...

There's absolutely no getting around it — ethics and psychological research are inextricably linked. So you really can't blame those pesky examiners for making you learn about it. Well, you probably could, but it would be a bit harsh. Anyway — learn it, then if anyone tries any nasty research on you at least you know your rights. Knowledge is power, my friend.

Research Questions and Hypotheses

***OCR people need to know what's on these pages.** If you ever design a psychological study, you need to make sure that you're really thorough, so that no smug cleverclogs can say that it's "just your opinion". It's really hurtful... so I've heard.*

Selecting a Research Question is Very Important

All research is conducted in response to a specific question, or a set of **research aims**.

1) An **aim** is a statement of a study's purpose — for example: "to study the difference in exam results between students who use revision guides and students who don't".
2) Producing a research question **beforehand** makes it **clear** what the study intends to investigate. For example, "is there a difference in exam results between students who use revision guides and students who don't?"

Hypotheses are Theories Tested by Research

Although the **research question** states the **purpose** of a study, it isn't usually **precise** enough to **test**. What is needed are clear statements of what's actually being tested — the **hypotheses**.

RESEARCH HYPOTHESIS (or EXPERIMENTAL HYPOTHESIS)

The **research hypothesis** is proposed at the beginning of a piece of research and is often generated from a theory. For example — "there is a **difference** in exam results between students that use revision guides and those that don't".

NULL HYPOTHESIS

The **null hypothesis** is what you're going to **assume is true** during the study. Any data you collect will either back this assumption up, or it won't. If the data **doesn't support** your null hypothesis, you **reject** it and go with your **research hypothesis** instead.

Very often, the null hypothesis is a prediction that there will be **no relationship** between key variables in a study — and any correlation is due to **chance**. For example — "there is **no difference** in exam results between students who use a revision guide and students who don't".

(Note: It's quite usual to have something you **don't actually believe** as your null hypothesis. You assume it is true for the duration of the study, then if your results lead you to reject this null hypothesis, you've **proved** it **wasn't true** after all. If the data forces you to **reject** your null hypothesis, then you accept your **research hypothesis** instead.)

If your null hypothesis was that two variables **aren't** linked, your research hypothesis would be that they **are** linked. Or you can be more specific and be a bit more precise about **how** they are linked, using **directional** hypotheses.

DIRECTIONAL HYPOTHESIS (also called ONE-TAILED HYPOTHESIS)

A hypothesis might predict a difference between the exam results obtained by two sets of students — a group that uses a revision guide and another group that doesn't.

If the hypothesis states **which group** will do better, it is making a **directional prediction**.

For example, you might say that "students who use a revision guide will get **higher** exam grades than students who don't" — this is a **directional hypothesis**.

Directional hypotheses are often used when **previous research findings** suggest which way the results will go.

No one was more surprised than Kevin when his one-tailed hypothesis turned round and tried to eat him.

NON-DIRECTIONAL HYPOTHESIS (also called TWO-TAILED HYPOTHESIS)

A **non-directional hypothesis** would predict a difference, but wouldn't say which group would do better.

For example, you might just say that "there will be a **difference** in exam grades between students who use a revision guide and students who don't" — this is a **non-directional** hypothesis, since you're not saying which group will do better.

Non-directional hypotheses can be used when there is **little previous research** in the area under investigation, or when previous research findings are **mixed** and **inconclusive**.

Variables and Experimental Design

Extraneous Variables** Can **Influence Results

1) A **variable** is anything that has a value that can **change** — e.g. time of day, number of words recalled, etc.
2) A hypothesis states a possible **relationship** between an **independent variable** (**IV**) and a **dependent variable** (**DV**).
3) An **independent variable** is a variable **directly manipulated** by the researcher.
4) A **dependent variable** is a variable that you think is **affected** by changes in the independent variable. (So the **DV** is **dependent** on the **IV**.)
5) For example, in the hypothesis 'time of day influences ability to remember word lists', the variables are the time of day (the **IV**) and the ability to remember the list of words (the **DV**).
6) In this example, variables other than the time of day could also influence memory ability, e.g. the level of background noise. These variables, that can affect the results of the investigation even though they're not part of the research aim, are known as **extraneous variables**.
7) If an extraneous variable **correlates** with one (or both) of the **hypothesis variables** it can lead to false conclusions being drawn. Extraneous variables that cause this to happen are known as **confounding variables**.

***Extraneous Variables** May Be Introduced by **People**...*

Extraneous variables can be introduced by either **researchers** or **participants**:

RESEARCHERS

Researchers may introduce extraneous variables if they **behave differently** towards different participants, **test** them in **different ways**, or give them **different instructions**. It's important that all the research procedures and instructions are **standardised** (see p.217) to avoid this problem.

PARTICIPANTS

Participants may vary from each other in many ways, e.g. **age**, **intelligence**, **interests**, **motivation**, etc. If the memory of one group was tested in the morning and a different group in the afternoon, the results could just be down to **differences in the participants** rather than the time of day. It could be, for example, that the people tested in the morning were more intelligent.

This problem can be avoided by **randomly allocating** participants to conditions, so that the differences 'even out'. Alternatively, using a **matched participant research design** (see next page) can prevent participants introducing extraneous variables.

*...or by **Research Situations***

Extraneous variables can also be introduced by the **situation** (**situational variables**), or caused by **order effects**:

SITUATIONAL VARIABLES

The **situation** that the research takes place in can affect the results of the study. For example, in a test to see the effect of time of day on memory, if one group were tested in a noisy room and the others in a quiet room, the results could be influenced by the noise level rather than just the time of day. This is known as a **situational variable**. Situational variables can be controlled by including them in the **standardised procedure**.

ORDER EFFECTS

In some experiments, participants may have to **repeat** a task. For example, the **same participants** might be used in two memory tests at different times of the day. In this situation, participants may become **bored**, and so do **worse** on the later conditions. Or, the **practice** they get may **improve** their results. Either way, the results may be affected by the fact that the participants have **already done** a test before. These are known as **order effects** and can introduce extraneous variables.

Order effects can be removed by careful control of the **order** in which participants experience the **conditions**. For example, if there are two conditions, A and B, half of the participants take part in A first, then B — the other half take part in B first, then A. When the results of the participants are **combined** the order effects **even out**. This is known as **counterbalancing**.

Variables and Experimental Design

*There are **Three** Main **Research Designs***

Experiments normally involve at least two groups — an **experimental group** where the independent variable is changed, and a **control group**, where the independent variable is kept constant, for comparison. However, **different designs** can be used, which has an effect on which conditions the participants take part in:

***Repeated** Measures*

1) All participants take part in **all of the conditions** in the study.
2) This provides lots of **data**. Also, if there are **different results** between the conditions a researcher can be sure that this **isn't** just because differences between the participants have introduced **extraneous variables**.
3) However, results may vary between the conditions because of **order effects**. Also, participants are more likely to realise the research aims and show **demand characteristics**.
4) Order effects can be removed by **counterbalancing**, where different participants do the conditions in different sequences — so any order effects should 'balance out'.
5) However, sometimes repeated measures are **impossible**, e.g. if the independent variable is gender.

***Independent** Measures*

1) Each participant only does **one** of the research conditions.
2) This means they are **less likely** to realise the research aims, and won't show **order effects**.
3) However each participant provides **less data**, and if there are different results in one condition this may be because extraneous variables have been introduced by variations in participants' **characteristics**, e.g. they are more intelligent.
4) This problem can be minimised by **randomly allocating** participants to groups (to balance out participant differences), or by **pre-testing** them to make sure they are similar.

Matched Participants

1) Each participant only takes part in **one condition**. However, the participants in each condition are **matched** in terms of age, intelligence, etc.
2) This means that results from this design shouldn't be affected by extraneous variables introduced by **participant differences** or **order effects**.
3) However, finding matching participants is **difficult** and **takes time**.

Practice Questions

Q1 What is a null hypothesis?

Q2 What is an extraneous variable?

Q3 What is counterbalancing?

Exam Questions

Q1 Outline how extraneous variables can be introduced to experiments by participants and the steps that can be taken to prevent this happening. [8 marks]

Q2 State a one-tailed hypothesis for research into the effect of different noise levels on memory. [3 marks]

I'm all confounded now — it's extraneous stuff this experimental design...

I'm not going to lie to you — there's more exciting stuff in psychology than designing experiments. But if we didn't design experiments properly, we wouldn't get any results worth mentioning and you'd miss out on all those interesting theories and stuff... OK, there's a possibility that I might be clutching at straws here. I'll stop. You're just going to have to learn it.

Probability and Significance

AQA and OCR. *Inferential statistics let you make an 'inference' (or educated guess) about whether your results show something significant, or if they're due to chance. The fun just doesn't stop...*

Inferential Statistics** are about Ruling Out **Chance

1) You can never be 100% certain that results aren't all down to chance. So instead of 'proving' a hypothesis, you have to be content with finding out whether it's **likely** to be true. This is called **statistical significance**.
2) If your results are statistically significant, it means that you can **read something into them** — they're unlikely to be just down to chance.
3) If your results are **not statistically significant**, it means they could have happened by chance rather than being the effect of changes in your independent variable, so you can't really read anything into them.

*Use **Statistical Tests** to Find Out if Your Results **Mean** Anything*

OK, it's not easy, this bit — so stop texting people and concentrate...

- The first thing you do is write out your **null hypothesis** (see p.221) — this is the theory you want to **test**.
- In a statistical test, you assume your null hypothesis is **true** (for the time being, at least).

  (So a null hypothesis might be *"rats that eat poison and rats that eat sugar pellets are equally likely to be ill"*.)

- Next you choose a **significance level** — this is a **'level of proof'** that you're looking for before you read anything into your results.
- The smaller the significance level, the stronger the evidence you're looking for that your results aren't just down to chance.
- A significance level is a **probability**, and so is a number between 0 and 1.

  (Probabilities near 1 mean things are very **likely**, and probabilities near 0 mean things are very **unlikely**.)
- Significance levels are always **very small** — usually 0.05 (5%) or less. (Because a significance level is very **small**, events with probabilities smaller than the significance level are very **unlikely** to happen.)

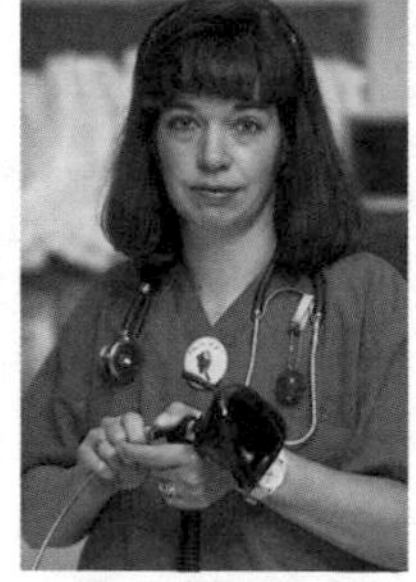

I didn't inhale, honest.

- You then turn all your experimental results into a single **test statistic** (p.226-229).
- Then you can find out how likely this test statistic is (and so how likely your results are), **assuming the null hypothesis is true.**

- If the probability of getting your results (assuming the null hypothesis is true) is **less than the significance level**, then they must be **really unlikely** — and so it's pretty safe to say that your null hypothesis **wasn't true** after all.
- This is what stats-folk mean when they talk about 'rejecting the null hypothesis'. (If you reject your null hypothesis, you assume your **alternative hypothesis** is true instead — see p.221.)

- If you reject your null hypothesis, you can proudly shout out that your results are **statistically significant**.

  (So rejecting the null hypothesis above would mean that *"rats that eat poison and rats that eat sugar pellets are not equally likely to be ill"*.)

- If you **don't reject** the null hypothesis, it means that your results could have occurred **by chance**, rather than because your null hypothesis was wrong.
- If this happens, you've proved **nothing** — not rejecting the null hypothesis doesn't mean it **must be true**.

- Using a significance level of **0.05** (5%) is okay for most tests.
- If the probability of your results is **less** than this ($p \leq 0.05$), then it's **pretty good evidence** that the null hypothesis **wasn't true** after all.
- If you use a significance level of **0.01** (1%), then you're looking for **really strong evidence** that the null hypothesis is untrue before you're going to reject it.

Probability and Significance

There are Two Types of Potential Error

It's possible to make errors when you're deciding whether or not to reject the null hypothesis.

A **Type 1 error** is when you **reject** the null hypothesis when it was **actually true**.
The significance level gives you the **probability** of this happening.
This is why significance levels are **small**.

A very small significance level (e.g. 0.01 or 1%) is used when you need to be very confident in your results, like when testing new theories.

A **Type 2 error** is when you **don't reject** the null hypothesis when it was **actually false**.
This can happen if your significance level is **too small** (e.g. if you want very strong evidence of the need to reject a null hypothesis and so use a 0.01 significance level).

Choosing significance levels is a **compromise** — if the level you choose is **too big** you risk making a Type 1 error.
If the significance level you choose is **too small**, you could make a Type 2 error.

There are Various Ways to Test Significance

1) Remember that you can never be 100% sure that a hypothesis is correct — it's always possible that results are just due to **chance**.
2) Significance levels are assigned to establish the **probability** of the result being due to chance, and if this is acceptably low (e.g. 5%), then you can reject the **null hypothesis**.
3) **Inferential statistical tests** help to decide whether to accept or reject the null hypothesis. However, there are many **different tests** and it is crucial that you use the **correct one** for your data. We'll get to the specific tests over the next few pages.
4) You use inferential tests to calculate what's called an **observed value** (the value you get when you carry out the test on your results). The observed value is then **compared** against a **critical value**, which is provided for each test in a **critical value table**. This indicates whether or not the results are significant.
5) In some tests, if the observed value is **more than** the critical value, the results are considered to **be significant**. In others, the observed value must be **equal to or less than** the critical value to **show significance**.

Her date's significant lack of arms, legs and head was no matter to Julie, who just needed someone to lean on.

Practice Questions

Q1 What does it mean if the results of an experiment or study are not statistically significant?

Q2 What two significance levels are commonly used in statistical tests?

Q3 Name the two types of error that can be made.

Q4 What is a critical value table used for?

Exam Questions

Q1 What is meant by $p \leq 0.05$? [2 marks]

Q2 Outline the two types of error that can be made when deciding whether to reject the null hypothesis. [6 marks]

There's a high probability that you'll be able to infer this stuff is important...

So, got all that? If not, have a read back over the pages again until it sinks in. In a very small nutshell, you can't ever rule out the fact that your results are down to chance, but you can ensure that the likelihood of that is as small as possible. And, joy of joys, there are some lovely statistical tests over the page to show you how it's done. I know, I know, I'm spoiling you.

Inferential Statistics

AQA and OCR again. *If the thought of statistics makes you want to run for the hills, then take a ticket and get in line. Unfortunately the hills aren't an option, but really, the stats bit isn't so bad if you stick with it. Honest.*

Several Things *Determine Which* ***Inferential Test*** *Should be Used*

Inferential statistics allow you to make an educated guess about whether or not a hypothesis is correct. Deciding which inferential test you use for your data is determined by the following factors:

Research Design

Research may have either **related measures** (if a repeated measures or matched participants design was used), or **unrelated measures** (if an independent measures design was used).

Research Aims

Some inferential statistics test whether there is a **significant difference** between two (or more) groups of scores:

- For example, 'did the participants in group A have significantly higher average scores than those in group B?'.
- This is what happens in an **experiment**. The IV is manipulated to see if it produces **changes** in the DV that are significantly different from the **control condition** (or other experimental conditions).

Some inferential statistics test to see if there is a **significant association** between two (or more) variables:

- For example, whether they occur together more than would be expected by chance.
- This is what we look for in **correlation studies** — to see if two variables are positively or negatively associated, more than would be expected by chance factors alone. If they are, a **significant** correlation has been shown.

Level of measurement / type of data

The results of a study can be collected in different ways, which affect how they can be analysed.

- **Nominal data** — This is the most basic level of measurement — a **frequency count** for completely **distinct categories**. For example, in a study where a confederate pretends to need help, you could assign each passer-by to either an 'altruistic' category (if they helped) or a 'non-altruistic' category (if they did nothing).
- **Ordinal data** — All of the measurements relate to the **same variable**, and measurements can be placed in ascending or descending **rank order**, e.g. on a **rating scale** for aggression where 1 = 'not aggressive' and 10 = 'extremely aggressive'. But you can't say a person with a score of 10 is twice as aggressive as a person with a score of 5, just which one was **more** or **less** aggressive.
- **Interval data** — Measurements are taken on a scale where **each unit is the same size**, e.g. length in centimetres. Interval data places participants in rank order **according to the differences** between them, e.g. in a race, participant 'F' was quickest, in 15.8 seconds and participant 'B' was second, in 16.5 seconds. Technically, an **absolute zero point** is needed to make judgements about whether one score is twice that of another. When we have this (e.g. 0 seconds, 0 centimetres, etc.) then we call it a **ratio scale.**

Spearman's Rho *is a* ***Correlation Coefficient***

To work out (and then test the significance of) **Spearman's rho** correlation coefficient, you need values for **two different variables** (e.g. hours of revision and average test scores for 10 students).

a) The values for each variable are placed into **rank order** (each variable is ranked separately). The lowest value for each variable gets rank 1 (and in the above example, the biggest value will get rank 10).

b) The **difference** (**d**) in ranks for each student's variables is calculated. (So a particular student may have done the most revision, but got the 3rd best results, in which case the difference in ranks will be d = 3 – 1 = 2.)

c) The value of d for each student is **squared**, then the results are added together (to get $\sum d^2$).

d) Then the special **Spearman's correlation coefficient** calculation is done, which is $r_s = 1 - \frac{6 \times \sum d^2}{N \times (N^2 - 1)}$ (where N is the number of students).

e) To find out whether the result is **significant** (and so whether the variables are linked), you compare the outcome of that nightmarish calculation with a **critical value** that you look up in a **statistics table**.

Inferential Statistics

The **Wilcoxon Signed Ranks** Test — A Test of Difference for **Related** Data

The Wilcoxon Signed Ranks test is used when a hypothesis states that there'll be a difference between two sets of data, when the data is ordinal, and when the experiment is a repeated measures or matched pairs design.

Example: A group does a memory test with two methods of memorising, in a **repeated measures** design:

	Participant no.	1	2	3	4	5	6	7	8
No. words recalled	Method 1	6	5	10	6	8	5	9	8
	Method 2	7	7	8	8	7	6	9	9

1) The **difference** between each participant's two scores is calculated:

Participant no.	1	2	3	4	5	6	7	8
Difference	1	2	2	2	1	1	0	1
Sign (+/-)	-	-	+	-	+	-		-

Always subtract in the same direction, noting if the result is a positive or negative value. Any differences of zero are removed from the results.

2) The differences are given a **rank** to show their **order** — the lowest gets rank one. Ignore +/- signs.

Difference	1	2	2	2	1	1	0	1
Rank	2.5	6	6	6	2.5	2.5		2.5
Sign (+/-)	-	-	+	-	+	-		-

When there are a few of the same number, calculate their mean rank. e.g. Here, there are four 1s, which should be rank 1, 2, 3 and 4, so they all get the mean rank 2.5.

3) **Total** the **ranks** for the positive differences and for the negative differences. The smallest is the **observed value of 'T'**.

> Total negative differences = 2.5 + 6 + 6 + 2.5 + 2.5 = **19.5**
> Total positive differences = 6 + 2.5 = **8.5**
> So, the **observed value of T = 8.5**.

4) The observed value must be **less than or equal to** the **critical value** to be significant.

- Critical values for each number of participants can be found in a **special table** that you'll be given.
- The number of participants is the actual number of people **taking part** in the trial, so 8 in this case.

Sarah wanted to work out the observed value but had totally forgotten which bottle was which.

Practice Questions

Q1 Why do differences in research aims determine which inferential test to use?

Q2 Name the three different types of data.

Q3 What do you need to be able to work out Spearman's Rho?

Q4 What sort of data would you be investigating if you decided to use the Wilcoxon Signed Ranks test?

Exam Questions

Q1 Explain why the Wilcoxon Signed Ranks test is used for research with repeated measures designs. [2 marks]

Q2 Explain the difference between ordinal and interval data. [4 marks]

I guess stats why they call it the blues...

Actually, that's a bit unfair. I'm sorry. All this stats stuff is dead useful — a good understanding of research methods and how they can affect your results is really important for this course as a whole. And even better than that, there's only a few more pages to go to the end of the section, after which point you can have a lie down until you recover. See, it's not so bad.

Inferential Statistics

These pages are for AQA and OCR. *Just two more inferential tests to learn on these pages. To make it a bit easier, we've worked through an example for each. Breathe in, breathe out, breathe in, breathe out, rank, significance, data, easy.*

The **Mann-Whitney U Test** is Used with **Ordinal Data**

The **Mann-Whitney U Test** is a test of difference (or of similarity) for **unrelated data**. It focuses on **ranks** and is used when you have **ordinal** data.

Take a look at the following example:

Two groups took part in a study investigating whether drinking a **vitamin drink** once a day for 4 weeks improved performance on a **verbal memory** test compared to a group who had not had any vitamin drinks.

Number of words recalled	Vitamin group	19	13	9	12	21	15	14
	No vitamin group	7	5	10	8	6	11	18

Firstly, the Data Needs to be **Ranked**

The data is ranked regardless of the group each score is in. Start with the **lowest score** (in the example it's 5) and give it a rank of '**1**'. Then the next lowest score gets a rank of '2' and so on.

Number of words recalled	Vitamin group (A) (rank)	19 (13)	13 (9)	9 (5)	12 (8)	21 (14)	15 (11)	14 (10)
	No vitamin group (B) (rank)	7 (3)	5 (1)	10 (6)	8 (4)	6 (2)	11 (7)	18 (12)

If some of the data values are the **same** then you have to use an **average** rank. E.g. if the 3rd and 4th values are the same then you'll use 3.5.

The **Ranks** for **Each Group** are then **Added Up**

Look at the **ranks** associated with the vitamin group's scores and **add** them up. Then do exactly the same for the no vitamin group.

Sum of ranks in **vitamin group** (R_A) = 13 + 9 + 5 + 8 + 14 + 11 + 10 = 70
Sum of ranks in **no vitamin group** (R_B) = 3 + 1 + 6 + 4 + 2 + 7 + 12 = 35

When you think about it, if the vitamin group really did show **better** verbal recall then their scores will be **higher** than the no vitamin group. This means that the **ranks** of the scores in the vitamin group will also be **higher**.

The Mann-Whitney U test then uses the following scary-looking formulas:

$$U_A = N_A N_B + \frac{N_A(N_A + 1)}{2} - R_A$$

$$U_A = (7 \times 7) + \frac{7(7 + 1)}{2} - 70$$

$$U_A = \mathbf{7}$$

$$U_B = N_A N_B + \frac{N_B(N_B + 1)}{2} - R_B$$

$$U_B = (7 \times 7) + \frac{7(7 + 1)}{2} - 35$$

$$U_B = \mathbf{42}$$

N_A is the number of people in group A
N_B is the number of people in group B
R_A is the sum of the ranks for scores in group A
R_B is the sum of the ranks for scores in group B

You need to select the **smaller** of these, 7, and call it '**U**'.

The observed U must be **less than or equal to** the **critical value** to be **significant**. Critical values can be found in a table that you'll be given in the exam. In this case, the critical value is **6**, so there's **no significant difference** between the two groups.

Inferential Statistics

The **Chi-square Test** is Used with **Nominal Data** and **Independent Samples**

There's no better way of explaining this than showing you an example. So, hey presto...

> A student is interested in seeing whether finding reality TV programmes **entertaining** is related to being either **male** or **female**. His results are shown in the table below.

The **chi-square test** tests the **null hypothesis**. In this example, the null hypothesis would be that there's **no association** between finding reality TV entertaining and being male or female — this is shown by the **expected frequencies**. Under the null hypothesis, the expected frequencies show that **equal amounts** of men and women find reality TV entertaining, and equal amounts do not.

	Men	Women	Totals
Finds reality TV entertaining	19	35	54
(expected frequency)	(27)	(27)	
Does not find reality TV entertaining	41	25	66
(expected frequency)	(33)	(33)	
Totals	60	60	120

The expected frequencies are worked out using the following formula:

$$E = \frac{\text{row total} \times \text{column total}}{\text{overall total}}$$

John was stunned that the "chai test" involved more than just "add boiling water and brew for 4 minutes".

You Then Just Have to Put the Numbers into a **Formula**

The chi-square (χ^2) is calculated using yet another scary-looking equation:

$$\chi^2 = \Sigma \frac{(O - E)^2}{E}$$

O is the observed frequency
E is the expected frequency

So, for each pair of observed and expected frequencies, take the expected score away from the observed score, square this and then divide by the expected score. Do this for all the observed and expected pairs — then add up all your answers (that's what the Σ means).

If you work through this example, χ^2 turns out to be **8.62**. You can then use a critical value table to see if this is significant (it is, so the null hypothesis is **false**).

For a reminder on critical value tables, take a look at p.225.

Practice Questions

Q1 What type of data is a Mann-Whitney U test used on?

Q2 When would a researcher use a chi-square test?

Q3 How do you calculate an expected frequency?

Exam Question

Q1 Ian is interested in whether there is an association between being an only child and having a pet.
Suggest a null hypothesis and a suitable inferential test for this study. [4 marks]

Just to throw another spanner in the works, you say "kai", not "chi"...

...but this isn't an inferential statistical test speaking exam (and thank goodness for that, by the way), so that's useless info. What will help, though, is knowing what each statistical test is used for. So, the Mann-Whitney U test is for ordinal data and the chi-square test is for nominal data. Mann-Whitney, ordinal, chi-square, nominal. Breathe in, breathe out, easy.

Analysis of Qualitative Data

These pages are for AQA only. *Qualitative data involves anything other than numbers, e.g. words, sounds and pictures.*

Observational Methods Can Provide Qualitative Data

1. NATURALISTIC OBSERVATION Participants are observed in their **natural environment**, normally without their knowledge.

Several design issues are involved:

1) **Sampling of Behaviour**. Researchers may use **event sampling**, where they only observe and record the particular events of interest. **Time-interval** sampling is used if the observation is over a long period of time.
2) **Recording Behaviour**. Researchers may make notes, or complete pre-made forms to record how often something happens. A problem with this method is that researchers may **miss** some behaviours or **disagree** over behaviours, so video or audio recordings may be made.
3) **Rating Behaviour**. Behaviours need to be described and placed into **categories**, e.g. solitary play, cooperative play, etc. Researchers can do a **frequency count** of how many times each behaviour is observed.

ADVANTAGES / DISADVANTAGES

a) The observation is in the participants' natural environment so there is **ecological validity**.
b) Participants don't know they're being observed so should behave naturally and not show **demand characteristics**.
c) There is **no control** over any of the variables so **cause and effect relationships** cannot be established.
d) Observers may be biased in how they interpret behaviours. So, it's important to establish **inter-observer reliability** by comparing two or more observers' recordings to ensure that they're similar.
e) For **ethical reasons** naturalistic observations can only be done where people would **expect to be observed**.

2. PARTICIPANT OBSERVATION An observer **joins the group** they are studying. They may be known to the group or hidden.

ADVANTAGES/DISADVANTAGES

a) Insights about groups may be found that other methods couldn't show, but it can be more difficult to record data.
b) However, 'hidden' observation raises **ethical issues**.
c) If the researcher is known to the group then they won't **behave naturally**.
d) Equally the researcher may get emotionally **attached** to the group, and become **biased**.

3. INTERVIEWS The structure of an interview can vary.

1) **Fully structured** — a set sequence of questions with **closed answers**, i.e. multiple-choice (this is quantitative).
2) **Informal/Unstructured** interviews — the interviewer asks questions with no set structure and answers are **open**, i.e. the person being interviewed can respond in any way.

ADVANTAGES/DISADVANTAGES

a) Fully structured interviews are **quick** and **easily analysed**, but the structure **limits** how the interviewee responds.
b) Unstructured interviews can provide lots of **detailed**, **insightful** qualitative data, but this is **hard to analyse**.
c) To **compromise**, both open and closed questions can be used.
d) Researchers must make sure that questions are not **ambiguous**, **double-barrelled** (combining more than one issue in a single question) or **leading**.

4. CASE STUDIES These involve the **detailed study** of an individual, or small group using many different methods*.

ADVANTAGES/DISADVANTAGES

a) Lots of **data** may be obtained, providing detail that other methods can't give.
b) This may give insight into unique cases and **unusual situations** which may help to develop theories, e.g. case studies on children who were **socially privated** have shown its **effects on their development**.
c) Researchers have very **little control** over variables in the study and can mistakenly identify **causal relationships**.
d) Results can't be **generalised** to the rest of the population.

*E.g. interviews (structured and/or unstructured), observations, psychometric tests (e.g. intelligence tests), experiments, etc.

Analysis of Qualitative Data

*It's Difficult to **Objectively Analyse** Qualitative Data*

1) Once **quantitative data** is collected it can be **easily** and **objectively** analysed.
2) However, **qualitative data** (such as an interview transcript) is much more difficult to analyse **objectively**.

Qualitative Analysis Involves Subjective Decisions

Qualitative analysis can involve making **summaries** and identifying key **themes** and **categories**. For example:

1) Analysis of a transcript or video involves identifying statements — e.g. feelings, jokes, criticisms, etc. Different researchers may read different things into the statements.
2) Such analysis may give the basis for **hypotheses**, e.g. about what may be found in other sources / other things the participant may say — the hypothesis formation is therefore **grounded in the data** (but could still be subjective).

Criticisms

1) How do you decide **which categories to use** and whether a statement fits a particular category?
2) How do you decide what to **leave out** of the summary, or which quotations to use?

These are **subjective** decisions and researchers may be **biased**, possibly showing statements or events **out of context**.

Strengths

1) Qualitative analysis preserves the **detail** in the data.
2) Creating hypotheses during the analysis allows for new **insights** to be developed.
3) Some **objectivity** can be established by using **triangulation** — other sources of data are used to check conclusions (e.g. previous interviews). With more sources researchers can cross-check their interpretations.

Content Analysis** is a Way to **Quantify Qualitative Data

1) When analysing a transcript, **coding units** can be established, e.g. 'references to cultural stereotypes'. These phrases are given **operationalised definitions**, e.g. 'defining a cultural stereotype'.
2) A **frequency count** of how many times each coding unit occurs in the transcript can be done, producing **quantitative data**, which can then be **statistically analysed** — this is known as **content analysis.**

Strengths — A **clear summary** of the patterns in the data may be established. Statistics provide a more **objective basis** for comparisons and statistical tests may show, for example, that a coding unit is **significantly** more frequent in one source of data than in another.

Criticisms — Subjective judgements are still made to define coding units. Also, reducing the data to particular coding units removes detail, and the true meaning of things may be lost when taken **out of context**.

Practice Questions

Q1 What is naturalistic observation?

Q2 Explain the difference between structured and informal/unstructured interviews.

Q3 What are the advantages and disadvantages of case studies?

Q4 What is content analysis?

Exam Questions

Q1 Explain why the analysis of qualitative data can be subjective. [2 marks]

Q2 Give one advantage and one disadvantage of content analysis. [4 marks]

Case study — leather, brown, handle, wheels... but thinks it's still a cow...

Phew, that's a whole lot of stuff on analysis of qualitative data. Which makes me think it must be important. It shouldn't be too bad to learn — four observational methods, a little bit on objectively analysing the results and an even littler bit on quantifying them. Learn that and it's job done. For now that is — there are still a few pages left before you can totally relax.

Presenting Data

AQA and OCR only. *It's all very well investigating the effects of the 'sarcastic clap' on a live interpretive dance performance, but you need to be able to present your results in a way that makes them really clear.*

Data Can Be Presented in Various Ways

1) **Qualitative** data from observations, interviews, surveys, etc. (see pages 230-231) can be presented in a **report** as a '**verbal summary**'.
2) The report will contain **summaries** of what was seen or said, possibly using **categories** to group data together. Also **quotations** from participants can be used, and any **research hypotheses** that developed during the study or data analysis may be discussed.
3) When **quantitative** data is **collected** (or **produced** from qualitative data, e.g. by a **content analysis** — see p.231), it can be **summarised** and presented in various ways. Read on...

Tables are a Good Way to Summarise Quantitative Data

Tables can be used to clearly present the data and show any **patterns** in the scores.

Tables of '**raw data**' show the scores **before** any **analysis** has been done on them.

Other tables may show **descriptive statistics** such as the mean, range and standard deviation.

Table To Show the Qualities of Different Types of Ice Cream

	Quality (score out of 10)		
Type of ice cream	Tastiness	Thickness	Throwability
Chocolate	9	7	6
Toffee	8	6	7
Strawberry	8	5	4
Earwax	2	9	8

Bar Charts Can be Used for Non-continuous Data

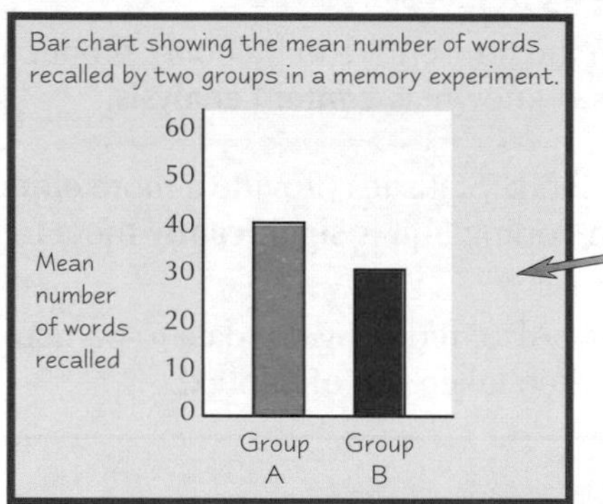

Bar charts (bar graphs) are usually used to present '**non-continuous data**' — when a variable falls into **categories** rather than being measured on a numbered scale.

This bar chart shows the number of words recalled by two different groups in a memory experiment.

Note that the columns in bar charts **don't touch** each other. Also, it's preferable to always show the **full vertical scale**, or **clearly indicate** when it isn't all shown (otherwise it can be **misleading**).

Histograms are for When You Have Continuous Data

Histograms show data measured on a '**continuous**' scale of measurement.

This histogram shows the time different participants took to complete a task.

Each column shows a **class interval** (here, each class interval is 10 seconds), and the columns **touch** each other.

All intervals are shown, even if there are **no scores** within them.

It's the **height** of the column that shows the number of values in that interval.

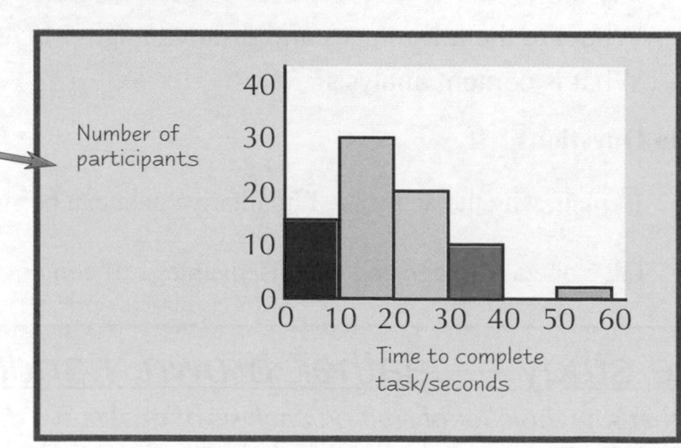

Presenting Data

Frequency Polygons are Good for Showing *More Than One* Set of Data

Frequency polygons are similar to histograms, but use **lines** to show where the top of each column would reach.

It can be useful to combine **two or more** frequency polygons on the same set of axes — then it's easy to **make comparisons** between groups.

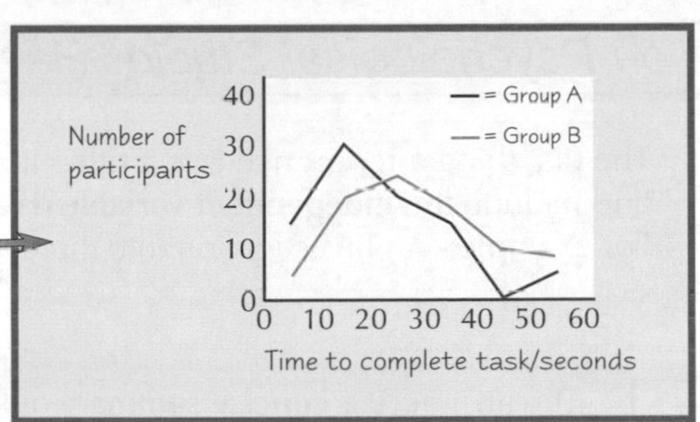

Scattergraphs Show *Relationships* Between *Co-variables*

Correlation is a measure of the relationship between **two variables**, e.g. how closely **exam grades** are related to **amount of revision**. A correlational coefficient is produced — these range from **–1** (a perfect linear **negative** relationship) to **+1** (the same, but **positive**). In a **correlational study** data can be displayed in scattergraphs.

1) **Positive correlation** — this means that as one variable rises, so does the other (and likewise, if one falls, so does the other).
Example: hours of study and average test score.
This correlation coefficient is roughly **0.75** (close to +1).

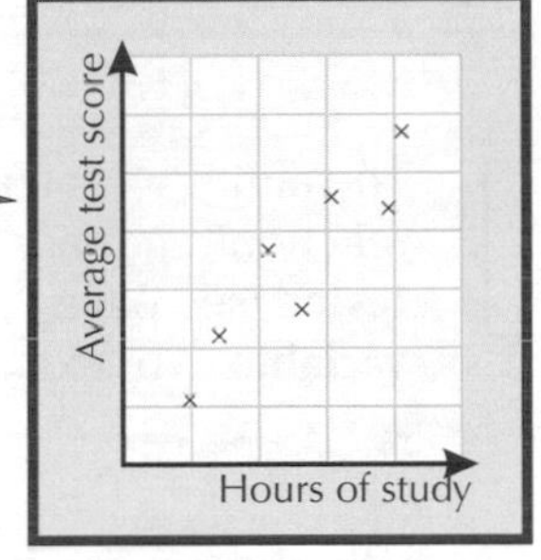

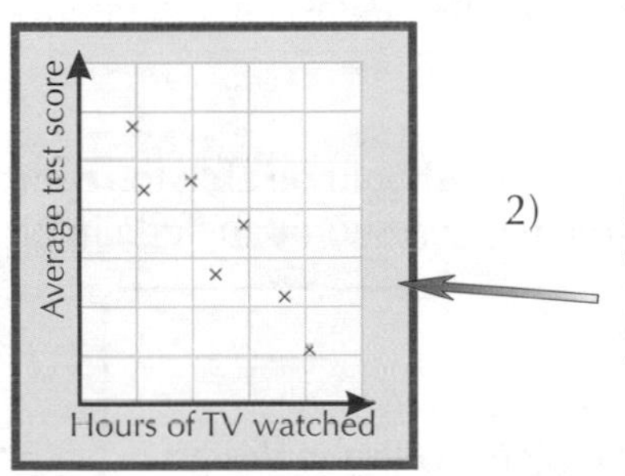

2) **Negative correlation** — this means that as one variable rises, the other one falls (and vice versa).
Example: hours of TV watched each week and average test score.
This correlation coefficient is roughly **–0.75** (close to -1).

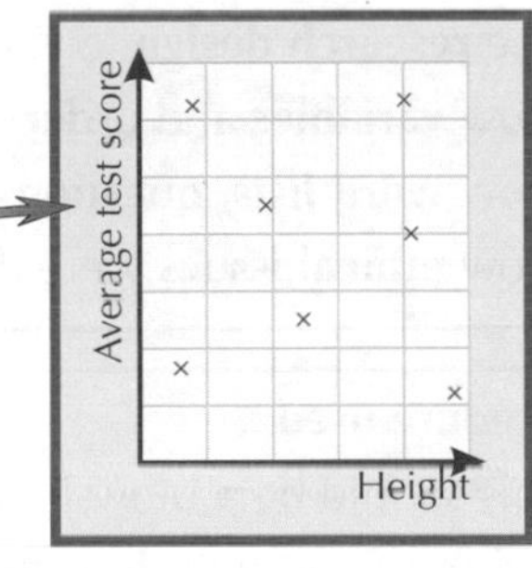

3) **No correlation** — if the correlation coefficient is 0 (or close to 0), then the two variables aren't linked.
Example: a student's height and their average test score.
This correlation coefficient is roughly **0.01** (close to 0).

Practice Questions

Q1 What kind of data is shown on bar charts?

Q2 What type of data do histograms represent?

Q3 What is the difference between a negative correlation and no correlation?

Exam Question

Q1 Describe three ways of summarising quantitative data. [6 marks]

What? They want numbers and charts as well? Are you having a graph?

Producing a graphical representation of results means that you can identify trends and correlations without having to trawl through endless reams of numbers. There's nothing worse than trying to work out 'what it all means' when all you really want to do is go downstairs and have a bowl of soup. But if you pop it on a graph, you can be at your saucepan in seconds.

Reporting on Psychological Investigations

AQA people only. *Once the research study has been done you'd think that'd be the end of it and the poor overworked psychologist could have a break. But no — the study has to be written up and it has to be done in a certain way.*

Reports** on Psychological Studies Have a **Specific Structure

Title

The first thing a report needs is a **title**. It should say what the study's **about** and include the **independent variable** (**IV**) and the **dependent variable** (**DV**). For example, 'An Investigation into the Effect of Hunger on Reaction Times'.

Abstract

The abstract's a **concise summary** of the report (often no more than 120 words), telling the reader about the research and findings without them having to read the **whole report**. It should include brief descriptions of the **aims** and **hypotheses** of the study, the **method**, and a summary of the **results**. The abstract should also contain interpretations of the findings and any significant **flaws** in the study. A lot to fit into a small space...

Introduction

The introduction is a general **overview** of the **area** being studied, including **existing theories**. It should also discuss a few **studies closely related** to the current study.

Aim** and **Hypotheses

The aim is a sentence stating the **purpose** of the study. For example, 'To investigate whether reaction times are affected by hunger levels'. The hypothesis is what's actually going to be **tested** (see page 221), and should include the **independent variable** and the **dependent variable**. For example, 'There is no relationship between hunger levels and reaction time'.

Method

The method describes **how** the research was **carried out**. Someone should be able to **replicate** the study by following the method, so it needs to be **detailed**. The method should include information on:

The **design of the investigation**, for example:

- The **research method** used, e.g. field experiment, interview.
- The **research design**, e.g. repeated measures, and any potential problems with the design.
- How **variables** and **order effects** were **controlled**, e.g. counterbalancing, randomisation.
- How **word-lists**, **questions**, etc. were chosen.
- How **ethical issues** were dealt with.

The **procedure used**:

- This should be a blow-by-blow account of **what happened** each time a participant took part.
- It should start with **how** the researcher and the investigation were **introduced** to the participant and how **informed consent** was obtained.
- It needs to include what was **said** to the participants (the standardised instructions), how the study was **carried out** and how the participants were **debriefed**.
- The method should also contain details of how the **data** was **recorded**.

The **use of participants**, for example:

- The **number** of participants used.
- The **demographics** of the participants, e.g. age, employment, gender, etc.
- The **sampling method** used (see p.214).
- How participants were **allocated** to **conditions**.

The **resources used**, for example:

- The **materials** used, e.g. questionnaires, pictures, word lists, etc.
- Any **apparatus** used — it's often useful to include diagrams or photographs of these.

Reporting on Psychological Investigations

Results

The results of the study can be reported as **descriptive** or **inferential** statistics. Descriptive statistics include **tables**, **graphs** and **charts** (see p.232-233). Inferential statistics (see pages 226-229) involve doing **statistical tests** on the data. The results section needs to include explanations of **why** certain tests were chosen, e.g. because the study was looking for a correlation. The **results** of the test — including the observed value, the critical value and level of significance should also be included.

Discussion

The discussion covers a range of things including:

- **An explanation of the findings** — **summarising** the results and **relating** them to the **aim** and **hypothesis**. The null hypothesis should be accepted or rejected in the discussion. Any **unexpected** findings should also be addressed and explained here.
- **The implications of the study** — for example, whether the study relates to **real life situations**, e.g. interviews, exams, etc.
- **The limitations and modifications of the study** — any **problems** or **limitations** need to be explained, along with modifications that could **improve** the study.
- **The relationship to background research** — the results need to be related to the **background research** covered in the introduction. The data should be compared to other data and comments made on whether or not the findings of the study support the findings of other studies.
- **Suggestions for further research** — at least two ideas for further research should be included.

References

The references section contains a list of all the books, articles and websites that have been used for **information** during the study. It allows the reader to see where the information on the **research** and **theories** mentioned in the report (e.g. in the introduction) came from. References should be presented in **alphabetical order** of first author's surname.

Appendices

Any **materials** used, e.g. questionnaires or diagrams, can be put in the appendix. **Raw data and statistical test calculations** also go here.

General Tips

The report should be written in the **third person**, e.g. 'the participants were asked to recall numbers' rather than 'I asked the participants to recall numbers'. The language used should be **formal**, e.g. 'the participants in the study were an opportunity sample', rather than 'the participants were basically anyone we could get hold of.'

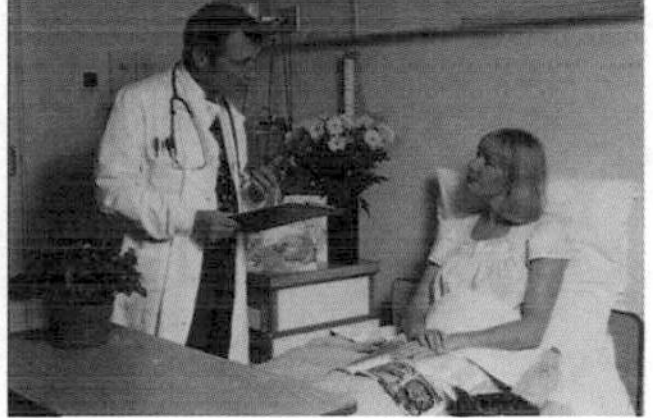

When Ellie said she needed help with her appendix, a hospital trip wasn't what she had in mind.

Practice Questions

Q1 What should be included in an abstract?

Q2 In which section of a report would you find an overview of the research area?

Q3 List six things that should be included in a method.

Q4 Name two types of statistics that could be included in the results section of a report.

Q5 In which section should materials such as questionnaires be included?

You've achieved your aim and reached the end of the section — result...

If you're the kind of person that has their own special celebratory dance for moments of crowning glory or achievement, I suggest you perform it now — because this is the end of the really statty stuff. If you've made it this far and learned everything in between then you are now (unofficially) an unstoppable psychological research machine. And very smart, too.

Using Psychological Knowledge

These pages are for Edexcel and OCR. *So, we have loads of psychological knowledge. But what's the point of it, I hear you cry. Well it turns out that it can be used for all kinds of things which, as usual, have practical and ethical implications.*

Psychological Knowledge Can be Used for **Drug Therapy...**

1) The **biological approach** suggests that mental disorders are a result of **chemical imbalances** in the brain.
2) This has led to **drug development** and means that many of these imbalances can now be **treated**.
3) This has benefited many people who suffer from mental disorders. For example, the development of the drug **chlorpromazine** to treat **schizophrenia** has allowed many schizophrenics to function within society using the drug to control their symptoms — previously they would have been placed in mental health institutions.
4) Drugs are usually only administered after patients have been **fully informed** about the **effects** of the drug (including side effects, potential risks, etc.) and have given their **consent**.
5) However, drugs can be administered by **force** if a patient has been **sectioned** under the 1983 Mental Health Act. This only happens in extreme cases where a patient's behaviour is a **danger** to themselves or others.
6) Drug therapy has been criticised for treating the **symptoms** of mental illness rather than tackling the **root cause**. Szasz (1960) argued that the biological approach ignores the underlying causes of mental illness and uses the **labels** of illness (e.g. 'schizophrenic') as a form of **control** over individuals who act differently to the majority.

...to Create a **Token Economy...**

1) A **token economy** is a system that's used to **alter behaviour** through **positive reinforcement**.
2) Each time an individual displays a desired behaviour they're given a token which can be exchanged for a **reward**.
3) This encourages the person to repeat the behaviour, i.e. the behaviour is **reinforced**.

	Ayllon and Azrin (1968) – Token economy in a psychiatric ward
Method:	45 female schizophrenic patients received tokens for 'good' behaviours (e.g. making their beds). These could later be exchanged for **rewards**. Tokens were taken away for bizarre behaviour. Naturalistic observation was used to assess the effectiveness of this procedure in changing behaviour in the hospital ward.
Results:	The women, who had been institutionalised for an average of 16 years and displayed bouts of screaming, incontinence, aggression and low social skills (e.g. eating by shoving their faces into the food), showed a massive **improvement** through the incentive of receiving privileges.
Conclusion:	Token economies can exert control over behaviour in a way which can give patients back a sense of dignity.
Evaluation:	Ethically speaking, it has to be considered whether the ends justify the means. Depriving patients of rewards may be seen as infringing on their **human rights**. However, it may be justified if the outcome is that the patients get back their independence.

...and to **Change Behaviours** Through **Classical Conditioning**

1) **Classical conditioning** can be used to change negative or harmful behaviours.
2) This is done by creating **new associations** with the behaviour. For example:
   - **Phobias** can be treated by forming associations between the **feared stimulus** and **positive outcomes**, e.g. relaxation rather than panic. This is known as **systematic desensitisation** (see page 82).
   - **Addictions** can be broken by forming **negative associations** with the addictive behaviour. E.g. alcoholics are often given a drug that causes nausea when it's taken with alcohol. The patient then associates alcohol with nausea, even after treatment has stopped. This is known as **aversion therapy**.
3) These therapies demonstrate a **positive use** of psychological knowledge as the aim of them is to help people.
4) However, there are still **ethical issues** to consider, such as the **distress** experienced by patients during systematic desensitisation or aversion therapy.
5) Classical conditioning is also used for more dubious reasons. **Advertisers** exploit classical conditioning principles in order to create positive associations with products, which may or may not benefit the consumer.

Using Psychological Knowledge

Psychological Knowledge Affects **Practitioner-Patient Relationships**

1) Different types of therapists see their **role** in relation to the patient very differently. For example:

- Traditionally, **psychotherapists** believe that their influence on the patient should be **minimal**. They aim to allow the patient to make their own rational and informed decisions. They remain 'blank screens', whilst the patient is the **active** one in a therapy session.
- **Behaviourists** believe themselves to be in **control** of the responses of the patient by managing the environment around them. The patient is **passive** in a therapy session.

2) However, **in practice**, the distinction between the two is blurry.
3) **Both** approaches involve a relationship where one person is trying to change another's actions, thoughts or feelings.
4) This creates an **imbalance of power** which can (and has) led to cases of sexual, financial and emotional **abuse**.

Psychometric Tests Use Psychological Knowledge to **Rate Individuals**

Psychometric tests try to measure factors such as **ability**, **aptitude** and **personality** to compare individuals and predict future behaviour. However, the results of these tests and how the scores are used can be **controversial**. For example:

During WW1 **Yerkes** tested 1.75 million US army recruits to test their suitability for different roles in the army. His results showed an **average mental age** of **13** for white American recruits. He also found **ethnic differences** in the results, which allowed nations to be ranked according to how immigrant recruits had performed in the test. Immigrants from **Northern Europe** performed **better** than those from **Eastern** and **Southern Europe**. Some people used this as an argument for tougher immigration laws and a justification of **racism**.

1) **Gould** (**1981**) carried out a **review** of Yerkes' work and found that his testing methods were **flawed**.
2) The tests **lacked content validity** as they largely measured **general knowledge**, which required experience of American culture, rather than **intelligence**.
3) Immigrants from Southern and Eastern Europe had, in general, arrived **more recently** than immigrants from Northern Europe. This meant they were less likely to be familiar with American culture and less likely to perform as well as Northern Europeans in the tests.
4) The tests also **lacked reliability** as the procedures were **unstandardised** (see p.217). This led to some people having **less time** than others to complete the test.

Psychometric tests can provide some useful data but they're not always great, often failing to measure what they aim to. If they're not designed carefully, they can be unreliable and have validity issues.

Practice Questions

Q1 Give one benefit and one criticism of the use of drugs to treat mental disorders.

Q2 Give two uses of classical conditioning in changing behaviour.

Q3 What is a psychometric test?

Exam Questions

Q1 Describe two ways in which psychological knowledge can be used beneficially. [8 marks]

Q2 Describe ways in which psychological knowledge can be used to exert social control. [12 marks]

Wanted — conditioning to form positive associations with revision...

So there you have it — this psychology stuff isn't just here to torment you, there's actually a purpose to it all. Lots of purposes in fact, and you need to learn them. Ooh, get me — telling you what to do. It's almost like I'm trying to change your actions and thoughts like one of those therapist types. It's all about the imbalance of power you see. Mwah ha ha...

Is Psychology a Science?

AQA, OCR and Edexcel — this is for you. And it's a real slippery rogue of a topic. Before you can decide whether psychology's a science, you need to know what science is — and no-one seems to have quite agreed on that either...

Science is about Establishing Truths

1) Scientific research should be **objective** — independent of **beliefs** or **opinions**.
2) So, the methods used should be **empirical** — based on **experimental data**, not just theory. The best way to make sure of this is to carry out an experiment that collects **quantitative data** and has strictly **controlled variables**.
3) This means that you should be able to establish **cause** and **effect**.

However, it's **hard** to make an experiment completely **objective**. **Rosenthal and Fode (1963)** showed this in an experiment on psychology undergraduates. They were told to train some **rats** to run a maze, and that some of the rats were **genetically pre-disposed** to be **better** at **learning** than others. Actually there was **no difference** between any of the rats, but the students' **results** showed that the supposedly more **intelligent** rats did **better** in the maze task. This shows how researchers can bring their own **biases** and **expectations** to an experiment.

Scientific Theories Should Have Validity and Reliability

1) All scientific work must undergo **peer review** before it's published — it's sent to **experts** in the field (**peers**) so they can assess its **quality**.
2) Poor research **won't pass** peer review so it won't get published. This helps to **validate conclusions** — it means published theories, data and conclusions are more trustworthy.
3) Other scientists then read the published research, and try to **repeat** it. This tests whether the theory is **reliable**. If it is, then the results should be **replicated** every time the experiment is done — this shows that the findings **aren't affected** by **time** or **place**.
4) If the replica experiments provide evidence to back it up, the theory is thought of as scientific 'fact' (**for now**).
5) If **new evidence** comes to light that **conflicts** with the current evidence the theory is questioned again. More rounds of **testing** will be carried out to see which evidence, and so which theory, **prevails**.

Popper (1969) Argued that Theories Should be Falsifiable

1) **Popper (1969)** argued that theories are **abstract**, so it's impossible to **prove them right** through **empirical research**.
2) Instead, he claimed that a theory is **scientific** if it's **falsifiable** — if it can be proved **wrong**. So, every **test** of a theory should be an attempt to **falsify** it.
3) This sounds a bit weird, but if you think about a **non-scientific** psychological theory then you can see how it fits. For example, Freud's theory that schizophrenia is a defence mechanism is **non-falsifiable** — you can't prove it wrong because it's based on the unconscious mind.

Kuhn (1962) Argued That a Science Should Have a Paradigm

To be a science, a subject should have some basic **key assumptions** or **principles** — a **paradigm**. This is **reductionism** — the idea that a **complex explanation** can be **reduced** to a smaller level. For example, all theories in the **biological approach** boil down to the assumption that **behaviour** is the product of **genetics**, **hormones** or the **nervous system**.

Kuhn (1962) argued that there are **three** different **stages** of science:

1) **Prescience** — the subject isn't a true science because it has lots of **different**, competing **approaches**.
2) **Normal science** — an overall **paradigm** is established. This means there's general **agreement** about **theories**, and appropriate **research methods** are used to **develop** the knowledge.
3) **Scientific revolution** — research evidence that **challenges** the **current paradigm** ends up **changing** the paradigm, so the subject returns to the **normal science** stage. For example, Newton's laws were the dominant paradigm until Einstein's theories revolutionised physics.

There are still lots of **different approaches** in psychology. People **don't agree** on the key assumptions of the subject, so according to **Kuhn** it **can't** be a science. This suggests that psychology is still in the **prescience** stage.

Is Psychology a Science?

There are **Problems** With Doing **Research** on **Humans**

Psychological research is very **different** to the research in **other sciences** — humans are **complex**, so it's **hard** to find **general laws** for their behaviour.

1) **Sampling** — scientists can't study every occurrence of something, so they need to use **samples** that **represent** what they're looking at. This is fine if it's something like carbon or gravity. The problem in psychology is that humans **vary** a lot, and in different ways — e.g. age, gender, culture or class could all be explanations for a person's behaviour. This makes it really **difficult** to **generalise** to the whole population from small samples.
2) **Operationalisation** — operationalising variables means **defining** them in **measurable** terms. However, **human behaviour** is often hard to define, so it's questionable whether things like **motivation** or **love** can be operationalised accurately. This means that human behaviour is a very **difficult variable** to **control**.
3) **Procedures** — experiments focus on just a few specific variables, so they're **simplistic** compared to real life. The lack of **ecological validity** means you might never see genuine behaviour in a controlled experiment.
4) **Participant variables** — people bring their past **learning** and **experiences** to experiments. They may try to figure out what the experiment's about and **change** their behaviour — **demand characteristics**. People's behaviour also changes if they know they're being watched — the **Hawthorne Effect**. **Social desirability bias** is when people change their behaviour to make themselves look better, e.g. more generous.
5) **Experimenter effects** — the experimenter can **influence** participants without meaning to, by giving out subtle **clues** about how they should behave. This means you can never know for sure if behaviour is genuine.

Some **Psychological Approaches** are More **Scientific** than **Others**

Very scientific ↑ ↓ Not very scientific

Biological — empirical methods are used which get quantitative data, e.g. brain scans. This means results can be replicated and aren't affected by participant variables such as past experience. The theories are falsifiable.

Behaviourist — only looks at observable behaviour, not thought processes or emotions, so the methods are empirical. E.g. animal studies get quantitative data and falsifiable theories. However, participant variables can have an impact on results.

Cognitive — empirical methods are used, e.g. memory tests, so findings can be replicated and the theories are falsifiable. But, it's hard to isolate the variables because it's hard to separate cognitive processes. Also, participant variables can affect results.

Social — some experimental methods are used which get quantitative data, e.g. Milgram's (1963) study. Other methods are based on observation and get qualitative data, e.g. studies that look at prejudice. This means the variables can be difficult to operationalise and control.

Psychodynamic — theories are based on abstract concepts that can't be tested, e.g. the unconscious mind. This means they're non-falsifiable. The non-experimental research methods (e.g. dream analysis) produce qualitative data and are unreliable, so the findings can't be replicated or generalised.

Practice Questions

Q1 What is peer review and what does it help to do?

Q2 Outline Popper's argument about scientific theories.

Q3 What suggests that psychology might still be in the prescience stage?

Exam Questions

Q1 Describe one psychological approach that can be said to be scientific. [6 marks]

Q2 Discuss the extent to which psychology is a science. [25 marks]

Revision is boring — attempt to falsify that one...

So, you might have to answer the question of whether psychology is a science or not. Trouble is, the answer isn't a simple 'yes' or 'no'. Instead, you'd have to give a selection of arguments for and against, demonstrating how carefully you've revised this topic and how clever you are. So unless you've a particular desire to look like a plonker — I'd learn these pages.

The Nature-Nurture Debate

***OCR and Edexcel**. This has got to be one of the biggest debates of all time — are you the product of your genes or your environment... Sadly, the conclusion is a bit less exciting than you might expect — it's probably just a bit of both.*

The **Nature-Nurture Debate** Has a **Long History**

Firstly, let's just get the definitions of **nature** and **nurture** absolutely clear:

- **Nature (genotype)** — **innate** characteristics determined by **physiological** and **genetic** factors.
- **Nurture** — the influence of the **environment** and **learning** experiences.

1) Philosophers have debated for centuries about **how far** human behaviour is the product of **innate characteristics**, and how far it's the product of the **environment**.
2) For example, in the 18th century there was debate between **nativists** and **empiricists**. **Nativists** like **Jean Rousseau** argued that all human characteristics were in-born. **Empiricists** like **John Locke** claimed that everyone is a '**blank slate**' when they're born, so the **environment** 'writes' unique characteristics onto us.
3) Nowadays, almost all psychologists accept that **nature** and **nurture** must **interact**, because personality and behaviour seem to be influenced by **both**. Studies on rats have demonstrated this:
   - Rats raised in **bare**, dark cages have been compared to rats that grew up in **stimulating** environments.
   - It's found that the rats raised in the unstimulating environments do **less** well in problem-solving tasks and **learn** much more **slowly** than the other rats.
   - This suggests that **environment** can affect **innate genetic potential**.
4) The debate now focuses on **how far** particular characteristics are influenced by nature or nurture.

It's **Hard** *to* **Separate Nature** *and* **Nurture**

Nature and nurture **interact** to form a person's character. Exactly **how** they **interact** is up for debate though...

1) **Gottesman (1963)** suggested that people have a **reaction range**. This means everyone has a certain **genetic potential** for things like intelligence and height — the **genotype**.
2) The **environment** determines **how much** this potential is fulfilled (how people turn out) — the **phenotype**.
3) For example, someone with a **high** genetic potential for intelligence, who didn't go to school, may have the same **IQ** as someone with **low** genetic potential for intelligence, who received a good education.

1) The **diathesis-stress model** suggests that people have **genetic predispositions** for disorders like schizophrenia.
2) A person with a **higher diathesis** (**vulnerability**) is **more likely** to develop the trait, but whether they do depends on the amount of **stress** they **experience** (i.e. the environment).

1) One influence can sometimes **override** another. For example, **phenylketonuria** (PKU), is a **genetic** metabolic disorder that can cause brain damage.
2) But if the person **doesn't eat** particular **proteins**, then the disorder **won't** get **worse**. This shows how **environment** can **override** a **genetic disposition**.

Determining how far nature or nurture control characteristics can be complicated by **genotype-environment correlations** — correlations between a person's genes and their environment, which make it difficult to establish which has the greatest influence over a characteristic. **Plomin et al (1977)** identified **three types** of genotype-environment correlations:

1) **Passive** — people with similar **genes** (e.g. members of the same family) are likely to experience similar **environments**. For example, two siblings may be aggressive because they have both **inherited** aggressive tendencies from their parents, or because their parents' predisposition towards aggression means that they provide a hostile home **environment**.
2) **Reactive** — **genetically determined** characteristics may **shape** a person's **experiences**. For example, people **react** more **positively** towards **attractive** people, so the kind of environment a person experiences depends partly on their **inherited** characteristics.
3) **Active** — people with particular **inherited** tendencies might **seek out** certain **environments**, which will then **shape** their behaviour just as their genetic background does. **Bandura (1986)** called this **reciprocal determinism** — environment determines behaviour and behaviour determines environment.

The Nature-Nurture Debate

Nature-Nurture *Influences* Can be *Studied* Using *Different Methods*

Family studies

- If **family** members **share** a trait more **frequently** than unrelated people do, then this could imply a **genetic influence** for that behaviour. For example, **Solyom et al (1974)** showed that phobias can run in families.
- However, similarities between family members may actually be the result of their **shared environment** — relatives might **learn** the behaviour from each other through **observational learning**.

Adoption studies

- These compare an **adopted child** with its **biological** and **adoptive parents**. If it has more **similarity** with its **adoptive** parents then this would imply that **nurture** is **important**, because they share the same **environment**.
- **Similarity** with the **biological parents** suggests that **nature** is more **important**. **Plomin et al (1988)** showed that adoptive children show a **stronger** correlation for **IQ** with their **biological** parents than adoptive parents.

Twin studies

- **Identical** (**MZ**) **twins** share **100%** of their **genes**. **Non-identical** (**DZ**) twins share about **50%** of their **genes**. So if **MZ** twins are more likely to **share** a characteristic than **DZ** twins, it implies a **genetic influence**. This is shown by **concordance rates** — the number of twin pairs who **both** have a particular trait. For example, **Holland et al (1988)** found a **56% MZ concordance** for anorexia, compared to **5% DZ concordance**, which suggests that **genes** influence the development of anorexia.
- However, if a trait was **completely genetic** then MZ concordance would be **100%**, so their behaviour must also be **influenced** by **environment**. For example, people might treat them **similarly**. Because of this, it's more **useful** (but also more **difficult**) to do research on twins who **haven't** been brought up **together**.

Different *Psychological Approaches* Fall on *Different Sides* of the *Debate*

1) **Biological** — emphasises **genetically** determined brain structures and processes. **Evolutionary** psychology states that many behaviours, e.g. aggression, are genetically influenced because they have **survival value**. However, the **environment** influences brain **development**, so learning can **override** genetic predispositions.
2) **Cognitive** — studies **genetically** determined mental processes, but accepts that the **environment** influences their **development** and **functioning**. **Piaget's** theory of **cognitive development** argues that **environmental** stimulation is needed for the **genetically** determined process of development to **unfold**.
3) **Psychodynamic** — Freud argued that personalities are the result of an **interaction** of nature and nurture. He emphasised the importance of **inborn instincts** and drives (represented in the id). However, he also said that **experiences** can result in **fixations** in the stages of **development**.
4) **Social** — behaviour and personality are influenced by **situation** and **who** you're with. The approach focuses on **nurture**, although it's also accepted that **personality type** and **temperament** can also affect behaviour.
5) **Behaviourist** — all behaviours are **learnt** through **conditioning**, apart from inborn **reflexes** and **instincts** (e.g. blinking). This approach falls most heavily on the **nurture** side of the debate.

Practice Questions

Q1 Outline three ways that Plomin (1977) thought nature and nurture might interact.

Q2 Outline two methods that can be used to study the influence of nature or nurture.

Q3 Outline two approaches that focus more on nurture than nature.

Exam Questions

Q1 Define the terms 'nature' and 'nurture'. [4 marks]

Q2 Discuss the nature-nurture debate in psychology. [18 marks]

I hope it's not nurture — this isn't a very stimulating environment...

Nature or nurture — this debate is as old as they get. Luckily, you only have to worry about it between now and your exam. So, I recommend you learn this stuff really well, walk into that exam room, add your thought to this endless debate in a knowledgeable and memorable way, then walk back out again and leave the experts to continue arguing about it.

Cultural Bias

***OCR and Edexcel**. The list of stuff to think about when you're designing an experiment goes on and on... and on and on. There's yet another thing to add on now — cultural differences. And these can throw up all kinds of issues.*

Psychologists** Have Often **Ignored Cultural Differences

Culture refers to the set of **customs**, **social roles**, **behavioural norms** and **moral values** that are **shared** by a group of people. As psychology developed in **western** countries, researchers would typically study people who were **available** — people from their own cultural background. Historically, there hasn't been much research to **compare** people of **different** cultures. There are various possible **reasons** for this:

1) Researchers **assumed** that people from **western** cultures are essentially the **same** as people in **other** cultures. So, whatever was found about people from one culture was **applied** to all other people.
2) It may have been assumed that **non-western** cultures were more '**primitive**' and less **worthy** of study.
3) Researchers who wanted to do **cross-cultural** research couldn't because they lacked **time** and **resources**.

Research Methods** Can Cause **Cultural Bias

Cultural bias can be the result of a researcher's **assumptions** and **research aims**.
Berry (1969) identified **two** main **approaches** to research which could lead to cultural bias:

Etic research

- **Etic research** is research from a specific culture which is then applied to other cultures to find **universal laws.**
- It's possible that there are lots of these. All humans have basically the **same physiology** and many behaviours are found in **all cultures**, e.g. language, attachment formation, aggression.
- However, because studies have to take **samples** of the population, it's **difficult** to **generalise** the findings to **all** cultures. If researchers do this, they could be guilty of **bias** in the form of an **imposed etic**.

Emic research

- **Emic research** is research based on a specific culture that's used to understand that culture from within. It isn't generalised to other cultures. Instead it studies **variations** in behaviour **between** groups of people. This avoids the problem of cultural bias through an imposed etic (i.e. making universal laws).
- However, bias may still occur by **exaggerating** differences **between** different cultural groups, and neglecting to look at the differences **within** the cultural groups.
- This is what happens in claims like 'people from country X are more generous than people from country Y'. Even if evidence showed that, on average, country X residents are more generous, it's still likely that many of them aren't, and that many people from country Y are. So it's important not to neglect the **variety** found **within** groups — individual differences.

The issue of **sub-culture bias** is also important — etic or emic bias for sub-groups **within** larger groups. For example, research on relationships might **focus** on studying **heterosexuals**, and so **neglect homosexual** relationships (**emic bias**). The findings might then be **generalised** to homosexual relationships, despite not having studied them (**etic bias**).

Studies** and **Theories** Can Show **Cultural Bias

Because most psychological studies have studied people from **western** cultures, a lot of them are **ethnocentric**. This means that they're **centred** around the one culture they're **based** in, and see it as the **norm**.

- Asch's (1951) research into **conformity** involved seeing whether people would **change** their answer to an **easy** question (judging the length of a line) to **conform** with the people around them. This study was **ethnocentric** because it only studied **Americans**. It showed **etic bias** because Asch **generalised** the results to members of groups that hadn't actually been studied.
- There was also **sub-culture bias** because it only studied **male** Americans — **female** Americans might act **differently**.
- **Further research** on this subject suggests that Asch's study was ethnocentric — **variations** in **levels** of conformity have been found depending on the **culture** being studied.

Milgram's (1963) study of **obedience** challenged the view that the German soldiers who had carried out the Holocaust must be inherently evil. Milgram found that people could commit evil acts because of the **situation** they were in, rather than because of their **character**. However, he used **American** participants in his study, and **didn't** take **cultural differences** between **Germany** and the **USA** into account, meaning that this was an **imposed etic**.

Cultural Bias

Cultural Bias Has Social Implications

Culturally biased **studies** will produce culturally biased **theories**. This has important **implications** for society because psychologists might be making claims that aren't actually true. It's especially problematic when biased views influence **psychological practice**, e.g. understanding and treating **abnormality**.

1) **Cochrane and Sashidharan (1995)** found that people of **African-Caribbean origin** in the UK were up to **seven** times more likely than white patients to be diagnosed as **schizophrenic**. The rate of schizophrenia in the Caribbean is **no higher** than in the UK, so it seems that African-Caribbeans **don't** have a **genetic predisposition** towards it.
2) **Littlewood and Lipsedge (1989)** found that African-Caribbean patients were often prescribed **stronger** doses of **medication** than white patients, even though their **symptoms** were the **same**. This suggests that their symptoms are **interpreted** as being more **severe** than they actually are.
3) These findings could be the result of **culture biased assumptions** influencing how people's behaviours are **interpreted**. It seems that all patients may be judged against **norms** for the **white population**, even if they're originally from a different culture.

There are Problems With Doing Cross-Cultural Research

Cross-cultural research can help to reduce cultural bias, but the results aren't always **valid**.

1) Even with a **translator** it can be **difficult** to **interpret** what participants say and do — some beliefs and customs may be difficult for people from other cultures to understand. This means that findings can be **misinterpreted** and research can be **ethnocentric** because the researchers judge behaviour against their own **cultural norms**.
2) **Cross-cultural replications** of studies are difficult to do. **Smith and Bond (1988)** argued that perfect cross-cultural replications are impossible because **procedures** will have different **meanings** to people in different **cultures**. This means that studies can lack **validity** — they might not be testing what they aim to test.

There Are Ways to Reduce Cultural Bias in Research

Cultural bias usually **isn't intentional**, so it can be difficult to prevent. However, there are ways to **reduce** it:

1) Samples should be **representative** of the groups you want to generalise the results to — they should include all relevant sub-groups.
2) **Berry (1969)** recommended conducting research in **meaningful contexts** and using **local researchers** who are part of the culture being studied. This **avoids** the problems of an **imposed etic**.
3) However, these measures can be **costly** and **time-consuming**.

Practice Questions

Q1 What is the difference between etic and emic research?

Q2 What is ethnocentrism?

Q3 Outline one example of culture bias in psychological research.

Q4 Explain some of the difficulties encountered in cross-cultural research.

Q5 What can be done to reduce cultural bias in psychological research?

Exam Question

Q1 Discuss the issue of cultural bias in psychological research [18 marks]

Cultural bias — too much theatre and art, not enough revision...

So to do a super-duper psychological study you need to make sure that your research is neither etic nor emic, that it doesn't show sub-culture bias and it isn't ethnocentric. No problem. Assuming that you know what etic, emic, sub-culture bias and ethnocentric mean. Actually — it's pretty difficult even then. But knowing what they mean is the first step. So learn them.

Determinism and Free Will

OCR people can choose to look at these pages, of their own free will... *It's probably best if you do look at them though, even if you don't really want to. Team Edexcel don't need to bother — you're done for this section.*

There's **Debate** About **Whether** People have **Free Will**

Psychology aims to explain **why** people **behave** in certain ways. The **free will vs determinism** debate centres around whether people can **choose** how to behave, or whether what they do is **influenced** by **other forces**.

Free will

People are able to **choose** how to behave — their behaviour **isn't** a response to **external** or **biological** factors, and **isn't** influenced by **past behaviour**.

Comments on free will

- People can **explain** behaviours in terms of **decisions** and **intentions**.
- However, **free will** is **subjective** — someone might **think** they're **choosing** how to behave, but actually be **influenced** by **other forces**.
- Some people with **psychological disorders don't** appear to have **free will**, e.g. people with **OCD** feel that they **can't control** their thoughts and actions.

Determinism

All of the physical events in the universe (including human behaviour) occur in **cause and effect relationships**. So, our thoughts, beliefs and behaviours are determined by **past events** and **causes**. This is a **scientific** view that implies that complete knowledge of a cause and effect relationship will mean you can **predict** future behaviour in the same situation.

Yes, Colette had in fact chosen to wear this of her own free will.

Comments on determinism

- The determinist approach is very **scientific**. Other scientific subjects (e.g. physics) have shown that events in the **physical universe** operate according to **lawful, cause and effect** relationships.
- However, determinism is **unfalsifiable** — it can't be proved wrong (see page 238), because it assumes that events **can** be the **result** of **forces** that **haven't** been **discovered** yet.

Different **Psychological Approaches** Fall on **Different Sides** of the **Debate**

1) Most psychological approaches are **determinist** to a certain extent, because they look for **patterns** and **causes** of behaviour. If the answer was always just that behaviour was down to free will, psychologists wouldn't have much to study.
2) Saying that, most approaches do **acknowledge** the existence of **free will**.
3) **Soft determinism** is the viewpoint that **both** free will **and** determinism influence behaviour, depending on the situation. Most **psychological approaches** hold this view, just to different **degrees**:

1) **Behaviourist** — **Skinner** claimed that behaviour is **determined** by the **environment** and is the result of **punishment** and **reinforcement**. Everyone has a different **history of reinforcement**, so knowing this about someone would allow you to **predict** their behaviour (e.g. whether they'll become addicted to gambling). If the environmental **conditioning** changes then their **behaviour** will also change.
2) **Psychodynamic** — **Freud** argued that behaviour is **determined** by **unconscious forces** (**psychic determinism**). For example, if you forget to go to a dentist's appointment, you might consciously think it was an accident. But Freud would claim it was actually determined by **unconscious influences**, e.g. you didn't really want to go. However, he also acknowledged that behaviours have many causes, including **conscious intentions**, e.g. a person can **choose** to have psychoanalysis.
3) **Biological** — Behaviours are **determined** by biological influences, e.g. genetics and brain structure. For example, **schizophrenia** has been linked to genes and brain structure abnormalities. However, **free will** is also acknowledged as having an **influence** on many behaviours.
4) **Cognitive** — Behaviour is the result of both **free will** and **determinism**. The approach looks for **patterns** in how the brain **processes** external information, and what **behaviours** this leads to. However, it acknowledges that people use cognitive processes like **language** to **reason** and make **decisions**.
5) **Social** — Behaviour is the result of both **free will** and **determinism**, depending on the situation. For example, you could **choose** to drive to the bank (free will), or you could do it because of an **external force** like someone holding a gun to your head. **Bandura (1986)** called this **reciprocal determinism** — you can **seek out** certain situations and choose your environment, but your behaviour is also **influenced** by what's **around** you.

Reductionism and Holism

Reductionism is About Explaining *Complex* Things in *Simple Terms*

Reductionism

Reductionism is the **scientific** view that it should be possible to explain **complex** things by **reducing** them to their most **simple** structures or processes. In psychology this means explaining **behaviour** by boiling theories down to some **basic principles** — e.g. **addiction** is caused by **conditioning**. Testing this in an experiment means that it's possible to establish **cause and effect**. However, experiments are often **unrealistically simplified** and **ignore** other **influences**, so they may not be testing real behaviour.

Holism

Holism is the argument that human behaviour is more **complex** than the processes that other sciences study, e.g. chemical reactions. This means it should be viewed as the **product** of **different influences**, which all **interact**. Trying to **separate** these influences by just studying one of them means that complex behaviour can be **misunderstood**, so a holistic approach avoids this problem. However, it's **difficult** to **test** integrated theories because you can't **isolate** the **variables** — this means it's **hard** to establish **cause and effect**.

Different *Psychological Approaches* Fall on *Different Sides* of the *Debate*

1) **Behaviourist** — all human behaviour (except biological reflexes and instincts) is shaped by the environment through the processes of classical and operant conditioning. This is **environmental reductionism**. Other possible influences (e.g. genetic, social) are ignored.
2) **Biological** — all behaviours can be explained as the product of biological influences like **genetics**, **brain structure** and **brain chemistry**. This is **physiological reductionism**. It aims to establish **cause and effect**, but it **ignores** other influences on behaviour, e.g. behavioural or social.
3) **Cognitive** — the brain's cognitive processes are compared to the working of a computer — **machine reductionism**. There is input, various stages of processing, and then an output. This is reductionist because it doesn't explain why humans function **differently** to computers, e.g. they can forget.
4) **Social** — your behaviour is influenced by the people around you. This is a form of **environmental reductionism** — it's assumed that behaviour is the **product** of **situation**, so other factors like cognitive function or genetics aren't studied.
5) **Psychodynamic** — the approach is **reductionist** because it argues that all **personality development** can be traced back through the **stages of development** to **childhood experiences**. However, Freud also emphasised that personality is the result of **interaction** between the different **components** of personality (e.g. the id and the ego), which is a more **holistic** view.

It may be that **multidisciplinary research** is the best way to find explanations for human behaviour. This involves **integrating** the explanations from different disciplines — e.g. **sociology**, **psychology**, **physiology** and **biochemistry**. This is useful because **behaviours** may be **caused** by many **different factors**, and it could be that some people **respond** more to some factors than others. However, integrated experiments can be **complicated** to carry out, and it might **not** be possible to establish **cause and effect**.

Practice Questions

Q1 Outline the arguments for the existence of free will.

Q2 Explain the difference between reductionism and holism.

Q3 Is the behaviourist approach reductionist? Explain why.

Exam Questions

Q1 Discuss the influence of free will on the different psychological approaches. [18 marks]

Q2 Discuss the extent to which different approaches in psychology are reductionist. [18 marks]

Jump, Willy, jump...

That's a quote from the 1994 hit film Free Willy, where Willy the killer whale exercised his free will by jumping over the wall of his enclosure to freedom. Or maybe he just did it because Jesse told him to. Or maybe his behaviour was the product of his genes and his nervous system. Or a holistic integrated combination of everything. Or maybe it was just in the script...

Do Well in Your AQA Exam

As the title suggests, these pages are for AQA people only. And they're all about how to do well in the exam. Lovely.

*There are **Two Units** in AQA A2 Psychology*

The Unit 3 (Topics in Psychology) exam has eight questions

1) There'll be **one question** on each of the following topics — Biological Rhythms and Sleep, Perception, Gender, Relationships, Aggression, Eating Behaviour, Intelligence and Learning, and Cognition and Development.
2) Don't worry though — you just need to choose **three** of these questions to answer. Each one is worth **25 marks** and could be either a **single question** or a **two-part question**.
3) The exam lasts for an **hour and a half**.

You'll be marked on the quality of your written communication in all three answers.

The Unit 4 (Psychopathology, Psychology in Action and Research Methods) exam is split into three sections

1) **Section A** is on **Psychopathology** and you'll have to answer **one 25 mark question** out of a choice of **three**.
2) **Section B** is on **Psychology in Action** — again, you need to answer **one 25 mark question** out of **three**.
3) **Section C** has one **compulsory** question on **Research Methods**. It's worth **35 marks** and is split into **several parts**.
4) The exam lasts for **two hours**.

You'll only be marked on the quality of your written communication in section A.

*The **Number of Marks** Tells You **How Much to Write***

1) The number of marks that a question is worth gives you a pretty good clue of **how much to write**.
2) You get **one mark per correct point** made, so if a question's worth four marks, you need to write four decent points.
3) In the Research Methods Section (Unit 4) there's no point writing a huge answer for a question that's only worth a few marks — it's just a **waste of your time**.
4) For the longer essay-style questions, make sure that you've written **enough** to get good marks, but don't waffle.

*You Need to Meet Certain **Assessment Objectives***

Just as in AS, there are three assessment objectives covered by the two units — **AO1**, **AO2** and **AO3**.
The way that a question is **worded** can give away which assessment objective is being tested.

AO1 is about the facts and theories

These questions test your **knowledge and understanding of science**. You get marks by **recalling** and **describing** psychological knowledge, such as theories, studies and methods. For example, you might get asked to **describe a theory** of depression. To get the marks, you'd simply need to describe what the theory proposed and describe its key features. What you don't need to do is evaluate the theory — that'd just be a waste of time that you could use elsewhere, and you wouldn't get any extra marks.

AO2 gets you to apply your knowledge

AO2 questions are slightly different in that they get you to **apply your knowledge and understanding** of science. It's likely that these questions will begin with '**discuss**' or '**evaluate**'. Rather than just recalling stuff, e.g. listing relevant experiments, you've got to **apply your knowledge** to the situation in these questions. So, you'd need to use the experiments you've come up with to **support your argument**.
You also might have to apply your knowledge to situations you've not come across before. For example, you could be asked to assess the **validity**, **reliability** or **credibility** of a study that's new to you.

AO3 is about 'How Science Works'

'**How Science Works**' focuses on how scientific experiments are carried out. You need to be able to suggest appropriate **methodology** and know how to make sure measurements and observations are **valid** and **reliable**. You could also be asked to **analyse** and **evaluate** the **methodology** and **results** of a study described in the exam. When you're doing this, don't forget about things like **ethics** and **safety**.

Do Well in Your AQA Exam

An *Example Answer* to Show You What to Aim for...

See pages 12-13 "Development of Perception" for more about this answer.

1 (a) Outline one cross-cultural study into the development of perceptual abilities. *(10 marks)*

(b) Outline the nature-nurture debate in relation to explanations of perceptual development. *(15 marks)*

(a) Segall et al (1966) investigated whether the Müller-Lyer illusion has a cross-cultural effect. They showed the Müller-Lyer illusion to a group of South Africans and a group of rural Zulus, and asked them which line was the longest. Most of the urban South Africans identified the line with the inwardly pointing arrows as being longer than the line with the outwardly pointing arrows, even though the lines were actually the same length. Segall et al believed this was because they were used to an environment dominated by straight lines (e.g. in their buildings) and interpreted the diagram in 3D. In other words, they saw one line as a corner receding away from them, and the other as a corner projecting towards them. The brain interprets the line receding away as being further away, so interprets it as being larger than the image it forms on the retina.

Get straight into gaining marks by introducing the study you're going to outline.

The Zulus were less susceptible to the Müller-Lyer illusion than the urban South Africans — a large proportion of them identified the lines as being the same length. Segall et al believed this was because they were less familiar with an environment made heavily from straight lines (e.g. their huts were circular) so didn't apply size constancy in the same way as the urban South Africans. This meant that they didn't perceive any difference in the length of the lines. Segall et al saw this cross-cultural difference in perception as evidence that perceptual abilities are developed in response to the environment. In other words, perception is the result of nurture.

This question is worth 10 marks so make sure you write enough — a couple of sentences won't do.

(b) Some psychologists believe that the development of perceptual abilities such as depth perception and visual constancies are the result of nature — they're innate abilities. Others believe that they are the result of nurture — we learn them through interaction with our environment. There are studies to support both sides of this debate.

For example, Gibson and Walk (1960) investigated the development of depth perception in babies. They created a 'visual cliff' and investigated whether six-month old babies would crawl over the 'deep' side. They found that babies were reluctant to crawl over the deep side, and concluded that babies could perceive this as a drop. From this, they concluded that depth perception is the result of nature. However, the babies that Gibson and Walk tested were 6 months old so could have learnt depth perception by this age.

The question's about the nature-nurture debate so include evidence for nature **and** for nurture.

Campos (1970) addressed this problem by using a different measure of depth perception. He measured the heart rate of babies who could and couldn't crawl on both sides of the cliff. He found that the heart rate of babies who couldn't crawl didn't change on either side of the cliff, suggesting that they are not aware of the depth. However, the heart rate of babies who could crawl dropped on the deep side, suggesting that older babies are aware of the change in depth. Campos concluded that as only the older babies appeared to be aware of depth this shows that depth perception is learned and therefore down to nurture.

The conflicting findings of these studies and many more (e.g. Segall et al (1966) suggests perceptual development is the result of nurture, Bower (1985) suggests it's the result of nature) mean that no conclusion can yet be drawn on whether perceptual development is the result of nature or nurture. In fact, many psychologists now believe that perceptual abilities could come about by a combination of the two.

Sum up your answer with a brief conclusion — but don't just repeat everything you've said.

... And Some Pointers About What to *Avoid*...

1) It's important to remember that it's not just a case of blindly scribbling down **everything** you can think of that's related to the subject. Doing this just **wastes time**, and it doesn't exactly impress the examiner.
2) You only get marks for stuff that's **relevant** and **answers the question**.
3) So, read the question a couple of times before you start writing so that you really understand what it's asking.
4) Try to **structure** your answer in an **organised** way. If there's one thing that examiners find worse than a load of pointless information, it's being unable to make head or tail of an answer. So, before you start, jot down a **plan** of what you want to write so you don't end up with a really jumbled answer.

Do Well in Your Edexcel Exam

These pages have been created especially for Edexcel people to help you do well in your exam. That's nice isn't it...

There are **Two Units** in Edexcel A2 Psychology

You'll be assessed on the quality of your written communication in the extended answer questions in both units.

The Unit 3 (Applications of Psychology) exam has four sections

1) There'll be **one section** on each of the following topics — Child Psychology, Criminological Psychology, Health Psychology and Sport Psychology.
2) You'll need to choose **two** of these sections and answer **all** of the questions in them. Each section is worth **30 marks** and contains **short answer** questions as well as an **extended answer** question.
3) The exam lasts for an **hour and a half**.

The Unit 4 (How Psychology Works) exam is split into two sections

1) **Section A** is on **Clinical Psychology**. It's worth **45 marks** and contains **short answer** questions and an **extended answer** question. All the questions in this sections are **compulsory** — you don't get a choice.
2) **Section B** is on **Issues and Debates** — again, it's worth **45 marks** and contains **compulsory short answer** questions. However, in this section you get to **choose** which of two **extended answer** questions to answer.
3) The exam lasts for **two hours**.

The **Number of Marks** Tells You **How Much to Write**

1) The number of marks that a question is worth gives you a pretty good clue of **how much to write**.
2) You get **one mark per correct point** made, so if a question's worth four marks, you need to write four decent points.
3) There's no point writing a huge answer for a question that's only worth a few marks — it's just a **waste of your time**.
4) For the longer essay-style questions, make sure that you've written **enough** to get good marks, but don't waffle.

You Need to Meet Certain **Assessment Objectives**

Just as in AS, there are three assessment objectives covered by the two units — **AO1**, **AO2** and **AO3**. The way that a question is **worded** can give away which assessment objective is being tested.

AO1 is about the facts and theories

These questions test your **knowledge and understanding of science**. You get marks by **recalling** and **describing** psychological knowledge, such as theories, studies and methods. For example, you might get asked to **describe a theory** of depression. To get the marks, you'd simply need to describe what the theory proposed and describe its key features. What you don't need to do is evaluate the theory — that'd just be a waste of time that you could use elsewhere, and you wouldn't get any extra marks.

AO2 gets you to apply your knowledge

AO2 questions are slightly different in that they get you to **apply your knowledge and understanding** of science. It's likely that these questions will begin with '**discuss**' or '**evaluate**'. Rather than just recalling stuff, e.g. listing relevant experiments, you've got to **apply your knowledge** to the situation in these questions. So, you'd need to use the experiments you've come up with to **support your argument**. You also might have to apply your knowledge to situations you've not come across before. For example, you could be asked to assess the **validity**, **reliability** or **credibility** of a study that's new to you.

AO3 is about 'How Science Works'

'**How Science Works**' focuses on how scientific experiments are carried out. You need to be able to suggest appropriate **methodology** and know how to make sure measurements and observations are **valid** and **reliable**. You could also be asked to **analyse** and **evaluate** the **methodology** and **results** of a study described in the exam. When you're doing this, don't forget about things like **ethics** and **safety**.

Do Well in Your Edexcel Exam

An *Example Answer* to Show You What to Aim for...

This is the sort of question you can expect to get in your Unit 3 exam:

See pages 186-187 "Privation" for more about this answer.

1 (a) Describe and evaluate research into privation. (12)

(a) All research into privation comes from case studies. For example, Curtiss (1977) studied a girl called Genie who, up until the age of 13, had been tied to a chair and locked in a room. She had been abused, and hadn't been allowed to talk. After she had been discovered, she was cared for in hospital and spent 4 years living with a foster family. She managed to develop some language skills and her social skills improved.

Another example is Koluchova's (1972) case study of twin boys who were locked in a cellar until they were found aged 7. They had been beaten and not fed properly. They were hospitalized and went to a school for children with extreme learning difficulties. They received a lot of care, their development began to improve, and as adults they were able to form relationships and function normally in society with jobs.

Koluchova's (1972) study has been criticised as not being a true case of privation. The twins had each other to bond with, so were able to form an attachment with each other. Research into privation can also be affected by emotional attachments. For example, Curtiss and Koluchova should have remained detached and objective when studying the children. Realistically this would have been difficult to do (Curtiss looked after Genie for many years) and their judgements might have been quite subjective. This reduces the reliability and validity of the research.

One of the main problems of research into privation is that all research has to come from case studies, as privation can't be reproduced in experimental situations for ethical reasons. This means the results of research can't be generalised to the wider population, as each example is unique. Also, control of variables isn't possible in case studies.

Another problem with using case studies is the data they provide is retrospective. The findings rely on memory, so some details may have been forgotten, and the details that are remembered are often subjective. This problem is compounded by the fact that as privation involves child abuse, the people who have the most information may be unwilling to provide it. All of these factors reduce the reliability of the data.

On the other hand, there are benefits to using case studies to research privation. For example, case studies have high ecological validity as they are real-life situations. They are often highly detailed and can provide a lot of data. Case studies can also have real-life applications, as they provide information that can be used to inform and improve the treatment given in subsequent situations.

Don't open with a general or meaningless sentence — get straight into gaining marks.

The question asked you to describe 'research', so include more than one study in your answer.

You've been asked to describe **and** evaluate, so make sure that you do both.

Evaluations need to include positive points too — not only problems.

Stop writing once you've answered the question — don't add irrelevant detail to fill up the space.

... And Some Pointers About What to *Avoid*...

1) It's important to remember that it's not just a case of blindly scribbling down **everything** you can think of that's related to the subject. Doing this just **wastes time**, and it doesn't exactly impress the examiner.
2) You only get marks for stuff that's **relevant** and **answers the question**.
3) So, make sure you read over the question a couple of times before you start writing so that you really understand what it's asking.
4) Try to **structure** your answer in an **organised** way. If there's one thing that examiners find worse than a load of pointless information, it's being unable to make head or tail of an answer. So, before you start, it might be worth jotting down a quick **plan** of what you want to write so that you don't end up with a really jumbled answer.

The examiners were really impressed with Jane's knowledge of phobias. It was too bad the question was on addiction.

Do Well in Your OCR Exam

Last but not least, these pages are here to make sure you lovely OCRers do super duper well in your exams. Enjoy.

There are **Two Units** in OCR A2 Psychology

You'll be marked on the quality of your written communication in both units.

The Unit 3 (Options in Psychology) exam has four options

1) There'll be **one section** on each of the following options — Forensic Psychology, Health and Clinical Psychology, Psychology of Sport and Exercise and Psychology of Education.
2) You'll need to answer **two questions** from one option and **two questions** from a second option. Each question is worth **25 marks** and is split into one **10 mark part** and one **15 mark part**.
3) The exam lasts for an **hour and a half.**

The Unit 4 (Approaches and Research Methods in Psychology) exam is split into two sections

1) **Section A** is on **Research Methods**. There'll be a passage setting the scene for a potential research project. You'll then have to answer a set of **short answer** questions worth **40 marks** in total.
2) **Section B** links Approaches, Perspectives, Methods, and Issues and Debates in psychology. You'll have to answer **one 40 mark** question from a choice of **two**. The questions are **structured essay questions**.
3) The exam lasts for an **hour and a half**.

The **Number of Marks** Tells You **How Much to Write**

1) The number of marks that a question is worth gives you a pretty good clue of **how much to write**.
2) You get **one mark per correct point** made, so if a question's worth four marks, you need to write four decent points.
3) There's no point writing a huge answer for a question that's only worth a few marks — it's just a **waste of your time**.
4) For the longer essay-style questions, make sure that you've written **enough** to get good marks, but don't waffle.

You Need to Meet Certain **Assessment Objectives**

Just as in AS, there are three assessment objectives covered by the two units — **AO1**, **AO2** and **AO3**. The way that a question is **worded** can give away which assessment objective is being tested.

AO1 is about the facts and theories

These questions test your **knowledge and understanding of science**. You get marks by **recalling** and **describing** psychological knowledge, such as theories, studies and methods. For example, you might get asked to **describe a theory** of depression. To get the marks, you'd simply need to describe what the theory proposed and describe its key features. What you don't need to do is evaluate the theory — that'd just be a waste of time that you could use elsewhere, and you wouldn't get any extra marks.

AO2 gets you to apply your knowledge

AO2 questions are slightly different in that they get you to **apply your knowledge and understanding** of science. It's likely that these questions will begin with '**discuss**' or '**evaluate**'. Rather than just recalling stuff, e.g. listing relevant experiments, you've got to **apply your knowledge** to the situation in these questions. So, you'd need to use the experiments you've come up with to **support your argument**. You also might have to apply your knowledge to situations you've not come across before. For example, you could be asked to assess the **validity**, **reliability** or **credibility** of a study that's new to you.

AO3 is about 'How Science Works'

'**How Science Works**' focuses on how scientific experiments are carried out. You need to be able to suggest appropriate **methodology** and know how to make sure measurements and observations are **valid** and **reliable**. You could also be asked to **analyse** and **evaluate** the **methodology** and **results** of a study described in the exam. When you're doing this, don't forget about things like **ethics** and **safety**.

Do Well in Your OCR Exam

An *Example Answer* to Show You What to Aim for...

See pages 114-115 "Offender Profiling" for more about this answer.

1 (a) Describe two different approaches to offender profiling. [10]

(b) Discuss the use of offender profiling in criminal investigations, using a case study to illustrate your answer. [15]

(a) One approach to offender profiling is the American top-down approach. This classifies offenders into two groups — organised and disorganised. It suggests that organised offenders tend to be intelligent, socially and sexually competent, live with somebody and plan their crimes. Disorganised offenders are less intelligent, socially and sexually incompetent, are loners and are more likely to behave impulsively and not plan crimes in advance. These groups are used to compare information from new crime scenes to make judgements about the criminals involved based on past experience.

Don't open with a general or meaningless sentence — get straight into gaining marks.

Another approach is the British bottom-up approach. In this approach the crime scene is used as a source of information, revealing details about the offender's everyday life and characteristics. A profile of the offender is built up from this information by making judgements about their possible characteristics, e.g. their personality characteristics, their criminal history, where they live, and details of their social, domestic and employment situation. For example, the location of crime scenes is seen as providing information on where the offender lives — a circle is drawn around an offender's crime scenes on a map, and the offender is often found to live in the middle. This is known as circle theory.

The question asks for two approaches so make sure you describe two.

(b) Offender profiling has been used in many criminal investigations to help catch and convict offenders. They are suitable for use in cases involving murder, rape, stalking and arson.

For example, John Duffy was responsible for 24 sexual assaults and 3 murders between 1982 and 1986. Canter was asked by the police to generate a profile of the offender, as forensic evidence suggested they were all committed by one person. The profile was created using the British bottom-up approach and the profile details were very similar to Duffy's actual circumstances and characteristics, making him appear to be a much more likely suspect than he would otherwise have been. For example, the profile suggested that the offender would live close to the first three crimes, be in his mid to late 20s, be knowledgeable about railways, have a criminal record that included violence, be small and feel physically unattractive and be interested in martial arts. All of these things were true. The profile helped the police to catch Duffy.

The case study can be any one that you want — as long as you can write enough about it.

However, offender profiling can be mis-used and has lead to suspects being falsely arrested and imprisoned, e.g. in the case of the Rachel Nickell murder. Another problem is that profiles can only be used for a limited range of crimes and aren't suitable for use in crimes motivated by material gain such as robbery and theft.

Add examples to back up your points.

Holmes (1989) looked at 192 cases where offender profiling had been used to see how effective it is. In 88 cases arrests had been made. However, offender profiling only contributed to 17% of these 88 arrests. Many people are also dubious about the use of offender profiling. For example, Copson (1995) found that many senior police officers did not believe that offender profiling was useful in solving crimes — they believed that forensic evidence and routine police work were much more effective.

This question is worth 15 marks so make sure you write enough — a couple of sentences won't do.

In conclusion, offender profiling can be used in criminal investigations to identify offenders. However, it's not always successful and can only be used for certain crimes.

Sum up your answer with a brief conclusion.

... And Some Pointers About What to *Avoid*...

1) It's important to remember that it's not just a case of blindly scribbling down **everything** you can think of that's related to the subject. Doing this just **wastes time**, and it doesn't exactly impress the examiner.
2) You only get marks for stuff that's **relevant** and **answers the question**.
3) So, read the question a couple of times before you start writing so that you really understand what it's asking.
4) Try to **structure** your answer in an **organised** way. If there's one thing that examiners find worse than a load of pointless information, it's being unable to make head or tail of an answer. So, before you start, it might be worth jotting down a quick **plan** of what you want to write so that you don't end up with a really jumbled answer.

Index

Index

Index